Internet Fraud Casebook

Internet Fraud Casebook

THE WORLD WIDE WEB OF DECEIT

Edited by
Joseph T. Wells

WILEY

John Wiley & Sons, Inc.

For general information on our other products and services or for technical support, please contact our Customer Care Department within the United States at (800) 762-2974, outside the United States at (317) 572-3993, or fax (317) 572-4002.

Wiley also publishes its books in a variety of electronic formats. Some content that appears in print may not be available in electronic books. For more information about Wiley products, visit our web site at www.wiley.com.

Library of Congress Cataloging-in-Publication Data

Internet fraud casebook : the World Wide Web of deceit / edited by Joseph T. Wells.
    p. cm.
  Includes index.
  ISBN 978-0-470-64363-1
  1. Internet fraud–Case studies.   2. Computer crimes–Case studies.   3. Computer security–Case studies.   I. Wells, Joseph T.
  HV6773.I573 2010
  364.16'3–dc22   2010013506

Printed in the United States of America

10 9 8 7 6 5 4 3 2 1

To James D. Ratley, my friend and colleague

Contents

All profits from the sale of this book go to the ACFE Foundation, which provides scholarships to deserving students. They will become tomorrow's fraud fighters

Preface

Let me admit one thing up front—I am a computer Neanderthal. As a matter of fact, when I graduated from college nearly four decades ago, these electronic wonders (that now manage nearly every aspect of our lives) had not even found their way into business school curricula.

My, how times have changed. But one thing that has stayed the same is the definition of *fraud*, which has been a part of our lexicon for eons. Simply put, it is an intentional false statement used to deprive an innocent victim of money or property. What is completely new is how people are now victimized. In other words, it is the same song but with a different verse.

Before the advent of mail, it was usually necessary for the fraudster to deliver a spiel to the potential victim face-to-face. When letters came in to existence, the crook only had to invest in a postage stamp to remotely defraud the victim. Not now. Anyone with a computer can deliver faceless phony pitches to millions of people almost instantaneously over the Internet—at little or no cost. Moreover, without proper security (as if there were really such a thing), thieves can tap into bank accounts, credit cards and most of the world's cash.

Although former U.S. Vice President Al Gore has taken great pains to discredit the rumor, many people actually still believe that he "invented" the Internet. The truth is that it began in 1969 as an experiment between the University of California at Los Angeles and Stanford Research International. In 1974, the term *Internet* was used for the first time. But the network didn't really take hold until 1988—when it was opened to commercial interests. By now, nearly 2 billion computers are connected worldwide, a number that continues to grow rapidly.

There are few inventions in history that have brought so much benefit to mankind. Conversely, the Internet is increasingly being used for evil. Cyber attacks in various forms are now commonplace. We've listed the typical schemes in the front of this book with a graphic we have dubbed the "Internet Fraud Tree." A glossary of computer-related terms is also included at the end of the book.

No good data exists on the number of Internet crimes but according to most experts, they are growing in number and sophistication. And as with other criminal activity, efforts to control Internet fraud always seem to lag behind; crooks try hard to be ahead of the game.

This is not unique to Internet crimes. Airport security gained importance after repeated attempts were made by terrorists to hijack and/or destroy planes and passengers. Physical screening became the norm but it was not (and is not) foolproof. Richard Reid, the so-called "shoe bomber," was one step above — pun intended — prevention measures of the time when he walked aboard an airplane with explosives concealed in the heel of his shoe. Now, every man, woman and child must remove their shoes to have them x-rayed before boarding a commercial aircraft. And then came the "underwear bomber," who unsuccessfully attempted to blow up a plane. This serves to illustrate that those who are determined to commit crimes will likely try to find a method that works.

With Internet fraud prevention, there isn't (and likely won't be) nirvana. Just as soon as the good guys think they've developed the perfect solution, the bad guys will prove them wrong. That leaves us with learning from the past so we will recognize the Internet fraud scams that have occurred and take appropriate measures. Put another way, education is the best fraud prevention tool.

As you will see in the following pages, Internet fraud is not committed by electronic machines but rather by the people using them. However, computers are a vital aspect of the miscreants' schemes and our efforts to catch them. If we are able to identify who is behind the keyboard, bringing them to justice most frequently involves traditional investigative methods — victim and witness interviews, methodically gathering evidence, undercover operations and confrontation of the suspect.

This is the arena where I am not a Neanderthal. For those of you who may not have kept track, I am entering my fourth decade in the anti-fraud field. I've conducted thousands of investigations. And although each has been different, they are also much the same in the approach to solve them.

First, an allegation is made. It is then evaluated to see if the facts, if they are proven, would constitute fraud. Assuming so, there begins the methodical process of gathering the evidence. In almost all situations, the documentary proof is gathered first. Next the investigation moves in a manner similar to rings on a tree trunk, beginning on the outside with interviewing witnesses who are the least culpable and working inward, toward the suspect or suspects.

People with limited experience in conducting investigations are likely to skip directly from the initial allegation to a confrontation with the suspect(s), omitting the crucial middle steps. The problem with this approach should be obvious: With no evidence to prove otherwise, the fraudster is likely to deny involvement. The pinnacle of an investigation is to conclude with a legally binding admission of guilt. Although many cases are made in court without a confession, getting one is the goal.

In this book, you will see many and varied examples of how Internet fraud is uncovered and investigated. Most cases were resolved, but not every one. Some fraudsters confessed; others stonewalled. Many were convicted while some escaped justice. Of those adjudged guilty, punishment was adequate for some; others received a slap on the wrist. But that is the lot of the criminal justice system — you can't win 'em all.

The cases to follow were written by members of the Association of Certified Fraud Examiners, the world's largest anti-fraud organization. These authors are in the trenches every day across the globe fighting fraud in an uphill battle. Were it not for them, the climb would be even steeper. The stories you will read were carefully selected. To protect privacy, key names have been changed.

Thanks first goes to those who have given of themselves and their time to provide these compelling stories for *Internet Fraud Casebook: The World Wide Web of Deceit*. Ms. Laura Hymes of the ACFE research staff deserves special recognition for her job as the book's project manager and for her superb editing skills. Were it not for Ms. Hymes, it is unlikely this work would be in print. Thanks also go to John Gill, head of the research department and to Ms. Andi McNeal, his second-in-command. And I'd be remiss if I didn't thank personally Jeanette LeVie, my trusty assistant of 19 years, who has been indispensible to me; and to James D. Ratley, the ACFE's president and my friend of a quarter-century.

If you investigate Internet fraud, are responsible for its early detection or prevention, if you educate others or if you simply have an interest in this fascinating topic, you will find much valuable information between these covers. Although I don't have a crystal ball, I'm going to make an almost sure-fire prediction. As use of the Internet grows, so will the problem of fraud.

Joseph T. Wells, CFE, CPA
Founder and Chairman
Association of Certified Fraud Examiners
Austin, Texas, USA
April, 2010

Internet Fraud Tree

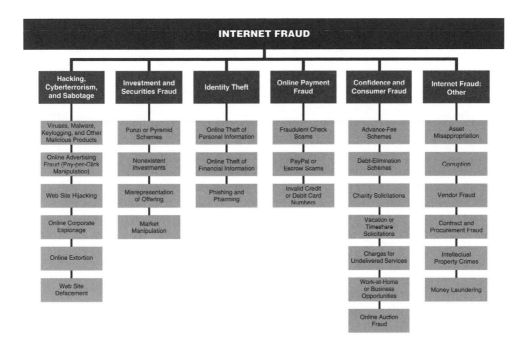

Phantom Figurines

JOHN OUELLET

She was a widow with three grown sons. Her late husband left her with a tidy inheritance that would have been sufficient for most women, but not for Eleanor Wallace; she was far too motivated and independent. At a mere 63 years old, she wanted more from life than idle contentment.

He was unhappily married and living on the western side of Michigan, some 200 miles from Eleanor. Like Eleanor, Roland Granger was not one to let life pass by without noticing him. He was two years younger than her, with a head for business and an eye for women.

Eleanor was refined; Roland was brash. She was tall and slender; he was compact with a burgeoning belly. She took great pride in her appearance and kept her hair smartly colored and coiffed. He was gray, balding and often disheveled. She chose her clothing carefully, for appearance and fit, while he kept the appearance of a weekend golfer in mid-July on the 18th green. In a bit of a character turnabout, it was Eleanor who preferred the informal "Ellie." He insisted on "Roland" for its formality, because most nicknames lacked respectability, and others he thought were just plain silly.

They met at an antique show. He was a seasoned pro, having been in the business with his wife for several years, and Ellie was still green. She used the money left to her by her late husband to start up her own business. Her sons warned her against such a venture. After all, she was getting on in years and had no experience — better to hand it over to an investor and live on the dividends. But Ellie had more trust in her own instincts than those of a stranger.

Ellie Wallace's business was really more of a consignment shop. She took in trinkets and gadgets, knickknacks and doodads. Those items she liberally called *antiques* had no place among Roland Granger's genuine artifacts.

Roland was smooth. His glib ways made it easy for him to sell and for folks to buy. He knew his merchandise and priced it right. Anyone near his booth was a buyer — or so he reasoned. They just didn't know it until they heard his pitch. But he wasn't condescending. He didn't argue, tussle or mortify. Most of those who waved him off often returned later for small talk and perhaps a purchase or two.

Ellie was impressed. She was a more striking figure than Roland, but she was stiff and uncomfortable in the role of salesperson. She had little confidence in her business acumen and none in her products. During a respite in his day, Roland challenged himself: "See that piece you've got?" he asked Ellie, pointing to a costume brooch. "I'll sell it for a glass of wine with you after the show." He took it back to his booth and returned an hour later with $45.

A House Divided

It was a sordid affair that blossomed into a model business arrangement. Roland left western Michigan, and his wife of seven years, and moved into Ellie's modest ranch home in a town 35 miles north of Detroit. They married within a month. Ellie Wallace thrilled at changing her name to Ellie Granger.

If Ellie's sons were nervous about her delving into the business world, they were downright horrified by this new addition to an already turbulent time in their mother's life. Their horror quickly turned to fury. Her three sons were small businessmen, and each had been taken advantage of one way or another — burned by partners, ripped off by employees, manipulated by lenders or cheated by suppliers. If there was a fraud one of the three hadn't fallen victim to, they had at least of heard of it. They had very strong suspicions about Roland Granger.

And yet they had no proof. They had no criminal history on this character, no references and no background checks. Jeff, the youngest, suggested — with tongue in cheek — hiring a private investigator. The other two thought hard about it but declined. How could they? How insulting would that be? Still, this Roland Granger was an unknown. He had come into their mother's life from nowhere. And why? For selling a brooch? He had left behind a wife and a business. How long before he did the same to their mother?

The boys downplayed their concerns, choosing to be tactful. However, hints — though unheeded — were not unheard. "Roland's right," she barked at them one night during a family dinner, "you're all just afraid of losing your inheritance!"

And with those words, sides were chosen, battle lines drawn.

Internet Auction Figures

When Roland Granger married Ellie Wallace, he took over her sinking consignment operation in the small, quiet town and turned it into an antique boutique called Classic Collections. Ellie opened a scrapbooking shop two doors down. With his background in antiques, Roland restructured Ellie's business. Consignments would be a sideline to get people in the door and, to focus the market more, Roland suggested ceramic figurines as their staple product. But Ellie was skeptical. Not just any figurines, he assured her, high-end figurines, retired figurines — Lladros, Wee Forest Folk and Hummels.

Although sales at Classic Collections's strip mall location were respectable, Roland didn't think they were reaching enough people, so he took the show on the road — where he was more comfortable and successful. He established a new customer base while reviving his old one. He used newsletters and e-mail to keep in contact with them, informing them of new products in his inventory and even serving as a middleman in procuring hard-to-find items.

It was around this time that online auctions began appearing on the Internet. Roland saw the advantages immediately. He had a core of buyers who were, for the most part, well-off but ornery collectors. Complaints about his business were few and revolved around his prices. To keep the small niche market coming back, he begrudgingly sold below his asking price at times. On the auction sites, he could let the system take the haggling out of the equation.

Once again, Ellie was skeptical. She was just getting comfortable with the standard business model. But she eventually concurred, not that her concurrence was requested. She was very hands-off with the business, except for filling in on occasions when Roland was away. Sales were brisk and profits considerable — better than she could have done — something she never hesitated to let her sons know. Her intermittent stand-ins at the shop ended when Roland hired two young employees.

Vanishing Act

At the time, I was a special agent working in a Detroit FBI resident agency office, which focused primarily on child pornography, child enticement and related interstate matters. As the only dedicated computer crimes unit in the area, we were the repository for computer frauds, as well. We began receiving complaints from the Internet Fraud Complaint Center (IFCC), a clearinghouse operated by the FBI.

Ironically (and seemingly counter-intuitively), the IFCC will forward complaints to the local, county and state agencies with jurisdiction, but not to the local FBI. Thus, eBay complaints were handed over to me whenever I stopped by the task force office. The eBay complaints I received on Roland Granger focused on Classic Collections after a two-week online auction that sold his rare and expensive ceramic collectibles. The volume of complaints submitted in just over a week and the difficulty of an interstate case like this one, meant the county happily passed along the complaints to me.

One mid-morning, I returned to the FBI office after attending a meeting with the task force, where I was handed another IFCC complaint. When I came in, I walked past a fellow agent who was consoling an irate and visibly shaken, elderly woman and two young men. I cringed upon hearing the names *Roland Granger* and *Classic Collections*, anticipating my first face-to-face meeting with three very ill-tempered victims. The woman, however, wasn't an ordinary victim. She was Eleanor Granger, who, I learned shortly thereafter, was not filing a complaint for the eBay fraud (she had no idea it had even occurred), but about her husband who had vanished with the entire proceeds from their bank account. The young men were two of her sons.

Through a two-way mirror, I listened intently to the interview. At first blush, I was sure Eleanor and her sons were eyebrow deep in a conspiracy; this trip to the FBI was just to establish a line of defense. As I heard Eleanor explain it, she and her husband of six years had built up a substantial business and accumulated about $220,000, which was deposited in a joint account at a local bank. Two days ago, her husband vanished during lunch. Concerned that night, she called their best friends, Averill and Linda Burkhart. Averill happened to be the head teller at the bank where the Grangers had their account and had seen Roland just that afternoon around one. Averill told Ellie that over the past few weeks Roland had come into the bank to withdraw large amounts of cash. Roland claimed he was purchasing very expensive pieces for the store. Each time, Averill recommended that Roland obtain a cashier's check for security reasons, but Roland wanted cash.

"How much did he withdraw?" Ellie demanded.

"All told? 'Bout a quarter of a million."

"You can't do that!" Ellie screamed, "That was my account."

"And his," Averill countered. "We filled out the CTRs by law. His name is on the signature card. It's a joint account. It was all done legally."

"What did he say to you this afternoon about where he was going?"

"Nothing. Just said this would be the final payment on the items. Then he withdrew the last sixty grand."

Mounting Complaints

When they left, I spoke with the agent who took their complaint and explained to her my current involvement with Roland Granger. We agreed that given Ellie Granger's unmistakable rage and the mountain of third-party complaints against Roland Granger, she was probably not a coconspirator. I called Ellie the next day and informed her that I would be handling the case. She was relieved someone was taking her problem seriously, though I didn't immediately tell her the bank was correct in stating the crime was not in Roland withdrawing money from the joint account: I knew that wouldn't go over very well.

And I needed time to wrap my head around the mounting eBay complaints coming from a wagon wheel of directions. There were the IFCC complaints being funneled to the cybercrimes task force. The task force, in turn, gave victims my name and contact information (which I advised them to do), so I was receiving direct calls. I had asked the IFCC to forward the complaints directly to me, which sometimes they did and other times they did not. The state and local agencies were also receiving complaints from the victims and IFCC. I eventually got them, as well.

There was a problem of victims unintentionally filing multiple complaints, due to the time delay and number of agencies involved. For example, John Q. Smith initially reported to the IFCC that he purchased Lladros "The Happiest Day" under screen name *HardcoreBuyer* on Monday for $450. A week later, he reported directly to his local law enforcement agency in New Jersey that on the last day of the auction, he purchased Wee Forest Folk "Haunted Mouse House" for $800 using screen name *BestBuy*. These duplicates were easily overlooked at first glance.

Before this case, I knew of Excel — and had even seen spreadsheets — but I never envisioned using it myself. However, I knew I needed a scorecard to organize all the information. With help from the FBI administrative experts, I set up a spreadsheet that included screen name, real name, item purchased, amount paid, date and time of bid, method of payment, U.S. mail used (yes or no) and the all-inclusive miscellaneous column for printouts of e-mails with Granger, letters, certified mail receipts and canceled checks.

This spreadsheet proved invaluable. Not only did it keep me and the data organized, but I was able to identify and eliminate double complaints, which cases had the elements necessary for mail or wire fraud and list the evidence I had to support each complaint as interviews were conducted and responses to grand jury subpoenas came in. A secondary benefit came up when the Assistant United States Attorney (AUSA) used my spreadsheet in drafting the eventual criminal complaint and federal pretrial services used it their sentencing and restitution report.

Modeling a Case

Up to this point, I hadn't approached an AUSA for a prosecutorial opinion. I knew I had a fraud based on the sheer volume of complaints, but I had no concept of how it was committed, and I wouldn't go to an AUSA without solid preliminaries. I also needed an approximate dollar loss. There is usually a threshold amount that the U.S. Attorney's office sets on financial crimes; if a case doesn't meet the threshold, an AUSA won't take it. It varies by district, type of financial crime and extent of the crime problem. It is never a hard and fast rule, and I recommend taking a strong stance if a case is declined because the loss is below the threshold. I've never met an AUSA who isn't swayed by a passionate and driven investigator. If a case is declined by the federal government, then it must be prosecuted locally or not at all.

While doing data entry, I needed to unravel the scheme to defraud, if there was one, and determine if it fit the elements of mail fraud or wire fraud. These were the two federal statutes I knew the government would pursue, because bank fraud was not applicable and because mail and wire fraud laws are extremely broad; they are the workhorses of federal white-collar crime prosecutions.

Bid Winner

At that point I had more than 40 victims. My spreadsheet was populated with information from filed complaints, but I needed someone to fill me in. Ellie was not going to be helpful. She was just learning the extent of the fraud from the irate victims who began calling her at Classic Collections when she took over operations. Plus, she was miffed at the FBI for not looking into the money Roland withdrew from the bank account. My decision on who to interview first was logical — I picked the person who lost the most money.

Joy Minot of Eugene, Oregon, lost $23,718 on nine Wee Forest Folk figurines, and she was eager to fill me in. She had been a serious collector for more than seven years and was considered one of the foremost experts in the country. About three years before, she heard that Classic Collections had some very rare pieces, which she purchased without a problem. She was so impressed with Roland Granger that she kept in contact with him via e-mail, and even with an occasional phone call for other collectibles. When she made her bids (and won) on the figurines from the estate sale in Phoenix that Granger advertised he had been entrusted to liquidate, she felt no anxiety. And his recommendation that she meet him at a hotel in Phoenix to pick up her high-value figurines was another gesture of his professionalism. But the exchange would have to wait until after the two-week eBay auction was complete, which, of course, she understood.

When the meeting came, he didn't show up at the hotel. When Joy requested that the front desk call his room, they told her they had no reservations for Roland Granger currently, in the past or in the foresee-able future. Her heart sank when the horrific realization started to set in. Her anger at herself was soon replaced by her fury at Roland Granger, and I learned through dozens of similar statements that victims of fraud can have more rage than victims of violent assault. That is because fraud is the only crime requiring voluntary victim assistance; these people felt like fools.

Joy returned home and set up a Web site dedicated to Roland Granger's auction misdeeds. I already had most of the victims' names, but Joy's Web site supplied me with background on the scheme. It was a feast that led to another challenge. Although the victims were eager to talk to me, it was difficult to keep them on track, and, because 99 percent of the interviews were over the phone, I spent a lot of time listening rather than interviewing. At first I saw this as a sound approach because the victims all seemed to want to vent. And it would have been a good rapport-building technique were it not for the volume of interviews I had to conduct. Immediately after interviewing Joy Minot, I felt I had enough information to contact an AUSA. He wasn't as enthusiastic as I had anticipated. His response was, "Maybe Granger couldn't get down to Phoenix or maybe he just forgot."

"But I have dozens of complaints," I argued.

"It's been what, less than three weeks since the auction? So he's late getting the orders out. What's his story?"

"He's got none," I said. "He emptied out his bank account and fled."

At least that got his attention. The AUSA's comments weren't from a lack of interest; he was acting out the prosecution in his mind and playing devil's advocate. There is a fine line between a fraud and a breach of contract, which would have been a civil matter, not a criminal one. I understood his point — a catalog of complaints on a spreadsheet wasn't going to be enough. I had to prove the Phoenix estate auction was a part of Granger's scheme to defraud, or I had to at least make a strong case for that possibility.

Proving a Negative

I had arrived at the classic impasse of proving a negative. The best approach was to conduct due diligence. According to my victims, Roland Granger's inventory of figurines available for the auction was worth hundreds of thousands of dollars. I was sure that such an estate auction would be newsworthy for someone, somewhere. So while I wrestled with corralling my victims, I queried the Internet, Phoenix newspapers, obituaries, trade magazines and even called a special agent with this expertise to do some digging.

While doing the homework, I developed a line of questioning for my interviews that stuck to the facts. It was a violation of Interviewing 101 to prepare questions in advance and not a strategy I had ever employed, but it was necessary. I found it good practice to keep this list of questions at the ready because Joy had put my name and number on her Web site, and I was fielding an influx of calls. The questions included the basics from my spreadsheet for confirmation, a brief synopsis of the sale, e-mails or letters exchanged and the method of payment.

The victims flooded me with faxes of eBay bids, payment statements and e-mails from Granger announcing that the victims were high bidders and would receive the figurine(s) shortly via FedEx. (Use of FedEx nullified the mail fraud statute, unless a U.S. mail letter preceded or followed.)

For my presentation to the AUSA, I adopted the military strategy of "shock and awe." My spreadsheet was like the sci-fi thriller, *The Blob* — expanding daily — but I wanted to present the AUSA with overwhelming evidence, not overwhelming data. I interviewed more than 20 of the victims on numerous occasions. Due to time constraints, I stuck to those who purchased multiple figurines or lost large amounts of money. The victims came from 14 states, England and Australia.

But copies and faxes weren't going to cut it. I had no doubt some folks who had heard of the fraud were going to jump in and claim to be victims. I needed grand jury subpoenas for canceled bank checks, credit card statements, wire transfers, cashier's checks, money orders, PayPal and Billpoint. I even subpoenaed the airline for Joy Minot's ticket to Phoenix and the Phoenix hotel's guest register for the week in question, both to verify Joy's story and to attack a potential defense by Granger.

As if Roland Granger's gall wasn't enough, I found two more appalling aspects to this fraud: More than a few times he sold the same figurine to the highest bidder, the second highest bidder and the third highest. While employing delaying tactics on victims like Joy, he was contacting other bidders and telling them the winner had reneged. To pad his nest, he then called a third bidder and repeated the claim. Granger's second big mistake was to invite three victims to that fictitious rendezvous in Phoenix.

Interviews follow general rules, but often they are dictated by the investigator's assumptions about who will be most cooperative and have the most information to offer. I knew Granger had two employees who, according to Ellie, were very active in the operation of Classic Collections. The question was, how loyal were they to Granger? Not very, I was happy to learn.

The Witnesses

Mark Mollencamp was 23 years old and worked on Internet sales for Granger. As fate would have it, he was under investigation by Immigration and Customs Enforcement (ICE) for trading child pornography. ICE had called my office a few weeks earlier to ask if we had information on him. I was glad to have the leverage, and used it freely during my interview with him. Mollencamp's statement brought the scam together nicely. Roland Granger, it seemed, was a serious online gambler. He talked openly to Mollencamp about hoping one day to play in big poker tournaments. Granger's sales before the two-week eBay auction were legitimate, and one day shortly after Christmas, Granger told Mollencamp of the big estate sale in Phoenix. He handed Mollencamp catalogs and circled the figurines to be listed on eBay for the auction. Mollencamp didn't see the actual figurines and didn't think Granger had traveled to Phoenix before his disappearance. Mollencamp also verified the double and triple sellings.

Granger's second employee verified Mollencamp's information in a separate interview. Both employees were promised a $4,000 bonus at the conclusion of the auction, but neither was paid. They last saw Granger heading out to lunch the day he disappeared.

I had enough at this point to shock and awe the most cautious AUSA. Computer forensics was becoming a hot-button topic at the time, so I finished up the case by seizing and examining the five networked computers at Classic Collections. The forensic examiners discovered incriminating e-mail and evidence to corroborate the motive Mollencamp suggested: thousands of online poker downloads.

Restitution and Bankruptcy

Granger was indicted by a federal grand jury in the Eastern district of Michigan on mail fraud and wire fraud charges, but he was a fugitive for more than three and a half years, until he was arrested outside Los Angeles, California. He pleaded guilty to single counts of mail and wire fraud and received the following sentence: restitution to 85 eBay bidders in the amount of $144,688.31 (my spreadsheet had 112 victims, but some of them had insufficient evidence); restitution to Wells Fargo Bank for charge-backs from Billpoint in the amount of $9,785.39; restitution to eBay in the amount of $27,878.01; and restitution to PayPal in the amount of $140,909.89. Total restitution was $323,261.54, which was conservative, based on the investigation and Granger's own admission. So incensed was the federal judge by Granger's outlandish acts and lack of remorse that he vacated the pretrial service's recommendation of 37 months of confinement and sentenced him to the maximum of six years.

Not accounted for in the sentence were the losses suffered by Ellie Wallace. (She changed her name back before I even had my spreadsheet completed). In filing Chapter Seven, her attorney and accountant estimated her financial losses at $415,800. She was able to satisfy creditors in the amount of $21,400.06, which she scraped together from savings. Unfortunately, the courts, attorneys, pretrial services and accountants could not put a price on Ellie's emotional damages.

Lessons Learned

I learned valuable organizational, technical and personal lessons from this case. I knew the wire fraud and mail fraud statutes but became overwhelmed when victims began discussing second- and third-bidder options, PayPal, Billpoint and other Internet auction jargon. I had never bid on an online auction site, and I needed to ask questions of the victims, eBay and PayPal to plan my investigation. I became shameless in acknowledging my ignorance, and eBay was unsurpassed in their cooperation.

When the numbers became overwhelming, Excel came to my rescue. I know there are many tools available that perform an assortment of data management and analysis, and I'm not advocating any in particular, but Excel does the basic grunt work well. However, keep in mind that it's easy to burden the individuals who read your spreadsheet by including too much information. The next stop after overwhelmed is confused, and then frustrated. Let the spreadsheet be a snapshot, something to provide the gist of the case over a cup of coffee. As TV's legendary Sergeant Joe Friday said, ``Just the facts.''

On the personal level, I found the victims of this fraud were often enraged beyond rational thought. At times, I caught myself treating the matter lightly, and more than one victim chastised me for my insensitivity. So I learned patience and added a new dimension to my empathy.

Had I not been actively involved with learning about cybercrime and working with the task force, I would never have received the case, let alone successfully investigated it. For cybercrime, identity fraud, child pornography and the like, task forces are the most effective tool law enforcement has to encourage sharing and learning — and if we are not doing that, we aren't doing justice to the justice system.

Recommendations to Prevent Future Occurrences

Roland Granger was able to defraud a very savvy, highly intelligent, well-organized group of serious collectors. They knew his track record when it came to eBay auctions, and it was a very good one. And to this day, the question is, was his six years of honest auctions a prelude to this one big score? His victims say it was; Granger isn't talking; and I'm not sure. But there are a few imperatives and suggestions that bear mentioning for both the casual and practiced bidder:

1. *Know the site.* There are dozens of online auction sites, including Ubid, Bidz, ePier and eBay. Each Web site has a degree of security to reassure customers. Learn the security measures, especially the ones that deal with seller rules of behavior, and how payments are made.
2. *Know your seller.* Granger had six years of on-the-up sales. To have him come up with an estate sale from Phoenix raised no suspicions. And his prices were not greedy. It's hard to catch a thief who is patient and judicious. But as the adage goes, "just because you're paranoid doesn't mean they're not trying to get you." If you've checked out the seller the best you can, check out his product, too.
3. *Know your product.* Though you can't inspect it online to view the condition or confirm its existence, you need to know legitimate price ranges.
4. *Network.* I found the collectors in this case had a vast and widespread network that ran efficiently and effectively when instituted. Unfortunately, it was activated too late, in this instance, because no one wanted other bidders to get a leg up at auction. The Collectors Information Bureau is an excellent resource and it publishes a trade magazine with a circulation of more than 7,000 collectors and retailers. A quick note to the Bureau from a "paranoid" collector to inquire about Granger's sale could have sent the hounds out.
5. *Keep all transactions, including e-mail, bid submissions, payment receipts and all mailed envelopes.* For banks, this is standard operating procedure, and I advise it for anyone who trades online; they will be needed to prove mail fraud.

On the law enforcement side:

1. Unless you are an online auction expert, don't try to come off as one. Ask a lot of questions from anyone you can. Even the stupid ones.
2. Local police departments may not have the expertise to investigate online auction Web sites, but county, state and federal agencies usually do. However, no one knows the Web site like the Web site administrators. Reach out to them before, during and even after the investigation to stay on top of things. The software and controls are changing even as you read this.

(continued)

(continued)

3. If you're going out to the subject's place of business, be aware of computer search and seizure laws and techniques. Most of the bigger frauds will involve networks, so have a network expert standing by as well.

4. Local police departments should develop fraud awareness Web sites, forums and community outreach programs to educate their citizens, especially the elderly.

5. Contact as many victims as you can and determine if the group of victims (collectors in this case) has a national or local association. These are amazingly efficient sources of information.

6. Prosecutors know the law, but don't rely on them to know how the crime was committed. Provide them with evidence — testimonial, circumstantial and direct — in the most organized form possible. Get as many of the original documents as you can and develop a filing system. Judges and juries may be even less savvy and more apt to be overwhelmed by the technical jargon in an Internet fraud case. Remember, it's just a fraud. The Internet is only a vehicle, so don't let it bog down the case.

While Granger was a fugitive, I contacted a high-profile television program that features at-large fugitives to ask if they would be interested in airing the story. The screener I spoke with was enthusiastic and said it was a crime many people could relate to. It had added commercial appeal because Granger had a nasty past that included three marriages (Ellie only knew of the second one), theft of valuable antiques from his first wife and money from his second and a stint in prison that included attempted murder of one of his guards. However, the producer called me back and declined to air it. "People who buy things online from strangers deserve what they get," he said, and nothing I said could sway him.

Sympathy for victims of Internet fraud runs that gamut. The judge in Granger's case gave him the maximum sentence; the television producer thought the victims were fools. It's hard to know who you'll encounter if you become a victim.

About the Author

John Ouellet is currently a supervisory special agent with the FBI in Detroit. His 23-year career has run the gamut from investigative duties to violent crime to counterterrorism, and he has worked on numerous task forces, including identity theft and mortgage fraud. Prior to the FBI, Mr. Oullet was an Army Infantry Officer. He is married with four children.

CHAPTER 2

From Russia with Love?

ERNESTO F. ROJAS

Victoria and her young daughter, Anna, lived in Novosibirsk, Russia. Since her divorce a few years ago, life for Victoria had been one of stumbles, bad relationships and financial difficulties. She worked as a clerk in a perfume store and shared an apartment with her parents. While her sisters and brother went to college, embarked upon professional careers and married other professionals, Victoria became more and more frustrated and tried to find a way out of her situation.

During a visit to the house of a friend who had Internet access, Victoria learned about the growing phenomenon of online dating and she began to develop a fantasy escape from her difficult life. She attended a public program to learn English and began to use the Internet at the local library. Once she had a stronger vocabulary, she joined Internet dating services that catered to international clients. She had professional photographs taken by a local glamour photographer and added them to her profiles on various Web sites. Soon she began to receive messages from prospective suitors interested in meeting her. Being a statuesque woman in her late twenties made her attractive to many men looking for a partner. Soon she met an American man online who wanted to visit her in Russia and meet her family.

Robert was an electronics technician in California and was looking to meet a Russian woman because his recently deceased wife was also from Russia. He had a conservative lifestyle and was very devoted to his young daughter; as a result, he felt that Victoria — whose daughter was about the same age as his — could be a good candidate to date and possibly marry. He traveled to Russia and met Victoria and Anna and invited them to visit him in Los Angeles. Once Victoria arrived in America, she realized that Robert was not rich, but rather a very hardworking man with a comfortable middle-class lifestyle. Her dreams of a sports car, boutique dresses and a life of leisure were not going to come true with Robert. She packed her bags and returned to Novosibirsk.

Victoria's trip to California taught her that not every American was a millionaire, and life in the United States was not really that much different from post-Soviet Russia. She returned discouraged by her failed attempt but armed with a great deal more information, a working command of English, an American wardrobe and — what would later prove most valuable of all — a basic understanding of American family law. A new chapter was about to begin for Victoria.

More Than a Name Change

Victoria had a new obstacle to overcome after her return to Russia: She was now part of the U.S. government's immigration database. If she were ever to return, the authorities would know she had visited the country with a U.S. citizen she met online previously. To overcome this potential problem, Victoria made some changes to her life. Equipped with her new English skills, she moved to Moscow with Anna and landed a job as an office assistant in an international oil company. She rented a small apartment in the suburbs and tried to make a living as best she could, but her champagne taste and poor money-management skills started to catch up to her.

A friend at work suggested that, with her looks, she could do some modeling for the many advertising agencies that were opening their doors as the Russian economy grew. She looked into it, and discovered her friend was right. Victoria was frequently hired for modeling assignments, which kept her away from her daughter for a longer part of the day. She quickly found out that modeling paid better than office work, so she moved full time into that job. In addition, she began "dating" clients of the modeling firm, enhancing her income even further.

A few years later, Victoria decided to change her name to Irina to fit the life she had developed in Moscow and to disconnect from her old self. She used a friend who worked in the government to obtain a new set of identity documents. However, age was catching up to Irina, and being a model over thirty was not well received in Russia. At that point, Irina knew what to do, how to do it and whom to target.

The Captain

James Mitchell was a successful man. He was a senior pilot for one of the top three airline companies in the world, a decorated military captain, and he had a number of inventions and investments that made his life very comfortable. James's passion was flying; he was a young aviator and a graduate of the U.S. Navy Fighter Weapons School (also known as the Top Gun school), and, in his forties, he still relished the feel of an airplane under his command. As a senior pilot, he could select any route around the world, and would frequently swap with his peers to break up the monotony of flying to the same city again and again. Being a former Navy pilot, he had not lost the charisma and swagger that appealed to the ladies, despite being in a great deal of pain after the recent loss of his wife to a catastrophic illness. His friends encouraged him to start dating again, especially because he was still young. One of them convinced him to join an international dating Web site because he flew internationally so often. "Even if it doesn't turn up your soul mate," his friend told him, "at least you'll have someone to dine with the next time you're in, say, Moscow."

A few weeks later, James was planning for an upcoming flight to Moscow and decided to look into meeting a Russian woman online. Like his friend said, it would beat eating dinner alone. While browsing his potential matches on the Web site, Irina's photograph caught his eye. He read her online profile and was impressed by her level of success as a single mother. "What's the worst that could happen?" he thought as he sent her an Internet message.

Hook, Line and Sinker

Irina had become quite skilled in assessing the background and net worth of her clients and companions; small hints, like watches, shoes and clothing, would tell her the potential for a relationship in which the primary beneficiary was going to be her. When she met James at a restaurant named Dostoevsky in the Red Square district of Moscow, her interest was piqued. He was well-dressed, and she already knew from reading his Internet dating profile that he was a pilot. Things were looking up, but she wanted to play it safe and did not take the evening beyond dinner that first time. At the end of the meal, she gave her business card to James and suggested that he call if he wanted to have dinner again on his next visit.

A few weeks passed while James thought about his meeting with Irina and the nice conversation they had over dinner, and he decided to call her. He told her he was flying to Moscow again and invited her out a second time. She said she would be delighted and suggested they meet at the same restaurant. Irina knew she had a fish ready to bite and was going to try to hook it.

After their dinner, Irina asked James if he wanted to go dancing at a nearby club. Since he had taken a 36-hour layover, he knew he could safely have a drink or two and be ready to fly in time, so he agreed. By the end of the night, James was hooked and invited Irina to visit him at his home in Winnetka, Illinois. She submitted her passport to the U.S. authorities and was granted a 30-day visitor's visa.

It was early autumn and the leaves were just turning gold in the northern suburbs of Chicago, a beautiful time of year. James met Irina at O'Hare airport's immigration area and escorted her to his Mercedes; they drove to his house so she could rest from the 14-hour flight. As they passed through the double wrought iron gates of the driveway, Irina knew she had made a great catch. James showed her to her room and had his housekeeper take up her bag.

The next day, James took Irina on a tour of Chicago and some of its landmarks. During her 30-day visit, James became quite attached, and when it was time for her to leave, he proposed marriage. Irina was delighted by the prospect of finding someone who would take care of her for the rest of her life. But what she had not mentioned to James — and would not ever mention — was that she had developed a liking for much younger men and had a relationship in Moscow with a young college student named Sergei. In addition, her plan was not to marry and live happily ever after, but to marry and divorce, American style.

Irina returned to Moscow, and a few weeks later flew back to Chicago with Anna to marry James. After a small wedding, they settled into the Winnetka house. Irina began to implement her plan of action, and her first request was for a laptop computer, which James gladly purchased for her.

The Honeymoon Is Over

That June day began as most June days in Chicago — light rain in the morning and hot by early afternoon. Irina was busy on the Internet using instant messaging (IM) to chat with her family, friends and Sergei. The time difference between Chicago and Moscow was convenient because it was early in the day for her, no one was home, and she could chat for several hours, until it was time to decide what to do about dinner.

As the month wore on, Irina executed her plan. She constantly asked James if he would buy her a new car — almost to the point of annoyance — until she broke down his defenses and he agreed to buy her whatever car she wanted. As soon as she was able to go into the city and meet new people, she befriended a woman close to her age who was going through a bad divorce. Irina began to visit her new friend, Candace, and found out about her life. Candace described various problems that her former husband had saddled her with, like credit cards being maxed out, unpaid property taxes and other financial woes. As Irina heard more, she decided to research the things that could happen in American divorces, using the Internet as her primary research tool.

Three months later, she was ready to put her studies to the test. She picked a fight with James by accusing him of being unfaithful with a member of his crew, not an uncommon occurrence in the airline industry. During James's ordeal, she threw a number of household objects at him. Once the argument was in full swing, she called 911 and asked the police to come because her husband was being violent. When officers arrived, they asked James to leave for the rest of the day and spend the night at a hotel. James was confused and didn't understand what was going on; he initially thought there was a misunderstanding and called his new mother-in-law for advice on how to get along better with his wife. Irina's mother told him that the way to reassure Irina of his commitment to her was to adopt Anna. Being the devoted husband that he was, James began to look into the requirements.

Three months later, an attorney had prepared the adoption papers, and they were signed by James and Irina. The two had reconciled and were living under the same roof again. That lasted a short time before Irina began insisting on being added to the house title. At this point, James's patience was running out and he finally started to doubt his new wife's sincerity. He decided to contact an attorney; the attorney spoke to him about the legal implications of his actions so far and recommended that James also speak to an investigator who specialized in family law; he recommended my firm.

Two Is Better Than One

We decided on a two-pronged approach: a physical investigation and a forensic one, for which I was primarily in charge. The physical investigator, Carla Edwards, followed Irina for several days on her outings around the city, and one aspect of the daily routine caught her attention — Irina was visiting a number of different banks and branches around the city. To her, this seemed very peculiar since James said that she only had one bank account, which they shared, and did not have any business ties in the United States.

James's attorney, Dave Phillips, wanted me to see if there was any information of value on Irina's home computer. Dave was not very familiar with electronic evidence and asked me if there were any e-mails that indicated what Irina was thinking and with whom she was communicating.

As part of my standard procedure, I treated the electronic evidence as if it was going to be presented in court. My team and I began by photographing and documenting Irina's laptop, which James sent to us, and then created a forensic image of the hard drive. To do this, we removed the drive and connected it to a write-blocking device, which prevented information from being written to the hard disk, thus preventing modification or deletion of any data. Once the forensic image was created, we ran it through a software program that allowed us to view the contents of the hard drive and see data that was not normally visible to the computer user.

I discovered a familiar but disturbing sign of tampering — an eraser program had been run on the laptop. These types of programs are designed to permanently erase files from the hard drive without leaving any evidence of their existence. After this finding, I halted my normal routine and ran a program that searches for anti-forensic products, logic bombs and other nefarious tricks that attempt to destroy evidence during a forensic examination. Although the courts have determined that anti-forensic tools are evidence of self-incrimination in computer investigations, their presence complicates the processing of a case. The report generated by the software program confirmed the presence of anti-forensic tools, and the installation dates were just after Irina received the laptop from James. After discussing my findings with Dave, I began to treat the investigation as a criminal one and worked under the assumption that Irina was trained in sophisticated anti-forensic techniques.

A Revealing History

My next step was to recover as many deleted files and file fragments from the hard drive as possible and prepare them for examination. This process took me 48 hours, but it yielded a treasure trove of deleted content and more than 90,000 pieces of evidence to be reviewed and examined, including — most important — Irina's Internet history files. It appeared that she had been regularly deleting her Internet history, but I was able to recover it; I saw the Web sites she was visiting and the full extent of her malicious behavior. In the recovered content, I found photographs, e-mails, online chats, access to foreign bank accounts and other files that began to paint a better picture of her activities while married to James. I uncovered the online research she conducted into divorce in the United States and ways to protect her interests. There were graphic e-mails and IMs she shared with Sergei, her Russian boyfriend, and even nude photographs of herself that she sent to him online. I found messages exchanged between Irina and her mother about persuading James to adopt Anna because it would result in child support and more alimony when Irina filed for divorce. And then there were transfers of money from the bank account she shared with James to multiple accounts in her name and those of her family members.

Annulment and Deportation

After several months of investigation, James had enough evidence against Irina to file a motion for annulment of his marriage in the Cook County Court, and a hearing date was set. It was unusual for marriages to be annulled, but in this case it would also terminate Irina's foreign spouse visa and reverse James's adoption of Anna.

I was the principal witness for the plaintiff in the annulment hearing and I walked the judge through the steps involved in locating the evidence on Irina's laptop and determining the dates she had accessed Web sites and sent messages. This was important because I was able to place Irina at the keyboard on the first day she received her computer, having an Internet chat with her lover in Russia, and sending explicit photos of herself. After one day of testimony, our side rested and it was time for the defense attorney to ask me questions. He had a difficult time rebutting the evidence, and most of his questions were related to the possibility of someone else placing the Internet history on the computer, for example, James, in order to avoid a potentially costly divorce. I was able to show the defense attorney how the time stamps ruled that out and explained how the process of imaging prevented the alteration of files. That was the end of the defense's questioning.

At the time, I did not know that an Assistant District Attorney (ADA) was listening to the particulars of this case in the back of the courtroom. About a week later, I received a call from the DA's office asking me to testify before the grand jury. Apparently, in the process of hiding her fraudulent intentions from James, Irina had broken several laws — including a few federal computer crimes statutes — and the DA was interested in prosecuting the case. I appeared before the grand jury a few months later and presented my evidence, and an indictment was returned for various offenses. After a warrant was issued for her arrest, Irina fled Illinois and was last heard of in California. A short time later, a notice of the annulment reached the Department of Homeland Security and her permanent residence card was revoked. A second arrest warrant, this one for a fugitive illegal alien, was issued for Irina. To date, she has not been located, but a car she stole from James was recovered in Arizona. I am confident that if she stays in the United States, Irina will eventually be caught.

Lessons Learned

This particular case brought to my attention a problem faced by those with a high net worth — the possibility that someone is entering a romantic relationship for the wrong reasons. Marrying for money is nothing new, of course, but with Internet dating, it has become much easier for people to be taken advantage of financially. It is difficult to protect against this fraud because human nature tends to lower a person's defenses when romance is involved. These cases are also hard to detect because the victims often do not want to recognize that they have been conned by a loved one.

(continued)

(continued)

It is becoming more common for international couples considering marriage to conduct checks into each other's backgrounds to make sure there are no undisclosed skeletons in the closet. Organizations like the World Association of Detectives and other reputable companies can help verify the backgrounds of potential mates. In this particular case, Irina's name change would have been a red flag that might have led to the discovery of her earlier visit to the United States.

Recommendations to Prevent Future Occurrences

In a world where the Internet connects us all, more and more couples are falling in love across national borders, particularly in Western countries. People with significant assets — a subjective term that varies from country to country — should consider hiring a professional to run a background check on romantic interests met online. According to psychological experts, it is easier to deal with deception earlier in a relationship than once a permanent commitment has been made. Unfortunately, Internet dating Web sites that claim to provide background checks can be either very superficial or nonexistent because they reduce the "inventory" offered to the prospective customer.

About the Author

Ernesto F. Rojas is the founder and president of Forensic & Security Services Inc., a firm specializing in electronic forensic investigations, extracting data from cell phones, GPS receivers and computer systems of all sizes. Its primary focus is in the fraud arena and cases that involve fraudulent data. Mr. Rojas has more than 25 years of experience in electronic and information systems and has done security-consulting work for private and government organizations. He is recognized as an expert witness in the state and federal courts. He may be reached at efrojas@for-sec.com.

CHAPTER 3

Behind a Smoke Screen

JAY DAWDY

Johnny Lee was the son of a peasant farmer in Yunxiao County in the province of Fujian, China. Brett Sinclair was a hardworking, white-collar professional living in Manhattan's Upper East Side. Johnny was uneducated and poor but worked hard and made a decent living by Yunxiao's standards, even if the industry he worked in was a bit shady. Brett had an excellent education, a great job and made plenty of money, but he was known as a cheapskate by his friends. He tried to save a few bucks wherever he could.

These two 25-year-olds lived in different worlds, but they both had a secret, and, unbeknownst to them, they also had a connection. The twosome was linked together at opposite ends of a complex network of people, companies and technology involved in the counterfeit cigarette trade. Simply put, Johnny made counterfeit cigarettes and Brett bought them. But the larger story was a far more complicated tale of a global black-market industry that had exploded through the use of the Internet.

Johnny Lee's secret was that he went to work every day in an illegal operation inside a cave hidden by the thick forests in the Yunxiao countryside. Inside that cave was a fully operational cigarette-manufacturing facility that cranked out counterfeit cigarettes by the millions each year. These cigarettes were produced with well-known U.S. and European cigarette labels, but they were 100-percent counterfeit. Even though producing counterfeit cigarettes was illegal in China, it was a highly lucrative business for the locals, and it beat the hard labor and low pay that went along with peasant farming. In fact, hundreds of locals worked in the industry because they could earn a far better living as counterfeiters than in the other limited opportunities that were available. Additionally, the chances of getting caught were slim, and the punishment was light if that happened. In other words, the cost-benefit ratio for counterfeiting cigarettes made sense.

I came to understand that Johnny was just one small piece of a much larger network of production and trade in counterfeit cigarettes around the globe. Even though it was in an illegal industry, Johnny's employer, Shin Tao Exporters, was vertically integrated and sophisticated. In addition to making the cigarettes, Shin Tao grew their own tobacco in Southern China, Vietnam, Laos and throughout Southeast Asia. And Shin Tao had a robust and growing customer base. They exported to distribution channels across the world — principally to cities in Russia, Eastern Europe and more recently a number of African countries, including Kenya and Tanzania.

Of course Johnny didn't know much about the global trade in counterfeit cigarettes or the many layers of exporters and smugglers between him and Brett — who was buying his cigarettes on the Internet. Johnny was simply keeping his nose to the grindstone and trying to make a good living. In his mind, he was doing his job, providing for his family and trying to hide the secret of his illegal activities.

Brett, however, more than 10,000 miles away in a different environment completely, was attempting to do more than make a living. He was trying to make enough money to buy a co-op on the Upper East Side — not easy in Manhattan's hot real estate market. Brett was tech savvy, smart and driven. He worked hard, tried to save as much money as he could and did almost everything on the Internet. He shopped online, ordered his groceries online, traded stocks online and did his banking online. Hell, he even dated online. Another thing that Brett did online was buy his cigarettes. In Brett's mind, everything was cheaper and more efficient online — especially buying cigarettes. Cigarettes sold online were much cheaper, in part because there were no hefty local taxes assessed on them, unlike the cigarettes Brett sometimes purchased at the corner newsstand in his neighborhood.

Sometimes the smokes Brett bought online tasted a little funky, but overall, they weren't too bad. And they looked like the real thing, even though the packages they came in were from some faraway places, like Thailand, Russia and many of the old Soviet countries with names Brett couldn't pronounce. It was true; Brett was a cheapskate who bought his cigarettes online, but he did it for understandable reasons.

Shin Tao

Brett and Johnny were linked indirectly because Brett was buying the cigarettes that Johnny was making for Shin Tao. What Brett didn't know, or for that matter, what Johnny didn't know, was that Shin Tao was just one small player in a worldwide industry. Counterfeit goods in general were a major export from China, and cigarettes were just one of the many black-market industries that had grown significantly in the past 20 years.

Shin Tao was one of hundreds of small counterfeit-cigarette entrepreneurs that had sprung up in the countryside of Yunxiao over the years. To get started, producers only needed a few cigarette machines, the raw materials to make the product, people to feed the machines, and a good place to hide the production facilities. The buyers were easy to find and the profit margins were great. There were hundreds of companies just like Shin Tao operating in and out of Yunxiao, combining to produce what some experts estimated at more than 450 billion counterfeit cigarettes per year.

Shin Tao was owned and operated by a few entrepreneurial locals who had several other production facilities around the Yunxiao countryside. Although this was big business, and the local officials knew what was going on (and were being paid to turn a blind eye), Shin Tao and the other counterfeiters were cutting into government revenues, so they had to operate in hidden locations — like caves, basements and other discrete spots located throughout the countryside.

But the Shin Tao founders were smart, careful and astute businessmen. As they grew, they established multiple covert operations. In the event that one location was discovered by the authorities, they could simply shut it down and continue their production elsewhere. And, in fact, the founders of Shin Tao were just one of many players on the lowest level of the massive production and distribution network in the counterfeit-cigarette trade. Shin Tao sold its cigarettes mainly to overseas buyers in Russia, Eastern Europe and Africa — the same places from where Brett's cigarettes were being shipped.

Over the years, Shin Tao had evolved from a local seller into a global wholesaler, producing a fake product at a far lower cost than the real thing and selling it at a profit to distributors around the globe. The products it sent to customers in Russia, Kenya and Tanzania tended to stay in-country; however, the cigarettes going to Eastern Europe were distributed to the United States and around the globe via the Internet. These Eastern European importers were more commonly referred to as smugglers. They were a new wave of entrepreneurs who made the big money in the counterfeit-cigarette business, selling to end consumers around the world.

The smugglers were based in Belarus, Georgia and Uzbekistan. In a short time, they had perfected the art, science and technology of trading black-market goods. These criminals had plenty of experience fencing counterfeit goods in the past, and they had developed a robust distribution network. They had perfected the use of one of the most efficient and cheapest distribution systems mankind had ever seen — the Internet.

The Eastern European middlemen hired a group of young programmers and Internet geniuses to develop Web sites to sell the illicit booty. The smugglers mainly bought from China and sold their products in the United

States. Their Web sites, online ordering interfaces, shipping and logistics capabilities would have made Amazon, Google and Yahoo! proud. The sites were everywhere and the sellers were prodigious in their ability to fill orders and ship cigarettes. And it started with the massive supply of counterfeit cigarettes coming out of China, including those from Shin Tao Exporters.

What the counterfeiters and smugglers didn't count on was the victims — multiple types of victims — getting tired of being ripped off. The legitimate cigarette manufacturers were, of course, being victimized in the form of lost sales to the counterfeiters. Local municipalities, particularly in the United States, that collected heavy taxes on cigarettes sold in their jurisdictions were also victimized by the lost tax revenue. And last but not least, the end buyers, like Brett, were being victimized, and many of them didn't even realize it. Although they were buying cheaper smokes online, the counterfeit cigarettes were unregulated and contained much higher levels of nicotine, carbon monoxide and other toxins than the originals, creating serious additional health concerns (as if smoking wasn't bad enough already).

The Gathering Storm

Victims were finally wising up, and they decided to do something about it. This was not a case in which there was an "aha moment" when a discovery was made that resulted in an investigation. The counterfeit market had been around a long time, but in the last few years, the counterfeiters had become much more sophisticated in mimicking the real product. As a result, they were able to sell more and more cigarettes. The supply increased rapidly as more counterfeiters popped up and realized the profit margins to be made by selling tobacco online.

As the Eastern European smugglers started exploiting the Internet as their distribution tool of choice, the trade in counterfeit cigarettes in New York and other U.S. cities exploded. With the perfection of the Internet as a distribution mechanism, the counterfeiters and smugglers began to seriously cut into the profit margins of the legitimate companies.

And as the counterfeiters multiplied, the established cigarette manufacturers around the world began to explore new ways of stopping them. The counterfeiters and smugglers were not only cutting into their profit margins, but the legit manufacturers were losing control of their brands, marketing and distribution networks.

Simply put, the genuine manufacturers were losing the battle to the counterfeiters and smugglers and they needed creative solutions to the problem. Other big players were also losing to the counterfeiters — state and local tax authorities. They were not collecting the taxes they were owed on the sale of counterfeit cigarettes, and cigarette taxes were a big source of tax revenue. As we know, the taxman doesn't like it when he doesn't get his cut. What resulted was a strange mix of bedfellows as clients, and some new and creative ideas for investigation. That's where my team came in.

New Challenges

During my investigative career, I had seen numerous frauds, worked on interesting and unique cases, and run into many nefarious characters. But when I received a call from a new client requesting that I run an undercover operation to buy cigarettes over the Internet, I remember thinking, "Wow, this is something different."

This case, in a nutshell, involved investigating the improper sale of counterfeit cigarettes over the Internet through a variety of Web sites, but no one knew who was behind the sites. Our client wanted to identify the responsible parties, go after them, and shutdown their networks. What we didn't know at the time was that, in addition to counterfeiters and their improper distribution methods, we would also uncover a vast network of questionable characters across the globe who were stealing products and selling them over the Internet. These schemes resulted in the selling of illegal and dangerous merchandise to unsuspecting consumers who usually thought they were simply getting a good deal.

After some research on my end and detailed briefings with the client, we realized that the Internet could be used as a powerful tool for the distribution of counterfeit goods. But we also came to understand that the Internet could be used as a superior investigative tool and a platform for conducting undercover operations.

Our assignment was relatively simple: Go online, identify the most prominent Web sites selling a certain brand of cigarettes, pose as consumers, and buy a predetermined amount of cigarettes to be delivered to addresses in New York City. We also carefully documented our purchases and receipts and engaged in dialog with the sellers whenever possible to gather information about their locations, modes of operation and any other background that might later be useful to our investigation.

I put together a team of mostly younger investigators who seemed to be online constantly. This team identified the Web sites in question and embarked on a very controlled and documented undercover-buy operation through the Internet. Working with the client, we developed a specific ordering protocol, documentation requirements (including capturing screen-shots of every relevant Internet page), and a purchasing method. After receiving the cigarettes, we followed a detailed chain-of-custody process, carefully cataloging the product receipts along with the ordering documents, taking video and still photos and packaging the evidence for delivery to outside counsel.

The sellers didn't know or care who we were. They didn't check age requirements or worry about local taxes that should have been levied. The sellers had been operating with impunity for years and had no apparent fear of being investigated or caught; they were just trying to sell as many counterfeit cigarettes as they could.

To do the buys, our investigators used their own credit cards designated solely for this case, and we had the cigarettes delivered via U.S. mail. We obtained new credit cards upfront for this purpose and then canceled them after the project to avoid any subsequent unwanted billing. We then examined the products received to identify the sellers and their locations when we could. The sellers included a variety of overseas smugglers, counterfeiters, gray-market dealers and sovereign groups that were selling goods in violation of several laws.

While attempting to investigate to the source of the counterfeiters and smugglers, we engaged in interesting chats over the Internet and collected some useful tidbits of intelligence about them, but for the most part they were wary of providing details about their locations and business activities.

My group of investigators — most in their twenties — loved this engagement. They were able to surf the Internet at work and rack up amazing bonus points and frequent-flier miles on their credit cards from the high volume of purchases we were making. They also had some funny stories about the reactions of their local post offices and neighbors, given the number of suspicious-looking boxes they were receiving from Eastern Europe. One of my investigator's neighbors wanted to stage an intervention because she thought his smoking habit had gotten out of control. "How could one boy smoke all those cigarettes?" his neighbor, Delores, asked him repeatedly.

Redemption and Raids

Ultimately, we were successful in documenting the counterfeiters and identifying a plethora of groups that were assisting the smuggling and distribution operations in the United States. Our investigative work resulted in the shutdown of a number of illegal Web sites. I wish I could say that our investigation made a big dent in identifying and shutting down the vast network of smugglers in Eastern Europe and the producers in China, but that would be too good to be true.

The fact is that although our work was vital in terms of assisting counsel in closing a number of Web sites with U.S. ties, new Web sites popped up daily. Additionally, many of them operated outside the United States, so the legal jurisdiction and ability to impact their operations was complicated and difficult at best.

However, we had a number of successes, particularly in the United States and within New York City. One of them involved Brett Sinclair's local newsstand. You see, Brett was actually one of my undercover investigators. Much to his neighbor Delores's relief, he actually had a good excuse for buying so many cigarettes — and he wasn't smoking all of them! Brett was working for the good guys the whole time, purchasing cigarettes, documenting his buys and continuing to investigate the source of counterfeits, just like the rest of my team.

In one particular instance, after doing some online buys, receiving the cigarettes, and engaging the supplier in online chatting, Brett learned the products bought from this Web site were being distributed via a warehouse in Brooklyn, New York.

After obtaining permission from the client, we engaged in additional investigation of the storage facility in Brooklyn. We sent a surveillance team to the location, documented trucks coming and going, wrote down license plates, collected video evidence, and followed some of the outgoing trucks to their next destination for delivery. A few of them went right back across the river into Manhattan and delivered cigarettes to local newsstands and neighborhood bodegas, which were selling the counterfeit cigarettes and making great profit margins. Sure enough, one of the newsstands was right down the street from Brett's apartment; the investigation had really come full circle.

With the assistance and approval of the client, we presented our findings to local law enforcement, which subsequently raided both the warehouse and the retail locations; confiscated the counterfeit products; and closed a number of the warehouses, newsstands and bodegas that were selling counterfeit products.

Lessons Learned

This case made me appreciate the reach and distributive power of the Internet for the dissemination of counterfeit goods. Although we were investigating counterfeit cigarettes, this could have been any other counterfeit merchandise. The Internet as the medium through which these products were sold provided cover for the individuals committing the fraud. The perpetrators were hard to trace because they hid behind their Web sites and offered little information about their identities or operations. However, we also learned that the Internet can be a powerful tool and a mechanism for

(continued)

(continued)

launching online and undercover investigations; it was the primary investigative tool employed in this case. Through our undercover purchases and subsequent Internet-based investigation to isolate and identify the offenders, we were able to stop future sales, dismantle Web sites and confiscate counterfeited and stolen products.

By capitalizing on the anonymity of the Internet, we used the fraudsters' tools to catch them. This brought out another reinforcing lesson for any investigation, which was to think like the fraudster and use their tools and methods against them. In this case, the perpetrators were sophisticated Internet-based smugglers, so we used the Internet against them. By performing most of our investigation online, we were able to collect valuable evidence that helped shut down their operations. Had we tried to contact these smugglers on the phone or approach them in person, they would have run for the hills. Instead we approached them in the way they were most comfortable — through the Internet.

Another important focus in this investigation was to appeal to the criminals' sense of greed. They were in business to sell counterfeit cigarettes and make money, so they were gullible to our undercover operation — and willing to sell to almost anyone. That, of course, backfired. However, if fraudsters think there is something in it for them, they are usually more than willing to unwittingly succumb to undercover operations.

A key ingredient to the success of this case — including the ultimate seizure of counterfeit products and capture of local merchants trading counterfeit goods — was the support of local government authorities. They had a vested interest in the case, but it was important to get them on board from the start. The threat of being put out of business and the attention of the authorities were, in many ways, more powerful deterrents to the criminals than the civil remedies that our client could employ. This lesson can apply to any investigation. It's important to think about who your allies are: law enforcement, other victims who are willing to pay for your services or cooperation by a related party who may have relevant information. The more interested parties and allies you have on your side (and frankly the more authority figures and deeper pockets your side has), the stronger your chances of success will be.

This case also made me realize that, even though we were not able to stop each player involved, as investigators we can make progress in small increments. It's important to keep working hard, pushing back, and being aggressive. And even if you can't completely solve the problem — as in this engagement — achieving smaller successes, such as closing a group of Web sites and the identification of local merchants who were buying from these sites, was in fact progress. Our success was also a major deterrent to others trading in this space.

Recommendations to Prevent Future Occurrences

From a consumer standpoint, this case reinforced that old maxim of buyer beware. This is especially true when buying anything over the Internet. Consumers should know who they are dealing with and what products they are buying before making any Internet-based purchases. It's easy for fraudsters, black-market purveyors and other scam artists to take advantage of the Internet's anonymity; consumers must take extra steps to ensure they are buying legitimate products from legitimate sellers.

From our client's viewpoint — the manufacturers and retailers who were being defrauded by Internet counterfeiters — this investigation supported several recommendations to prevent future occurrences. Below are steps that similar businesses should consider taking:

1. *Develop a robust tracking and monitoring program to track counterfeit activity that may be occurring with your products.* The Internet has made this a much more efficient process, and it can be done more cost-effectively than the traditional gumshoe investigative methods of the past. Programs and personnel can be put in place to detect new Web sites selling counterfeit products and to monitor activity on existing ones.

2. *Engage in active and relentless investigation and enforcement to combat counterfeiting.* Although it may seem like a never-ending battle, your actions will pay dividends in the long term and help keep the counterfeiters at bay. The Internet has made the investigative process more efficient, meaning you can do more with less. Plus, the costs of not engaging in counter-offensive investigations are too great.

3. *Partnerships with city, state, and federal government or other key allies are important and can pay huge dividends.* Engaging the authorities in your investigative initiatives can be very beneficial.

4. *Combat both supply and demand.* This is not specific to the counterfeit trade in cigarettes, but it is important when investigating fraud of any kind. Where there is demand for products or proceeds of fraudulent activity, there will be fraudsters ready to meet the need. In our case, following the investigation to the demand — the newsstand buyer who was purchasing counterfeit cigarettes — was the flip side of following the supply chain back to Shin Tao in China. Ultimately, if there is no demand, there will be no supply.

My key recommendation is establishing stronger fraud prevention. One of the most effective tools I've encountered is to increase the perception of detection. If fraudsters think they are likely to be caught and the punishment outweighs the benefits of the crime, they are less likely to engage in fraudulent behavior. In any investigative effort or in the implementation of any preventive controls and procedures, this concept should be part of the overall plan. By aggressively investigating fraud and following through with enforcement actions, you increase the perception of detection, which is a key to substantial savings in the future.

About the Author

Jay Dawdy, CFE, CMA, is the president of Gryphon Investigations. He has more than twenty years of finance, accounting and investigative experience and concentrates on complex financial, litigation support, due diligence and fraud investigative cases. Mr. Dawdy served as an instructor in investigating financial fraud at Baruch College and presents and writes frequently on fraud investigation and prevention.

Cars, Cards, Chemicals and Crayons

AL STERNBERG

Mark Hagen was a 21-year-old resident of Hillside County. He attended Hillside Technical Community College but had not completed his studies. Mark worked at the Hyland Steakhouse as a take-out window employee. He was on probation for speeding to elude police and was known to have a history of break-ins and drug abuse. As a deputy sheriff, I had become acquainted with Mark during a fraud examination earlier that year that resulted in his arrest. When I spoke to Hagen's father, he told me he had bailed him out of trouble on many occasions and he was no longer welcome at home because Mark had assaulted him. Mr. Hagen told me to have the courts throw the book at his own son.

Jerry Settles was a 22-year-old transient and friend of Mark Hagen. In December, he was sleeping on the couch in the apartment that Hagen shared with a housemate, Ginger Taylor. Settles had a small child with an ex-girlfriend, but the child and the ex-girlfriend lived in a town on the coast. Settles had some previous run-ins with the law in a nearby county. He made a difficult living on a cash basis as a tattoo artist and kept the tools of his trade in Mark's apartment.

The Benefits of Early Morning Banking

I never thought to ask Paula Searcy why she chose 3:00 one morning in the first week of September to do some online banking. In any event, she did — and discovered that a fraudulent purchase for $110 was charged against her account to purchase something from a Web site called Euro Parts. The transaction posted only two hours earlier. She immediately contacted Euro Parts and spoke with Georg Lindemans about the unauthorized transaction. He was very cooperative and gave her a description of the car accessories ordered and the address of where the goods were supposed to be shipped. Due to the prompt discovery of the fraud, the order was stopped.

She notified her bank and filed a police report with the Hillside County sheriff's office.

I happened to be receiving incoming fraud reports at the sheriff's office that week. I classified Paula's case as workable because the shipping address was a house just down the street from hers. At the time, I was tracking a series of cases in which victims reported receiving packages they did not order. The packages contained consumer electronics, such as digital cameras, cell phones and computer gear — all billed to the victims' credit or debit card accounts. After tracking Internet protocol (IP) traffic patterns used by the perpetrators in Paula's case, I concluded the offenders were either war driving (seeking out unsecured wireless networks to use for anonymous Internet access to commit crimes) or placing orders from another state or country. This type of crime makes sense only if the fraudster is local, mobile, and able to intercept packages, or if he has a coconspirator who can intercept the packages. This local offender can either place the order himself or instruct others to place it for him. In a local case such as Paula's, when there is no relationship between the victim and suspect, the victim's identity has usually been stolen locally as well. This mystery offender was worth hunting despite the low value of the attempted fraud and the stopped shipment.

Following an Online Trail

I contacted Georg at Euro Parts and asked him to e-mail me details about Paula's order and to confirm the IP origination data. Georg was highly cooperative and told me he was happy to see someone in law enforcement trying to track this sort of crime. The fraudster had ordered three novelty European-style vehicle registration plates and had requested unique names for each plate. Georg forwarded several e-mails sent to Euro Parts by the offender. Georg even strung the offender along about the order, drawing out more e-mail IP traffic and evidence of the attempted wire fraud. The IP data we were able to gather included dates, timestamps and time zones. The offender was using the e-mail address admin@euroresearchltd.com. The use of *admin@* was unusual because most fraudulent e-mail accounts involve anonymous services such as Yahoo! or Hotmail.

Using www.geobytes.com/ipLocator.htm, I confirmed that the Cable Com sub-IP address used by the perpetrator was local. Next I used the Whois tool on www.arin.net and found out that Cable Com was also the Internet service provider (ISP) for the originating e-mail order. Whois is a function that lists Web site registrant data, technical contact information, date of registration and hosting server data. Most Whois data is provided on an honor-system basis and cannot be taken strictly at face value. I ran the novelty plate names, looking for nicknames in my agency database, Facebook and MySpace, but found nothing. I next went to www.eurore-searchltd.com and found this:

Euro Research Limited

To enter the site you must be pre-approved. Please have your username and password ready and click here to enter when ready.

DO NOT give out your site username to anyone, EVER. We currently monitor IP Address activity per username, should we suspect you have given out your username you will be contacted and possibly banned.

You need to be referred by a previous customer to join the site, you may contact the admin if you have username or password issues.

Once you have been approved you will receive an ERL based email address and password, you are expected to place your orders and ask questions through this email address only.

Let us know if you have any questions.

To login to your ERL based email please click here.

There was no other information on the homepage regarding what customers buy or do there. The explicit warnings and instructions seemed designed to warn off casual visitors.

Using the Firefox browser toolbar, I clicked *view*, then *page source*. This function electronically decodes a Web site into text format and displays the underlying code used to construct the page. I was looking for hidden content, metatags and true e-mail/hyperlink paths. Meta tags are used to hide webpage construction code the page's author does not wish to display on the open page. Occasionally, a meta tag reveals an author's name. Other meta tags hide keywords used to snag the interest of search engines. I noted a meta tag identifying the Web site as "your local source for fine chemicals." I took this to be a weak euphemism for illegal drug distribution and sales.

I conducted a Whois search on www.register.com to see who was responsible for the Euro Research Web site and discovered that the registrant was an entity called Streaming Power. Whois also showed that the record was created via a domain registration service in March. Domain servers were also on Streaming Power. I noticed the use of *admin* as the contact for www.euroresearchltd.com, which implied that the user was the administrator and controller of the Web site. The members' *click here* link led to a sub-Web site hosted at Streaming Power, which indicated the Streaming Power servers and hosting were integral to operation of the Euro Research Web site. The source code revealed that clicking on the *contact the admin* link led to admin@euroresearchltd.com, the same e-mail account used by the suspect in the original crime.

Based on this preliminary investigation, I obtained court orders signed by a superior court judge to compel Streaming Power and Cable Com to identify customer and user account data. I served these on the companies in late September. By November, I had heard nothing and resubmitted the orders Thanksgiving week. This time, Streaming Power's corporate attorney contacted me right away and sent the compliance data disk overnight.

Around this time, I came down with an illness that kept me out of work for nearly three weeks. I took the disk from Streaming Power and my case file home. While recovering, I had plenty of time to conduct an electronic investigation, reach out to others for information, and eventually type the drafts of search warrants and arrest warrants on the suspect.

The Credit Card Lifter

I reviewed the data from Streaming Power and found that the creator of www.euroresearchltd.com used the e-mail address cclifter@hushmail.com to create the Web site. From this brazen name, standing for "credit card lifter," I formed a working hypothesis that the Web site was used for trafficking drugs and stolen identity data. (Note that a hypothesis is only that — it could be correct or incorrect; but at least it is something to work with.) I checked the e-mail hosting service and found it to be a service that incorporates encrypted messaging. I also found the following residual e-mail content (excerpted):

```
From: yhrtvui Service <service@yhrtvui.com>
To: euroresltd <admin@euroresearchltd.com>
Message-Id: <redacted>@yhrtvui.com>
Date: <redacted> 12:54:32 -0700 (PDT)
<redacted> has made a comment on BMW 328i new muffler
zound: i can't believe you missed crushing that camera.
```

I immediately was struck by the BMW reference. Earlier that year, I charged Mark Hagen with three fraud felonies that involved making false statements to victims. He would sell them BMW parts and accessories, take their money, and never ship the goods. He met the victims on a BMW aficionados' Web site. At the time, Hagen's MySpace page had a reference to a BMW 328i. The three victims who filed complaints were from out of state.

Based on this recovered e-mail content, it appeared that somebody had opened an account on YouTube using the name "euroresltd" and the e-mail address admin@euroresearchltd.com. Euroresltd posted a video clip, another person with a YouTube account commented on it, and YouTube automatically sent the comment to admin@euroresearchltd.com. Euroresltd appeared to be an abbreviation for Euro Research Limited.

I went to YouTube to look at the BMW video and saw that it was the only video this euroresltd had posted. The BMW in the video appeared to be black. It drove over the camera, turned around, and a hand picked up the camera before the video clip ended.

The compliance data from Streaming Power included the following e-mail sent by a euroresearchltd.com sub-account:

```
From: <admin@cclifter.streamingpower.com>
To: beth@<redacted>
Subject: remember me!?
Reply-To: admin@cclifter.streamingpower.com
Date: <redacted>14:35:10 -0700

hello beth,
my name is mark, i ordered from you a couple of times,
you may recall me as river.2c0@thuderpel.com that email service sucks
so i am trying again from my new one. If you're still in the business,
i'd like to do a new order from you, can you verify if the price is still right?
i'd like to order 5 grams of ``2c-i'' and 5 grams of ``DOI'' to
make a total of 10 grams...in the past this was $980 and we did this thru moneygram.
if it's cool, let me know what name you want me to send the money to and where.
also can you send me a new price list.
```

This appeared to be an uncoded message to a narcotics source to tell Beth that he was contacting her from an e-mail address she was not familiar with and showing his credentials by providing his old e-mail address and his first name. I conducted a little Internet research on 2C-I and DOI; I discovered they are exotic, rare designer drugs that have hallucinogenic and psychedelic effects. 2C-I is considered an analogue of 2C-B, another psychedelic that is on my state's controlled-substances list. The e-mail sender identified himself as Mark, which strengthened my suspicions it was Mark Hagen. I also noticed that the admin@cclifter.streamingpower.com e-mail address was added to www.euroresearchltd.com as a user on the same date that the e-mail was sent. I added the solicitation to purchase drugs to my working hypothesis.

During my previous investigation, I found user names and nicknames for Mark Hagen, including the name "marksman," on MySpace and the BMW fan Web site. I went to MySpace's "friend finder" service, searched for marksman, and quickly located Hagen's MySpace page. The thumbnail view featured a photo I knew to be of Mark Hagen.

Insanity and Bulls**t

I ran a Google search on euroresltd and was led to a blog maintained by www.thedopehead.com. I ran a query in the blog on euroresltd and pulled up numerous postings and posting strings. One of the posters on the Web site made the following statement:

> Re: idiots & a****les
> smok6e on <redacted> Oct 23, <redacted> 5:27 pm
> whoa, i looked up marksman and euroresltd dude they post from the same IP dude whut u think we're smokin . . . .

My query on euroresltd also provided a detailed photo essay from October 2008 and a list of items he ordered or bought, including variants of psilocybe mushrooms — a Schedule-I controlled substance. He was quite proud of his accomplishments and posted photos of his equipment and his growing operation. He even posted a photo of his bedroom. Manufacturing and growing Schedule-I controlled substances expanded the scope of my case. Further perusal of blog threads revealed that euroresltd had angered others, including smok6e who went to the trouble to link marksman and euroresltd by IP address. I made a separate query on marksman and found numerous postings going back a long time, including one that said, ''you can also find him on a bunch of other forums by typing 'research chemicals' into google.'' I did just that and located some useful posts, one of which led me to this entry:

> Marksman
>
> wannabe (guest)
>
> IP: Logged Jul 07 <redacted, previous year> at 7:48pm
>
> Botanical exploration
> Anyone looking for any botanical products, if you don't see them on the inventory i can usually find them from someplace, i got super ebayer rating just email river.2c0@thuderpel.com

The e-mail address was the same one in the e-mail to Beth.

In early December, I finally received the compliance material from Cable Com and traced the IP address to Ginger Taylor, with a North Hillside apartment as the service address. A second IP address in the documents was associated with an apartment in the same building. Taylor's account was canceled in late October.

One of my colleagues told me that Mark Hagen was currently living with Ginger Taylor in the same apartment on the Cable Com documentation.

I drove by the apartment and saw Hagen's black BMW 328i parked in front. DMV records showed the car was registered to Hagen's father.

I had one of my crime analysts pull employment records on Hagen and discovered he was working at Hyland Steakhouse in North Hillside. I formed an additional working hypothesis that he obtained stolen bank and credit card information from his job. I checked the restaurant's hours; they serve lunch and dinner only, from 11:00 AM to 10:00 PM I figured Hagen would most likely be a late sleeper, and that a visit around 8:00 AM should catch him at home. On the strength of my experience raiding scores of identity theft locations, I thought Hagen would have considerable evidence of his crimes stashed in his "safe house" base. I also thought that Hagen would have additional evidence in his car because he had to be mobile when harvesting packages off other people's porches.

Based on the confluence of evidence and data I had found up to that point, I believed that there existed a strong likelihood and probable cause that the unknown suspect behind the euroresearchltd mask and Mark Hagen were one and the same. A magistrate judge agreed with me, signing search warrants for Hagen's apartment and car. He also signed felony arrest warrants for the original crimes; one count was for identity theft, reflecting Paula Searcy as a victim, and the other count was obtaining property by false pretenses, reflecting Euro Parts as a victim.

The next morning, I met with other raid participants, including the Hillside police department fraud and forgery unit, since its officers would have interest in an identity thief operating in their city. Hillside's cyber crimes unit came out to help with collection of computer gear. I was also joined by a few other sheriff's office investigators, a supervisor who would serve as the officer in charge, and a Hillside uniformed patrol officer. It is always good practice in search warrant operations to have a uniformed officer with you at the front door. We also brought a federal agent with us for his electronic crimes expertise. It is a separate crime to lie to a federal agent, a great advantage for us if the apartment occupants gave statements.

The Jig Is Up

At the apartment, we knocked on the front door and not-so-subtly announced our office and purpose: "POLICE! SEARCH WARRANT! OPEN THE DOOR!" A young man opened the door. He was not Mark Hagen. We entered and began to secure the apartment. Ginger Taylor was in the shower. Hagen's room was locked. We called out to him to open the door, and when he finally did, he was groggy from being awakened. We got everyone calmed down and secured. We identified the man who opened the door as Jerry Settles. I went over the details and scope of the search warrant with Settles, Hagen and Taylor and gave them a copy to read while we commenced the search. The Hillside uniformed officer kept watch over the apartment occupants.

At this stage, my practice is to conduct a walkthrough of the premises, take photos detailing the condition of the place, and assess which areas would most likely yield the evidence. I zeroed in on Hagen's bedroom and the living room. Evidence was packaged and identified based on where it was found and collected. Hagen's bedroom looked just like the photos I'd seen on the Dopehead forum on the Web. We sent a team to search Hagen's car. Hillside's cyber crimes unit worked on documenting and collecting the computer equipment, and we seized several computers and hard drives. No fraud evidence was found in the BMW.

During the search, I looked through the bottom bureau drawer in Hagen's room and discovered five Hyland Steakhouse triplicate order slips with imprints of the fronts of credit and debit cards, including card numbers, expiration dates and names. I found a printed private MySpace message from a person using a nickname that exactly matched one of the novelty license plates ordered with Paula Searcy's card. I found numerous pay stubs for Mark Hagen showing he worked at Hyland Steakhouse.

We also found a considerable amount of marijuana-related drug paraphernalia scattered in plain sight in Hagen's bedroom and on the dining table. Hagen acknowledged the paraphernalia on the table in the common area was his. I showed Hagen the bankcard imprints and asked him why he had them. He said he got them a few months ago and never used them.

The cyber crimes unit supervisor scanned computer networks in the area and found there were at least four unsecured wireless networks within range of the Taylor-Hagen apartment. This showed how easy it would be for Hagen to piggyback on other people's accounts.

Jerry Settles asked to speak with me in private. He told me he suspected that Hagen ordered something with one of the card numbers but had the item shipped in Settles's name to the apartment. I found a cell phone on the floor near the dining table, and Settles claimed it as his. I wrote down the phone number and returned it to Settles at the end of the search. I found a Pyrex container full of marijuana in Settles's box of tattoo equipment, which he initially blamed on one of his clients but later claimed responsibility for. Hillside police charged him with drug possession.

Felonies, Felonies and Felonies

When we were finished with the search, I gave Taylor a copy of the inventory we seized and informed Hagen that he was under arrest and would be going to jail. On the drive downtown, Hagen asked me to explain the charges to him. I went over the elements of the crimes and told him the five credit card imprints were each separate, additional fraud felonies. I told him that because he had so many charges, his punishment grade would be beefed up to a more serious fraud felony level.

I'll never forget Hagen's next statement: "These are *felonies?*"

When I came into his holding cell to inform him of his additional misdemeanor charge of possession of drug paraphernalia, he told me he suspected Settles had gotten into his room and used one of the card numbers to order glass marijuana pipes and bongs. Hagen told me the lock he had on his bedroom door was to keep his housemates out of his room and his stuff. He also asked if he could call his job to let them know he would be late that evening.

After booking him, I sent off inquiries to my crime analyst and bank fraud investigator contacts to try to identify the cardholders. I made an appointment to meet Hagen's boss, Marie Bass, the proprietor of the Hyland Steakhouse. I went to the restaurant that evening and showed her copies of the card imprints. She told me she recently saw video surveillance of Hagen suspiciously leaning over something in the take-out area, his workspace. Bass said she searched his area and found some crayons that looked like they had been used sideways, as if to make imprints. Bass wanted Hagen prosecuted for stealing the card numbers. She also wanted to make an example to other employees that such behavior is intolerable.

The next day, I was able to identify and interview the cardholders. All wanted to prosecute. Each victim had paid with credit or debit cards at the Hyland Steakhouse take-out window. One victim identified more than $300 in fraudulent charges on her card in late November to Media Town, a site that sells downloadable music and movies. Another card number was used to make purchases at two Web sites, Glass Bowls and Groovy Glass. I looked at the Web sites and identified their wares as obvious marijuana pipes. Another card was used to make a fraudulent purchase at Cell-Tel, a cell-phone service provider. I later tracked another transaction to Shroom Haus, a Midwest supplier of psychedelic spores and grow equipment. I spoke to Hagen's neighbor, whose Cable Com account Hagen had piggybacked, and he also wanted to prosecute. I did not contact, nor charge on behalf of, Glass Bowls, Groovy Glass, or Shroom Haus.

My contact at Cell-Tel sent me data showing the stolen card number was used and declined to try to make an $80.07 payment on a prepaid wireless phone account. The phone number was Jerry Settles's. Settles neglected to mention this payment to me in our conversation. I called Settles on his cell phone and asked about the Media Town transactions. He denied them but said Hagen had a lot of music on his computer and did a lot of downloading. I spoke with him about the use of one of the stolen card numbers to pay his cell-phone bill. He claimed that he gave Hagen cash because Hagen wanted to pay the bill with his credit card.

I charged Hagen with six additional counts of identity theft for the five cardholders and the piggybacked neighbor. I charged him with another count of obtaining property by false pretenses for the Media Town fraud, and finally decided that felony common law forgery was the best charge to file on behalf of his employer. This charge described Hagen's acts of forging the card numbers onto the triplicate forms he took with him. When I served the new warrants upon Hagen, he insisted that Settles had committed the Media Town fraud and that I needed to look at his iPod. I also obtained felony fraud warrants against Settles for the prepaid phone payment and the Media Town purchases.

Sentencing

Mark Hagen pleaded guilty to seven counts of identity theft, two counts of obtaining property by false pretenses, and one count of common law forgery, all felonies. He spent four months in jail and was released to a term of probation. Settles and Hagen kept pointing the finger at one another. With the stronger case against Hagen disposed of, the prosecutor eventually dismissed the charges against Jerry Settles. Ginger Taylor was not charged.

Lessons Learned

Identity thieves can be found! There is an infrastructure to electronic crimes and nearly all frauds. This infrastructure of communications, phones, computers, safe houses, transportation, food, utilities, employment and other purchases and activities is laced with weak seams. My method is to go where I expect to find the seams, probe for those weak points and then rigorously exploit any mistakes made by the offender and hunt him or her down. Hit the offender with the best charges you can make and move on. The Mark Hagen case was an excellent example of how to identify places likely to have weak seams. His crimes were both high and low tech. Such a mix is not uncommon, even in highly complex fraud schemes.

Forming working hypotheses is a good approach for shaping an investigation; the key is to know when to change or abandon a hypothesis. The hypothesis that Hagen was trading identities for illegal drugs never completely came together. I was unable to link Hagen to any more of the mail drop incidents, but those hypotheses, nevertheless, provided valuable information and helped my case progress.

> ## Recommendations to Prevent Future Occurrences
>
> When going out to restaurants, pay with cash or use a credit card. Never use a debit card because, if someone steals your information, the fraudulently drafted funds will come directly out of your account. Using online banking to periodically check on transactions and balances is a good practice. All identity theft victims should file police reports and submit a complaint to their bank. Report details can be of great value to an investigator.
>
> Web-based businesses should be cooperative with law enforcement in cases of Internet fraud. Information these companies possess can be the key to unlocking the whole case.
>
> The commendable response and willingness of Hyland Steakhouse's manager to have her employee charged with theft of customer identity data is actually rare. Until this case, I'd never had an employer demand charges, usually because managers do not want the company to be seen as a victim. Businesses should seek prosecution. It sends a signal to the other employees that fraud and theft will not be tolerated. Hopefully, Mark Hagen's next employer will check his criminal record and not make the same mistake.

About the Author

Al Sternberg, CFE, graduated from UNC-Chapel Hill with a BS in Criminal Justice Administration and Psychology, and then joined Wake County Sheriff's Office. He became a Certified Fraud Examiner and an investigator specializing in a number of fraud crimes. He is currently assigned to the homicide/major crimes department as a senior investigator. He trains fellow officers on advanced methods of fraud investigations at Wake Technical Community College.

CHAPTER 5

Small-Town Boys

ANDREA LEE VALENTIN

Buzz and Felix, two dull-witted local troublemakers, enjoyed creating a ruckus in their small Virginia town of Walden during their teens. They frequently got into trouble in school — when they made it, that is — and parents with teenage daughters steered them clear of the duo. However, after they somehow graduated from high school, the young men both moved away for a few years and came back as productive citizens. They surprisingly managed to grow up to be hard-working adults. Buzz and Felix were still known to enjoy late-night outings and flashy cars and clothes, but otherwise they kept to themselves. Both were very good tippers at the local restaurants and were friendly and helpful to their neighbors. The townspeople believed Buzz and Felix, in their early thirties, were traveling salesmen who made frequent trips all over the East Coast. They were strong technology users and usually had a cell phone, laptop, or other technical device in hand.

When they returned to Walden, Buzz told Felix, "This is the best place for us right now. It is centrally located so we can easily travel to Atlanta, New York and Miami as needed." But Felix did not know exactly how important their location was in Buzz's plans.

Thrown Together by Fate

USA Choice Payments, Inc., a privately held company based out of Greenwood Village, Colorado, specialized in payment systems providing an alternative to traditional brick-and-mortar banking by offering complete payroll services for businesses entirely through the Internet. The company was created in the early 1980s and was a pioneer in the alternative payment industry. Unfortunately, as management found out, there were a few unpredictable threats lurking in USA Choice's business model that would jeopardize its reputation as innovators in the arena of fraudulent activity prevention and detection. Today, USA Choice Payments remains a leader in alternative payments; however, managers are much quicker to admit that, at times, the fraudsters appear to be one step ahead. Hence, the company developed a greater focus on surpassing compliance by placing the emphasis on total fraud-lifecycle management.

Rhiannon, a young and hip mother in her twenties, was juggling family, work and school. Financially, things were very tough, and many times she and her husband went without dinner so their children could have a special treat instead. When their computer's antivirus software came up for renewal, Rhiannon said to her husband, "Let's wait to renew that next month. What can happen in a month?"

Mark Andrew was heavily involved in the Christian music industry, traveled frequently, and often logged onto his laptop to do a little online banking at his favorite coffee shop that provided free wireless Internet access. He was a long-time customer at People's Bank of North America. Mark traveled the United States as well as Canada and Central America for his ministry work. While on the road, Mark sang and played music for many poor communities. One of his favorite sayings was, "Authority is granted by God. You must be very careful not to give your God-given authority to the devil, who will constantly try to trick you into giving it up." Little did Mark know that the same principle rang true for online banking passwords and unsecured, public Internet connections.

Zoe and Damon were entrepreneurs in the holistic-medicine business and contemplated starting a Web site to sell their merchandise. Damon said to Zoe one night over dinner, "I found some great webmaster options, but a large number appear to be overseas. What do you think — is it safe?"

How were all of these individuals connected to USA Choice Payments, Inc.? None of them had ever heard of the company, let alone employed its online payroll services. But they quickly became acquainted with the downside of the Internet world, and with the name USA Choice Payments.

A Ruined Cup of Coffee

Most people have at least dabbled in online banking for their personal or business needs. Many fraud investigators are familiar with online account takeovers and have read case studies on the use of shell companies to embezzle money. Rarely do we find connections to account takeovers and shell companies where embezzlement is *not* part of the fraud equation. The case presented here involves a less-publicized way shell companies can play a part in fraudulent account takeovers.

Imagine this: You grab your coffee one Saturday morning and settle in to pay some bills online. You log in to your bank account and see your balance is short by close to $1,500. After a frantic review of your account history, you see an online transfer to an unknown bank account with the note "Payroll — George Smith." This is your personal bank account, you do not know anyone named George Smith, and you certainly did not perform an automated clearing house (ACH) transaction to him. What do you do now?

This situation has occurred in some form or fashion to online banking users throughout the world. Financial institutions first detected the scheme when account holders called them to dispute outbound ACH transactions on their personal or business checking accounts; the institutions, in turn, sent out requests to the numerous receiving banks to pull back the funds. USA Choice Payments, Inc., was the end recipient of a few such requests, which prompted a review of the account holders' activities. At the time, nothing seemed out of the ordinary to the personnel examining the transactions, so no further action took place. But when I joined the company a few months later and received a phone call regarding a possible fraud scheme, I decided to take the review of our accounts a few steps farther.

Now, let us find out what ruined those cups of coffee.

Making the Right Connections

I have always been an advocate of information sharing. This case highlighted how working together with other investigators who may potentially have valuable pieces of the fraud puzzle can streamline your investigation and improve the quality of your company's fraud-management lifecycle as a whole. My examination began when an investigator from a large traditional bank called me regarding complaints he had received from customers, which he managed to trace back to an account managed by USA Choice Payments, Inc. This investigator, Wu Lee — with People's Bank of North America — indicated that he had numerous customers who were startled by abnormal transactions while reviewing their account history. These customers claimed they did not share their passwords with anyone and did not know Johnny Smith, George Smith, Rita McDonald, or Colin Gonzales — all supposed employees to whom Lee's customers made payroll transactions using USA Choice Payment, Inc.'s alternative payment system. Lee informed me that in each case, the same IP address was used to initiate the funds transfer, but only some of the money was sent to accounts with USA Choice Payments, Inc. I began to get the idea that this case was larger than first thought.

After a complete review, I was able to connect a number of additional accounts to the same group of individuals. I said to myself, "Surely this is not fraud; the activity appears normal and these are lower-risk accounts." But something did not seem entirely right, so I decided to do some extra digging and called an investigator at another financial institution, 1st Loan & Trust Bank, to ask about some ACH deposits going to a few of the accounts under review at USA Choice Payments, Inc. I was shocked to find out that the 1st Loan & Trust fraud investigator, Tina Drew, was working a case that fit the exact profile, except that the majority of the funds were sent to another payment-services company. I gave Drew some of the information shared by Lee, and she exclaimed, "We have lost more than $100,000 so far to this Johnny Smith!" From there, Drew, Lee and I shared what we knew and helped each other complete our cases more quickly than we could have dreamed had we been working alone.

Gone Phishing

After discussing my findings with my new contacts, I was absolutely convinced that I was onto something. I continued to dig. A major breakthrough in the case was the discovery of Web site logins from the same IP address on a large group of USA Choice Payments, Inc.'s accounts. While this IP was different from the one supplied by Lee, the activity still seemed odd — particularly because the IP pointed to a small town in Virginia. This was strange because the account holders had addresses on record all over the United States. I sent off multiple requests to the Internet service provider to obtain more information or a contact in their fraud department but had no luck. Since the case was going nowhere, I felt strongly that the accounts and the IP address had to be clues to the case Drew, Lee and I were discussing. It was time to reach out again to my new contacts.

Drew was excited to hear of my IP connections because she had found transactions made by the same address in her case. Drew told me she had spoken with local police investigators in Virginia who were very interested in Drew's IP connections and said they already had two suspects identified. The suspects were both young men with possible connections to organized crime in Miami. My ears perked up with the mention of a Florida-based mob because the activity I was seeing on our accounts was in Miami. I said to myself, "Surely this is no coincidence." According to Drew, one of the young men in question, Buzz, was allegedly running a money-laundering ring that included almost all of the nightclubs in Walden and the surrounding area. The local investigators were under the impression that Buzz's friend, Felix, was not aware of all of the activities going on but that he was involved in a small way and, at the very least, benefiting from the fraudulent activity. Now it was time to call Lee and share what we had learned.

Lee had spoken with one of his victims, Mark Andrew, and learned that he had responded to a phishing e-mail, inadvertently giving away his online banking password. Rhiannon, subsequently, called Drew at 1st Loan & Trust to report that her and her husband's life savings of $1,396 had vanished from their bank account with a memo "Payroll — George Smith." "I was saving that for my children's vacation to Disney after my graduation this spring," Rhiannon wailed. Rhiannon told her story to Zoe, a lifelong friend, over coffee. Zoe, who never banked online but did use 1st Loan & Trust, vowed to check her account history via the bank's 800 phone number when she returned home that morning. When she called, Zoe discovered that the business checking account she shared with her partner, Damon, had a large transaction that she did not recognize. Zoe visited the bank branch the next morning and spoke with the branch manager, who explained that the transaction was a payroll disbursement to a Rita McDonald. "Rita McDonald. Who is that?" cried Zoe. "Well, it says here that this transfer was made by your partner, Damon," said the branch manager. She assured Zoe they would look into the transaction and get back to her as soon as possible. The branch manager then passed this information to Drew. When Drew followed up on the complaint, Zoe denied responding to an e-mail asking for login information. "I could not have done it, especially because I have never even used online banking." Zoe quickly called Damon who swore he did not make the transaction but said he did have an online login. In fact, Damon said, "I just confirmed my login information via an e-mail the other day." Zoe and Damon's funds went to an account at another alternative payment provider; however, I suspected the pattern of withdrawals would prove an obvious connection to this scheme, as well, and our friends Buzz and Felix would be on the receiving end.

Coming out of Their Shell

Government investigators began to put together cases, and at the time of this writing, a grand jury hearing was pending for one of the perpetrators. The scheme totaled more than $250,000 for USA Choice Payments, Inc., alone. There were elements of identity theft, shell company usage, debit card fraud, connections to organized crime and Internet fraud in this intriguing case. While it is impossible to be sure that all victims have been accounted for, the last dollar amount I heard involved in this scheme was upward of one million dollars in losses to individuals and businesses. These losses — absorbed by the financial intuitions, ultimately, and not the victims in this case — are just a small piece of the total fraud costs every year.

Our investigation revealed that Buzz and Felix had managed to obtain legitimate incorporation papers for a handful of shell companies from a state government office. Each company was set up using multiple stolen identities to complete the first step of the scam. Next, they used these companies as a means to send payroll to their many different employees through alternative payment systems. It was unclear how many parties were involved in the creation of accounts (opened with the names of employees) at multiple organizations, such as USA Choice Payments, Inc., and other smaller alternative payment systems; however, it was quite evident that identity theft was the motive. We suspected that the identities of the victims whose personal details were used to set up the accounts were acquired either by searching Google or a public records database. Their ''employers'' all had Web Sites making them look like legitimate businesses (perhaps they even were actually selling the items advertised on the sites).

The funds for these payroll transfers were obtained from multiple business and personal checking and savings accounts with large financial institutions in the United States. The victims in this case are just a sample of the types of unsuspecting online banking users who fell prey to what we believed was a phishing scheme; this assumption was later confirmed, thanks to a confession from Felix to law enforcement. It turns out that while Felix was not aware of the money-laundering activities with the nightclubs, he was technically savvy and allegedly was able to develop viruses to capture the online banking passwords of many individuals through a phishing scam. The passwords and user names he obtained were able to sustain him and Buzz for more than two years in a comfortable lifestyle. It appears that the Walden residents were only partially incorrect. Buzz and Felix certainly were no salespeople, but they had managed to sell the townspeople the idea that they were good citizens.

At this writing, Felix is facing multiple felony charges under the Computer Fraud and Abuse Act and multiple identity theft charges. He is expected to obtain a lighter sentence than Buzz, but could still spend up to 20 years in prison for some of his charges. Buzz, the mastermind, is facing conspiracy to commit mail fraud, multiple counts of mail fraud and conspiracy charges, in addition to money laundering and identity theft charges. The charges against Buzz are still mounting as additional victims are uncovered and he will probably be charged with more counts relating to the allegedly forged state incorporation papers.

Lessons Learned

Information sharing is vital. Without tips received from other investigators, I could not have compiled my case. However, ensure that you do not violate various privacy laws in the process. I made many useful contacts during the investigation, and my excitement in my career choice was renewed. So often

(continued)

we investigate false positives and — if we are lucky and do our jobs well — prevent the small frauds, so when a large case comes along, it can be quite exciting!

A number of internal controls existed at both the entry and exit points of USA Choice Payments, Inc.'s operations, including multifactor authentication, customer identification programs, ACH fraud monitoring and limitations on the dollar amount and frequency of transactions. The red flags of account takeovers, shell companies and ACH fraud are difficult to combine into a concise list; however, the uniqueness of these schemes should make the activity unmistakable when reviewed with a skeptical eye. The top three clues for a scheme of this nature are:

1. Inconsistent loading activity for payroll
2. ACH return requests
3. Tips from other investigators (if someone tells you something is not right, do not stop looking until you are certain the activity is legitimate)

This case taught me many valuable lessons, including the fact that internal controls do little to prevent sophisticated schemes if the company's anti-fraud personnel are not aware of the purpose of them. Second, investigators must be encouraged to share information to increase their ability to spot and detect fraud faster in the future. Third, companies must stay in tune with their environment and constantly update and create lists of red flags for each type of fraud if monitoring is to be effective at all.

Recommendations to Prevent Future Occurrences

While it will never be possible to eliminate fraudulent activity completely, it is imperative for companies to work together with law enforcement and other financial institutions to minimize their exposure to such schemes, or we will surely see fraud increase exponentially over the coming years. Here are key ways your company can identify and prevent payroll ACH and account takeover schemes from occurring:

- Conduct due diligence.
- Monitor ACH debit returns closely.
- Use fraud case studies to instruct others in your organization.
- Teach customers how to protect their passwords against phishing schemes and viruses.

(continued)

(*continued*)

Encourage employees to conduct due diligence on other organizations with which they do business as well as on clients and customers. This goes beyond Know Your Customer (KYC) and USA PATRIOT Act requirements in that, whenever possible, you should gather as much information as you can to know with whom you are dealing. You will want to know what types of fraudulent activity your industry peers and their colleagues have encountered in the past. For a payroll client, you will want to know how many employees they have and how they structure their payments to establish company norms and best practices, which will make it easier to monitor activity outside these parameters. Constant assessment of the organizations connected to your enterprises will allow you to assign the appropriate risk, which will allow investigators to spot abnormal activity easier. Conduct your due diligence periodically, not just once.

Another great way to strengthen your investigators' skills is by providing avenues to conduct — and encouraging the practice of — periodic reviews of fraud case studies, especially if your organization is at risk for those types of schemes. Investigators should be encouraged to join professional organizations and participate in regular training to enhance their opportunities to increase their personal fraud IQs. Financial institutions, in particular, need to increase their internal and external education about viruses and phishing schemes and urge consumers to protect their accounts by keeping their passwords secure.

About the Author

Andrea Lee Valentin, CFE, has more than 10 years of experience in the financial services industry with a focus on research, investigations and compliance. With a BA in Accounting from the University of Central Florida, Mrs. Valentin went on to obtain an MBA in Economic Crime and Fraud Management from Utica College in New York. Today, Andrea uses her passion for fraud fighting in her role at FSV Payment Systems, Inc., by leading the fraud and operational compliance divisions and is the cofounder of Virtual Fraud Detection Services.

Dangerous Diet

NANCY E. JONES

Anoop Dugar lived at 23 Crawford Gardens in the small Springdale suburb of Harrisburg, Pennsylvania. He was a quiet, polite, and considerate child who grew up attending the local public schools. When Anoop was in elementary school he excelled in writing, entering and winning several contests. He also entered read-a-thons for charity events and won those. In his middle-school days he was the winner of several local and national spelling bees. His parents traced their roots to India and were proud of him and his older sister. Anoop was devoted to academics and steered clear of physical activity. He was an avid reader who spent huge amounts of time alone. When he graduated from high school he was significantly overweight and had been teased incessantly because of his size. Following graduation, he convinced his parents to allow him to live in the basement of their home and was employed as a night auditor for local hotel chains. His sister became a reporter for CNN News. Much of his free time was spent watching various Pittsburgh athletic teams on television and, on the rare occasions when he was seen in public, he usually wore clothing that supported Pittsburgh teams. The houses on Crawford Gardens were well-maintained family homes. Neighbors came and went and saw very little of Anoop. Residents did not have the faintest idea that the soft-spoken son of Amal and Charu Dugar was turning to a life of crime. In fact, he was about to be exposed as a mastermind in a major wire fraud case by his sister in a CNN report.

Anoop, it seems, had a dark side. He began using hotel customers' credit card numbers to purchase personal merchandise. Moreover, when customers reserved rooms with their credit cards but paid in cash upon check-in, Anoop would pocket the cash, charge the room to the credit card, and manipulate hotel records to cover his activity. Anoop waived indictment and pleaded guilty. Days later, CNN got a hold of these facts and Anoop's sister reported from the district court. The district court attributed a loss amount of nearly $918,000 to Anoop's actions. He accepted responsibility for a portion of this loss but objected to nearly $811,000 of it. He argued at sentencing and on appeal that he should not be responsible for the total because the prosecution had not fully proven the amount he stole. This argument worked to reduce his sentence from 30–36 months to 18–24 months.

After serving 23 months in Somerset State Prison, Anoop returned to his parents' basement in central Pennsylvania and was under court-supervised probation. While he had been in prison, there were repeated calls to the police for domestic abuse at his parents' house, but his mom never pressed charges against the father; she was a very submissive wife. While Anoop was incarcerated, his dad divorced his mom and made several trips back to India. Anoop stayed in contact with his dad, and his mom became quite dependent on Anoop after he was released from prison. She encouraged him to find employment and to continue to focus on losing weight, as he had done while jailed. Charu was struggling to make ends meet now that her husband had left her.

About a month later, Anoop was hired at a local nutrition store called General Nutrition Supply (GNS) about ten miles from his home. As Anoop gained retail experience, he began to see opportunities to return again to the dark side. He wanted to be an entrepreneur and was unhappy having to work for GNS. He became dependant on steroids and worked out daily at the local gym. The expense of his dependency wore on his finances, and he rekindled his life of crime. He convinced his mother to open a storefront on eBay selling supplements and told her he would help support the business as a buyer. But she didn't really know that she was letting Anoop's illegal activities develop unhindered.

Local Market

In midsummer a new diet pill called NixObi was introduced as an over-the-counter weight-loss aid. Immediately after it hits the shelves, Local Market — a supermarket chain with 150 stores in the Mid-Atlantic States — began reporting that they were unable to keep any of the product on the shelf. Within a 25-mile radius of Springdale there were more than a dozen Local Market stores, and one of them was in the same plaza as the GNS store where Anoop worked. I was working as the Vice President of Asset Protection for Local Market at the time, and my team was called in to determine why we were constantly out of NixObi.

The data analysts quickly determined that the NixObi pills were likely being stolen. A study of Local Market's purchases versus sales of NixObi reflected that very little of the product was selling, and the profit margin on the product was quickly eroding. Kurt Gentry, one of our data analysts, began gathering information about the weight-loss pill from various sources. Several Local Market detectives began reporting incidents of theft, and several stores claimed they were ordering more units than they were selling. When Kurt presented this information to me, I immediately assigned Investigator Andy Peters to the case.

The Beauty Queen

Andy began to investigate who might be stealing the product and where they might be selling it. A quick Internet search showed that eBay had already held about 350 auctions for this brand-new product. The very next day there were more than 400 packages of NixObi for sale online. Andy asked Kurt to review all of the auctions and determine which ones were within 200 miles of the Local Market marketing area. Kurt quickly determined that there was an eBay seller within 20 miles of several Local Market stores, known as "beautynutritionqueen23." Other items offered by this seller included health and beauty care items and general merchandise. Kurt let the Local Market detectives know that the seller lived near Harrisburg, and then he initiated contact with her. He sent her a message saying, "I have two questions. I live near Harrisburg and I am very excited to try NixObi as it is new to the market. I actually have kids in daycare in Harrisburg. Would it be possible to pick up the product at your house? Where did you get the product from? I have been skeptical to try diet pills, but the FDA approval helps me feel better with this one." The seller responded with, "We can meet somewhere if u win the auction and I can assure u that my NixObi is the real deal. Check my feedback."

Kurt bid on several products and won the auction. He completed his purchase through PayPal, through which he discovered the seller was Charu Dugar. Investigator Andy Peters searched her name in Local's system and discovered she had a store loyalty card. Using the search engine Zabasearch, he found her address at 23 Crawford Gardens in Springdale. The transactions on her loyalty card appeared to be normal shopping purchases made at normal times. Further investigation revealed another loyalty card for her address registered to Anoop Dugar. Anoop's card had excessive transactions in the Harrisburg area, and most were made overnight. Many of the purchases were for packing tape and envelopes. Andy Peters requested that Detective Walt Bradley review the closed-circuit TV (CCTV) footage of the transactions on this card. Bradley observed Anoop taking numerous items from the health and beauty care (HBC) aisle, concealing them in his clothing, and making purchases of tape and mailing envelopes. The detective thereafter viewed the surveillance at four other area stores and saw Anoop entering each store wearing a Pittsburg Steelers jacket, concealing NixObi and other products from the HBC aisle in his jacket, and leaving the store without paying. Kurt then analyzed the eBay sales for "beautynutritionqueen23" for the past 90 days; he found 1,319 items sold for $14,259. Kurt ordered additional products and received them in Duck Brand padded envelopes, which Anoop Dugar frequently purchased at Local Markets.

I then reviewed the evidence and asked Andy to contact the local police to discuss the matter with them. Sergeant Hope of the High Hill Police Department agreed to take the case and coordinate it with the other jurisdictions. He drove by Charu's address and noted a late-model, four-door, blue Honda Accord in the driveway. During parking-lot surveillance of one of the Local Market stores, Detective Bradley saw a blue Honda Accord pull into the lot. He recorded the license plate number and saw Anoop walk into the GNS store next to Local Market.

Sergeant Hope, armed with significant evidence, contacted Assistant District Attorney Brenda Peck. She requested that Local Market continue to purchase NixObi and let Anoop steal the product until he accumulated at least $2,000 in thefts, at which point the crime would become a felony. Investigator Andy Peters and I conducted a conference call with Local Market's Asset Protection personnel and outlined the case for them. We directed them to mark 18 frequently stolen HBC items, including NixObi diet pills, at eight Local Markets using invisible ink.

A few days later, Peters and Bradley went to a store to investigate the following:

1. The store reported their NixObi went missing during the overnight shift between July 25 and 26.
2. The store did not sell any NixObi on July 25 or 26.
3. Anoop Dugar's loyalty card showed a purchase at 2:01 PM on July 26.
4. Around 11:00 PM on July 26, "beautynutritionqueen23" posted two bottles of NixObi for sale on eBay.

Detective Bradley reviewed the CCTV and saw Anoop Dugar enter the store at 1:55 AM on July 26, walk directly to the HBC aisle, and conceal all of the NixObi and several other HBC items in his jacket pockets. He purchased mailing supplies and left in a blue Honda Accord.

Sergeant Hope presented the case evidence to U.S. Postal Inspector Larry Bond, who agreed to take the case because it involved using the U.S. Postal Service to ship stolen goods. Inspector Bond requested from Local Market all of Anoop Dugar's purchases of stamps and shipping supplies and a rough estimate of traceable retail losses. Kurt provided all the point-of-sale receipts for all postal supplies Anoop bought in the previous three months. He also continued bidding on eBay auctions for marked product. When he received the product from the auctions, he kept it unopened in the original envelopes, and turned it over to the police to be opened in their presence, thus preserving the chain of custody. When we did open the envelopes, we discovered that much of the merchandise had been removed from the boxes already. Detective Bradley arranged to have the Springdale police department inspect the trash at 23 Crawford Gardens during the weekly garbage pickup, so Gentry met Detective Bradley and Postal Inspector Bond at the Springdale Maintenance Garage to review what had been found. Evidence seized from the trash included three marked NixObi packages, numerous DVD sleeves and plastic wrap, Local Market receipts, Local Market bags, packaging supplies, addressed envelopes and eBay invoices and correspondence.

The Same Defense Twice?

At this point, Inspector Bond told me he had enough evidence to request search and arrest warrants for Anoop Dugar. A few days later the warrants were executed at 23 Crawford Gardens at 7:30 AM Anoop Dugar was taken into custody by U.S. Postal Inspectors and approximately $5,000 in retail products, packaging supplies, a Pittsburgh Steelers jacket and a computer were taken as evidence from the home. The eBay records were subpoenaed and revealed that Anoop had sold $104,000 worth of Local Market's merchandise. That afternoon Anoop Dugar was arraigned in front of the U.S. District Magistrate and pleaded not guilty.

At that time he was under court-supervised probation for his previous federal offenses. Weeks later the grand jury indicted Anoop under a violation of his probation and charged him with mail fraud. The indictment found that he knowingly engaged, and attempted to engage, in a scheme and artifice to defraud and to obtain valuable property, by means of false and fraudulent pretenses, representations and promises. Specifically, he — as a previously convicted felon under court-ordered supervision — had engaged in an Internet fraud scheme involving the sale of stolen goods. As part of his artifice to defraud, Anoop concealed his extensive criminal record from his victims. Another aspect of the scheme was advertising to innocent customers that he possessed an inventory of goods. He was willing to sell these goods at favorable prices when, in truth and in fact, he did not have lawful possession of these goods because they were stolen from various businesses. He also lied to his probation officer and concealed material facts regarding his employment, income and fraudulent activities.

Eventually Anoop pleaded guilty to the charge of mail fraud, but again he argued that he should not be responsible for the entire $104,000 because the government had not proven the amount beyond a reasonable doubt. The judge, who had presided over Anoop's previous cases as well, disagreed and committed him to the custody of the U.S. Bureau of Prisons for a term of 33 months.

Lessons Learned

This case was intriguing because it proved that traditional investigative skills and techniques can be effective in combating modern Internet crimes. The investigative team followed the same fundamental steps, which included gathering evidence, determining how the crime occurred, identifying the suspect, developing the case for prosecution and proving damages. The difference was that specialized techniques for tracking merchandise flow and Internet activity were used. The process of marking our products with the ultraviolet invisible ink, although labor intensive, was critical. It provided the chain of custody that the District Attorney's office needed to establish the crime. As a result, we learned that we needed to be able to identify our product once it reached the black market. We are currently working on a long-term solution for this issue.

At the time of this investigation, we had just begun using data analysis in theft cases. We discovered that there was a significant difference between handling traditional (physical) evidence and electronic (intangible) evidence. We capitalized on the ability of data mining to tap into various sources. This included information primarily intended for marketing, not loss prevention. Our team's skillful coordination of gathering and protecting evidence, especially electronic, led to a successful outcome. Data mining has continued to evolve and Local Market has placed more focus on Internet crime as a result of this case.

Both the private and public investigators had to work very closely together. Key members of the team were the Internet auction site investigators. Their efforts and cooperation with both law enforcement and the internal investigators made this a solid case. The laws that protect the privacy of Internet sites and their clients proved to be a challenge. Anoop was exploiting antiquated laws and the anonymity of the Internet to sell stolen goods. The investigation was delayed by several weeks while the team went through painstaking efforts to obtain the evidence necessary to prove the government's charges. Resources had to be diverted from other projects to devote the proper time to building this case. From a supervision level, managing the risks throughout the investigation required constant focus and attention.

Recommendations to Prevent Future Occurrences

Advances in technology and the Internet have challenged corporations to find solutions to protect their assets. In the retail segment, e-fencing has become common and retailers have had to devise investigative strategies to combat the issue. At Local Market, large-scale losses and the sale of stolen products on the Internet prompted us to develop a strategy to fight organized retail theft (ORT). Cyber cops are a part of our strategy and we are devoting significant portions of our budgets toward such efforts. Investigative units are a common part of loss prevention annual budgets. Building relationships with online auction sites is an important step.

This epidemic cannot be solved solely by retailers fighting these cases in stores and in the judicial systems. Both state and federal laws are in the process of being revised to make it less bureaucratic to work through these cases and to make it less challenging for both private and public investigators. Legislation is needed to impose reasonable duties on online marketplaces to collect information that law enforcement can use to prosecute e-fencers. Legislation is also needed to define ORT as an offense separate from traditional retail theft. Tougher legislation could deter ORT by giving law enforcement greater authority to pursue criminals and make it more difficult to resell stolen goods on the Internet. In this case, Anoop was only charged with violating probation and mail fraud. Current theft legislation was not adequate to prosecute, and racketeering laws did not fit either. State and federal criminal statutes could give law enforcement and prosecutors the tools they need to effectively punish perpetrators.

To win the fight against shrink (missing or stolen merchandise), retailers should have the right tools. Petty shoplifters are motivated to steal for personal consumption whereas organized retail thieves have different motivations; based on my experience, ORT is often conducted by drug addicts. These drug-dependant shoplifters sell their products on popular Internet auction sites that act as clearinghouses for stolen goods. This rising tide of theft and shrink brought us to two conclusions:

- The largest source of shrink is employee theft, but it is very closely followed by organized retail theft.
- Improved data analysis, digital CCTV and investigative staff are the top loss prevention tools to address the issue.

The financial losses inflicted on the retail industry via Internet fraud are growing in size and scope. It is a daunting task to fight this war on organized retail theft and e-fencing as loss prevention teams attempt to do more with less. Clearly, this case demonstrates that retailers must commit adequate resources to asset protection to have a chance to overcome the growing threat of Internet fraud.

About the Author

Nancy E. Jones, CPP, received a BS degree from Worcester State College, Massachusetts, and is a certified teacher. She began her career in retail security in 1970 and has worked for three major East Coast supermarkets. As the Vice President of Asset Protection, she is responsible for protecting the assets of a company that includes 250 stores located in the mid-Atlantic region.

7

The Suburban Spoofer

JAMES B. KEITH

The decision to immigrate to the United States from Angola was an easy one for Domevlo Lukamba's parents. Angola, a south-central African nation, was impoverished and had experienced an intense civil war since 1975, when the country — which had been a Portuguese territory — gained its independence. The war raged until 2002 and had taken its toll on the social and civic fabric of the fledgling nation. At the time the Lukambas emigrated, the United Nations estimated that 80 percent of Angolans had no access to medical care and more than 1 million people needed assistance to avoid starvation. Survival was the motivating factor that drove the Lukambas to the United States with their 16-year-old son.

The family settled in Chicago and opened a beauty salon. They were hardworking people who took advantage of the opportunities available to them in a country where only the limitations people imposed on themselves could hold them back. The Lukambas' business was successful and they were able to move into a home in a middle-class neighborhood in the suburbs.

In his mid-twenties, Domevlo was tall, good looking and well spoken. He had finished high school in Chicago but had a difficult time adjusting to the disparity between what had been a life of fear in Angola to one of peace, tranquility, freedom and prosperity in the States. He was in another world, but he still carried remnants of the dread he felt before he moved — it was like waiting for the other shoe to drop. Psychologists refer to this condition as *posttraumatic stress disorder* (PTSD). He learned to adapt the survivalist street smarts he developed in Angola to life in a free and democratic society. He maintained contacts with some of his relatives in Angola and had formed new connections and a network of fellow African immigrants in Chicago. Life was good, and it became easy — too easy — once he learned how to work the system.

Domevlo had a couple years of college under his belt and was living part-time with his parents and the remainder with his girlfriend, the mother of their young son, on the campus of Southern Illinois University. He had taken a few computer and IT courses but decided not to follow through with his degree. However, what he learned about computers opened up a whole new world to him, one he would learn to take advantage of criminally.

Domevlo's problems adjusting to the American lifestyle manifested themselves in a lengthy adult criminal record in the short period since his seventeenth birthday — the age of adulthood in the eyes of the law in Illinois. He had adult arrests for theft, aggravated assault, aggravated robbery, unlawful restraint, kidnapping, attempted theft by deception, aggravated discharge of a firearm, criminal trespass to a motor vehicle and criminal damage to a vehicle. He had an outstanding warrant for a traffic offense and was on felony parole for unlawful use of a weapon by a felon. His last arrest was for domestic battery on the campus of Southern Illinois University after he assaulted his girlfriend. As victims of domestic violence often do, Domevlo's girlfriend denied being struck by him, but witnesses told police what actually happened. At the time of his arrest, he was holding a credit card and a checkbook that he was using for identity theft. His possessions eventually helped us identify him as the perpetrator of a major Internet-based identity theft case that took place across multiple states.

The Survivor

Things were getting back to normal in LaPlace, Louisiana, after Hurricane Katrina wrought mass destruction on a level not seen before. A Category-5 hurricane, Katrina swept through LaPlace — in St. John the Baptist Parish along the east bank of the Mississippi River in the New Orleans metropolitan area — leaving in its wake great hardships for the people who stayed to rebuild. Patricia Frank, 55 years old, had lived in LaPlace ever since she moved from Kansas at the age of 13 with her parents. Before Katrina, Patricia had already survived one major Category-5 hurricane, Camille, in 1969. She recalled in a raspy voice — ravaged from years of smoking — that "we never left for either hurricane and after Katrina we were without electricity for two months."

She easily progressed in and graduated from East St. John High School. After graduation, when she was 17 years old, she met 22-year-old Michael, a Vietnam veteran who was the brother of one of her friends, and they married after a brief engagement. Patricia explained the short courtship by saying, "We didn't have to get married. I wasn't pregnant — we were in love!"

After they were married, Patricia worked in a bank's accounting department until she had her first child. Michael took a job in the local steel mill as an electrical maintenance supervisor, where he has worked ever since. They bought a historic home that was built more than 130 years ago and raised two daughters in it. Their first daughter was born five years after they were married. Both of their girls went on to graduate school and became professionals.

Patricia Frank was the epitome of a survivor. She was a small-town girl with rural values who knew how to dig in deep when times got tough. After her first child was born, she became a housewife and maintained the family's finances. She was a newcomer to the Internet and online banking. She was a world away from, and completely naïve to, the frustrations she would come to experience as a victim of identity theft.

An Unexpected Move

On a normal Tuesday in February, Patricia Frank called the Olympic Gardens, Illinois, police department to say that she was a victim of identity theft. Her initial report indicated that she had received a letter from her bank, Capital Financial, thanking her for keeping them informed about her change of address to 20200 Main Street, Olympic Gardens, Illinois. Mrs. Frank had not even visited Olympic Gardens, had not moved recently and did not make the changes to her checking account, which she had opened in 1972.

Patricia immediately notified Capital Financial that she had not requested the change of address. The bank representative she spoke with told her that her certificate of deposit worth more than $7,000 had been transferred to her checking account. Her online account information had been changed, including her personal identification number (PIN), e-mail address and telephone numbers. A request was submitted for checks to be sent to the Main Street address in Olympic Gardens, and there had been several attempts to move funds out of the checking account. The bank representative informed Patricia that he had called one of the new phone numbers added to her account and spoke with a male who identified himself as Pat Frank. Shocked, Patricia promptly closed the account.

Patricia also learned that the new Main Street address and telephone number on her checking account were used to open a credit card in her name with Citibank, and there had also been an attempt to transfer $3,000 from her Bank of America credit card. Patricia complained to her local police department in Louisiana and was advised to file a report with the Olympic Gardens, Illinois, police as well. Thus began my investigation —

as an officer in Olympic Gardens — which would ultimately lead to the discovery of losses totaling more than $100,000 to various victims as well as the arrest and prosecution of a suspect for federal criminal charges.

A Checkered Past

The first thing I did was try to determine who lived at 20200 Main Street in Olympic Gardens, using an online public records database to which the police department subscribed. I entered the address and a report was generated that showed the owner of record for the property was Marian N. Lukamba. I also checked the two telephone numbers that were added to Patricia's bank account. One of them was registered as a cellular telephone number for Marian N. Lukamba. There was no registration information for the other phone number, but it was assigned to the same company, B-Cellular.

The report also listed a summary of Marian's relatives, so I conducted searches on them as well. The report I generated in the same database for Marian's son, Domevlo Lukamba, indicated that he had been arrested for the unlawful use of weapons by a felon and had been sentenced to three years in the Illinois Department of Corrections. I conducted a computerized-records search for his driver's license through the Illinois secretary of state and a criminal-history check through the Illinois Department of Corrections. I learned that he had a suspended license, had an extensive criminal history and was on parole for the charge of unlawful use of a weapon by a felon. He had state and federal arrest numbers and had an active warrant for his arrest for a traffic violation. His last arrest was at Southern Illinois University just a few months ago for domestic battery and resisting arrest.

My next step was to contact the last place he was arrested, the police department for Southern Illinois University. I phoned and spoke with a savvy veteran street sergeant, John Venditti, who was Domevlo's last arresting officer. Venditti told me that he arrested Domevlo Lukamba after responding to a complaint of a domestic dispute at a campus residence. When he arrived he met with Lukamba and his girlfriend, the mother of their child, who had clearly been battered. Lukamba denied hitting her, but witnesses said he struck her in the face with his fist several times. When Venditti attempted to handcuff Lukamba, he resisted arrest and had to be tackled to the ground. When officers searched Lukamba at the police station they found a debit card in the name of Reginald Barker and a checkbook in the name of Lynn Jackson. Venditti confiscated both items.

Repeat Victim

A couple of weeks after Patricia Frank filed her original report with us, I contacted her for a follow-up interview. She told me she closed her original checking account with Capital Financial and opened a new account with them. The first statement she received for the new account showed a fraudulent charge for a cell-phone bill in the amount of $481. She closed that checking account and opened yet a third one. She talked with a fraud investigator from her bank, Mario Davis, with whom I later spoke. Davis told me that the information changes to Patricia's checking account were made online and through phone calls to Capital Financial. He provided two Internet protocol (IP) addresses that were used. Having the IP address provides law enforcement investigators — if they are armed with a grand jury subpoena — with the information needed to locate the company providing the Internet access, and who the subscriber is. It will include the name, address and telephone number for the account. Davis also told me the new telephone number on Patricia's checking account. I recognized the number as the cell phone number listed for Marian Lukamba.

I decided to conduct a garbage pull at 20200 Main Street, which consists of contacting the disposal company responsible for picking up the garbage for a given address and requesting that they turn it over to police officers after it has been collected from the curb and placed in the garbage truck. The courts have recognized that there is no right to privacy once refuse has been picked up for disposal from the residence. A garbage pull is not one of a police officer's favorite things to do, but it can yield very useful information and evidence — as was the case here. The garbage pull yielded a shipping statement addressed to Robert Black from a sportswear company for the purchase of a Chicago Bulls jersey and overdraft statements from a bank addressed to Domevlo Lukamba at 20200 Main Street. The shipping label indicated the jersey was shipped to 20200 Main Street under the name Robert Black and paid for with a Chase MasterCard; the last four numbers of the card were listed. The contact number for the purchase was the cell phone number listed to Marion Lukamba. Chase MasterCard sent out an affirmation request to the cardholder — who turned out not to be Robert Black — and learned that the account holder had not given permission for his credit card to be used for this purchase. The account was closed as an account takeover.

Because the mailing address on Patricia's bank account had been changed to 20200 Main Street, correspondence from the bank was diverted to that address. That constituted mail fraud, a federal offense that fell to the jurisdiction of the U.S. Postal Inspection Service. I suspected the U.S. Postal Service would uncover more victims whose mail had been diverted to the

20200 Main Street. I decided to contact a friend of mine who was a postal inspector, Mark Kline.

Special Delivery

Special Agent Mark Kline was a gritty, down-to-earth, keep-your-nose-to-the-grindstone law enforcement professional who was not afraid to get involved in a tough case that presented a challenge. He had a keen wit and a sharp mind for names and details. The first time I met Mark, he rolled several boxes of reports and evidence into my police department after we realized we were pursuing the same suspect in a case. Mark had many contacts in the banking and credit card industries and had worked on a number of complex financial-crimes cases. He told me that the Postal Inspector's Office would have jurisdiction in my case and agreed to work it with me.

Special Agent Kline conducted a "mail cover," which involved monitoring the mail sent to and from the 20200 Main Street address. Mark found that Domevlo was receiving several credit card statements in various names from Capital Financial, so I contacted the investigators at Capital Financial and they requested that the post office intercept the mail. After one week, the mail cover resulted in 68 pieces from Capital Financial. Most were addressed to different people, but all went to 20200 Main Street.

I called Capital Financial's lead fraud investigator, Mario Davis, and got his permission to open the letters. They pertained to multiple credit card accounts, and eleven of them actually contained credit cards in different names. Capital Financial's fraud investigation team developed a spreadsheet of the compromised accounts with correspondence sent to 20200 Main Street, which totaled sixteen accounts and more than $100,000. I asked Mario how he thought the identity thief acquired the victims' account information, and he said it was probably obtained through a phishing scam. Such scams — also known as *spoofing* — are accomplished by sending an e-mail, text message or other communication to victims posing as their bank and requesting verification of their account information. The victims respond by unwittingly forwarding personal information, such as name, birth date, Social Security number, address, telephone number, account number and PINs.

During the mail cover we also intercepted a letter addressed to Reginald Barker, the name on the debit card that Domevlo Lukamba had in his possession at the time he was arrested for domestic battery at Southern Illinois University. The letter contained a bank statement. I contacted the bank and learned that two checks totaling $10,000 had been deposited to open the account; both had been returned unpaid.

Three months had passed since Patricia Frank filed her original report. Patricia was upset and said that her Discover credit card had also been compromised — the address was changed to 20200 Main Street and the credit limit had been increased. I immediately phoned a friend who was an investigator with Discover Financial, Bill McDonough. He a 26-year retired police detective from Bloomingdale, Illinois, with a forte for financial crimes investigation.

Bill looked into Patricia's account and learned that Discover had closed it as an account takeover. The perpetrator had made a request for an emergency authorized-purchaser card to be sent to the 20200 Main Street address in the name of Domevlo Lukamba; McDonough said the card had already been delivered. He checked Discover's database and learned that there were two other requests for emergency authorized-purchaser cards to the 20200 Main Street address in the name of Domevlo Lukamba, along with credit-lines increases. Both of those cards had also been sent but were not scheduled for delivery by DHL for another two days. One of the Discover cards was in the name of Kevin Reed — a name I recognized from Capital Financial's spreadsheet of account takeovers. The second was for Keith Applequist with a request to send an emergency authorized-purchaser card in the name of Domevlo Lukamba.

I decided it was time to contact the Cook County state attorney's office to seek approval for a search warrant. I called DHL and scheduled a pick-up of the two packages from their terminal before they were delivered to 20200 Main Street. Our plan was to have one of our police officers pose as a DHL deliveryman and attempt a controlled delivery of the two packages. Immediately afterward, we would execute the search warrant. We coordinated our plan with members of the Cook County Sheriff's Department Emergency Response Team, which routinely provided specialized assistance to suburban Chicago communities upon request.

The next day, officers from the Olympic Gardens Police Department, Cook County Sheriff's Department and special agents from the United States Postal Inspection Service served the search warrant at 20200 Main Street. After breaching the front and back doors of the residence — which was empty — we began our search. We found a photograph of Domevlo Lukamba and mail addressed to him in one of the bedrooms. We also seized a laptop computer; a desktop computer; several thousand dollars in cash and checks; credit cards; and almost one hundred pages of computer printouts containing addresses, phone numbers, account numbers, passwords and PINs for many of the victims we had already identified. The printouts came from Domevlo Lukamba's e-mail address — the same one he used to file fraudulent credit card applications. One of the credit cards we recovered was an emergency authorized-purchaser card for Lukamba on Patricia Frank's account. The items were seized and entered into evidence. Although Domevlo Lukamba was not at home when the warrant was served, his parents arrived shortly after we began the search. We asked them to have Domevlo contact the police department, but not surprisingly he didn't.

The Flood Gates Opened

A few days later, information about the case began to pour in. Since Lukamba did not contact me after the search, I called his parole agent and we met to review the case. The parole agent spoke with Domevlo's parents, but they said they did not know how to contact their son; the agent then spoke with his supervisor and obtained a parole violation warrant for Lukamba.

I learned that another credit card company discovered two fraudulent requests for emergency cards to be sent to Lukamba at 20200 Main Street. Several banks provided me with video footage from local branches that showed Lukamba requesting fraudulent cash advances against the credit cards that had been sent to his parents' home. At one bank he even signed his name and put his thumbprint on the receipt.

I developed grand jury subpoenas for the IP addresses used to contact the defrauded credit card companies and learned that Marian Lukamba was the subscriber. While sifting through this new information, I received another call from Patricia Frank; she had yet again been the victim of another account takeover.

I spoke with special agents from the Federal Bureau of Investigation about Domevlo, and they conducted a background check on the Lukamba family. The agents learned that Domevlo Lukamba was not in the United States legally and could be subject to deportation proceedings.

Based on our overwhelming evidence, I sent a bulletin to law enforcement agencies in the Chicago metropolitan area announcing the arrest warrant for Domevlo Lukamba, which included his photograph and a description of his fraudulent activities. Shortly thereafter, I was notified that he had been arrested in a nearby community. Lukamba was questioned by Postal Inspector Mark Kline and he confessed to the various account takeovers we were investigating. He identified himself in the surveillance from various banks and admitted to taking cash advances against other people's credit cards and checking accounts.

Mark obtained an indictment for Domevlo Lukamba through the U.S. Attorney's Office that included charges of identity theft, credit card fraud, wire fraud and mail fraud. Domevlo Lukamba pleaded guilty and was sentenced to three years of federal incarceration. He faces deportation once his sentence has been served.

Lessons Learned

I gleaned many lessons working on this case. Experience taught me that Internet fraud is nefarious in nature. The psychological cost to the victim, as well as the time, effort and money needed to repair the damage caused by an identity thief can be devastating. In this case, Domevlo Lukamba easily preyed on his victims by obtaining their financial information through a phishing scam. The breadth of personal information Lukamba had about his victims was astonishing and included addresses, telephone numbers, birth dates, Social Security numbers, personal identification numbers, passwords and account numbers. Consumers should be aware that their banks and financial institutions will not send out requests for them to verify personal identifiers because they already have that information. They have no need to request verification.

The number of victims and the amount of information recovered indicated the relative ease with which Lukamba was able to commit his frauds. With the personal information he obtained, he conducted full account takeovers that allowed him to transfer funds; change billing addresses, e-mail addresses and telephone numbers for the accounts; and have additional credit cards sent to him. He was also able to conduct application fraud using the victims' information to open new accounts.

A major challenge in investigating Internet fraud is that victims, suspects and witnesses can be in multiple jurisdictions. However, Internet frauds can be resolved successfully if the investigators use a combination of computer research, traditional investigative tools and interjurisdictional law enforcement cooperation.

This case required an inordinate amount of resources, time and labor to investigate. Credit card companies, financial institutions, telephone companies and Internet service providers were slow to react to our requests because they were trying to protect the privacy of their customers. Obtaining subpoenas for the information was another time-consuming task in and of itself.

Investigators should think about preservation of electronic evidence. Have trained forensic computer technicians conduct a proper search and seizure of electronic devices. Send letters to e-mail providers asking them to preserve e-mail in suspects' accounts. Delays in obtaining information result in law enforcement having to play catch-up when the suspect is several steps ahead. Once the information is obtained — which can be months after the original request was made — it takes time to analyze and report it, giving the suspect time to move and close cell phone or Internet providers. It is easy for suspects to exploit service providers by using stolen identities, which can make it difficult to identify and zero in on the actual perpetrators of the crimes.

Recommendations to Prevent Future Occurrences

- Be careful providing personal identifying information unless you have a trusted business relationship with a company. Never respond to a phishing communication. Visit www.antiphishing.org to learn more. If you have suspicions about a message you receive, the easiest way to verify its legitimacy is to call the company directly. Most companies can also be contacted through their Web site.
- Protect your personal identification as the valuable asset that it is. Check your credit history on a regular basis. The law allows you to obtain a free credit report once a year; place a fraud alert on your credit report if you suspect a problem.
- Subscribe to a credit-monitoring service.
- Learn the different ways in which identity thieves obtain information.
- Keep the number of credit and debit accounts you maintain to a minimum and keep a photocopy of the cards in a secure place.
- Use a shredder to dispose of any mail or documents containing personal identifying information.
- Go to the Federal Trade Commission's Web site to learn more about identity theft: www.ftc.gov/idtheft.
- If you discover that you have been a victim of identity theft, file a police report as soon as possible and maintain the documentation of fraudulent activity.
- To help reduce the ability of fraudsters to use stolen credit cards, legislation should be considered that would require credit card companies to imbed the account holder's photograph in a computer chip in the credit card. When used at a point of sale, the photograph would appear so the salesperson could make a positive identification.

About the Author

James B. Keith, MPA, CFE, is a fraud investigator for the Illinois Department of Insurance, Workers' Compensation Fraud Unit. He has a master's degree in public administration from Governors State University in University Park, Illinois, and a BA in education from the University of Wisconsin, Superior.

Don't Mess with Texas

KASONDRA N.D. FEHR

Trina Johnson was 32 years old when she started working for the Lewis Staffing Agency. Her past to that point had been shaky at best. Being a single mother wasn't easy, but after her only daughter turned 13 years old, Trina was able to get back into the corporate world and work full time. She had previously worked part time at various corporations in Houston in the receivables department and when she was off, she enjoyed working with her church. Trina graduated from high school near the top of her class and obtained a bachelor's degree in business administration and public relations, but had not found work in her field of study. She even considered going to law school at night.

Trina eventually secured a temporary position with Corydon Corporation as a credit manager responsible for the collections of specific segment clients. They were bigger than Trina was used to working with, but she was confident that she was up to the job.

Around the same time she began working at Corydon, Trina met Rhonda Davis in a beauty salon on a Saturday afternoon. Like Trina, Rhonda was a woman of spiritual belief and, to Trina's pleasant surprise, a part-time preacher. The two became friends instantly. Trina joined Rhonda's congregation and attended services often. One morning in April, Trina noticed that her new friend was a little troubled. Rhonda said she had a lot on her mind and had recently learned that the company she worked for was going to relocate its offices farther away; she was considering resigning. Trina was deeply upset by this news — Rhonda had become her closest spiritual friend. Wanting to help Rhonda, Trina told her that she would try to help get Rhonda a position at Corydon Corporation. Two months later, Rhonda was contracted through a temporary agency as Trina's assistant in the credit department.

Rhonda was nine years older than Trina. She had a small frame but a commanding, rough voice. Although Rhonda did not smoke, her voice sounded like she had a three-pack-a-day habit. Rhonda had minimal education and no set career path; she had made ends meet as an accounts payable clerk over the years. When Rhonda was hired on at Corydon, she had been divorced for two years. After 15 months of contractual employment through the temporary agency, Corydon offered her a full-time position.

Trina enjoyed working closely with Rhonda and within 18 months her interest in Rhonda had grown into an obsession. Trina even changed her life insurance policy to include Rhonda as a 50-percent beneficiary, cutting her only daughter's share in half.

Abuse of Power

Corydon Corporation was a large international conglomerate with many business segments, each of which produced its own revenue stream. Because of the size and complexity of the company, management created a customized accounting system. Each segment had its own credit department with a line-management system in place for internal direction and communication.

The credit department to which Trina was assigned was managed by Jesse Clark, and the primary metric of success used in the department was the Receivables Aging Report that communicated the number of days receivables were outstanding. The clients Trina was responsible for varied in size. Some were large international companies and others were small and locally based.

As a credit manager, Trina had great authority with clients. If she e-mailed her contact at a company and said that Corydon would like to receive some of their aged or outstanding receivables through an Internet-banking transfer, why would a client question it? Most of Trina's clients paid by check but they were not averse to paying with an online transfer if an invoice was past due. So Trina requested just that — and jumped on her opportunity to generate funds to impress the woman she had grown fond of and didn't want to lose. Trina's plan was to build a house of worship so Rhonda could preach full time.

Because she knew that some of her clients might not be familiar with Internet banking and the process for making online transfers, Trina sent e-mails to the accounts payable representatives at the targeted companies with the instructions for transferring funds online; there were 11 of them in total. Not so coincidentally, Corydon Corporation's new Internet banking account was the same as Trina Johnson's personal account. In the beginning Trina forwarded the new banking instructions only to clients who went into bankruptcy. These payments would be easy to cover up because Corydon wasn't expecting to receive the funds and she could write them off without suspicion. But it didn't take long for Trina to become brave enough to e-mail fraudulent bank instructions to her other clients.

The Handover

Part of the function of the credit department was to review collection efforts made on major clients' accounts. Traditionally this happened quarterly, but with the dramatic increase in business in the past few years, it had unfortunately become an annual event. It was during one of these reviews that Jesse Clark, Trina's manager, asked about one of the receivables for Powell, a major client. Trina responded that the check must have gotten lost in the interoffice mail because she had sent it to the lockbox a few weeks earlier. Jesse's suspicion was raised because he knew Powell had to reissue another check recently, again because it was lost on Corydon's end.

Jesse was also unhappy with Trina's performance in recent months. He couldn't put his finger on it but something wasn't quite right, so he decided to move her to a different segment with new accounts to manage. Doug Brown was slated to take over Trina's accounts. While this transition was occurring, Jesse was thinking about how to reduce the department headcount because business had started to slow down. Only a handful of people were being considered for the layoffs, and Rhonda's low seniority put her near the top of the list.

During the handover of accounts, Trina told Doug and Jesse that two of her clients had multiple problems and that she would like to resolve them herself. Jesse was skeptical but agreed to let Trina finalize the issues with Powell and Axis.

Doug had a tough time at the office after the handover. Employees in other departments were uncooperative. After many meetings with operations, Doug learned that Trina had been aggressive with the operational staff to the point that no one wanted to work with the credit department.

Shortly after the handover, Jesse asked Doug and Trina for an update on the Powell and Axis accounts. Trina was panicking. She had received the payments as Internet transfers — one from each company — to her personal bank account many months earlier. How was she going to write off the amounts without attracting suspicion? She had already lied about the lost checks to Jesse and couldn't risk the truth surfacing. Then there was Rhonda's church to consider. Construction had started at the site and the Web site was being designed; Trina had to pay many contractors to keep her plan in motion. Jesse insisted that both Doug and Trina go to Powell to pick up a replacement check for the lost payment and, while there, Trina was to introduce Doug to the Powell accounts payable supervisor, Vivian York. Jesse wanted to know what was going on and he knew that he would not get answers until Trina was completely out of the picture. The meeting was arranged for later in the week; Trina knew she was on borrowed time.

Mysterious Payments

On the same day the Powell meeting was arranged, Doug was surprised to receive an e-mail from Corydon's treasury department stating that the missing Axis payment of $129,747.24 had been received. Treasury had scanned a copy of the details as an attachment. Doug looked through the supporting documents and was puzzled by the calculator tape (with handwritten notes) that accompanied the check. He also thought it was strange that Axis paid with a cashier's check. Doug forwarded the documents to Jesse and then called him to discuss the calculator tape. The handwritten words next to the amounts said "Axis, Powell and Strickland." While there were various calculations and notations, the amount of $129,747.24 appeared next to "Axis," $118,770.32 appeared next to "Powell," and $78,412 appeared next to "Strickland." Jesse and Doug both agreed that the calculator tape was strange, but neither of them understood the comments and decided not to pursue it.

The day of Trina and Doug's meeting at Powell's offices was beautiful and sunny with almost no humidity — a rare day for the millions of people who live close to the Gulf of Mexico. Doug was supposed to meet Trina at Powell's Houston office at 1:00 PM and he was right on time. He parked in the visitors' parking area and went into Powell's main reception area. Doug checked in with the receptionist, who informed him that Trina had already been there but returned to her car for a moment and would be back shortly. Doug took a seat and waited.

Trina came off the elevator a few minutes later and apologized to Doug, saying she had forgotten something in her car. Trina also told Doug that she had already received the check from Vivian right before the meeting and that they could leave after introductions were made. Trina signaled her readiness to the receptionist, who called Vivian York to announce her visitors. Vivian came out moments later and took them back to her office.

Doug first apologized for the trouble of Corydon losing the two previous checks. Vivian was sympathetic and said, "That's okay; it happens sometimes." There was some small talk but, for the most part, Vivian was in a hurry because she had another meeting to get to. The three exchanged good-byes. On the way to the elevator, Doug asked Trina to see Powell's check. Trina looked through her briefcase and day planner but couldn't find it. She said, "I must have left it in my car when I went down earlier." That seemed extremely unlikely to Doug, but he followed her to the main parking lot. Trina led Doug to her car (a BMW 7 Series that she claimed she bought after winning a lawsuit), and picked up a plain envelope that was lying on the back seat. She handed the envelope to Doug; he looked inside and immediately had a sinking feeling. It was a cashier's check that looked very similar to the Axis check. Doug made no comment except to thank Trina for arranging the introductions. He took the replacement check and assured Trina he would put it in the lockbox.

Doug went back to his office and quickly faxed a copy of the Powell check to Jesse. Both the Powell and Axis cashier's checks were from the same bank — sequentially numbered — and the Powell check amount matched the figure next to Powell's name on the calculator tape submitted with the Axis check. Jesse reviewed Trina's customer account records and another recent receivable jumped off the page — a payment with a cashier's check on the Strickland account. Jesse thanked Doug for the information and said that he would take it from there. Jesse met with various levels of management and the consensus was to terminate Trina at once and figure out the damages later.

Security Breaches

When I was brought into the Corydon case as an investigative auditor, Trina was no longer an employee, which meant I was not able to interview her. I was told that Trina had been fired several weeks ago and we needed to determine the extent of her criminal actions.

The investigation team was composed of me and my colleague Adrian. We were given the facts that had already been gathered. At the start, we only knew "who" and even then we could not rule out the possibility of accomplices. We divided the investigation into four parts.

1. Details of the redirected payments
   - People involved
   - Motivation and opportunity
   - Financial institutions involved
2. Financial effect
   - Determining the scale and totality of the scheme
   - Concealment of the redirected customer remittances
3. Other testing
   - Forensic review of certain computers
   - Review of system transactions of the targeted clients

4. Review of processes
   ◆ Write-offs
   ◆ Cash application
   ◆ Credit management

Adrian started reviewing the credit and collection process and asked Jesse for an overview of Trina's job responsibilities, while I focused on her computer. I was hoping to recover any evidence that might have still existed. This was the first forensic review that had ever been performed at Corydon Corporation — history was in the making. I was also aware that the district attorney's (DA) office had been contacted and Trina's bank records were being subpoenaed, so I hoped to have more information to work with soon.

Adrian's review of the credit department's processes revealed multiple internal control breaches:

- *Write-offs*. Trina was able to directly instruct, without supporting documentation or authorization, the write-off of customer receivables.
- *Cash application*. There was no procedure for the proper handling of client checks outside the company lockbox. Some of the checks owed to Corydon were even made payable to credit managers. When the automated clearing program for the lockbox did not clear the receivable, the exceptions were not fully investigated. Instead, the cash applications clerk communicated directly with the related credit managers for subsequent processing instructions. Finally, credit balances were transferred between customer accounts unnoticed.
- *Credit management*. User profiles in the accounting system allowed credit managers more than viewing access to the books and records. Trina was able to transfer money between accounts, although she should only have had viewing rights. Customer account notations by the respective credit managers varied in style, and collectability issues were not necessarily documented.

Deceptively Simple

I began my forensic review with the deposits that blew Trina's cover in the first place. With photocopies of the two cashier's checks in front of me, I started searching. The main questions going through my mind were: "Why would clients wire transfer funds to a personal bank account?" and "How did Trina convince them to do it?" What I discovered shocked me because of its simplicity. I found the wiring instructions Trina had e-mailed to the companies associated with the two cashier's checks. It became obvious why the clients changed their banking instructions — Trina told them to. She was, after all, a credit manager at Corydon Corporation so, why wouldn't they believe her? The targeted clients must have assumed that the online communication, sent from her Corydon e-mail account, represented the business decisions and processes of Corydon.

The e-mails she sent were short and to the point. Both Powell and Axis had normally remitted their funds via physical check; however, because she had established relationships with their accounts payable supervisors, Trina had no trouble getting them to switch to wire transfers temporarily. She just asked: "Any chance of getting a wire transfer on the old invoices?"

When the client said yes, Trina followed up with: "You are wonderful and to show my appreciation, I would like to take you for lunch whenever your schedule permits. Due to the delay in payment, the only two invoices I would like sent by wire transfer are the oldest from January and February. Attached are the wire instructions that I need these funds sent to."

The wire transfer form that Trina had attached was a simple Word document with only basic information:

WIRE INSTRUCTIONS FOR CORYDON CORPORATION	
Bank Name:	Bank XYZ (address)
Account Name:	Corydon Corporation c/o Trina Johnson
Account No.:	00xxxxxxxxxx
ABA No.:	11xxxxxxx
Reference:	Invoice numbers being paid
If you have any questions, please call Trina Johnson @ xxx-xxx-xxx (Credit Department Manager)	

While the bank account number was her own personal account, by giving both her name and the company name, she made it less obvious. So why did the bank allow a business wire transfer into a personal bank account? The DA's office asked just that and it turned out, much to our surprise, most banks at the time did not review the names on wire transfers because they were automated transactions. As long as the account and routing numbers existed and people did not complain, bank personnel would generally only review transactions if system errors occurred.

Once I had the bank account number and wire instruction details, I searched through Trina's computer for other electronic instructions. I identified more targeted clients and two other bank accounts in Trina's name. I cross-referenced her payroll files and learned that she had changed her direct deposit information three times during her employment history. This information was given to the DA's office to subpoena the other bank statements and we hit the jackpot; Trina had received wire transfers in the other two accounts.

God's Plan?

We discovered e-mails between Trina and Rhonda that solidified Trina's motive to commit the fraud. Countless e-mails from Trina to Rhonda had the same tone. Trina was clearly submissive to Rhonda and sought her love and approval. Trina commonly referred to Rhonda as "Pastor Davis" or "Overseer" and often thanked her for allowing Trina into her life.

The best piece of evidence, known as "Exhibit 33," was also found in Trina's e-mail server. It was a detailed, four-page e-mail to a pastor in a nearby city. The relationship between Trina and this pastor was not determined, but the letter outlined how Trina's life had recently been blessed by a "woman of God" and that Trina was so excited because "God had spoken" to her and given her a plan to follow. The e-mail was written in chronological order, and each time God spoke to Trina, money miraculously appeared in her personal bank accounts. God's plan included many perks for Rhonda. A new Lexus, a wardrobe and fully paid back taxes were just the beginning; the most extravagant item demanded of Trina by the Lord was a house of worship for Rhonda. Trina sought the advice of this pastor after explaining that her relationship with Rhonda had become estranged. She did not understand why Rhonda pushed her away after Trina had bestowed gifts to her, as commanded by God.

The question on my mind after finding this document was, where was Rhonda? I knew we needed to go through her computer, but much to my disappointment, Rhonda had been laid off due to headcount reductions three months before Trina was fired. Rhonda's computer had been wiped and reissued to another employee and her backup account on the server had been purged after 90 days of inactivity.

Intrigued by the mention of a new church in Trina's e-mail to the other pastor, I performed additional searches on Trina's computer and scored again. Temporary Internet files led me to the church's new Web site. Multiple pages detailed the construction timeline of the new church and the organizational chart of the people involved in the ministry. Rhonda was at the top with a beautiful picture that linked to her biography; Trina's title was "Audio & Tape Ministry" with other responsibilities in overseeing the Web site's design. I also found e-mails to and from the Web designer in Trina's computer with detailed instructions, as communicated to her by Rhonda. We couldn't wait to get the bank records from the DA.

The Bank Records

After we received Trina's bank records, we cross-referenced the deposits with her customer sales. We also reviewed two of Trina's other personal bank accounts and discovered hundreds of thousands of dollars of redirected client payments.

Corydon worked closely with the DA's office to build a solid case against Trina. Through information-sharing we learned that the bank account that received the majority of misdirected receivables was in the names of both Trina Johnson and Rhonda Davis. Signature cards were required for shared accounts and we already had other reasons to believe that Rhonda was involved in the fraud — primarily because of the material benefits she received from Trina. I searched through the bank documents and, sure enough, found a signature card with both Trina's and Rhonda's signatures. I matched their signatures on documents in their respective personnel files. After communicating this to the DA's office, Rhonda's personal bank accounts were subpoenaed — she had three accounts and had received $103,000 from Trina.

While tracing the funds that Trina electronically sent from her various bank accounts, we also discovered the new church's accounts. There were a total of four, and more than $500,000 had been transferred to them online from Trina. Besides payments to a number of contractors working on the church, other expenditures included furniture and a home-theater system for Trina's new house as well as ongoing payments for her leased BMW. There were even donations to other ministries in Texas.

The Final Tally

Thirty-seven of the identified misappropriations were wire transfers. By the end of the investigation we determined that Trina had targeted 14 clients and stolen more than $2.5 million over the course of three years. She opened three different bank accounts during the period, as outlined here:

Bank Account	Duration of Account	Amount of Funds Received
Account 1 (Trina's name only)	20 months	$45,000
Account 2 (Trina's and Rhonda's names)	34 months	$1,700,000
Account 3 (Trina's name only)	11 months	$819,000
		$2,564,000

The first and second accounts overlapped for a few months, as did the second and third. During the last 14 months of the fraud, Trina repaid invoices — totaling $925,927 using cashier's checks — mainly because of the many questions she received during credit meetings when Doug took over her accounts. She could not keep telling her manager that checks were getting lost in the mail. Too many wire transfers had hit her personal bank accounts, and Trina could not keep up with hiding them. She felt that she had to give some of the money back or risk being discovered. We reviewed the repayments she made to ensure no other victim clients were missed. The remaining funds in Trina's bank accounts were frozen and Corydon got back $360,000 from them.

The DA's office interviewed Rhonda. Her story was that Trina had told her she owned several oil rigs (handed down from her family) and that Trina wanted to help Rhonda build a house of worship. Rhonda thought it was a "dream come true." She confirmed that the church was being built but there was no more money left in the church's bank accounts. After the DA informed Rhonda that the money had in fact been taken from Corydon, she transferred ownership of her Lexus to the company. Rhonda was not prosecuted due to a lack of direct evidence connecting her to the fraud, and she had left Corydon before the scheme was discovered. The DA offered Trina a reduced sentence to disclose Rhonda's involvement but she stuck to her story that Rhonda had nothing to do with the fraud. However, we believed that Rhonda had to know about the fraud because:

- She was Trina's assistant at Corydon.
- Bank statements were mailed to Rhonda's house.
- She received a car and more than $500,000 from Trina.

Lack of Remorse

Before Trina spoke in front of a judge to be sentenced, several character witnesses testified on her behalf. One was a former supervisor under whom Trina worked at a different company. After he finished extolling Trina's virtues, the prosecuting attorney asked a basic question. "If you had a chance to hire her back, would you?" The supervisor looked around the courtroom as if to stall for time and then said, "Don't think I could do that."

When Trina took the stand she didn't offer a defense or an apology. She was arrogant, obstinate and disrespectful. She showed no remorse, offered no explanations and talked in circles. Trina's stance was that it was other people's fault. The judge was frustrated with Trina's cavalier attitude in the courtroom and sentenced her to 30 years in state prison. Restitution was set at $1.2 million.

Lessons Learned

- Credit managers can have a lot of clout. Their communications to clients regarding payment instructions need secondary monitoring.
- Credit managers should not be allowed to directly interfere with those who can apply collection payments against invoices.
- Many red flags were evident during the three years of Trina's fraud. Her performance evaluations had gone from "Excellent" in year one to "Good" in year two to "Poor" in year three. On Trina's third-year appraisal summary, her manager commented on her lack of follow-up and inadequate or nonexistent client notes. Trina was reprimanded for inaccurately communicating the timing of client payments and for not being transparent with her customer account notes in the accounting system. Much like at Trina's sentencing trial, her comments to management in response to these problems indicated that she was not to blame. In addition to her deteriorating performance at work, her colleagues noticed changes in Trina. Aftermath interviews revealed that Trina had become belligerent with coworkers. Interviewees were aware that Trina gave lavish gifts to Rhonda and that Trina bought Rhonda a Lexus. One colleague, who considered Trina a friend, visited her new house in the second year of the fraud and couldn't believe how big and beautifully furnished it was. Given Trina's demeanor, she thought that Trina might have been mixed up with drugs. The colleague also sensed Trina was confused about her sexuality.
- Every attempt should be made to encourage clients to pay their invoices by electronic data interchange (EDI) payments.

Recommendations to Prevent Future Occurrences

- Treasury departments should have procedures in place to ensure that clients' Internet transfers are going to the correct corporate accounts. For more advanced accounting systems, red flags like "no recent deposits" can trigger system reports for investigation. Further, the client listing should be divided so that confirmation calls can be made (bi-annually or annually — whichever is cost effective for the size of the business and its risk tolerance) by a separate department to verify that the correct banking instructions are still in place.
- Requests should go through the manager of the financial center or a credit supervisor for verification before exception transactions are performed. Further, the collections should be restricted to a few designated employees (segregation of duties) and only after a formal confirmation (independent

(continued)

(*continued*)

supporting documentation) is requested from the client. Finally, tolerance limits for charging off payment differences should be defined and investigated if higher.

- If clients insist on paying with manual checks, then a procedure to systematically mail them to a company-designated lockbox would be beneficial. If possible, credit managers and other internal employees should not be permitted to handle the checks.

- Credit managers should be required to document their communications regarding client payments. Checks and balances should be performed on the access rights of the credit managers to ensure that they cannot alter the accounts receivable ledgers.

- Finally, if background checks had been performed on Trina — either by the temporary agency or Corydon Corporation — she would have been exposed as a repeat offender of fraud. She had embezzled, in different ways, while working for two other companies. Corydon Corporation was victim number three, which was the primary reason she was sentenced to the maximum jail time. As the sayings go, "Three strikes, you're out," and — more important — "Don't mess with Texas!"

About the Author

Kasondra N.D. Fehr, CFE, CGA, CFI, is a compliance audit manager at Schlumberger Limited. She joined the company in 1997 as the Controller over Canadian Seismic operations and was transferred to the Internal Audit department based in Sugar Land, Texas, in 2001 where she began her career in financial fraud investigation. Ms. Fehr has traveled the world to investigate financial crimes. She has investigated many types of internal crimes and has worked closely with law enforcement agencies in several countries. In 2006, she moved to the Compliance Department of Schlumberger.

CHAPTER 9

Hot Wire

RYAN W. MUELLER

Adrian Vargas was a young man with big dreams. Originally hailing from Texas, Adrian was a proud Marine who served two tours of duty in Iraq. Despite being overseas for several years, Adrian remained close to his relatives, and many people would have described him as a family man. Originally, Adrian joined the Marine Corps in search of excitement and adventure. In spite of the miles between his Marine base and his home in El Paso, and the even longer distance between his locations on tours of duty and family, Adrian maintained close ties and frequently sent back letters and gifts. This pattern held true after his discharge when Adrian began sending home illicitly obtained funds and unknowingly assisted investigators in tracing the proceeds of his crimes.

After four years of service with the Marines, Adrian received an honorable discharge, and the world could have been his oyster. However, life after service proved to be stressful, as reported by Adrian himself in his sentencing hearing. He had money troubles and difficulty readjusting as a civilian. He missed the adventure and liveliness that the Marines had provided him, and eventually found a new outlet for his restless energy that also helped solve his money issues — identity theft.

Onward and Upward

Founded in a basement in Alberta by two friends eager to break into the online funds-transfer industry, www.OnlineMoney.com quickly became a runaway success. Other service providers were abandoning high-risk merchants and their attendant customers with increasing rapidity. Online-Money was quick to step in and fill this ever-widening gap, and it soon outgrew the basement and opted for more spacious accommodations above a car wash. The sky would prove to be the limit, and quickly OnlineMoney found itself in a multilevel office building with a number of dedicated departments and business units. Eventually, it would move to even more spacious and luxurious locations, both locally and internationally. Before this final move, I would discover Adrian's treachery in our customer database and assist in bringing him to justice.

Night Watch

I was initially employed with OnlineMoney as a customer service representative, aiding customers with the setup and navigation of their accounts and finishing my university homework between calls. Within a few years, I had demonstrated a knack for dealing with difficult customers, pursuing debtors and locating fraudulent or otherwise suspicious accounts. I was promoted to the investigations unit and promptly placed on the night shift, riding the rookie desk as the newest addition to the team.

Despite its somewhat negative effect on my social life, working nights offered the first crack at all the best cases, as this was when the majority of identity theft or other victims notified us of their unfortunate discoveries. It was also the prime time for fraudsters with day jobs to try their luck against our identity and bank verification systems with varying degrees of success.

I was working yet another 3:00–11:00 PM shift, collating data on an active investigation in Broward County, Florida, when my desk phone rang. I lifted the receiver, pressed the queue button, and said, "Thank you for contacting OnlineMoney Investigations. How can I help you?"

"Ummm. Hi, Ryan, " came the reply from our receptionist. "I have an investigator employed with a Marine credit union on hold claiming several bank accounts have been compromised. Can you take the call?"

"Put him through, please."

Information Deployment

I began by asking the bank investigator for a brief summary of the issues and how he had come to feel the charges against the accounts were unauthorized. I asked this because we received several calls a day that were simply cases of buyer's remorse. Frequently, these remorseful buyers would involve their banks, and even law enforcement, in an attempt to negate their purchases. Other times, an overzealous bank employee would call us to check up on the products their client was purchasing to ensure they were not controlled or prohibited by the bank. At this point, I thought I had heard it all.

The gentleman proceeded to outline the five Ws (who, what, when, where and why) of the case so far. The evidence supporting his claim that the transactions were not authorized seemed solid; all of the identities used to establish accounts belonged to Marines on active duty in Iraq at the time. Being perhaps the most compelling evidence I had heard up to that point in my career, I quickly dispensed with my usual cynical phone persona and got down to business.

I closed all accounts with a few keystrokes and employed a variety of techniques to isolate a clear trail to the identity of the perpetrator and assess the possibility of criminal proceedings. The majority of OnlineMoney's account products were designed to be as user friendly to increase conversions and decrease abandoned signups. This left the intrepid investigator with a very lean sample of "tombstone" data to work with that typically consisted of:

- Name
- Date of birth
- Social Security number or other identification number
- Phone number
- Address
- E-mail address
- IP address
- Security questions and password
- Bank account or credit card information

It helped that the perpetrator had registered multiple linked accounts, leaving a wider trail of unique attributes to investigate. I set about my task, following every lead as far as it would go, and then following the next one.

Investigators in the online space are like investigators anywhere; the case load dwarfs the available resources, the budget isn't written to give you more than last year, and the coffee in the pot is always two hours old. Given that I was not employed by law enforcement, the toolkit that I had access to was limited, to say the least.

Our chief methodology when dealing with a concentrated third-party fraud was affectionately named Search and Destroy. Essentially, it consisted of following links among accounts and running checks on the customer data attributes present on those accounts until a perpetrator was identified. Once that was accomplished, all I had to do was prove that the individual — or someone known to him — was involved in the scheme and lawfully lean on him until he either admitted the wrongdoing or squealed on his friends. Not the most sophisticated approach, but when life gives you lemons, you need to supply your own sugar and water.

The hottest data attributes were typically:

- Phone number
- Social Security number
- Address

- IP address
- Password

By *hottest* I simply mean these gave the most useful results when investigated. As a first step, I ran a search of our system for all transactions submitted in the last 30 days, using the credit union routing number in question, and further pared down that list by eliminating accounts that were registered prior to the alleged fraud being reported. In past investigations, I had netted a good line on the perpetrator simply by identifying which account had been signed up and operated first. I can't count the number of times a fraud ring started with one debtor who got to know the system via their initial shady account operating.

Trip Wire

This approach bore fruit yet again when I found an account signed up in Adrian's name that did not have any transactions but was linked to several suspect accounts by a telephone number. All accounts registered with OnlineMoney required that a recorded call be placed to the account holder and certain information be verified. I looked up the phone numbers to which verification calls had been placed for every account in the questionable group; several of them were in Adrian's name or surname. Many of the addresses used also turned out to be connected to Adrian. I began to think that either I was incredibly lucky, or my perpetrator was a bit of an amateur.

Doing a computerized search on Adrian's full Social Security number, I was able to confirm his employment with the USMC; tracing several of the IP addresses yielded hits to Marine bases or public libraries near Adrian's home. The net was beginning to tighten, but I still needed more proof. Externally, the investigation was proceeding nicely. The initial complainant at the credit union had forwarded the case to the Naval Criminal Investigative Service (NCIS) for completion, but not before Ted and I compared notes.

"So, Ted, I think I've got good news. I've identified a perpetrator," I said.

"Me too! Who's yours?" he replied.

"Adrian Vargas. Same as you?"

"Yeah, same as me. One of the sloppiest I've seen," he chuckled.

"Yes, me too," I laughed.

I informed Ted of what I would need for an official request to release my findings and wished him well, hoping we would meet under happier circumstances one day. But I still needed more proof to make my implication of Adrian irrefutable and ironclad. Turning to our phone records, I extracted the verification call conducted on every account under investigation. That same old lucky feeling was returning; the voice that confirmed Adrian's initial account sounded the same as every subsequent account. I felt like I was unwrapping presents when every call I extracted yielded the familiar voice I had come to know as that of Adrian Vargas. All that remained was to submit my evidence to NCIS and await the results.

Typically, any progressive service that provides online funds transfers only requires that a formal request for information be submitted by the enforcement agency investigating the case, on official letterhead, before releasing its records. Some circumstances will require a subpoena; however, solid legal precedent does exist for the release of records to the authorities, and most reputable service providers write this directly into their terms of use and privacy policies. (Law enforcement staff dealing with online investigators like me will probably find this information very useful.)

I called my new contact at NCIS to discuss the case and outline my requirements to release information. I learned that in addition to the rogue transactions and purchases made by Adrian within the OnlineMoney system, there were countless wire transfers from the compromised checking accounts to himself and to members of his family. Again, Adrian was earning a reputation as the sloppiest perpetrator I had seen.

The NCIS agent was very interested in the case I had built because there was very little evidence of the fraudulent wire transfers. My key evidence was the recorded phone calls, the account in Adrian's own name, and the IP records captured each time he logged into the fake accounts. These IP records, combined with surveillance video from the public locations from which he logged on, effectively placed Adrian at the scene of the crime. Coupled with his vocal confirmation of each account, including the stolen identity information, the prosecutable crimes were beginning to pile up.

Later that day, I received the official request for information from NCIS, which I stapled to the front of my case folder. After dropping it on the desk of my supervisor, I cut out for an early lunch, thoroughly satisfied with a pending successful collar and confident the approval process would take about as long as a leisurely cheeseburger down the street. Sure enough, on my return to the office, the proverbial rubber stamp had authorized the release of my evidence. I sent an e-mail to the NCIS with my full case attached. Then, I got back to work on other open files. Sadly, they were not all as amateur as Adrian Vargas.

Mission Accomplished

At the time that this case crossed my desk, I had about one hundred open investigations. Some were isolated instances of family members hijacking each other's accounts, some were high-dollar compromises in accounts, some were complex money laundering schemes, and the rest were concentrated fraud efforts, similar to that of Adrian, but with more sophistication. Unfortunately, not all of them were concluded as favorably.

Once all the data was collated from OnlineMoney's database and fully investigated, the identity of the perpetrator in this case was painfully obvious. Some criminals are exceptionally good at covering their tracks; Adrian Vargas was not one such criminal. Nearly every online vendor provided details that confirmed Adrian made the purchases in his own name. Additionally, the NCIS investigator had discovered that Adrian had made several wire transfers from the bank accounts in question using forged identity documents to himself and his family in Texas.

With the addition of the information from the vendors involved, the case against Adrian was as solid as anyone could hope. Having been in custody awaiting trial for a considerable amount of time, Adrian would now get his day in court. I felt a great sense of personal satisfaction about the investigation.

The defendant was indicted and eventually pleaded guilty to one count of conspiracy to commit wire fraud, one count of wire fraud and two counts of identity theft. Obviously, plea-bargaining was involved, as this represents a fraction of the charges originally laid against him. He faced up to 45 years of incarceration and $750,000 in fines. But Adrian was ultimately sentenced to 18 months in prison, five years of probation and ordered to pay restitution equal to the total loss. In this case, the risks and punishment did not justify the reward. The total loss incurred, and thus the total gain that Adrian could have hoped for, was $39,094 — a far cry from the value of a clean record and the possible fines he could have faced.

Lessons Learned

Several key lessons can be learned from this case by aspiring gumshoes and pros alike. The first is to act quickly, especially when efforts among several investigative agencies are involved. This limited the total loss faced by Online-Money and, in turn, the victims. Quick action on the part of the credit union investigator shut down one of the chief avenues employed by Adrian to obtain the illicit funds. And promptness by the NCIS resulted in the apprehension of the perpetrator before he was able to go on the lam to avoid capture.

Second, it *always* pays to keep complete records on customers and maintain a reliable audit trail. This is doubly true for investigators and business owners operating online where the bulk of your interaction with a customer is done remotely. Had OnlineMoney's system not tracked the data attributes it did, this case would have been significantly more difficult to resolve.

(continued)

A key feature of our system was that if customers were unable to successfully log in to their accounts because they had entered their password incorrectly, our computers captured that information. A sole individual or a small group often operates fraud rings and they will frequently enter the password of another account when logging in. One example of a different case in which retaining incorrect passwords proved useful was that of one customer gaining access to another customer's account. The IP address records were not conclusive enough to identify the culprit perpetrator, but when I realized the perpetrator's unique password was used in an unsuccessful login to the victim's account, I was able to move forward.

A final, high-level lesson to be taken from this case is not to sacrifice too many verification steps to drive customer acquisitions. I'm sure many professional investigators have crossed swords with sales and marketing staff in their organizations regarding conversion and abandon rates. At every stage of an online account signup or online purchase, potential customers will abandon the process if it proves too difficult or time consuming. Fortunes can be made or lost on abandon rates, so it is important that processes remain easy and user-friendly; but this should not involve sacrificing effective ''Know Your Customer'' procedures, especially in light of ever-changing anti-money laundering and counterterrorist financing legislation. Without effectively identifying the customer, there is no way to serve them well or investigate if things seem amiss.

In the case of Adrian Vargas, the absence of the recorded telephone verification could have made the case much more difficult or impossible to prosecute, and thus diminished the consequences he faced. This single procedure meant the difference between a manageable fraud loss and an unmanageable one.

Recommendations to Prevent Future Occurrences

Elimination of fraud, especially in the online environment, is a lofty goal not easily attained. In a brick-and-mortar operation, depending on the size of the business, it is essential simply to have employees interact with customers to sniff out fraud proactively before it happens. A fraud prevention team that is available 24 hours a day, seven days a week, could pay for itself in customer satisfaction and increased profits. In my experience, the majority of fraudulent activity is not discovered and reported during regular business hours. If having company personnel man a hotline is not feasible, there are many third-party reporting services available.

It is also important to provide employees appropriate training to deal with third-party investigative bodies and law enforcement. This should be approved by the company's legal team to ensure it is compliant with privacy policies and terms of use.

(continued)

(continued)

Online offenders can be transitory, and catching them is very difficult. Don't be caught unprepared by online fraud and allow perpetrators a longer lead time to cover their tracks and get away because the staff is not fully trained. Increase chances of recovering lost funds through restitution by affording this issue the urgency it deserves.

If you have the resources, set up a system of automated alerts that will notify you and your staff when a large quantity of purchases are made in a short time with a common attribute, such as a routing number or IP address. If you do not have the technical resources to do this, train your staff to keep an eye on the live customer environment and flag this activity manually. Remember, an ounce of prevention is worth a pound of cure.

Investigators often experience frustration because they solve a case, but it cannot be prosecuted due to jurisdictional snags or difficulties with online evidence. Too often, the perpetrator is located in a different jurisdiction than the victim, and the law enforcement agency that takes the police report is unable to make the arrest. This — coupled with the fact that the amount of loss suffered by individual victims is typically small — allows online perpetrators to operate with impunity because even if they are identified, the possibility of going to jail is low.

As often as possible, these types of cases need to be pursued by a law enforcement agency that has the ability to cross jurisdictional lines to ensure that the criminals can be brought to appropriate justice. Without the assistance of NCIS, my case may not have been successfully prosecuted, despite the litany of evidence gathered. If you come across a similar online case, try to involve a law enforcement agency that can prosecute it if you realize you can't.

About the Author

Ryan W. Mueller has been a fraud investigator for more than seven years, working exclusively in e-commerce and online payment processing. Ryan graduated from the University of Calgary in 2006 and is currently the director of Golden Apple Consultants, a consulting firm focused on online fraud prevention and investigation. E-mail him at ryan@goldenappleconsultants.com.

A Business within a Business

ALAN F. GREGGO

Since the creation of Internet auctions, internal theft as a cause of loss to businesses has exploded. According to a CNBC segment that aired a while back, reporters estimated that online e-fencing was a $37-billion-a-year business — and it's only grown since then. It is much more profitable and less risky for criminals to sell stolen merchandise on the Internet. An unscrupulous employee can stock his own Internet business from his employer's shelves; without proper detection and prevention measures, such activity can go on for months and years.

The crime of *e-fencing* occurs when employees or boosters steal merchandise from a retail store or distributor and offer it for sale on Internet auction Web sites or through their own online store. A *booster* is a person who shoplifts goods after they have been displayed in a store, as opposed to an employee who steals merchandise from the stock room.

Internet auction Web sites have increased the viability of selling stolen products by offering fencers a far safer method than taking the loot to pawn shops, swap meets or selling it out of car trunks. The Internet allows the thief a level of anonymity that in-person transactions can't offer. Experienced and crafty Internet sellers will not provide their real identities to auction Web sites when they create accounts for the purpose of selling stolen products. Luckily for investigators, e-fencing is a new enough trend that not all the players have the necessary prowess to conceal their identities, even when they try.

Fabio Benifico was an Italian citizen employed as the shipping manager in a U.S. distribution warehouse of Mille Grande — an Italian high-fashion design house. He was one of the last employees to have access to sealed shipments before they were placed on the truck and sent to stores. Fabio was a family man, and his family moved with him to the United States a year and a half ago. He had been selected by Mille Grande's leadership to come to the United States to learn more aspects of the business. Fabio was being groomed to take on more responsibility, and the company tradition was to immerse up-and-coming employees in the U.S. corporate culture so they could learn new skills and diversify their approach to business. Fabio was living the American dream; an expensive dream, but it was his dream come true. He loved his new house and enjoyed devoting time to his favorite hobby — computers. However, acquiring both the home and the computers ran up the family's expenses and became a source of stress for Fabio.

Surfing on the Job

Mille Grande was a purveyor of fountain pens, watches and fine cologne for men and women; the products were typically sold in upscale designer boutiques. Not far from Fabio's warehouse Sarah Gray, a sales employee in a Mille Grande boutique, happened to be looking around an online auction Web site one day and noticed high-end cologne, watches and fountain pens for sale, so she copied down the seller's information. She thought it was interesting that the online seller lived in the same city from which her shop's Mille Grande shipments came.

At the time, I was working as the head of Mille Grande's loss prevention department, so Sarah called me to report what she had found online. When I asked her what she suspected, she said that she didn't know if there was anything improper about the auction site, but that it just looked odd to her that someone so close to the corporate distribution center was auctioning off Mille Grande products.

After copying down the details Sarah could provide, I contacted Scott Pilson — a seasoned investigator who had been with Mille Grande for more than eight years — and assigned him the case. I was confident in his abilities, especially because he had worked Internet investigations in the past. We checked out the auction site together, and it did look suspicious. We both knew that not only was this seller unauthorized — Mille Grande did not sell their products for less than the manufacturer's retail price — but we also suspected the merchandise was most likely stolen; Mille Grande did not believe in selling through auction sites. We were shocked that this Web site had 44 items up for auction dating back six months. The seller's transactions prior to six months ago were not available to the public. The big question was — where and how were the products leaking from the company?

I asked Scott to fill out a seller's information request on the auction site, and he discovered that the seller was registered as Fabio Benifico. That name struck a chord with me. I had been to the warehouse in the last year and met a new shipping manager from Italy named Fabio, but I was not sure of his last name. It was apparent that we needed to do more digging into this connection, so I asked Scott to meet me at the Mille Grande warehouse and distribution center.

Failed Controls

The next day, Scott and I arrived in the warehouse parking lot and drove around the back of the building near the loading docks. The door was propped open and no employees were in sight. Once we went inside, we signed in and met with the warehouse manager. We conducted an assessment of the warehouse and found that employees were not being subjected to random purse, lunch bag and backpack searches, as mandated by company policy. Scott also discovered that the camera system for the building was unplugged and not being used. These were significant violations of the company policy and Mille Grande's basic fraud prevention program. I discussed the matter with Scott and we concluded that merchandise could easily have been stolen directly from the warehouse — by the very employees responsible for protecting it. It was time for a more detailed investigation.

During our visit I confirmed that the shipping manager was Fabio Benifico. He had two employees under him who helped load and unload trucks. The products that Mille Grande shipped into the warehouse from Italy consisted of high-end colognes, pricey fountain pens and Italian-made watches with fine Swiss movements — expensive merchandise that was easily concealed. I could not believe that there was no security lock-up for the merchandise after it was received.

We learned that the two employees who worked for Fabio both left for lunch at the same time every day, leaving Fabio alone. It was during the second half of the day that outbound shipments were routed to Fabio's area to be sealed and addressed to one of the boutiques or department stores. He had complete and unchecked access to the merchandise before it went onto the truck. Scott began searching the shipping log for reports from stores that their shipments had shortages. Sure enough, that shipping log was kept up by none other than Fabio. A quick review confirmed our suspicions: It was loaded with reports of shortages.

I accessed the Internet to search for other auctions that were offering Mille Grande's products and found only a few individual offerings of one or two items. None matched the complexity and variety of Fabio's auctions. His included the company logo, product cases and warranty information. The other auctions looked like used personal items that the owners were trying to sell. Fabio's auction had 44 brand-new items with original packaging and warranty information. I contacted the company's wholesale and marketing divisions to ensure we had no other authorized sellers.

Scott and I organized the evidence and prepared to interview Fabio Benifico. We had the Internet auction Web site's seller information reports, the shipping log, and the obvious lack of controls in the warehouse as evidence. However, we were lacking our pièce de résistance — a purchase from Fabio's auction site to confirm the theft. So Scott went to Fabio's Web site and placed a bid on a bottle of cologne. This extended our investigation a few days, but the delay was worth it. Fabio had no idea we were onto his scheme and the Internet transaction could not be erased.

Covering the Bases

Before interviewing Fabio, I spoke to personnel in Mille Grande's human resources and legal departments. I wanted to make Martin Jumper, our Human Resources (HR) director, aware of the investigation and to get an understanding from him about any of Fabio's potential performance issues. He also provided me with Fabio's application and hiring documents to review — I was looking for his level of education and interests in hopes of building a rapport with him early in the interview. My meeting with Martin also gave me an opportunity to read through the results of his preemployment background check, which can sometimes provide valuable information.

Next I spoke to a staff attorney, Angela Bishop, to ensure that my investigative techniques had not exposed the company to unnecessary risk. This step is particularly important in investigations that will likely result in prosecution and potential public relations or media coverage. I also asked Scott to review with Angela any extraordinary investigative techniques he used, such as the use of covert cameras or purchases of stolen product for evidence gathering.

Scott won the auction for the cologne; when it was delivered, we verified that the sender's address on the parcel was Fabio Benifico's home address. The cologne was boxed and shrink-wrapped in original company packaging. It was the best evidence we had in the case. We were ready to conduct the interview.

Across the Table

I contacted Fabio's supervisor to let him know Scott and I would be interviewing Fabio and gave him the reasons for the interview. I knew that if Fabio's boss told him to cooperate with Scott and me — both strangers to Fabio — he would be more likely to comply. Plus, it was a simple courtesy to let the supervisor know we'd be coming.

The interview was scheduled and I was going to act as the witness while Scott ran the show. "Good afternoon, Fabio, I'm Scott Pilson with the loss prevention department here at Mille Grande,'' Pilson said as Fabio entered the small office for his interview. Scott covered the usual introduction and the reason for the interview.

"So Fabio, tell me about this auction Web site Fabio's Fabulous Accessories for Less. It's registered in your name at your home address and it sells Mille Grande watches, pens and colognes.'' Fabio just stared at Scott, apparently unable to talk. "I'm not so interested in what you are selling today, but how many auctions you have had in the past; how much would you estimate you have earned?'' Scott was using a time-tested approach in confessions. He didn't ask Fabio if he'd committed a wrongful act; that would have led to a denial by Benifico. Scott assumed that Fabio had done it, so he just wanted to know how much he had sold.

"A . . . a . . . about $9,000,'' said Fabio. Based on his experience, Scott knew he was getting a soft admission from Fabio. He tried to further develop the admission by saying, "Tell me how often you removed merchandise from this building to post it on the Web.'' Again silence. Fabio just stared at the ground. Scott did not speak, but allowed the silence to work on Fabio. And notice that Scott didn't ask whether Fabio had removed merchandise; he asked "how often?''

After a few minutes Fabio said, "I only sold merchandise that I received with my employee discount coupons. My wife also bought a lot of merchandise and she didn't need it, so I was selling it to recover some of the money.'' Fabio looked down and would not make eye contact with Scott. Fabio denied that he was stealing; Scott, like most experienced interviewers, expected that to happen.

Scott tried to help Fabio rationalize about the facts of his new life in America and the long hours he was working. Scott told Fabio that the interview was his opportunity to explain exactly what happened truthfully so the company could understand why he did it. Pilson said that — although he could appreciate that a few items might have been family purchases — based on the value and condition of the merchandise on Fabio's auction, there was more to the story. He asked Fabio again, "How often did you remove merchandise from the shipments?'' There was dead silence in the room. Fabio glanced up quickly and then looked back down at the floor.

"Shall I rephrase the question for you?'' asked Scott. Fabio mumbled, "No . . . I mean . . . I take some every week.'' Scott thought about how big the loss was. He guided Fabio through a complete admission by outlining Fabio's need to support his expensive lifestyle, computer hobby and house payments. Fabio explained that it was just too easy to place some merchandise in his lunch cooler and carry it out at the end of shift. He removed the items from the outbound shipments before he sealed them. Pilson asked if he thought he would be caught, but Fabio said he was by himself a lot in the dock area and he never believed anyone would find out about it. Fabio did not think Mille Grande's management would have the Internet knowledge needed to discover the auction Web site, let alone connect him to it. He did not realize that other employees were taught awareness and integrity. They were the eyes and ears of the company, and passed along tips to loss prevention either in person or by way of the company's abuse hotline.

Fabio wrote a statement outlining his whole scheme. He confessed to stealing approximately $20,000 worth of Mille Grande merchandise and selling it on the Internet, but he said he made much less than the manufacturer's suggested retail price because he auctioned products off for the highest price he could get. We asked Fabio to sign the auction Web site's release of records form to allow us access to the complete history of Fabio's Fabulous Accessories for Less. Fabio agreed.

I submitted the release form to the online auction hosting service to access a complete report of Fabio's activity from the time he opened his auction site. This step was necessary because most Internet auctions limit the amount of information that a buyer can access about the seller. We could see from the Web site only a few months of activity and estimate the amount of theft activity from Fabio's sales, but we were sure we did not have the whole story. Even though he admitted to stealing $20,000, we were pretty confident the auction history would reveal a much higher total.

Good Behavior

The disposition and prosecution of this case was next on our minds, so we contacted Martin in HR again and explained Fabio's confession. Martin reviewed the circumstances with Fabio's manager and they decided to terminate Fabio for theft and violation of company policy for illicitly selling Mille Grande merchandise. They communicated the termination to Fabio and mentioned that they viewed his scheme as running a business from within the business and using the company's warehouse to stock his Internet auction Web site.

We summoned the police department and explained the investigation to the responding officers. They placed Fabio under arrest and obtained a search warrant for his house. The police returned merchandise worth just under $1,000 to us, which they discovered in Fabio's home. The police waited to formally charge him until the auction Web site's release was returned with the complete history of Fabio's business. When we received the records, the police charged him with $61,500 in theft — the auction site returned an additional nine months of sales history and we were able to prove $40,500 more in product stolen at our suggested retail price.

Fabio pleaded guilty to grand theft and embezzlement and was sentenced to five years of incarceration and ordered to make restitution of $60,000 after he was released. But the former employee only served 12 months of his sentence and after that was released for good behavior. As long as he makes his restitution payments, he will be on probation. If he stops paying back his loss, the judge promised him the comfort of his jail cell again.

Lessons Learned

Internet auctions can make it easy for employees to fence stolen products. Retail businesses should consider purchasing Internet crawling software that uses key trademark information to track down illicit sales of the company's assets. Also, having an Internet-savvy investigator on staff with the knowledge needed to investigate these crimes was worth the expense.

Each Internet auction service has its own rules and regulations for cooperating with investigations. Some hosts only cooperate with law enforcement officers and will not turn over information to loss prevention practitioners. The auction's release form, when signed by the suspect employee, is an effective tool in gaining necessary information.

I also learned to appreciate our employees as the best providers of information. This case began with an inside tip, so to encourage similar behavior in the future I recommended to management that Sarah receive a monetary reward for uncovering this large theft.

Recommendations to Prevent Future Occurrences

Businesses should have a written policy stating that theft of company property will result in termination and prosecution. The policies should also outline what is allowable and what is prohibited regarding the resale of company merchandise that employees acquire through discount programs, awards and gifts. Consider making an official statement about Internet auctioning to say it is a conflict of interest and subject to investigation and possible adverse action, including termination. Company policies and procedures should be read and signed by new hires.

I recommended that retail and wholesale businesses have a rewards program for employees and explain it publicly. The program should state the guidelines that need to be followed to receive a reward for providing tips about potential wrongdoing. This program should work in concert with the company's abuse hotline, allowing workers to provide anonymous tips and still receive a reward. The amount paid should be confidential to protect the integrity of the program.

(continued)

(*continued*)

Finally, distribution-center security should be reviewed monthly by conducting a risk analysis and evaluating the security cameras, shipping logs, door-locking systems and lockers reserved to hold expensive merchandise. Key facets of the distribution and warehousing center should be evaluated and the results should be reported to management. If appropriate measures had been in place at Mille Grande, we would probably have caught Fabio's thefts months earlier.

About the Author

Alan F. Greggo, CPE, CPP, provides loss prevention leadership and consulting services to retail and medical practitioners. He has more than 30 years of loss prevention and asset protection experience in the optical retail and mass merchandising fields.

Double Play

DELENA D. SPANN

Mollie Garrett was a talent in the corporate banking sector of one of the largest financial institutions in the nation. She'd moved up the ranks in Buck's Bank much faster than many of her peers. She was the consummate professional — dependable and well educated in her field — and she was considered the crème de la crème of the industry.

I met Mollie during the fall at a quarterly meeting attended by law enforcement and financial industry employees. As soon as we were introduced, I knew Mollie wasn't average — she was a graduate of one of the most prestigious universities in the state of Illinois and every detail of her demeanor expressed that she was accomplished and talented. A group of us sat at a table prior to the meeting and shared our work experience and our alma maters. I distinctly remembered Mollie, who said that she had received a bachelor's of science degree in accounting and minored in finance.

The group at the table engaged in friendly conversation. We were a diverse mix but we had one thing in common — we had come to share our expertise and experience in the area of fraud. We discussed the common features of some of our most recent investigations, new trends that had been discovered and the growing pains we faced in attempting to stay at least two steps ahead of the fraudsters. It was an insightful meeting.

As our discussion came to a close, Mollie approached me privately and said she wanted to help me with investing opportunities at her bank. She gave me detailed information about new options she had available, and I was impressed with her knowledge. We agreed that we would touch base in a few weeks or so to discuss it further.

Buck's Bank, Mollie's employer, had more than 50,000 people working in its domestic and global offices. It was so well run and successful that many other financial institutions used it as a model. In the first quarter of the year, the company grossed $1.3 billion in revenue. It had the reputation of a solid and stable financial institution, and I had no reason to suspect otherwise. When I met Mollie, I remembered an article I read a few months earlier in the *Financial Times* that said Buck's Bank had been one of the only financial institutions to have mastered the derivative and hedge-fund market. Buck's Bank was where I maintained my checking account.

Free Lunch for Fraudsters?

The following February, I was deployed on a two-week assignment to provide analytical assistance to an ongoing, high-profile white-collar crime investigation that encompassed a variety of fraud schemes committed by the suspects Roger Cranson and his brother, Thomas Cranson. The Cransons were involved in telemarketing fraud, mortgage and title transaction fraud and pump-and-dump schemes. The investigation, dubbed "Operation Money Bag," uncovered one of the largest fraud schemes cultivated in the South to date.

I was excited about being assigned to such a high-profile investigation. I estimated during my initial analysis that the fraud loss well exceeded $5 million and the attempted fraud totaled more $20 million, with more than 80,000 unauthorized bank drafts. During the first few days of the assignment, I was given the task of providing very detailed and specific analyses on a plethora of financial statements that had arrived the week prior. The work was tedious and exhausting — sifting through financial statements, Suspicious Activity Reports (SARs) and the like is not the most exciting job assignment. I had to work diligently, be precise in my findings, put in overtime and provide significant recommendations that would foster other investigative leads.

My first day was spent in a briefing with other investigators and analysts assigned to the task force to ascertain the direction the case was going. After a few productive meeting hours we had worked up an appetite and decided to go to lunch together. On our way to a restaurant, I stopped by an ATM to get some cash. When I punched in my PIN number and requested a withdrawal of $200, I received a message that I needed to contact a bank representative because the transaction couldn't be completed. I was startled — I knew I had enough money in my checking account to cover the request. My facial expression clearly told my companions that something was wrong.

The Investigator Became the Victim

I returned to the car my colleagues had rented and told them what happened. As we were driving to the restaurant I called the bank and asked about the message. I was told by the customer service representative that there were no available funds in my checking account. I was confused, embarrassed, angry and utterly dismayed. I simply could not imagine what had happened. Was I not the expert in fraud detection and analysis? How could this possibly happen to me? The bank representative said it would be best if I came into the branch to discuss the matter in person.

After lunch, one of my colleagues was kind enough to give me a ride to the nearest Buck's Bank branch. When I met with a customer service representative, I was asked the standard questions: "How may I help you?" and "Do you have an account with us?" I explained that I needed to speak with someone regarding a message I had received while attempting to get cash from an ATM.

She politely asked when and where I last used my debit card, if I paid any bills online and if I made any other transactions or transfers online. I said I had used the card at my local grocery store last weekend. I also used online banking to pay my mortgage and other miscellaneous bills, and I told the representative that I had used my card at a Buck's Bank ATM before departing on my business trip two days ago. The representative asked if I had used it at the main branch, and I told her yes, it was where I had initially opened my account several years ago. It was also the branch where Mollie Garrett worked.

The customer service representative said it was likely that my debit card had been compromised, and that it appeared as though there had been a key logger attached to my computer and/or IP address that retrieved my Internet banking information and pass code. I asked her how that could have happened, because my PIN number was supposed to be encrypted. I also thought that when I used online banking, the automated clearing house (ACH) terminal encrypted the pass code. The representative did not know how to answer these questions, but she assured me that an investigation would be opened.

I knew that I had to devise my own plan, so I contacted Mollie; I was certain she would make every effort to assist me in this matter. I also felt that Mollie and I had established a rapport when we first met. And we were supposed to meet in the upcoming weeks to discuss other investment opportunities — this would be the perfect time to kill two birds with one stone. I decided to do the following before meeting with Mollie:

- File a formal complaint with the Federal Trade Commission (FTC) based on the Internet Intrusion Laws. The FTC is the chief consumer-protection agency to protect against Internet fraud.
- File complaints with the three major credit bureaus (Equifax, Experian and TransUnion) and place fraud alerts on my reports.

- File a complaint with Buck's Bank to close the hijacked account and establish a new account immediately.
- Review consumer rights acts regarding Internet fraud to ascertain any other avenues that I needed to pursue.
- File an Internet fraud complaint with Consumer Sentinel — a consumer online database of Internet, phishing and spam victims.
- File a complaint with the Internet Crime Complaint Center, which is cosponsored by the FBI in conjunction with the National White Collar Crime Center.

The Tables Were Turned

After completing these tasks I phoned Mollie and explained what happened. I gave her specifics about the transactions, such as where they were made and what amounts had been paid. Mollie listened closely as I gave her the details. After I finished, she told me that she would help in any way possible to rectify the situation and to put my mind at ease.

But then Mollie said something strange. She told me that this was a way of life for the intruder. It happened all the time; I should not worry about it — it was only money. "Money comes and goes," said Mollie. I paused while I tried to understand how a person who was supposed to be a savvy banker could make such a statement to a customer whose account had just been compromised, let alone someone who was also a fraud investigator. Adding to the puzzle was that Mollie didn't seem interested in helping me. Our conversation came to a close; she did not give me any specific encouragement or tell me how she planned to address the problem. My confidence in Buck's Bank and Mollie was waning quickly.

As the days passed and I didn't hear from Mollie, I wondered why she seemed agitated and unsympathetic during our last conversation. On the third day of my assignment, a call came in on my cell phone from a number I didn't recognize. Normally, I did not answer unknown calls, but I thought it might be the bank. Indeed, it was Ted Ramon, an investigator at Buck's Bank. However, my guard was up, so wanted to I ask him a few questions before giving him any of my personal information. I asked for his direct office number, e-mail address and supervisor's name.

The bank investigator asked sarcastically, "Am I being investigated?" I replied, "You just never know who you're speaking to through a bunch of wires." And after what had transpired just three days ago, my new philosophy was to scrutinize everything, if need be. Ted assured me that every effort would be made to determine how my account was compromised, who did the compromising and how the culprit used my banking information.

Ted asked me very specific questions about my account, my debit card transactions, the account balance, online transactions and so forth, and I provided him with the requested information. As the interview progressed, I began to feel as if I were the criminal being interrogated. I was on the other side of the fence and realized at that moment how victims feel. I vowed to be more sympathetic when interviewing individuals who report frauds. As Ted continued with his questioning, I also realized that the interview technique he was using was one that I used with suspects. Wow! I had not imagined being victimized, let alone being considered a suspect by my interviewer.

Before our phone called ended, Ted asked me if there was anything else that I would like to add. I remembered the last conversation with Mollie and how strange I thought it was, and decided it was worth mentioning. Ted was quiet for a minute before he told me that when he received my case, it was marked as a non-priority investigation and that Mollie's was the final signature on the complaint. However, luckily for me, Ted decided — based on his own experience as a bank investigator and a fellow Certified Fraud Examiner — that every fraud case was important. He also told me that he would be assisted in the investigation by a cybercrimes specialist named Jake. I was beginning to feel better already.

After the conversation with Ted, I clearly remembered that I had last used my debit card at the bank branch where Mollie worked. As I recollected, when I was approaching the ATM in the lobby, Mollie had walked over and exchanged a greeting with me; she hovered near me as I used the ATM. After I made my withdrawal, I stepped aside for her to use the same ATM. It appeared as though she was checking for something, but what that was, I couldn't begin to imagine.

I now thought to myself, was there a skimming device on the machine? Is that how my information was compromised? Or did someone hack into my computer and log my every keystroke when I conducted Internet transactions? Were my passwords not encrypted, as Buck's claimed they were? Was my spyware not functioning at its capacity? I also had the nagging feeling that Mollie was not the consummate professional that she appeared to be. But what would her motive to commit fraud be?

Double Agent

As the investigation unfolded and new details began to surface, Ted provided me with some astounding information. Apparently when customers went to the main branch of Buck's Bank and used a particular ATM, the transactions were immediately duplicated on the bank's end — meaning that someone was retrieving stored and encrypted information from the customer via a skimming device attached to the ATM. Ted told me the device fit neatly over the card-swipe slot and the customer would be oblivious to it — and to the transaction duplication.

I also learned that I was the victim of another malicious act by the ATM skimmer. I had received a message on my home computer that the manufacturer of a software program installed on my PC had created an upgrade. However, unbeknownst to me, once I installed the "upgrade," hackers could track my keystrokes. When I made an Internet banking transaction, they had access to my account number and password. Jake, the cybercrime specialist on my case, was able to determine that the information from the ATM skimming device and from my hacked computer were going to the same place — the e-mail account of a Buck's Bank employee.

Ted reassured me that Jake was conducting more detailed analyses of this new information, and in the meantime shared some interesting facts he had uncovered about Mollie. Prior to being hired at Buck's Bank, she had been employed with Trust Dive Technology, a computer firm specializing in malware and spyware intrusions. Mollie was considered one of the top innovators at the company and was on the technology board at the Trust Dive Institution.

She was known as a go-getter of sorts at Trust Dive — a sought-after genius in her field. Ted confirmed that Mollie received a degree in banking and finance; however, she also earned a graduate degree in computer management systems. In addition, she had acquired several IT certifications — CISS and CQSA to name a couple. Mollie had not disclosed in her Buck's Bank employment application that she had worked for Trust Dive. Why hadn't she mentioned this? What else was she keeping secret?

After being employed with Trust Dive for four years, Mollie had resigned. Ted decided to dig deeper into her resignation and discovered that Mollie had been asked to leave the company because she infiltrated the computer systems of Trust Dive and sold their top clients' information to an industry competitor. It was revenge to get back at her boss when she didn't get a promotion that she felt that she deserved. Not only was she asked to resign, she lost her pension, had to pay restitution for the bonuses that she received, had to return the company car and relinquished her company stocks.

When the additional findings were uncovered, Ted scheduled a conference call including himself, me and Jake. Jake indicated that there had in fact been an Internet intrusion on my Buck's Bank account by an expert hacker who knew how to block his or her IP address. Lucky for us, Jake was experienced enough to know how to work around such defensive measures. The same hacker also changed the configuration of the bank's computer that was used to decipher my personal information. Yes, indeed, Jake confirmed that Mollie was the culprit behind these fraudulent actions. She had befriended me, used a skimming device to gather my ATM card information and hacked into my computer and Internet banking system to steal my money.

Sweet Relief

Ted Ramon wrote an internal report to the president and chief operating officer of Buck's Bank, alerting them to his findings. Mollie was notified that the bank had discovered her previous employment issues and her fraudulent actions. As a result of previous complaints regarding possible online fraud and identity theft, the bank had been conducting an Internet sting on Mollie's office computer for the past year. However, I did receive some relief. The bank deposited the money Mollie stole from my account into a new, interest-bearing money market account, and the president offered me a lower interest rate on my credit card. I was also given a free safe-deposit box, and the last few bills I paid online during the inception of the fraud were restored to my new account. Mollie was fired from Buck's Bank but, regrettably, no charges were filed against her.

When Internet fraud occurs via online banking and an individual's home computer, the trust and confidence the customer had in her financial institution is undermined. Depending on the scale of the attack, it can ruin the business relationship permanently. When this type of fraud occurs, there is usually a direct loss to the financial institution.

Lessons Learned

This was an overwhelming learning experience. When I met Mollie, I judged her by her appearance and later learned firsthand how true the old adage, ''never judge a book by its cover'' is. This distressing experience gave me different insights into how frauds are committed by the very elite, sharply dressed and well educated. Like so many others, I was almost conned by someone who exuded confidence. If it can happen to a fraud investigator, it can happen to anyone. I shudder when I look back and remember that this con artist wanted to ''help'' me with my investments. This whole episode could have been so much worse.

I also learned to be cautious of my surroundings when using public ATM machines. I now take the necessary precautions when using online banking and consistently — at least twice a week — check the balance of my accounts. The FTC and other organizations advocate consumer education

(continued)

(*continued*)
about the risks of online fraud and the legal measures that can be pursued if the perpetrators of the crime can be identified. I now use them as resources not only in my professional research but also in my personal dealings.

Most important, I learned what it is like to be the victim and, trust me, it isn't fun. I experienced the pain and confusion that comes from being taken advantage of by a fraudster and understand better the victim's point of view.

Fraudsters are constantly becoming more creative, but according to the Anti-Phishing Working Group, this fraud trend isn't new; it began about four years ago when scammers began to realize that some banks were taking cautious measures to reduce cyber attacks. The stricter our anti-fraud controls become, the more deviant the fraudsters' methods for subverting them will become. This is nothing new; criminals have historically tried to be a step or two ahead of efforts to catch them.

Recommendations to Prevent Future Occurrences

We should continue to take necessary precautions to ensure that we're well protected against fraud. Some measures are listed here.

- Financial institutions should enhance consumer security.
- Customers should review online accounts twice a week.
- Banks should offer online consumer education.
- A fraud detection and intrusion network system should be purchased by individuals who bank through the Internet.
- Online transactions should match checkbook withdrawals or deposits.
- Individuals should keep abreast of new fraud highlights within their financial institutions.
- Internet-banking customers should consider joining the Anti-Phishing Working Group.

About the Author

Delena D. Spann, MS, CFE, CCA, is regent emeritus and vice chair of the 2009–2010 Association of Certified Fraud Examiners' Board of Regents. Ms. Spann's fraud analysis expertise includes white-collar crime. She is employed with the U.S. Secret Service, Chicago Field Office, assigned to the Electronic and Financial Crimes Task Force.

CHAPTER

12

The eBay-Fraud Brothers

GERARD (JERRY) BUCHLEITNER

Adam and Jeffrey Yazco were brothers. They were less than two years apart in age and were the only children in a middle-class family in a suburb of Columbia, South Carolina. Adam was a senior in high school and had a very outgoing personality. Jeffrey was right behind Adam — a high-school junior. While Adam spent most of his time in school socializing and making new friends, Jeffrey was considered a loner. One thing students at school relied on Jeffrey for was troubleshooting their computer problems. But he had few social skills and, as a result, no real friends. Neither of the Yazco brothers, though, was by any means popular with the school administration. Both had truancy records and had been in trouble with the law. Vandalism and destruction of property in their neighborhood had their parents, both of whom had jobs, scrambling to keep their sons out of the local juvenile correctional facility. Mr. and Mrs. Yazco were instrumental in enabling — through the liberal application of attorneys' fees — Adam and Jeffrey to each receive one year of unsupervised probation for their crimes. The juvenile judge informed the brothers that, should any additional trouble follow them during their year on probation, they would both be spending time behind bars.

The neighborhood in which the Yazco brothers' vandalism occurred was used to these types of juvenile crimes. Many of the homes were abandoned in the 1990s and their upkeep was minimal at best. This led to a decrease in property values and an increase in crimes. Adam and Jeffrey had one thing in common with many kids who lived in the neighborhood and whose parents worked late — an abundance of unsupervised time.

After their juvenile court proceedings, both Adam and Jeffrey promised their parents that they would find after-school jobs. Adam found his first job in no time; he had such an engaging personality, after all. He was hired by a local discount retail store, BAM's Inc, to stock shelves in the evenings, usually from 4:00 PM to 9:00 PM. Mr. and Mrs. Yazco were relieved and hoped that maybe, just maybe, this would keep their son out of trouble.

When the Yazcos asked Jeffrey how his job search was going, he explained that he was not having the same luck as Adam had. In actuality, his computer was just too interesting to him; he didn't want a part-time job that would interfere with his time online. But Jeffrey was able to convince his parents that he was "in the running" for various opportunities, but would lose out when someone else at school was hired or because the business decided not to fill the position at the last minute. His luck was horrible, he claimed. That then left Jeffrey home alone after school day after day — it was just what he wanted.

Adam loved his first job at BAM's, and BAM's loved Adam's work. He was extremely helpful and friendly with the customers, and they praised him to his store manager. Management offered Adam extra hours, and then an additional day here or there. He was quickly promoted to a shift manager. The 18-year-old liked the money he was able to make and his new spending capabilities; he would come home with his paycheck and brag about it to his brother. "Check this out, Jeff. I'm getting that new CD I was telling you about. How's the job hunting going with you?"

"Don't you dare tell Mom and Dad," Jeffrey threatened, "but I'm not looking."

"What in the world are you doing here after school every day?" Adam asked.

"Just messing around on the Internet. I've found all kinds of things on here you can do to make money."

"Oh, yeah, like what?"

"Well, you've heard of those Internet auction sites, you know, the ones where you can put an item or items up for sale and people nationwide place bids on them?"

"You mean like eBay? What do we have around this place that's gonna make you money on eBay, Jeff?"

"I've been doing some serious thinking lately, Adam. It's not so much what junk we *have* around here, but what we *don't have*! Secondly, it's not how much money I can make, but how much *we* can make! And, most of all, Mom and Dad don't have to know what we do. I can make them think I got a job. They'll never know."

Adam's interest piqued he couldn't resist. "I'm all ears, bro. Tell me more!"

Entrepreneurial Spirit

Brian Andrew Mistoff grew up in a farming family just outside of Greenville, South Carolina, during the 1950s. The grueling, day-to-day, tedious work of managing a farm with his father was not his idea of a career. Mistoff was restless at the age of 18. He noticed that his family had to travel into town to buy staple items for the farm every weekend and the process took an entire day. And hauling those huge bags of rice from the truck to the house was not his idea of a great time. No sir, Mistoff was not going to do that his entire life. He longed for something more challenging.

When he was 19 years old, Brian married his high-school sweetheart, Marilyn. They both agreed that farming was not in their future. Mistoff realized that the only grocery store in town, located on Main Street, was getting everyone's business. What if Mistoff started his own, but put it outside the town? That way, everyone coming into town would have to pass by it on their way. Plus, he was raising so many cows and chickens on the farm, why not offer his customers fresh meat as well? When Brian told Marilyn his idea, she endorsed it right away. The Mistoffs chose their location, renovated the building and set their business plan in motion within a year. Brian hired his family members as meat processors and cutters and BAM's Inc. became a reality.

Brian and Marilyn Mistoff owned their first business, and it was just what they envisioned. As word of mouth spread through the community, most of the townspeople began patronizing BAM's. The store's signature product became fresh-cut meat. As business exploded, the Mistoffs invested and managed their money to the point that they could hire new staff members and then open a second store on the opposite end of town. Throughout the 1960s, the business became more and more profitable. BAM's stores began opening in other towns around Greenville and a few years later, the Mistoffs purchased land and built their first distribution center. BAM's catered to the young and old alike, and began adding grocery items, mainly canned and boxed products. People of every age eventually came to identify BAM's by the large statue of a cow in front of each store staring out over a flock of cars in the parking lot. Children wanted their parents to take pictures next to a BAM's cow as soon as they arrived. The Mistoffs' vision of a friendly, neighborhood store became the place to shop in upstate South Carolina. BAM's grew to more than 250 stores throughout the region, and eventually had a workforce of 15,000 employees. The product line expanded and the company catered to clientele from lower to upper-middle class families. In every city where BAM's operated, it was in the top three in market share.

However, the larger a company becomes, the more the opportunities there are for both employee dishonesty and customer shoplifting. When an employee steals from a company, it is known as *occupation fraud* or *internal theft*. When a customer steals, it is *external theft*. In general, 55 to 60 percent of retail companies' losses are from internal theft; 35 to 40 percent come from external theft; and the rest is due to operational errors, spillage, breakage, incorrect shipments and so on. BAM's was no exception.

FBI Tip

To minimize their losses, BAM's management established a loss prevention department and I was the regional loss prevention manager based out of Columbia, South Carolina. While I was sorting through some of my endless paperwork one day I received a phone call from Tom Flannery at the Columbia branch of the FBI. He informed me that an investigator for eBay, the Internet auction site, contacted him to report a suspected fraud. Individuals were posting items for sale on eBay, collecting money from the winning bidder via Western Union transfers, but not shipping the merchandise. The eBay investigator was able to trace the IP address of the computer used to set up the auctions to the Yazco residence in Columbia. Tom was calling me because he suspected that one of the Yazco brothers worked at a BAM's store in the area; he wanted to know if I could look into Adam Yazco's records to help develop a fraud case. I looked up Adam in BAM's employee database and, sure enough, he worked at a store on Fleet Street. I told Flannery I'd be happy to help with the investigation.

After hanging up the phone, I contacted my supervisor, John Groverton, the director of loss prevention for BAM's. I filled him in on what Flannery shared with me, and Groverton asked that I keep him informed of the investigation along the way. When our conversation ended, I sat back in my chair and took a deep breath. "Wow, I wonder what will come of this one. Well, time to get started!" I picked up my coat and notebook and headed out the door, straight for the Fleet Street BAM's, thinking along the way of what my next steps might be.

Caught on Tape

I hit the ground running. I verified through the store's employee list that Adam Yazco was still employed there. I decided to focus on the Western Union reports and closed-circuit TV (CCTV) tapes first. According to Flannery, Adam was receiving Western Union payments from Internet auction bidders but not shipping the products to them. I was hoping to find a record of Adam cashing these payments either in the store's paperwork or on the surveillance tapes or both. According to BAM's procedures, Western Union records were kept for six weeks and categorized as *sent* and *received*. Each day, the bookkeeper printed a copy of both reports and filed them for safekeeping. I was primarily interested in looking at the received Western Union reports; they would show the date, time, register number, cashier/bookkeeper ID number, receiver's name, sender's name and dollar amount of the transfer. I thought that if I found Adam Yazco's name in the received records, I might also find him transferring funds to another party. Therefore, I would need to review the sent Western Union files as well.

But what if a bookkeeper, for example, was in on the fraud with Yazco? If so, one of their ID numbers would consistently appear on the reports when Adam transferred funds. And what about his brother? Would he be involved in receiving Western Union payments at the store? There was another BAM's even closer to the Yazcos' home than the one where Adam worked. What would be found there?

I began looking at the Western Union records from six weeks ago and quickly found that Adam Yazco had received three Western Union payments at the Fleet Street BAM's. A week later, Adam started receiving more payments — his fraudulent Internet sales seemed to be increasing. In the six-week period for which we had records, Adam Yazco amassed more than $5,000 in Western Union transfers to BAM's Fleet Street location.

Next I reviewed the Western Union sent reports, but neither Yazco boy's name appeared on any file as a sender. While inspecting the Western Union reports for common bookkeeper ID numbers on Adam's transactions, I found that many different bookkeepers processed his transactions. Therefore, Adam Yazco appeared to be receiving money from his fraudulent eBay auctions and keeping it for himself without the involvement of other store employees. He was also not turning around and sending the funds to another person or location.

Then I collected the CCTV tapes that coincided with the dates of Adam's wire transactions. Sure enough, Adam appeared at the customer service desk, signed for the transaction, and was given the funds by various bookkeepers on different days. His body language gave away his actions — tapes showed him looking very nervous and glancing around. I organized my evidence for Flannery at the FBI by placing each day's videotapes with their corresponding Western Union paperwork in separate, large envelopes. The envelopes were labeled with Adam Yazco's name, BAM's store number and the date.

I sent my findings to the appropriate company executives and continued my investigation at the other BAM's store in the area, the one near the Yazcos' home. I found no evidence of Adam, but the CCTV tapes did show his brother, Jeff, picking up Western Union transactions from different cashiers and bookkeepers. The store's reports showed that the six weeks' worth of Western Union funds Jeffrey received at the second BAM's store totaled more than $3,000.

After gathering evidence from the two stores, I checked the Western Union transfers and CCTV tapes at other stores in the district, but did not find more of Adam's or Jeffrey's illicit conduct. My evidence indicated that in six weeks the Yazco brothers cashed more than $8,000 worth of Western Union transfers from defrauded Internet auction victims. The money came from individuals in multiple states and were cashed at the two local BAM's stores.

Two for One

At the end of my investigation, I sent an e-mail to the district manager, the vice president of operations, and my direct supervisor to recap my findings. They gave me permission to send my report, files and evidence to the FBI; a few days after I did so, I received a call from Flannery who said that warrants had been issued for the arrests of Adam and Jeffrey Yazco on federal wire fraud charges. They wanted to take Adam into custody first at the Fleet Street BAM's location as soon as he clocked out of work. Then they would go straight to the Yazcos' house to arrest Jeffrey. I reported this news to BAM's executives, and they requested that Adam's arrest take place in the parking lot so as not to disrupt business. I called the manager at the Fleet Street BAM's to inform him of the upcoming arrest and asked when Adam was working that week. The manager told me that Adam had been a no-call, no-show for three straight days. When the manager tried to reach Adam, his calls went unanswered. Undaunted, the FBI decided to arrest Adam and Jeffrey together, at home. A few days later, I learned that the brothers had indeed been arrested at home and charged with wire fraud.

The Yazcos were both tried in court as adults, even though Jeffrey was 17 years old at the time. Flannery told me that both pleaded guilty to their charges in a plea bargain. The court ordered them to pay full restitution to their eBay customers and to serve a two-year prison sentence, but they both received suspended jail time upon the successful completion of five years of supervised probation. They were also fined, but the amount was not disclosed.

Lessons Learned

The BAM's store where Adam Yazco worked was a high-volume location. Therefore, the staff and management easily overlooked the red flags that were raised by Adam's actions. The store's bookkeepers and managers, who were supposed to review the paperwork on a daily basis for accuracy and completeness, did not question the numerous Western Union transactions Adam received, although they appeared on the nightly Western Union reports. These should have raised suspicions because they involved an employee and should have prompted someone to contact the loss prevention department.

(continued)

This case also demonstrated the importance of maintaining CCTV systems. A substantial portion of our evidence against the brothers came from the surveillance tapes in two stores. Most important, BAM's had no program in place to check potential employees' backgrounds. The company had experimented with pre-employment screening in the past, but the executives did not allocate enough funds in the budget to permanently implement a process. If BAM's had pre-employment background checks at the time, Adam's prior criminal record would have surfaced and he would not have been hired in the first place. As Flannery and the FBI were preparing to arrest Adam they found a misdemeanor shoplifting conviction on his record. He had been caught stealing CDs from a local electronics store before he was hired by BAM's. These CDs, by the way, were photographed and placed for sale on a fraudulent eBay auction by the Yazcos, as were many of their other personal possessions. When the brothers received the wire transfers from eBay customers, they did not ship the CDs or other items to the buyers; they simply kept the money.

Recommendations to Prevent Future Occurrences

Although employee dishonesty is a pernicious problem that retail companies cannot completely eliminate, as a result of this investigation, we made the following recommendations to BAM's executive management to prevent future occurrences or losses.

STORE-LEVEL OWNERSHIP AND ACCOUNTABILITY

Paperwork from the customer service center should be audited and signed daily by both the head bookkeeper and a member of the management team. Such records include Western Union sent and received reports, orders sold and other similar documents. Red flags should be immediately reported to the district manager and the loss prevention department for further action.

STORE-LEVEL COMMUNICATION

This and other cases should be used to train bookkeeping staff and members of store management. The training seminar can be conducted by a member of the loss prevention department in each district at periodic managers' meetings. This would also solidify and strengthen the teamwork atmosphere that should exist between district or store management and the loss prevention department. Also, the managers could return to their stores and train their bookkeeping staff and lower-level management. These sessions would heighten employee awareness about the threat of fraud and would make staff members more alert to the red flags of common schemes.

(continued)

(*continued*)

AUDITING AND INSPECTIONS ON STORE VISITS

District managers, loss prevention personnel and corporate store auditors should follow up on store visits to inspect and review the customer service center daily and weekly reports to ensure policy compliance.

BACKGROUND CHECKS

Upper management should approve and allocate funds in the annual budget for a pre-employment background check on potential employees, at least those in key sensitive positions, such as store managers, bookkeepers and department heads.

HOTLINES

Companies should have a hotline number that employees or customers can call to report concerns about potential or actual losses. BAM's has since contracted with an outside agency to provide employees with a hotline service. Now reports of fraud are called into the BAM's corporate office, not the individual store, to ensure confidentiality and that each report is appropriately and accurately investigated.

The best recommendation for managers and others in key jobs to prevent fraud in the future is to be visible, attentive and involved. When those in positions of responsibility show empathy, ethical behavior and firm but fair treatment of their subordinates throughout an organization, there will be decreasing losses through fraud. The fraudsters will then have fewer opportunities and be less inclined to act on an opportunity in a business where adequate procedures and policies are in place.

About the Author

Gerard (Jerry) Buchleitner, BA, Criminology and Psychology, Indiana University of Pennsylvania, has more than 25 years of district and regional retail loss prevention management experience, including conducting background investigations for federal government agencies and for large corporations in the health care and telecommunications industries.

He is an active member of the ACFE, a published coauthor, has achieved the certified protection professional (CPP) designation, and is a public speaker at local colleges and universities to future criminal justice professionals. Jerry and his wife, Julie, live in Columbia, South Carolina.

CHAPTER

Not-So-Precious Metals

MICHAEL J. MOLDER

Cristoforo (Cris) Marino's parents died in an automobile accident when he was twenty-seven years old, leaving him, their only child, with an unexpected nest egg. Cris owned a successful computer consulting business and had neither the interest nor the ability to run his parents' specialty foods company, which consisted of a chain of three gourmet food shops and a catering service. Selling his parents' business left Cris with several hundred thousand dollars, most of which he invested in a variety of mutual funds offered through national fund management companies. Still, Cris had been intrigued by the financial markets for years, so he decided to keep some of the proceeds to put together his own portfolio.

About a year later, things were going fairly smoothly. Some of his stock choices were up; others were down a bit. Cris had invested all but about $50,000, for which he was trying to find something different — something tangible — an investment he could point to as his own. Cris considered real estate, but he wasn't sure he wanted to stay in the area and feared it would tie him down too much. He thought about art, coins and other collectibles, but he knew he lacked the knowledge to make informed investment choices. While reading one of his favorite online investment advice blogs, Cris found an option that met all of his criteria: mobility; ownership of specific, identifiable property; and a limited learning curve — precious metals.

The Deal

Federal Bullion & Coin, Ltd. (FBC) was a precious-metal dealer in Pensacola, Florida. FBC sold silver, palladium, gold and platinum, in both ingot form and investment-grade coins (such as the American Eagle or the South African Krugerrand). FBC offered direct delivery to the customer or, for an additional fee, arranged storage of the metal at a secure vault. There the customer's bullion would be commingled with other customers' metals, but, as each ingot and sealed coin bore a logged serial number, each customer's metal would be organized. One page on the Web site explained the process:

> Federal Bullion & Coin, Ltd., delivers the physical product you have purchased directly to you or a designated depository. *Coin for coin, ounce for ounce, period!* We do not use futures contracts, forward contracts, options or any other artificial means that would expose you to any other risks beyond price fluctuations in the marketplace. If, for any reason, our company becomes insolvent, your purchase would be unencumbered by corporate debt.

FBC offered just the kind of alternative investment Cris sought. As the company's Web site assured, this was not some kind of abstract purchase in a mining company or a futures contract. With FBC, Cris was buying actual metal. Unlike art or other collectibles, metals had a ready market with quoted prices available from a wide variety of sources on the Internet. Cris understood that, as with any investment, he was taking risks on the fluctuation of the market price of the metal, but unlike collectible coins, the value was unrelated to the particular coin in his possession.

Aware that the Internet is rife with frauds and fly-by-night operations, Cris initially established his account with a $2,000 deposit through PayPal, which prevented FBC from obtaining his credit card information. Cris's first outlay was a small one. He purchased one "unit" of U.S. Silver Eagles, consisting of five sleeves of twenty coins. The U.S. Silver Eagle has a face value of one dollar, is approximately 1.5 inches in diameter, and contains one ounce of silver. As a result, the value of these coins fluctuates with the market value of silver and, generally, is substantially more than the face value of the coin.

FBC charged a 5 percent commission on the total value of the transaction as well as delivery charges to ship the product to either the customer or the secure storage facility (storage charges were a separate fee if the customer elected that service). Cris, still cautious, elected to have the metal delivered to him, and two weeks later he received his package. Over the next several weeks, Cris monitored metal prices and by the end of the month, he had recovered most of the commission and delivery charges. Confident that FBC was legitimate, Cris began investing in earnest.

Welcome to the Family

When Cris transferred $50,000 to his FBC account, the metals broker paid attention. Before the funds cleared his bank account, Cris received a call on his cell phone. "Mr. Marino, I'd like to introduce myself," said a deep voice with a distinct drawl. "My name is Carmichael J. Fredrick, and I'm your account executive at Federal Bullion & Coin, Ltd. I'd like to welcome you to the FBC family of investors."

During that first conversation, Fredrick spoke with Cris for nearly twenty minutes without once soliciting an order for metal. They discussed Cris's background, his computer consulting company, and the death of his parents and subsequent sale of their business. At the end of the call, Fredrick promised to e-mail Cris some recent research on anticipated demand in precious metals and to call him back early the following week after the funds cleared the bank and were available for investment.

As promised, Fredrick was on the phone the following Tuesday, "Y'all get a chance to look over the research?" he asked.

"Yes, Mr. Fredrick, I did, and I'm intrigued by the potential shortages in palladium from restrictions on mining in Russia and increased demand from growth in cell phone manufacturing," Cris answered.

"Well, first, please call me Mike. Mr. Fredrick was my daddy. And I think palladium is a great choice. I'd also like to see you take a position in gold. It is an essential element in the production of semiconductors and other electronic devices. Everywhere you turn, there are more and more computers and electronics. As there's only so much gold available in the world, there's nowhere else to turn, and if the economy slows down, it's a great hedge against declines in other investments like stocks and currency."

So Cris placed his order, and Fredrick transferred him to a compliance officer to complete the transaction.

Compliance Check?

"Good morning, Mr. Marino, my name is Austin Goodwin. I'm a compliance officer with FBC. I have in front of me a purchase order that Mike Fredrick prepared and it's my job to confirm the terms of the transaction with you and make sure we've got your order correct. It says here that you wish to purchase 20 ounces of gold and 100 ounces of palladium." Cris agreed.

"You understand that FBC charges a 5 percent commission on the total price of your metal and a combined delivery charge on this order of $150 for insured, secure handling to its final destination?" Goodwin continued. Again, Marino agreed; Fredrick had already discussed these transaction fees with him.

Goodwin went on, "Now, I see that you have decided to have FBC arrange vault storage for you . . . a wise decision with this quantity of metal. It's very expensive to try to arrange adequate security on your own. I assume that Mike explained to you that we place customer metal with an entirely independent vault company called FundEx, which is located in Texas. We do so much business with FundEx that they have agreed to provide vault space to us free of charge. The only fee associated with secure metal storage is a handling charge of $75, which you will pay every time you deposit or withdraw metal from the vault. Now for your convenience, we will advance the FundEx handling fee from your FBC account, and FundEx will send you a depository receipt via overnight delivery confirming the metal and serial numbers of the ingots it is holding in storage for you. Is that all right with you?'' Again, Fredrick had already explained the storage terms to Cris and he readily confirmed the transaction with Goodwin, who thanked him for being such an enthusiastic customer and welcomed him again to the FBC family.

Deepening Relationship

Over the next three months or so, Cris's relationship with FBC flourished. He would hear from Fredrick at least once a week. They discussed a wide variety of topics from activity in the precious metals markets to the general economy. Cris was in and out of several different metals as prices fluctuated. Silver dipped before he could ship the coins from his original purchase back to FBC to sell them, so he took a bath on that investment. Palladium, however, rose steadily as Russia — true to expectations — curtailed production of the metal to push up the price.

About four months after his initial contact with FBC, Fredrick had him on the phone. Palladium had experienced a particularly sharp price spike, and Fredrick said, ''It's a shame you're a cash investor. With leverage, you could have quadrupled your profit.''

Cris had no idea what he was talking about. Fredrick explained further, ''FBC is a metals broker. We arrange the purchase and sale of precious metals for our customers on a commission basis. To customers like you, who understand the true potential in the precious metals markets, we offer a program that is actually provided by the vault company we deal with, FundEx. They offer financing using the metal they're storing for you as collateral for the loan. You can borrow up to 80 percent of the value of the metal using the equity in your account for the other 20 percent.''

Cris was interested, but also concerned about the risk of borrowing, which he raised with Fredrick.

''That's the best part,'' Fredrick responded. ''Since they hold the physical metal as collateral, and they are heavily involved in precious metal investing themselves, FundEx is able to offer the loans at very favorable rates. Unlike buying stock on margin from a brokerage firm, FundEx will advance funds to you at a half point over prime. You're not likely to get that kind of rate anywhere else.'' Flush with the success of his precious metals investments thus far, the thought of using somebody else's money for profit was appealing. Cris signed up for the leveraged investment program.

During the next two years, Cris steadily built on his initial cash. He tentatively used the equity in his account to leverage his metals positions at first. But before long, Cris had more than a quarter of a million dollars worth of metal in storage at the FundEx vault. Cris traded in and out of various metals on the basis of news reports of global events and Mike Fredrick's knowledge of the likely reactions of the markets to these events. Certainly, there had been some losses, but these were minor compared to the gains he had enjoyed in the majority of his trades. As a result, Cris was surprised to receive an e-mail from FundEx requiring him to remit $6,400 to meet his margin requirements.

All That Glitters Is Not Gold

Cris had been so focused on the investment side of his metals portfolio, he hadn't noticed the accumulation of storage and handling charges each time he bought or sold a position in a metal. Rereading the customer agreement, he realized that the storage charges had only been waived for his first six months as a customer, and had been steadily building ever since. Cris discussed the margin e-mail with Fredrick, who encouraged him to pay the $6,400 because inflation expectations would push the value of his metal up in the next few months, and he would recover the additional investment several times over. Cris sent the payment.

Six months later, and two years into FBC's leveraged-investment program, Cris realized that the inflation wasn't coming. Looking deeper, he recognized that his losses were mounting and the interest, transaction and storage fees had effectively eliminated any equity in his account. When he added in the margin calls he had satisfied, he realized that he had lost substantially more than his initial investment. Cris called Mike Fredrick and instructed him to liquidate the remaining positions. Fredrick encouraged him to wait — a recovery in the metal markets was around the corner. Cris, however, would not be deterred. Fredrick agreed to close the account and send a check for the balance. Cris anxiously awaited receipt of the funds. A week later, when he had still not received the money, he checked his account online. There had been no change. FBC had sold none of Cris's metal and the FundEx loan remained, accumulating interest day to day.

Cris called FBC again, but Fredrick wasn't in the office. Cris called the next day; Fredrick couldn't take the call because he was on the phone with another client. He didn't return the call. Frustrated, Cris called again and asked to speak with Austin Goodwin. Goodwin claimed to know nothing of Cris's request to close the account and assured Cris that he would get to the bottom of the problem, "I promise you, sir, if Mike Fredrick dropped the ball, we will cover any losses that might have accrued over the last week. I'll get back to you by tomorrow."

Goodwin did not call back the following day, or the next, or even the next one after that. Once again, Cris logged into the FBC Web site to check the status, but the system showed the account as "Unavailable." Fearing he was the victim of an investment fraud, Cris contacted counsel.

The Investigation

When Cris described his experience to me, I initially believed that he had been the victim of high-pressure, incomplete-disclosure sales tactics common in boiler-room operations. Although Cris was locked out of his online trading account, he had printed copies of all trade confirmations and loan renewals.

We analyzed the transactions, comparing the purchase and sale prices to historic pricing information available on the Internet, and discovered that Cris's purchases were, routinely, 8 to 10 percent above the spot price of the related metal and his sale prices were always 5 percent below. These premiums and discounts were in addition to the commission FBC charged on the sale. Our analysis of the loan renewals showed that, contrary to the representations in the compliance interviews, the loans did not renew "bi-yearly," or every two years, but rather every six months. FundEx charged a 1.5 percent origination fee with each renewal, increasing the annual interest rate 3 percent. Further research revealed that Austin Goodwin was not merely the FBC compliance officer; he owned the company. While the FBC promotional materials and Web site claimed FBC and FundEx were independent, Goodwin owned the financing entity also. Armed with these misrepresentations, we filed a class-action claim for fraud in federal court in Florida on behalf of Cris and all other similarly situated FBC customers.

Through the discovery process, we requested financial statements and tax returns for both FBC and FundEx, as well as a number of other accounting records, but the defendants and their attorneys stonewalled. Eventually, through a subpoena to the companies' accounting firm, we obtained copies of the tax returns and other FBC and FundEx financial records that the accountants had in their files.

Reviewing these documents, we discovered a curious thing. During the three-year period that the court had allowed us to investigate, FBC had generated approximately $10 million in sales. At the same time, the company recorded $2.7 million in metal purchases. Similarly, FundEx had recorded millions in interest and fee income, which was consistent with the millions in lending it would have done to support FBC's sales of metal. However, FundEx was supposed to be holding depository receipts from a secure storage facility as collateral for the loans, but the company did not show any expense for it.

The Jig Is Up

After obtaining and analyzing this documentation, we managed to locate Carmichael Fredrick. When Cris filed his lawsuit, Fredrick left FBC and moved to New Mexico, where we found him telemarketing penny-stock investments. No longer tied to Goodwin or FBC/FundEx, and fearing the appearance of a process server with a subpoena at his new job, he agreed to meet with us voluntarily at a bar after work. At the meeting, Fredrick acknowledged what we had already come to suspect: There had never been any actual precious metal.

FBC account executives would take orders from customers, using varying premiums and commission rates as incentives to decide quickly on the purchase. The account executive would pass the customer to Goodwin, who acted as a compliance officer to provide an air of formality to the transaction. Goodwin would then enter the ''order'' into a tracking program he'd developed himself. The tracking program would generate applicable ''loan'' documentation that Goodwin's sister would print and mail to the customer from her home in Houston. When customers like Cris logged into the FBC Web site, they were actually accessing the tracking program.

''What about the metal?'' I asked him.

Fredrick took another swallow of beer, ''There really wasn't any. Oh, Austin had a safe in his office where he kept a few thousand dollars worth of coins and bullion. Once in a while, we'd get a call from somebody who needed immediate delivery for some reason — like Cris's first order, or the crazy old lady from Boston who was giving her grandkids gold American Eagles as bar mitzvah presents. Other than that handful of coins and ingots, he would only buy metal when somebody actually settled an account and requested delivery of metal.''

Further conversation revealed that Goodwin managed a portfolio of precious metals futures based on the total metal ''held'' by FBC customers. He used these futures contracts as a hedge against sudden, unfavorable movements in the market price. ''Like,'' Fredrick explained, ''if there was a huge mine disaster in Russia, the price of palladium might spike, and we could get a whole bunch of people wanting to close out their positions.'' The value of the futures contracts would track the price movement of the metal and allowed Goodwin to satisfy a demand to produce actual metal if needed. Goodwin recorded the futures contracts as "purchases" of metal in the accounting records, which proved to be the basis for most of the $2.7 million in purchases on the books.

In the meantime, it was the account executives' job to try to convince customers to maintain their leveraged positions so that the interest accumulation and renewal fees would consume whatever "equity" appeared in the account, and to reinvest "profits" to generate more commissions. Goodwin rewarded the account executives with lavish parties, deep-sea fishing trips in the Gulf, and substantial cash bonuses.

About three months after our meeting with Fredrick in New Mexico, the court ordered a conference on our renewed motion to compel FBC and FundEx to produce detailed financial records. The judge was very angry when defense counsel appeared with no representative of the defendants. After several minutes of being berated, defense counsel acknowledged that he had been unable to reach his client for some time. We later learned that Goodwin had cleared out the bank accounts and fled when he discovered the accountant was producing documents in response to the subpoena.

FBC's landlord had sold the abandoned furniture and computer equipment before we found out that Goodwin had absconded with the remaining cash but the landlord had saved several boxes of old files, which he gave to us. From these documents we identified more than 700 other FBC/FundEx investors who had lost about $15 million.

Falling through the Cracks

With no defendant in sight and no funds to pursue, the civil litigation floundered, and the court ultimately dismissed the action. We tried to interest government regulators in pursuing criminal action against Goodwin in the hope that it might lead to some degree of restitution, but we discovered an unfortunate gap in the then-applicable regulatory structures. The Securities and Exchange Commission (SEC) lacked jurisdiction because the transactions did not involve the purchase or sale of a security. Similarly, the Commodities Futures Trading Commission (CFTC) could not pursue the matter because Cris and the other FBC customers had expressly purchased actual metal, and the CFTC's jurisdiction was limited to policing contracts for the future delivery of a commodity, not an obligation to deliver the product currently. Finally, we spoke to state and local criminal prosecutors. While they sympathized with the situation, there was no perpetrator around to arrest and limited evidence with a dubious chain of custody. Further complicating the matter was the issue of jurisdiction, as Cris and the vast majority of other

FBC customers were neither Florida nor Texas residents. In the end, there was no prosecution or restitution to satisfy FBC's defrauded investors.

Lessons Learned

Despite the fact that *Marino v. FBC et al.* ended so badly for the victims, the case presented a learning opportunity for both Cris Marino and my partner and I as his counsel. Cris realized the value of personal relationships in long-term, high-value arrangements. The Internet is a wonderful tool. It allows people to connect across thousands of miles instantaneously. Purchasing a simple consumer product through the Internet is a matter of a few mouse clicks. However, a long-term relationship or a substantial commitment of resources deserves the personal touch — a referral from a trusted family member or friend, a face-to-face meeting with the person on the other side of the transaction, a visit to the location. Investment transactions should not be conducted with the same ease or anonymity of small purchases.

Cris also came to understand how a ``long con'' operates. He believed that by initially purchasing coins in a relatively small transaction, he had verified the legitimacy of the FBC operation. While some frauds operate as a quick hit (such as a sale of stolen merchandise or passing a bad check), the more profitable ones need to age like a fine wine. Cris learned that FBC processed his initial transaction smoothly and promptly to allay his concerns about the legitimacy of the operation. Buoyed by that misplaced confidence, he made the larger commitment, giving FBC the big payoff.

Finally, Cris realized that information presented on a Web site is subject to manipulation. Cris relied on the FBC Web site for information about the pricing of precious metals, the amount of metal stored on his behalf, and the serial numbers of the ingots and coin lots. None of this information was even remotely connected to reality. The pricing information on FBC's Web site did not reflect actual spot prices for the products. The individual account information, including amounts and types of metals and the identifying numbers, were all complete fabrications.

As counsel, my partner and I learned that we could not underestimate the sinister nature of some people. When I became involved with this case, I had been an auditor, securities fraud litigator and Certified Fraud Examiner for nearly two decades. I had investigated and litigated dozens of alleged frauds, but my exposure to Ponzi schemes, overstated earnings and undisclosed liabilities had not prepared me for this case. I originally assumed that Fredrick and Goodwin were essentially businesspeople. I knew that they bragged, pressured and glossed over risks. But I wrongly believed they had a real operating business. It did not initially occur to me that FBC was a complete fabrication and the investments of Cris Marino, among others, were stolen from the start.

Recommendations to Prevent Future Occurrences

Short of investing solely in government bonds purchased directly from the U.S. Department of the Treasury, it is probably impossible for Internet-based investors to wholly protect themselves from fraud. There are, however, a number of steps they can take to mitigate their risks.

BACKGROUND CHECKS

The Internet is a remarkable tool for investigating prospective vendors and business partners. There are many subscription sites, such as Dun & Bradstreet, that can — for a relatively minor fee — provide background information on businesses. Alternatively, you can invest time rather than money and obtain a wealth of information from free sites. For example, if Cris Marino had checked the Web sites of the secretaries of state in Florida and Texas, he would have discovered that FBC and FundEx were owned by the same person. Similarly, a search on a mapping Web site would have shown that the mailing address of FundEx was in an unquestionably residential neighborhood of Houston. Although some businesses may be able to operate out of a home, FundEx was claiming to store large quantities of precious metals in a secure vault.

REGULATORY OVERSIGHT

There is a host of different, and sometimes conflicting, regulatory systems governing the conduct of investment advisors. While a number of regulatory agencies enforce differing degrees of oversight, they might nonetheless provide some degree of confidence that the entity itself is legitimate. And if a company violates the requirements of the regulatory body, at least there may be an enforcement mechanism to assist in recovery. Before investing significant money with an advisor, broker or fund manager, ask what government agency exercises authority. Then actually check with the regulatory body to make sure that the company is in compliance with applicable reporting requirements. Even if those reports turn out to be false, at least there may be assistance available with the investigation and recovery if things fall apart.

AUDITED FINANCIAL STATEMENTS

Audits are not an insurance policy against fraud, but if an investment company permits an independent examination of its financial records on an annual basis, it is more likely to be legitimate. Further still, a company's unwillingness to share the information with investors is a red flag that the advisor could have something to hide. It is not enough, however, to merely accept an audit report. If it is not performed by a recognized, established accounting firm, investors should verify the existence of the auditors with the state board of accountancy or the Public Company Accounting Oversight Board.

(continued)

FACE-TO-FACE CONTACT

The Internet provides unparalleled opportunities for research and convenient investing. You can analyze investments and portfolio performance in your fuzzy bunny slippers when you wake up in the morning. You can get up-to-the-minute news and place trades through a smart phone while you're sitting on a bus in traffic. But before you make a substantial initial investment, face time is an effective due diligence tool. Whether it is a meeting with an actual account representative or paying a visit to the office, this action provides an opportunity to take the measure of the person or firm with which you are entrusting your money. Had Cris gone to the trouble of visiting FBC, he would have known that the company ran its operations from a storefront in a strip mall. Even if Fredrick had arranged to meet Cris somewhere other than the FBC office, Cris would have seen that, without the scripts and other props that Goodwin prepared, Fredrick knew nothing of the precious-metal markets and was not a trustworthy investment advisor.

As more and more financial transactions are conducted over the Internet, individual consumers and investors need to be aware of the risks they face. Entrusting your money to an advisor whom you have not met in person — or to a company that you have not properly researched — is a dangerous decision. Likewise, fraud examiners and other anti-fraud professionals need to adjust their understanding of perpetrators to include this new breed of online criminals. While Web sites can give an air of professional legitimacy to common fraudsters, investigators should not be fooled by such tactics.

About the Author

Michael J. Molder, J.D., CFE, CPA, CVA, CFF, is a senior manager in the Business Advisory Services group of Marcum, LLP. Throughout his career, he has litigated, or aided counsel in, more than a hundred cases involving alleged fraud and financial manipulation. Mr. Molder has helped recover hundreds of millions of dollars for victims of fraud.

14

The Cool-Cash Syndicate

AUSTINE S.M. ADACHE

Yare Twizyila was a tall, lanky twenty-something who liked to sport an Afro hairdo and glasses because he thought it gave him an "old-school" look. He was the eldest of five children and the only boy, so he considered himself the head of the family. As a young man, he was eager to establish a name for himself and prove to his sisters that he deserved the authority he asserted over them — he just didn't want to work hard to earn it. He dropped out of high school because, by his own estimation, he was not cut out for words and numbers. He thought he was better suited for trading spare car parts in Nigeria's commercial capital, Lagos, so he moved downtown and made connections with traders. Through his new friends, Yare heard about informal computer classes offered at the local college and enrolled in one to try it out. With constant practice, he advanced appreciably and became familiar with the technology. A few months later he took a job as an attendant in an Internet café. His easy access to computers and the Internet at work further expanded his cyberspace horizons.

While Yare was acquiring his computer skills he was also developing a group of criminal friends who convinced him to channel his new prowess into fraudulent activities. He had one particular friend named Qiddsa Dodagi — nicknamed "Mr. Cool Cash" by colleagues and friends — who did nothing tangible for a living except to be on the Internet every day, yet he had more money and lived more comfortably than any of his hardworking peers. He drove a sleek, black BMW and owned a three-bedroom house in an expensive area of the city. Mr. Cool Cash's easy lifestyle and wealth lured Yare Twizyila into the world of Internet fraud.

Yare and Mr. Cool Cash became such good friends that Mr. Cool Cash revealed the source of his money — hacking into people's bank accounts. He taught Yare this art and science and Yare — with his knowledge of computers and the Internet — learned quickly. Together they amassed so many victims they were becoming a racket. To create their enterprise, Mr. Cool

125

Cash and Yare used three methods to break into people's bank accounts: phishing, card cloning and extrapolation.

Phishing

Phishing — a common Internet scheme directed at the fraudulent acquisition of privileged, sensitive, confidential or private information from an individual — was committed by Yare via text messages, e-mail or instant messaging (IM). His scheme involved posing as a genuine or trustworthy authority or company to persuade victims to provide their banking information. They sent mass e-mails to unsuspecting victims that were supposedly from their bank and requested they confirm their account details. By replying to the e-mails, people were essentially handing the fraudsters their money.

Card Cloning

Yare learned how to clone cards by printing, embossing or encoding a fraudulent credit or debit card with information from a genuine card. Typically, the data on a real card's magnetic stripe was copied onto another card without the cardholder's knowledge, or the card details were stolen from discarded receipts or directly from the card at a point of sale (POS) terminal or ATM. Yare was able to read, overwrite and encode an existing card with new details or information using a cloning machine.

Extrapolation

Because they knew that the 19-digit number — called the personal account number (PAN) — on a debit card was a combination of the issuing bank's code and the account holder's personal account information, Yare and Mr. Cool Cash made informed guesses until they hit on the right combination. They gathered some of the information from receipts littered around the ATMs and they used a hacking tool called a *net monitor* to generate numbers and test their validity. Once they confirmed on the Internet that the card was active, they began to extrapolate the personal identification number (PIN). Unfortunately some debit card users create PINs that are easily guessed, such as 0000, 1234, 1111, 1980 and 1970; fraudsters had two tries a day before they were locked out of the online login process. But given a long-enough period of time, they were able to guess the correct PINs.

Saving for a Home

Micah Jumo was a public servant with a demanding job in Lagos. He denied himself and his family luxuries in the hopes of one day building a home.

Micah had maintained a checking account with a leading Nigerian bank for nearly 10 years. He also used the checking account as his major savings depository and had a debit card associated with it. Because Micah was saving to buy a home, he guarded his debit card diligently against possible compromise and checked his account balance regularly. Toward the goal of owning a home, Micah had already purchased a plot of land in the suburbs. In a show of determination, Micah had commissioned the architectural design for the house — four bedrooms with a guesthouse — from a childhood friend who was an architect. He had even begun requesting building permits from the various city and planning councils that oversaw the process. He was hoping to start construction within a year.

One afternoon Micah went to the bank to make a withdrawal from his account, but the balance did not tally with what he expected. He was shocked to see it was short by an equivalent of about $12,000, and he knew perfectly well that he did not withdraw such an amount. He lost his temper with the bank teller and demanded an explanation. He was referred to the customer care unit, where he registered his complaint and requested to see the manager. After an exhaustive deliberation, the manager asked Micah to write a formal complaint. The manager ended their conversation by asking Micah to exercise patience while he looked into the problem.

The bank records showed that the money was withdrawn from Micah's account over the course of three days in amounts equal to $4,300, $4,300 and $3,400. The transactions were made through the Internet. Because Micah denied knowledge of the transfers, the bank manager referred the case for further investigation to the government agency in charge of economic and financial crimes. I worked there as an investigator and was given the case.

Can I Get Your Number?

From past investigations of similar crimes, I had learned that debit cards can be compromised directly or indirectly, intentionally or unintentionally, by a bank employee, a debit card owner or an external fraudster. I also knew that insider abuse was rare. Therefore, my initial hypothesis was that the culprit or culprits were outsiders. As the leader of the investigation team, I attended a briefing with Micah and heard his account firsthand. This meeting was also attended by key staff members from the bank.

After hearing the basics, I requested Micah's bank statements and transaction records; both showed that the three disputed transfers were debited from Micah's account for Internet purchases. This led us to an Internet-based payment facility — InterSwitch — and in turn to a Web site that sold pay-as-you-go cell-phone service. We requested that the phone company, Comsoft Limited, send us the Internet protocol (IP) addresses used to make the three purchases. We also asked for the buyers' names and e-mail addresses, although it was likely that the information provided would be fake. However, we knew the IP addresses could be traced to physical addresses with the help of the Internet service providers (ISPs). After following the trail backward, we identified two public Internet cafés as the site of the fraudulent transactions. Unfortunately, Internet café owners in Lagos were notorious for not maintaining records of their customers; we began surveillance on the cafés in the hope of establishing suspects, but to no avail.

While we were monitoring the Internet cafés, Comsoft returned the phone numbers that were used for the three fraudulent purchases. We traced one number to an apartment in downtown Lagos rented by a woman named Tifari Twiyzyila and paid her a visit. When my partner and I arrived and explained where we worked, we were invited inside by her. Upon my request, she gave me her cell phone and I scrolled through her contacts. Two numbers caught my attention — I recognized them from the list of numbers provided by Comsoft. The names associated with the two numbers in Tifari cell phone were "big brother" and "Janz." When I asked her who the two people were, she said one was her brother, Yare Twiyzyila, and the other was her brother's friend, Janzozo Danbola.

Falling Like Dominoes

After much prodding, Tifari reluctantly led us to Yare's apartment, and the scene that greeted us indicated that he was tipped off — furniture was askew and a radio was left playing as if the occupants had left in a hurry. However, we planted a surveillance device in the apartment and made it known in the area that we were leaving. About a week later, Yare resurfaced — an event that our surveillance device picked up — and we were able to speed over to his apartment in time to find him frantically packing his belongings, apparently trying to flee. We arrested him and discovered two of the Comsoft cell phones in his possession. While searching Yare's apartment, we found Janzozo Danbola's address and my partner and I immediately headed in that direction, leaving a forensics team to finish the search at Yare's home.

Janzozo Danbola made quite an impression on us when we parked outside his house. He was just stepping out the front door when we pulled up and was dressed in remarkably elegant clothing. Much to his chagrin, we added a pair of handcuffs to his fashionable ensemble. We found one of the Comsoft phones on Janzozo as well, and discovered that only minutes earlier he had sent a text message to a contact named Doncali. The message said, "Here are the card details 5678788889075657432. Expiry date 2010." When we asked him the meaning of the message, Janz said he had lost his debit card and was asking his friend Doncali to help him look for it.

Doubting this explanation, I sent another text message to Doncali from Janz's phone asking, "How soon, please?" Doncali immediately responded with, "Meet me at the Mobil filling station in one hour."

Putting my suspicions together, I came to the conclusion that Doncali was in possession of a debit card duplicator. Janzozo had somehow acquired the details of a debit card and sent them to Doncali to generate a fraudulent card. After presenting my theory to Janzozo, he admitted his role and told me what transpired. He said he stole information from the cards of unsuspecting victims and sent it to Doncali — except the PINs, which Janz kept to himself — to make fake cards. When a card was ready, Janzozo and Doncali met at an ATM to see if there was money in the account. Janz kept the PIN for this reason, so Doncali couldn't make a card and withdraw the money himself. If there was money in an account, Janz withdrew it and paid Doncali a percentage. Janz also informed me that Doncali met his clients at public places and made sure nobody knew where he lived or stored his duplicating machine.

We set up strategic positions around the rendezvous gas station and instructed Janzozo to meet Doncali, collect the cloned debit card, make the withdrawal and pay him. After that, he was to give Doncali the details of another debit card — which I gave to him — and we told him to stress the importance of getting the card quickly. We watched the meeting take place and then followed Doncali as he drove away. As he was driving, Doncali unnecessarily changed directions several times and stopped momentarily to see if he was being followed. However, we did not lose track of him. He parked in front of a two-story house with a panoramic view of the city. A few minutes after he went in the house, we entered the building and executed a search warrant. We arrested Doncali Ijabula and recovered the card duplicator.

When we were able to interview Yare Twiyzyila, he initially denied knowledge of the fraud. But when we confronted him with the volume of evidence that led to his arrest, he opened up and confessed to the crime. He said he used the extrapolation method on Micah Jumo's account to figure out the PIN — the year Jumo's first daughter was born. Yare also said that when he eventually hacked into Micah's bank account, he went to an Internet café on the other side of town to transfer the money, hoping that the transactions could not be traced back to him. Generally, debit card fraudsters prefer to make purchases on the Internet rather than withdraw money from an ATM to avoid the withdraw limit. Also, items purchased online can be sold easily for cash.

The arrests and confessions of Yare Twiyzyila, Janzozo Danbola and Doncali Ijabula indicated they were members of a larger fraud ring, and this led to two other major arrests, including that of ringleader Qiddsa

Dodagi (Mr. Cool Cash). The evidence we found on Mr. Cool Cash's laptop was what finally nailed him. We identified and traced some of the proceeds from stolen card information to Dodagi's individual bank account and to properties he bought. The perpetrators' accounts were frozen and their properties ordered for seizure by the court. When we sent the case to our legal unit, they drafted the appropriate charges and filed the case in court.

The Syndicate Dissolves

Qiddsa Dodagi, Yare Twiyzyila and the other members of the Cool-Cash Syndicate were charged for conspiracy, forgery and stealing. They hired a brilliant lawyer who employed every stalling technique in his arsenal, but justice prevailed in the end. Each member of the fraud ring was found guilty and sentenced to jail for terms ranging from three to seven years. The court ordered the forfeiture of the proceeds of the crime and restitution for the victims.

Lessons Learned

This investigation was an interesting exercise. It required time, energy, initiative and money and taught me how to best harness and employ our resources. I also learned new methods by which frauds were committed from my suspects when I interviewed them. The findings of this investigation made me take more precautionary steps in safeguarding my own debit card information, and I accordingly make the following recommendations to other users.

Recommendations to Prevent Future Occurrences

FOR THE FINANCIAL SERVICES INDUSTRY

- *Transaction alerts* — Each transaction conducted with a debit card can be sent to the card holder's cell phone as a text message. This allows individuals to immediately notice fraudulent transactions.
- *Money guard* — Provide customers with a 24/7 hotline to report unauthorized transactions. InterSwitch, the Internet payment service used in this case, has gone a step further to allow customers to automatically deactivate their cards if they suspect they have been compromised.

(continued)

- *Instant gratification* — Limit the amount of money that can be spent online in one day to a reasonable sum.
- *Non-instant gratification* — Purchases exceeding the instant-gratification limit could take three days to process, a period in which the cardholder would be asked to confirm the purchase.

FOR DEBIT CARD USERS

The following tips are useful in helping to have one's card secured and protected.

- *Transaction alerts* — Most banks offer to alert customers when transactions occur either with a text message or an e-mail, and customers are encouraged to subscribe to it.
- *Debit card and PIN safety:*
  - Safeguard and protect your debit card as if it were cash.
  - Immediately report a stolen or lost card.
  - Memorize your PIN. Do not write it down; someone may see it.
  - Change your PIN frequently.
  - Do not let your card out of your sight while paying for goods or services at merchant locations.
  - Get your card back after you use it at a POS or ATM.
  - Keep your vouchers and ATM receipts in a safe and secure place.
  - Do not disclose your PIN to anyone for any reason, not even to your bank. It can be illegal for any person or establishment to ask, demand or request your PIN.
- *Secured use of ATMs:*
  - Be vigilant when using ATMs to ensure that no one sees you enter your PIN.
  - Cancel the transaction if you are not certain of its safety.
  - Take the receipts of complete and canceled transactions; your debit card details can be copied from them if left behind.
  - Be very careful about receiving assistance. Do not accept help from strangers when you are using an ATM.
- *Online communication and transactions:*
  - Beware of e-mails asking for your PIN and card details. Do not disclose or send your PIN or account information in the body of an e-mail.
  - Confirm that a Web site has adequate security features before initiating an online transaction.
  - Avoid making online purchases in Internet cafés.
  - Be careful of e-mails purporting to be from your bank and requesting your account details and PIN. Report suspicious e-mails to your bank.
  - Ignore e-mails asking for your PIN to claim prizes or directing you to use your debit card at an ATM to claim a reward. Do not reply to such e-mails and do not click on any links in the messages; otherwise, your computer might be infected with a malicious virus.

About the Author

Austine S.M. Adache, CFE, is a deputy detective superintendent and lead investigator in the Advance Fee Fraud/Cyber Crime Section of the Economic and Financial Crimes Commission (EFCC), Nigeria. He has been involved in fraud investigation since 2005. He is currently in the Kano Zonal Office of the Commission.

Dastardly Design

PRABHAT KUMAR

By the end of his presentation, Alex Gomez had attained the undivided attention of almost everyone present at the Structural Engineers' Seminar (Asia Pacific) for the New Millennium. The topic was "Political Corruption and the Construction Industry in Southeast Asia." Albert Watanabe, head of Southeast Asian operations for Construction Consultants, Ltd., was among the audience members who were impressed by Alex's presentation. Construction Consultants, Ltd. (CCL) was a Hong Kong–based structural engineering consulting firm and was well known throughout Southeast Asia. CCL was founded by Edward Lim, a professional engineer. What started off as a small consultancy quickly expanded and, in a mere six years, Lim established his company as one of the most powerful and respected in Southeast Asia. As a knockout blow to its competitors, CCL acquired Nathan & Associates Structural Engineering, Ltd., the second largest such firm in the area.

More recently, Albert Watanabe's immediate subordinate, Ramesh Pillai, resigned because his wife had insisted on immigrating to Canada, where her parents had retired. This resignation created a vacuum that put incredible pressure and workload on Watanabe. As the regional country manager, he was responsible for the profitability and growth of the Kuala Lumpur office. However, he was also the regional director in charge of offices in Singapore, Indonesia and Malaysia; his new workload was causing him too much stress and he needed a right-hand man to independently run the Malaysian operation with minimal supervision.

A lunch break followed Alex Gomez's presentation, and Watanabe did not want to lose his opportunity to meet this dynamic speaker because, if the plan worked out, Watanabe hoped to hire Gomez and finally be relieved of his gargantuan workload.

Perfect Fit?

Watanabe, full of confidence, walked up and introduced himself to Gomez. After a brief conversation, Watanabe asked Alex to visit him in his office the following Monday at 10:00 AM, to discuss Alex leaving his position as the general manager with a local company involved in the construction of commercial complexes. For Gomez, Watanabe's proposition was a dream come true; since obtaining his BS in civil engineering from the University of Berkley and moving to Malaysia, he had been looking for a high-profile engineering firm that solely provided consultation, not construction. CCL had been on his radar for a long time and his meeting with Watanabe was truly a breakthrough — at long last his ambition was going to be realized.

CCL was possibly the best-suited firm for Gomez in his mind, especially because the salary offered was close to double what his previous employer had been paying him. For Watanabe — who was looking for a young, dynamic, self-driven person familiar with the Malaysian market and with expertise in structural design — Gomez had perfectly matched skills and experience, so Albert strongly recommended him for the director position in the Malaysian office and got approval from Hong Kong, pending a background check — which was never conducted.

After only eight months at CCL, Alex had demonstrated his uncanny skill in handling his clients and subordinates and showed the innovative creativity needed for structural designing. Watanabe did not feel it was right to make such a talented person undergo a background check and, thus, the first fatal mistake was made. But over the next five years, Gomez repeatedly proved his skills and he was highly looked upon by Watanabe and Edward Lim himself. Gomez was given a big bonus in appreciation of his design engineering effort for a prestigious client, and everything seemed to be going his way. The business was flourishing, and his subordinates hardly had the courage to go against his instructions; they knew he was connected with the higher authorities and that his orders were final. Watanabe's visits to the Kuala Lumpur office were mostly confined to meetings with major clients and, taking advantage of this, Gomez was running the office with absolute authority. In a nutshell, with the complete trust of his seniors on one hand, and the unprecedented level of control on the other, Gomez was fully armed.

Lunchtime Alarm

As usual, it was a busy day at CCL's Kuala Lumpur office and the staff was in a rush to complete a design for a renowned developer. Gomez was briefing a subordinate, Rayan Tan, about the final details and minor corrections that needed to be made and was in a hurry because Alex had a lunch appointment with an important client. Rayan assured Gomez that he would have the designs ready on his table for review by the time he got back from his meeting at 3:00 PM. As soon as Gomez was gone, his private telephone rang. Gomez, who normally kept his office locked when he was out, had left the door open as Rayan requested, in case he needed to refer to some of the files.

Although Tan had access to his boss's office, he did not answer the call because he felt it would have been a breach of privacy. But after half an hour, the phone rang again. Presuming Gomez might have left his cell phone behind and that an important client might be trying to contact Gomez, Tan reluctantly entered his boss's room and picked up the phone. No sooner had he done this than the caller started yelling, "Alex! It's Michael Wong here. Why are you doing this to me? Stop ignoring my e-mails! The renovation of my house is hanging in the balance because of your delay. How long do you expect us to stay in a hotel? Last week, on Monday, you promised to deliver the design by Friday and to have a meeting with our contractors but it is already Wednesday and there has been absolutely no response from your end."

"Sir, my name is Rayan, Mr. Gomez's subordinate, and he is not in the office at the moment. May I have your contact number and ask him to call you back?"

Wong, taken by surprise, said that Gomez had his number and to just tell him to return the call as soon as he got back. After that, as far as Tan could tell, the phone was slammed back onto the receiver. As a matter of habit, when he was talking, Rayan noticed the caller ID on the phone. He wrote the number in his diary and returned to his cubicle with some unease because the caller appeared to be an individual requiring a new design to complete the renovation of his home. CCL dealt only with contractors and builders, and apparently the caller was neither. To understand this mystery, Tan went through the list of active clients but did not find any by the name of Michael Wong. Despite this anomaly, Tan did not have time to delve into the matter further — he had pending designs to finish for Gomez. He engrossed himself in the project and left the issue to be handled by Alex, who returned at 3:00 PM sharp and was visibly upset. He headed straight for his office and, on the way, told Tan to see him there. Gomez had received a call on his cell phone from Michael Wong who mentioned his conversation with Rayan.

Gomez jumped into an explanation to Tan about how a crazy customer was on his tail and kept e-mailing him to get some work done despite Gomez's numerous assertions that CCL did not work with individuals unless they were building contractors or engineers. This explanation further bewildered Tan because Gomez volunteered it, which was against his basic nature as an authoritarian who hardly interacted with his subordinates. Tan was now suspicious.

Calling in the Big Guns

The following day, Gomez left for Indonesia to attend a three-day Innovative Construction Seminar. It was the perfect time for Tan to dig further to remove the doubts that clouded his mind. Rayan, uncertain as he was, contacted his old friend, Phillip Leong. They had been close for many years and had worked together in a well-established construction company, with which Phillip was still affiliated. Rayan met Phillip during lunch and briefed him about the incident. Together, they decided that Leong would contact Michael Wong in an attempt to get more information by posing as a consultant. Soon after lunch, Phillip called Michael's office and set up an appointment with him for the next day. During that meeting, Michael showed Phillip a structural design that had been proposed by Gomez that required modifications because Michael wanted a swimming pool inside the living area. Seizing this opportunity, Phillip assured Michael that if he could have a photocopy of the design, he would come up with new plan, pool included, despite the complications.

Michael told Phillip he could pick up a copy from the reception desk at around 5:00 PM. Phillip did so and passed it on to Rayan. Tan opened the envelope and was astounded to see that Gomez had stamped the design plans under CCL's name. This was most definitely against CCL's policies. "What I am going to do with this? Who should I contact? Who should I discuss this matter with? Would the cost of making this information known be too high for me?" These questions left him utterly perplexed and unsettled. It was a stressful night for Rayan; he still felt loyal to his boss.

The following morning, mustering up his courage, Rayan called Watanabe on his personal cell phone and said he needed to discuss something urgent and confidential. Watanabe, who was in Singapore, asked Rayan to wait until Gomez returned from Indonesia; Watanabe said Gomez would be the right person for Rayan to speak with. Rayan took a deep breath and managed to utter, "Sir, this matter involves possible wrongdoing by Mr. Gomez and I feel that his conduct could be damaging for CCL." Watanabe's first reaction was of disbelief because he hardly knew Rayan, apart from the fact that he had been Gomez's subordinate for the past four years. Nonetheless, he could not ignore Tan. Watanabe asked his secretary to book the earliest available fight to Kuala Lumpur and kept his departure confidential. By 1:30 the same afternoon, Watanabe had landed in Kuala Lumpur.

As instructed, Rayan was waiting for Watanabe at the airport with documents of CCL's current and past customers. These confirmed that Michael

Wong was not on the customer list. Watanabe alerted his boss, Edward Lim, who instructed Watanabe to probe the matter thoroughly and to establish the facts. In the meantime, Edward's office contacted Alex and asked him to visit the head office after his seminar before going back to Kuala Lumpur. This was designed to keep Gomez occupied and buy time for Watanabe to get some preliminary work done before launching a full-scale investigation.

You Can't Hide

I worked as the chief investigator in the forensic accounting division of my own firm; one of our core areas of services was computer forensics and Internet-based investigations. Watanabe consulted with us and requested we look into the matter. He told us that time was of the essence and he suspected the evidence of Gomez's actions would be found in his Internet history and e-mail correspondence. To maintain the secrecy of the investigation, Watanabe made special arrangements for us to visit and gather evidence after office hours. Based on the information provided by Rayan, the first place we looked was in Alex's locked wooden cabinet, where we found a stack of rough structural design sheets that were not related to any of CCL's known clients. Some of the documents we recovered pertained to Michael Wong's extraordinary house. Then my partner, Samir, and I began a complete and through forensic examination of Gomez's laptop. While we were searching his office, we found a number of ATM slips from Alex's bank account, indicating massive withdrawals over a period of seven months. Alex's salary could not account for such large transactions.

Because Gomez was dealing with outsiders, we assumed he would be communicating with them through the Internet and reasoned that we would find evidence thereof through the forensic review. Other than that, we hoped to find deleted files on the laptop that could explain Gomez's activity. Our first step was to create a duplicate image of the hard drives to review from our own office.

Based on information gathered during our search, interviews with Rayan and our understanding of the type of the case, we developed a focused search strategy and performed keyword searches. It was not a very complicated investigation because Gomez was not a computer expert, and we knew what evidence we were looking for. Once Samir and I reduced the search space by identifying and filtering known and suspect files through signature analyses, we turned our attention to searching for specific keywords. The words we searched for included: *design architect, civil construction, invoice, payment, consultation, fee, architectural design, building, house, structure, commercial complex, villas, bungalow, living area, interiors.*

File signatures were examined to evaluate whether the user attempted to hide files in plain sight by changing file extensions. We compared the file extension with its corresponding signature; since they matched, we were assured that no effort was made to obscure the file type.

As a part of our routine analysis, Samir and I also searched e-mail files; these leave traces on computers that provide vital information and, in this case, they revealed the modus operandi. We found traces of Gomez accessing his private e-mail service, Gmail. We also saw spreadsheet attachments to e-mails that suggested that significant amounts of data had been uploaded and downloaded through Gmail on various dates. We then conducted a series of experiments to determine the names associated with each message in the Gmail account and the result was astonishing. Numerous spreadsheets pertaining to CCL's debtors' ledger and other financial accounts were uploaded and downloaded on various occasions in the last three years. The resulting metadata analysis revealed the author as GMZ, which obviously indicated Alex Gomez. This was further confirmed when we discovered the laptop and its software programs were registered to GMZ. We recovered deleted invoices that were created by the same author. These documents were bookmarked and copied to our evidence folder, as was the metadata analysis. We also bookmarked several Web page entries relating to payments to an account at Bank of Commerce.

Gee, Look at This Gmail!

A detailed study and correlation of the evidence took hundreds of hours and revealed the followings facts about the fraud perpetrated by Gomez against CCL:

- At least 37 different individual customers were serviced by Gomez in the last 41 months.
- The customers were invoiced through Gomez's Gmail account but payments were received in the name of CCL.
- A parallel spreadsheet with detailed accounting information about various customers of CCL was maintained by Alex. Some of these customers' ledgers were affixed with the code "GMZ" in front of their name.
- A comparison of the ledgers with the GMZ code confirmed that these names did not appear in CCL's books of accounts.
- To hide the transactions, the accounts of the GMZ customers were stored and maintained on Gmail in the name of customergone@ gmail.com
- The invoices we retrieved were created by Gomez or through his laptop; the author of the invoices was "alexgmz."

- Gomez e-mailed his individual clients instructions to transfer payments online to a bank account at Bank of Commerce and attached invoices supposedly from CCL.

Watanabe contacted Bank of Commerce because CCL did not have an account at that financial institution. The bank gave us its records, which indicated Gomez had opened the account using a board of directors' resolution granting him the authority as the sole signatory. The bank's compliance officer told us she accepted an e-mailed copy of the resolution — not the original — because Gomez was on the board of directors. She assumed he was trustworthy. We later found a bogus, reprinted copy of the resolution with directors' signatures pasted onto it, shoved in the back of one of Gomez's desk drawers. This was the copy he had scanned and e-mailed to the bank. During the course of four years Gomez had earned almost $380,000 by providing services to clients under the guise of CCL. As investigators, Samir and I were left out of discussions regarding what actions CCL would take against Gomez. We later found out from Watanabe that the board of directors fired Alex Gomez immediately and gave our evidence to the local police. However, after months of indecision, the police decided the case was not large enough to warrant pursuing criminal charges. CCL did not press the matter with police because management did not want to attract the negative press.

Lessons Learned

Watanabe acknowledged his mistake in not conducting a background check before hiring Gomez. As it turns out, this would likely have prevented him from being hired in the first place because Gomez had been forced to resign from his previous employer, Three Aces Construction. At the time Watanabe heard Gomez give a presentation at the conference, Gomez had already been put on administrative leave. He was then asked to submit his resignation for accepting $10,000 in bribes from a subcontractor to approve inadequate construction materials.

Watanabe also admitted that he had been too preoccupied with his other branches to employ his old technique of surprise checks of the Kuala Lumpur office. Although Watanabe used to visit Gomez's office once a month, he did not interact with the employees or make them feel comfortable enough to report their concerns about Gomez.

(continued)

(*continued*)

Following the discovery of this scam, CCL's accounting system was revamped. The accounting departments of the various branches across Asia were put under the control of a director of finance at the head office in Hong Kong so their activities could be monitored daily. The number of well-trained and experienced staff in the internal audit and compliance department was also increased, so each of the offices could be audited once in every six months.

CCL also made it compulsory for employees to take an annual vacation, regardless of their workloads. A 24-hour hotline was created for employees to report suspicious activity, and staff members were given fraud awareness training. One of the most important measures taken by CCL in response to this fraud was to prohibit access by employees to their personal e-mail accounts from company computers. This step was taken because Gomez communicated with his personal clients from his office at CCL, and maintained their records in his Gmail account.

About the Author

Prabhat Kumar, CFE, CA, FCA, DIFA, is chief consultant with Alliance IFA (M) Sdn. Bhd. and has more than 18 years of experience in auditing, accounting and financial expertise. He has extensive experience of investigation and forensic accounting goes with the clients in Singapore, Malaysia, Cambodia and Brunei. Prabhat has been involved in the training of law enforcement officers from Royal Customs Malaysia on a regular basis, since 2005 and is a frequent seminar presenter across South and South East Asia on topics including fraud, evidence management, expert testimony and economic damage quantification. He has authored a book titled *The Accountant as an Expert Witness.*

16

The Reckless Clerk

OLEG LYKOV

Mikhail Dutov had just started climbing the career ladder. He was 22 years old, recently graduated from Plekhanov Academy of Economy (a prestigious Russian university), and had been hired in a starter position of customer relationships manager at a branch of WestBank, one of the largest banks in Russia. He had worked in the bank for about a year and people were sure he would be successful. Gossiping tongues, though, attributed his success to the fact that the branch manager was a family friend. An objective observer would have noticed that Mikhail lacked self-confidence and might easily fall under someone else's influence.

The branch where Mikhail worked was located in the center of Moscow, in a popular and crowded area. Mikhail's position was to assist customers who came into the branch and explain the bank's products and services to them, and to bring business into the institution. He was assigned sales targets and was reaching them quite well. Mikhail had recently started working with VIP clients, too. He was happy about his work and looked to his future with enthusiasm.

WestBank Conflict

Previously I worked as the Country Fraud Risk Manager in the Russian subsidiary of WestBank. The bank started corporate business in Russia several years ago and was ranked among the top 30 banks in the nation. When the bank decided to develop consumer business products, it formed a team of foreign and local specialists. The start-up team had to create the processes and products almost from scratch. Adoption of strategies used in other Eastern European countries took significant time and effort due to local requirements. By the time I moved to the consumer arm of the bank, the start-up group was being replaced by the business-as-usual team. Most employees were learning on the job — they often had no previous consumer banking experience. Aggressive sales targets sometimes pushed people to cut corners.

When I joined the consumer business department, the fraud risk management team consisted of two people — including me — and we needed at least four more. The lack of anti-fraud personnel meant we could run only critical routines and had no time to perform a thorough risk assessment of the new and changed products and procedures. We were in an open area where I was able to see the entire back office without even standing up. I sat side-by-side with my colleague — not even in those notorious cubicles, but in a truly open space. Each desk had a phone and we sat next to the collections unit, which spent the workday talking to clients who did not really want to talk to them. At least it was funny sometimes.

When I was hired, I was stunned to see the number of plain-text files containing data from daily transactions (several files represented various transaction flows for each day). It was not just a time-consuming exercise to find — it was simply impossible to look for patterns and analyze data. It was probably a more reasonable system when volumes were insignificant, but during only a few months the bank had doubled in size and was continuing to grow rapidly. Later it appeared that automating the reports was of critical importance — it gave us an opportunity to quickly gather the necessary information about the largest fraud case at the moment, and it meant feeding additional data flows into our system was only a question of a few hours.

Online monitoring of debit and credit card transactions took about 70 percent of my time and it was the only partially automated process. Factor in the manual review of credit card and loan applications and my entire working day would be gone.

Obviously something had to change. I realized the threat of heavy understaffing and was trying to fill the open positions, but there was a lack of experienced people on the market with English skills and a readiness to work for WestBank's low compensation. Also, the level of overtime in our bank was notorious. So my strategy was to hire younger people with basic or intermediate banking experience who were able to speak English to a certain extent, and then train them in fraud risk management.

WestBank offered a range of debit and credit products — plastic cards, loans, savings accounts and deposits. Clients' personal and transactional information was accessible through an internally developed software application and used by the client-facing staff — at branches, call centers and the back and middle office. Additional approvals were required to view the data of bank staff members and VIP clients.

Our clients used an Internet banking system to view their account balances, make wire transfers and execute other transactions. To access their accounts, clients had to enter their card number and PIN code. We could not change this login procedure at that time because it was defined by our head office.

Roots of the Problem

WestBank's consumer client base was growing rapidly but we did not have enough employees in critical units, and our sales targets were too heavily weighted in the compensation program. We employed poorly screened or unscreened sales agents. Aggressive plans and an inadequate bonus system for salespeople — bonuses could be paid regardless of delinquency status of the new client — laid the foundation for ignoring internal compliance requirements. Staff turnover was high, especially at low levels.

Within two months of me being hired, my sole subordinate decided to pursue other opportunities and left, and I was alone for almost six months. As the only employee in a department with six vacancies, I was only able to cover the most critical areas — monitoring card transactions and credit card and loan applications. Ridiculous as it sounds, even when we hired two new employees, they were not able to start working for almost a month because their network credentials and e-mail accounts had to be created overseas. I tried to push IT support to get my new hires operational faster and even engaged my boss to push from his level. Perhaps it would have taken longer without such efforts.

A reasonable person would expect something bad to happen in such circumstances. But surprisingly, the trouble didn't begin until I had two subordinates fully operational and familiar with internal procedures and systems.

Sounding the Alarm

One typically busy and snowy winter day another Russian bank contacted me and suggested that three wire transfers they received from WestBank were fraudulent. The employee said he was keeping them on hold until we confirmed their status.

I immediately contacted the customer, determined the wires were not authorized and began reviewing our other customers' wire transfers. There were a few distinctive features of the questioned items that made me sure we had a problem on our hands. The transfers were from an individual's current account but they were marked "for marketing research." Also, three of them were to the same beneficiary on the same date. When I contacted one client for information, he said he had not heard of the beneficiary and also told me he had trouble logging into the Internet banking system. We blocked his bank card (used to access the Internet banking system) and opened a fraud case.

Shortly after the case was opened, my operational unit supervisor, Sergei Krylov, came to my desk. "There is an issue, Oleg," he said. "We received a call from another bank. They suggested that several wire transfers they received today from one of our clients are fraudulent." A quick look at the wires alarmed me — there were several in amounts ranging from $1,000 to $3,500 with the same memo, "for marketing research." They were executed through the Internet banking system.

We continued digging and discovered two more customers with similar wire transfers made on the same date but to another beneficiary. Quite soon we realized about $140,000 had been wired out of the bank within a few days to various Russian banks from the accounts of six customers. We also found that several transfers were made to the same beneficiary, Artimons Ltd. There were four other beneficiaries, both companies and private individuals. We managed to stop some of the withdrawals, but others were already cashed.

Wires were sent to various Russian cities and to one of the Baltic States. Trying to reach the appropriate people in the beneficiary banks and convincing them to stop the transfers before they hit the recipients' accounts kept us busy in the beginning of the investigation.

If at First You Don't Succeed . . .

I reviewed wire transfers for the previous week and then for the month. The fraud appeared to have started three days ago. We had to call a number of clients and make careful inquiries about their wire transfers in order not to alarm them without necessity.

By the end of the day we had about $100,000 in confirmed losses (cash withdrawn from the beneficiaries' accounts) and about $40,000 held in a few banks waiting for our interbank messages. We were able to stop only transfers that were initiated on the date we started the investigation. The wire transfers were initiated using the Internet banking system where the account login credentials were changed shortly before the transfers. The account takeover was made via our call center after the fraudsters provided correct answers to security questions.

My priority was clearly stopping the fraud, but the problem was we had not been monitoring wire transfers due to the staff shortage. My first step was to hire a monitoring team of two people. They reviewed the wires while processing, looking for red flags, calling customers and escalating the investigation if the client could not be reached. Additional training and instructions were given to call center operators, and they were told to contact me if suspicions arose.

We also quickly hired two additional people to monitor wire transfers originating from the Internet banking system and other sources. This was our most successful step in preventing further losses. We implemented a process of parallel monitoring of wire transfers without delaying them.

Five batches a day were reviewed, and to automate the process I had to create an Access database to convert the text files (since wire transfer information came to us in plain-text format) and apply filters for known fraud criteria. I also designed the database to omit some types of payments (e.g., utility bills and taxes) and those below a certain amount (however, multiple payments under the threshold within the same day would still trigger the alert).

We applied additional controls to the customer information database. Access to high-wealth accounts was closed for everyone and reopened only after the individuals received a supervisor's and my approval. This drastic measure allowed us to regain control over access. However, as I learned at a later point, it did not stop the internal perpetrator — he had the right to access the VIP clients.

While trying to stop the fraud without suspending the Internet banking service, we followed a rather standard investigation plan. It involved calling customers, analyzing logs of connections to the Internet banking system, and reviewing records from the customer database. We formed a cross-functional team including fraud risk management, security and collections. Team members listened to numerous phone calls (comparing voices, determining the number of people involved, etc.) and checked IP addresses to map them and compare them to a customer's addresses.

Initially we had three theories for the cause of the fraud: phishing, customer fraud and occupational fraud (with or without external parties involved). After talking to the customers, analyzing their profiles and listening to phone calls, we focused on one theory — account takeover fraud with the involvement of internal and external parties. In other words, we had a thief among us.

We determined that fraudsters had obtained information from an internal informant and were using that information to penetrate our controls, take over Internet banking accounts and perform illegal wire transfers. The IP addresses used to connect to our online banking system were either from Internet cafés or dynamic addresses owned by various Internet providers, including mobile phone operators. Telephone numbers used to call to change the login credentials were mobile phones (in Russia information about those users was not in the public domain and could not be accessed legally by banks).

WestBank's phone records demonstrated that our phone operators were often ignoring red flags, such as hearing page-turning sounds before the individual answered security questions or quick answers to questions that would normally require time to recall (like the last transaction). We arranged for additional training to increase their vigilance, which resulted in a number of attempts of account takeover being prevented by the telephone operators.

Two months later, despite our efforts and fixing control gaps, we were still unable to find the internal perpetrator. We were no longer losing money to this scheme but attempts to steal from our clients were still being made. It was clear that the problem would not go away by itself.

A Lazy Caller

During these two months I had analyzed attempts to take over customers' accounts. I listened to the calls and checked the phone numbers, but they were made from mobile phones. The numbers were registered to fictitious people and were only used once or twice before the telephones were dumped. I had nearly exhausted my investigation methods, and was about to hand over the case to the authorities. However, during a routine check of the phone number used to change login credentials of one of our customers, I noticed it was not a mobile number. This meant a lot — there was a good chance this was going to give us a fraudster's address.

In a few minutes I knew the address from which the call was made. The apartment was located close to downtown and was registered to Ruben Abovyan. Interestingly, the beneficiary's name of the wire transfer was Kirill Rubenovich Abovyan, possibly the son of Ruben Abovyan (in Russian the father's name is used to form the middle/patronymic name of the child). This looked like a good sign for us and a very bad sign for them.

We contacted the beneficiary's bank and explained the issue to the security manager. After discussing the case with his bosses he agreed to help us. The plan was simple: We wanted to talk to the person who would come to their bank to withdraw the transfer.

Kirill called the bank to ask if the transfer had been deposited to his account and he was told that it was the bank's standard procedure to require the customer to visit the bank when a transfer amount is significant (he attempted to transfer $35,000).

Needless to say, when Kirill arrived at the bank we were waiting for him. We announced ourselves and asked him to discuss the transfer with us. He was cooperative when we asked if his father knew about his attempt to steal someone else's money.

Soon we knew everything he knew about the scheme. One of his friends gave him the necessary information to answer account security questions and warned him not to do it from home. Fortunately for us, Kirill was too lazy to think of a better method than calling from his father's apartment. He also knew that the information came from a WestBank employee whose name was Mikhail and was able to tell us the branch where Mikhail worked.

Catching the Rat

The branch was very small and only one Mikhail worked there. By lunchtime there were three of us sitting in front of him; a pile of papers (mostly meaningless but we needed something that looked like evidence) was in front of us and we were looking through it in silence. Mikhail was obviously nervous. His hands were visibly shaking.

As soon as we began the interview, Mikhail asked for a glass of water — he had quite a few during our discussion. Initially he tried to deny everything, but eventually confessed that he was copying customers' Internet banking information and selling it to an outside contact. Mikhail insisted he only received $800 for the information he provided. The amount seemed ridiculously low to me, but Mikhail stood firm and we had no evidence to disprove him.

The scheme was very simple. Mikhail used his access to customer accounts to look for people with high balances. When he found one he wrote down the information an outsider would need to answer verification questions. We had just created a new monitoring system to detect profile surfing by employees, but apparently it was not receiving all the input data needed to function properly, which was why Mikhail was not on our radar. It was a frustrating demonstration of the fact that internal data flows can surprise you in very unpleasant ways.

After we turned over our evidence to the police, it took them nearly two years to get a conviction and sentence. Six people who purchased account information and made fraudulent transfers were sent to jail for terms ranging from one to six years. Kirill received a one-year jail sentence. Mikhail got a suspended sentence, and the worst repercussion for him was the effect it had on his life — instead of being on the fast-track career path with a large bank, he could only hope to get low-paid positions with no-name companies that existed for too short a time to care about their employees' backgrounds.

We initiated many changes to our internal procedures, including monitoring the systems to ensure we had a complete picture of who accessed customers' data.

Lessons Learned

I learned a number of things from this investigation, primarily regarding Internet fraud. If I had known the following information earlier, I would have been much better equipped to tackle this case:

1. *The heavy understaffing for extended periods of time made it impossible to cover the important job functions, thus resulting in control gaps.*

(continued)

(continued)

A lack of staff means people are doing too much to be able to deliver high-quality work. Results of understaffing may not be visible immediately but will surely appear sooner or later, either in the form of non-compliance with internal rules or as fraud cases that could have been prevented or discovered much earlier. I am sure understaffing was the main cause of the fraud in this case.

2. *When you create a monitoring system, ensure that it catches each related data flow.* Check and double-check it. Learn the cycle of customers' information and make sure the monitoring system is capable of accessing and capturing the right data. Talk to back-office personnel and the information security manager. You may be surprised to learn the undocumented ways to access customer files. Do not blindly rely on IT developers and support. If your monitoring system omits just one source of data, it might become essentially useless. If our profile-surfing monitoring system had caught the needed information, we could have discovered Mikhail within a couple of weeks instead of two months.

3. *Keep a record of attendees to fraud awareness sessions and ensure that employees attend them.* Mikhail did not attend any, apparently because his branch managers were not happy to temporarily lose their staff and were practically sabotaging them. The tone at the top played a large role in this case.

4. *Establish good working contacts with the local authorities responsible for your office's jurisdiction.* It might save you time when you have to file a case.

5. *Know that your investigations may result in a criminal or civil case.* Keep your paperwork tidy and ensure your actions do not increase legal risk. Make sure you know exactly how far in your investigation you can go — at a certain point you may become required to report the criminal violation. Talk to your in-house lawyer and keep the lawyer informed about your investigative plans. It may save you from serious legal troubles.

Recommendations to Prevent Future Occurrences

STAFFING

Control units need to be staffed properly, including planning for vacation time and unexpected prolonged absences. This is was one of the first improvements we made as a result of this case. Unfortunately, management realized how serious the problem was too late.

PRIORITIZATION

Careful prioritization of control activities is required to ensure that the critical functions are performed in time. Implementation of and regular adherence to control checklists are important. Do not assume the signature in the checklist means the control activity was actually performed unless you did it yourself. I had to fire a team member when I discovered that documents were kept in his cabinet for a few days instead of being cleared on a daily basis. His checklist was in order, but he did not do his work in a timely fashion. Fortunately I decided to reconcile his checklist with other logs.

CHALLENGE ASSUMPTIONS

Comprehensively analyze new products and product changes prior to their implementation, using what-if scenarios and assuming there is at least one control gap. Do not forget potential internal collusion; segregation of duties cannot overcome this issue. The fraudster may be a trusted employee and others may collude with him or her without knowing they are participating in a fraud.

TRAINING

Track attendance at fraud awareness sessions in a computer database for easy administering and to ensure 100-percent attendance. Make sure management is setting the proper tone at the top. Partnering with Human Resources may help in this goal.

MONITORING

One of the best things a bank can do to improve its internal controls is to monitor profile surfing. The system should review channels capable of transferring money, including card-to-card, wires and internal transfers among accounts of different customers. Consider constant monitoring if there is a business case for it. If your bank provides internal transfer services to customers around the clock, then you may want to monitor this activity in real time.

About the Author

Oleg Lykov, CFE, is an Investigations Senior Manager in Microsoft's Financial Integrity Unit and is based in Russia. In his previous positions he was responsible for fraud risk management and anti-money laundering in the financial services industry. Mr. Lykov is a graduate of the Russian State Financial Academy. He has eight years of experience in fraud risk and anti-money laundering areas.

CHAPTER

Close Quarters

JOHN P. GRANCARICH

Imagine that your company is conducting an internal investigation into an employee's alleged access to prohibited Internet Web sites. One worker has filed a sexual harassment claim against another, and counsel has instructed a computer forensics examiner to determine if the allegations are true. The examiner visits the company's office after business hours, creates a forensic image of the suspect's computer and performs an analysis back at the lab; he finds that the allegations are true and the suspect did access inappropriate and prohibited Internet Web sites over an extended period of time. The case seems open and shut — but is it?

The practice of computer forensics, a unique hybrid of legal knowledge and computer science, is undergoing remarkable growth and facing tremendous challenges. New software, new technologies and more creative attacks and intrusions often leave the computer forensics examiner one step behind, constantly playing catch up and having to perform research quickly to follow the particulars of the investigation in progress. If we also factor in that many computer examiners are not investigators or fraud examiners by training, we begin to understand the enormous burdens that this new breed of professional faces with endlessly creative fraudsters and criminals.

This leaves us with the question of what we should reasonably expect a computer forensics examiner, or any investigator for that matter, to achieve in a scenario such as the one outlined at the beginning of the chapter. Should we expect the investigator to confirm or refute the allegations at hand and do no more? Or is it his or her responsibility to exercise professional skepticism and question what he or she finds and press further, perhaps even attempting to disprove his or her case theory? Part of the answer to this question lies in what those findings are. And as we will see from this case, things are not necessarily what they seem when it comes to Internet-related investigations.

Polar Opposites

Alan Merseaux lived the good life. Born into privilege and an only child, he bounced around Europe as a young boy while his businessman father moved the family around, making his way up the corporate ranks in the financial services industry. It was a thrilling way to live for young Alan, and he was enamored with this seemingly random yet exciting way of life. He developed a reputation as a bon vivant when he hit his teenage years, fond of parties and indulging in an impulsive and aimless lifestyle. Living in Paris one year and Berlin the next, the possibilities seemed endless.

When Alan was in his early twenties his parents divorced. His father stayed in Europe while Alan and his mother moved to California to be closer to her family. The divorce was difficult on Alan and left him feeling like the rug had been pulled out from under him. What happened to the good life? California seemed boring compared to Europe, and he was not particularly fond of Americans to begin with. "So typical," he would think when his new countrymen would do something he didn't approve of. Nevertheless, he needed to find work and enjoyed tinkering with technology and electronics. With some experience in computers under his belt from his years at university and a connection made through his father, Merseaux landed a job as a computer systems analyst at Meridian Technologies. It was something to do and a way to make some money. Sharing office space with him at his new job was Eddie Walters.

In contrast to Alan, Eddie had lived a life of hardship and challenge. Eddie's father left the family when Eddie and his two younger brothers were young. Being the oldest child left Eddie in the man's role in their house. He started working early in life to help his mother make ends meet. A high-school teacher noticed Eddie's talent at taking things apart and putting them back together in shop class and suggested he learn about computer repair. He did just that, and over several years developed his skills in various technical jobs into a full-time position as a systems analyst at Meridian. He could help his family; he couldn't be happier with the turn his life had taken. Alan and Eddie came from two different worlds and neither could predict how their paths would cross and set off an unpredictable chain of events.

Meridian Technologies began as a two-employee computer-repair shop in Los Angeles in the 1980s. Started by college dropouts, Meridian had the good fortune to be in the right industry at the right time and it grew by leaps and bounds. It provided services ranging from systems administration and technology outsourcing to software development and programming. A few years later, Meridian had grown out of its original space on a nondescript street and moved to a larger and more prestigious location in the central business district of Los Angeles. It had 375 employees and counted as its clients many of LA's premier companies.

A Disturbing Claim

Jon Randall, Meridian's director of human resources, was sitting in his office the afternoon of June 18th poring over staffing reports when he heard a knock. Looking up, he saw Alan Merseaux standing at the door.

"Hey, Alan, what's going on?"

"I need to talk to you about something."

"Sure, come on in and have a seat. Close the door behind you." Randall had been in this position for several years and had a finely tuned antenna for when something was up.

After both of them were seated, Alan began talking. His speech was slow and deliberate.

"For the last several months, Eddie has been going to porn sites and watching these graphic videos in the office. He looks at pictures on these Web sites too. I've tried to ignore it, but it's really getting to me. I asked him to stop a bunch of times and he just continues. I sit in the same cube as him, back to back, in the locked server room so even though I can't always see it when he's doing it I can hear it. I can't sleep at night, I feel sick and nervous when I'm here and I can't concentrate on my work anymore."

Randall looked at him and thought there might be something more. "Alan, is there anything else you want to me tell me?"

Alan sighed. "Two days ago he physically assaulted me in the office after I asked him again to stop. I feel very threatened, Jon."

Randall listened intently and then, with Alan still in the office, he called Tim Metzger, Meridian's in-house counsel. Metzger came in a few minutes later and joined the conversation. He asked difficult questions, sensitive questions, and heard what Alan had to say.

"Does anyone else work with the two of you in the server room? To your knowledge is anyone else aware of this?"

"No, it's just us, and I don't think anyone else knows about it. I didn't want to talk about it with anyone."

Metzger found the allegations extremely troubling — in addition to the physical and emotional toll these events were taking on Alan, if true, they would constitute harassment and potential liability for Meridian. In accordance with Meridian policy, Alan was immediately granted paid leave. After Merseaux left, Metzger and Randall were quiet for a few moments.

"We need to investigate this thoroughly," began Metzger. "If Eddie Walters is doing what Alan says he's doing we have a serious problem that needs to be addressed now. Who do we use to investigate a sensitive matter like this?"

Randall picked up the phone and began to dial.

Long-Distance Sleuthing

I was sitting in my office in New York late one afternoon when my phone started ringing. I looked at the display and saw it was Jon Randall. He only called me when there was a problem — as Meridian's resident corporate investigator, I was often tasked with conducting internal investigations and computer examinations. Randall explained the situation at Meridian's West Coast office, and I knew it was right up my alley. After getting the background on the situation I realized I had two immediate challenges: I needed to have Eddie's computer forensically imaged as soon as possible — it was getting late in the day — and the hard drive was 3,000 miles away.

After calling around a bit I found a trusted partner who could do the forensic imaging that night. I consulted with Randall and Metzger and decided to have Alan's computers forensically imaged, too. The reason is simple: When dealing with a claim such as Alan's, there was no way to determine at the beginning of an investigation what really happened. It was my job to preserve and gather the available evidence and reconstruct the events using that evidence.

While the forensic examiner was on-site imaging the computers, I worked with other internal resources at the company to preserve copies of server e-mails, e-mail backups, Internet proxy server logs and personal data on the network for further analysis. I was building my universe of information to work with.

The investigation was fast paced from the start, and too much for one person to do effectively. Plus the hard drives were on the other side of the country. The forensic examiner processed the image of Eddie's computer first while I developed an investigation methodology. I started by preparing the following for analysis: Eddie's Internet browsing history, cached images from his Internet activity and user-created folders in the event that he was saving files to his computer. It was a logical place to start and would relate directly to the claim.

I struck investigative gold right away. A review of images cached from the Internet revealed a substantial number of pornographic images viewed under Eddie's user account and of the type Alan had indicated in his complaint. There were also video files. On its face, the evidence supported Alan's allegations. But should I stop my investigation there? There were two ways to interpret these findings:

1. Eddie downloaded prohibited images and videos to his computer.
2. There were prohibited images and videos on Eddie's computer, but we did not have enough information to determine who put them there.

Role Reversal?

How can the second option be plausible if the information was located in Eddie's user account? I stepped outside of the digital realm for a moment and considered the physical layout of the work area and recalled that there were only two employees in a secured area — Alan and Eddie. Before coming to Randall about it, Merseaux alleged that Walters had been viewing prohibited material for several months. I thought about this point carefully; the time frame seemed too long to me. Why didn't he come forward at three months? Or at one month? If Alan felt harassed several months in, wouldn't he have felt harassed much earlier and come to Randall? Something didn't add up. I discovered another odd fact: Dozens of Alan's personal Yahoo! e-mails were cached on Eddie's hard drive. Eddie had also reimaged his own computer on the same day that Alan made the claim against him.

By then it was the next morning, and a long first night of work was behind me. I sat in my office and thought about what had happened up to that point. How did Alan's e-mails get on Eddie's computer? Was Alan using Eddie's computer to download the illicit materials? How credible was Alan? The pieces weren't fitting together yet and, after consulting with Randall and Metzger, we decided to examine Alan's computer as well. I continued to dig into Eddie's data while I readied myself for the results from Merseaux's. I didn't know what to expect.

The West Coast examiner called me later that day with some preliminary information. Given the serious nature of Alan's allegations against Eddie, I was more than a little surprised to hear the examiner tell me three very important and troubling pieces of information:

1. Alan's Internet browsing history indicated that Alan himself had visited various pornographic Web sites over a period of several months.
2. His hard drive had also been reimaged on the day he made the claim against Eddie.
3. A keystroke logger was installed on Alan's computer.

Things had just become a lot more complicated. I needed to assess what evidence I had and synthesize it into a chronology to move the investigation forward. The challenge was that the evidence I had at that point — all of it electronic — left me with gaping holes as to what was really occurring and I couldn't build a story without filling in some of those blanks. Alan's claim did have some merit, but now his credibility was questionable too. There were too many important concerns unanswered. I needed to broaden the scope of the investigation and put the key players in place and time. I continued to picture the physical area they both worked in, with access restricted to just the two of them, and my mind raced with the possibilities.

A Fruitful Harvest

My next step was to circle back to the recovery and harvesting phase of the investigation to identify and pull together various sources of evidence to build my case. For this second round I focused on the following:

- Domain controller logs, which would tell me who was logged into each computer and when
- Video of the public areas in the company that would help me track Alan's and Eddie's movements
- Floor plans of the office to help me get a sense of what the space looked like
- Access key records to various floors, offices and secure areas
- Interviews of Randall and Metzger

The ultimate goal was to divide what we knew and could prove versus what we did not know. Once I had the second round of evidence in hand, the pieces began to fall into place more quickly. I started with the physical security access logs to determine where each person was at various times and what doors they passed through during the day. In his discussion with Randall and Metzger, Alan stated that Eddie physically assaulted him in the server room for nearly 30 minutes, between 5:00 and 5:30 PM. My analysis of the physical access logs, however, showed that while Alan was in the server room from 5:00 to 5:30 PM, Walters was only there for five minutes.

I next looked at the domain controller logs for Alan's computer for the day of the alleged assault. When a computer is part of a Windows domain, the domain controller log displays a chronology of logins for that particular computer. (A Windows server domain is a group of computers running the Windows operating system that interface with a central directory database. This directory contains the user accounts and security information for the members of the domain. In a domain, the directory resides on a computer that is configured as a "domain controller" — a server that responds to security authentication requests.) The records on Alan's log showed that Eddie logged into Alan's computer twice on the day of the alleged assault. What was he doing? To find this out I merged data from the physical access logs, domain controller logs and the Internet history to show that Eddie had logged in to Alan's computer using his own account, run various searches for and installed keylogging software and then logged off Alan's computer. The keylogging software would capture Alan's keystrokes and save them to a file that Eddie could access later.

What about the reimaging of Eddie Walters's computer? A subsequent follow-up call to Randall established that just after Alan Merseaux made his initial claim in Randall's office, Alan, Randall and Metzger went to a conference room on the 14th floor to discuss the matter in detail from 2:00 to 5:00 PM. Eddie's computer revealed that he had reimaged his hard drive during that same time frame. Was this a coincidence, or did Eddie learn about the meeting somehow? A look at the access logs for the 14th floor showed that Eddie visited the floor during Alan's meeting and left via a different exit. He would have passed by the conference room and could easily have seen the meeting in progress.

Regarding Alan's personal e-mails that were found cached on Eddie's computer, it appeared that the keylogging software likely accounted for this. It provided Eddie with access to Alan's Yahoo! e-mail user name and password. Alan's screen name was unique and could be easily searched for online — I thought maybe given his questionable credibility I might find some Internet social-networking activity for him. And I did. Lots of it. He appeared on Web sites such as MySpace, Facebook and multiple dating Web sites. I even found one nude photo of him. I created an account on the Web site and preserved this significant piece of evidence.

His MySpace account was particularly revealing. It was a public profile that anyone could find by browsing through his posted information. I spent some time each morning for the next few weeks monitoring Alan's Internet activity and building a profile of him. Although he claimed physical and emotional distress when he made his complaint to HR, I found comments on his MySpace page that directly contradicted that:

- "Are you ready to party?"
- "So where will you be tonight? . . . I am your new stalker."
- "Thank you so much for the wonderful experience of last Saturday night."
- "We should go and have a blast tonight."
- "I had a blast with you guys! Where is the next party?"

Photo Finish

Then there was Photobucket.com. It is a Web site that allows users to upload, organize and label their pictures. Users can make their accounts public or private. Again, Alan had created a public site for anyone to see using his Yahoo! e-mail address as the profile name. After he made his claim to HR, he was immediately granted paid leave, and in subsequent follow-up calls Alan stated severe emotional and physical distress caused by the events in the workplace. He had also retained an attorney and was considering filing a claim against Meridian. But his Photobucket page told a different story: It contained a picture of Alan partying at a trendy hotel in New York City a week after his initial complaint — a period during which he was supposed to be in extreme distress.

I compiled the facts against both Alan and Eddie and set up a conference with Randall and Metzger. The evidence made sense and flowed chronologically to me, but I wanted to make sure I could explain any technical jargon in layman's terms. Before presenting a report for review, I asked myself, "If I had no prior experience in this field would I be able to understand this?" I also prepared a timeline that displayed the evidence in chronological order.

What I ultimately presented Randall and Metzger with was a story of two bad apples who, over a period of several months, both viewed prohibited pornographic images and videos from the Internet at the office. Then, for reasons unknown, they became involved in a workplace confrontation that escalated into Walters spying on Alan, and Merseaux filing a fraudulent claim for workplace harassment.

Randall and Metzger interviewed Eddie about what had transpired. The evidence of his Internet activity and his installation of the spyware on Alan's computer was shown to him piece by piece, and he was asked questions about each. (A standard investigative technique is to show evidence to a suspect one piece at a time instead of altogether; this builds psychological pressure.) But Eddie refused to answer any questions in the interview and was let go from Meridian.

Alan ultimately filed his threatened claim against Meridian, asking for several hundred thousand dollars. Meridian responded by showing Alan's attorney what we had gathered: the prohibited Internet usage, the MySpace posts and the picture at the hotel. The evidence clearly refuted his claims of physical ailments and emotional distress. To make the whole sordid episode go away, Meridian made a very low settlement offer to Alan, which he quickly accepted.

Some weeks later Randall was flying coach from Los Angeles to New York. Looking toward the front of the plane he observed a young, stylishly dressed man in first class having drinks and chatting up the other passengers. It was none other than Alan Merseaux, likely spending what was left of his modest settlement on a first-class flight to New York.

So typical.

Lessons Learned

The goal of any investigation is to discover and present the truth, regardless of which side it favors. If the evidence you discover appears sufficient to build your case, would you try to dig further or would you accept your findings at face value? The answer may be, "it depends." This case began as a harassment matter that evolved into a fraud investigation based on Internet use, and both the claimant and respondent turned out to be at fault. Certain characteristics of the case (the several-month period of prohibited Internet use Alan alleged of Eddie, and their close quarters in the server room) was enough for me to question the evidence and conduct further investigation. The investigator's job is to fit the pieces together, to make a whole out of the parts. To do that we cannot jump to conclusions — we must assemble as many facts as we can find into a cohesive story. We need to follow each investigation through to its end, even when we are not sure where the evidence is leading us.

Recommendations to Detect and Prevent Further Occurrences

The post-mortem on this investigation revealed two internal control weaknesses in Meridian's IT systems. The first was that the technical people were able to circumvent the Internet proxy monitoring service that other employees were subject to. Had this been implemented and managed properly, Eddie and Alan would not have been able to spend several months browsing various prohibited Web sites — behavior that was the catalyst for worse things to come for them and Meridian.

A closely related second weakness was the installation and use of an alternate Internet browser (Mozilla Firefox) rather than Meridian's default (Internet Explorer). Because Firefox was not subject to the same monitoring protocol as Explorer, Eddie and Alan used the higher-level rights that came with their technical positions at Meridian to avoid the watchful eyes of anyone in management.

Meridian has since corrected both of these weaknesses.

About the Author

John P. Grancarich, CFE, is the Practice Support Manager of Electronic Discovery Consulting at Paul Hastings Janofsky & Walker LLP. He has extensive experience directing and managing electronic discovery and investigative projects on a global scale, including computer examinations, analysis and reporting. He is a Certified Fraud Examiner and an EnCase certified computer examiner.

CHAPTER

18

Playing with Fire

HANK J. BRIGHTMAN

As a child growing up in the bustling city of Lagos, Nigeria, Tom Nakafe believed that he could accomplish anything he set his mind to. His father, Paul, was a successful and highly respected engineer who held a senior management position with an international petroleum corporation. Tom's mother, Larayna, had her own burgeoning medical practice and was considered among the top pediatricians in the region. Tom excelled at languages and fluently spoke English and French, as well as his native Hausa and Igbo. Much like his father, Tom had an outstanding grasp of algebra, trigonometry and calculus, the latter of which he had essentially taught himself during a holiday break at his family's luxurious summer house (in between soccer lessons with his older brother, Awayle, who played for Nigeria's national team). Tom was an exceptional athlete in his own right, regularly starting as a striker on his private secondary school's soccer team, despite being among its youngest members. He daydreamed that after finishing his undergraduate studies at Oxford, he would complete law school, study international diplomacy and ultimately work abroad, maybe even someday as an envoy at the United Nations in New York. Perhaps he could even join a local football club (provided the Americans understood the difference between his version of football and their own).

Staring out onto the rain-soaked, potholed main street of urban Vinington, New Jersey, through a dirty storefront window, Tom found it difficult to accept that nearly 20 years had passed since his childhood dreams had been forever shattered. The series of violent, bloody coups in Nigeria that ultimately silenced the upper-middle class and plunged his family, as well as the families of just about everyone he knew, into chaos felt like they had happened yesterday. Not that he was complaining. Tom considered himself especially lucky to have escaped Lagos with his life, unlike his mother, father and older brother — each of whom perished at different times but under the same circumstances (conviction for high treason against the reigning military government followed by execution).

He was also thankful that his boyhood friend, Yohimbe Aglean, had also found his way from Lagos to London, and then ultimately to New Jersey. Since they first spotted each other across a row of cabs at Newark's Liberty Airport (Tom was driving an unlicensed cab waiting for a fare, and Yohimbe was a skycap for a major airline), they had become inseparable. Yohimbe was good with computers, and — despite the fact that he had no working papers required of immigrants — had enrolled in several advanced courses in Web design and language programming at the local community college.

Given their shared and steadfast commitment to success, coupled with Tom's penchant for trade and Yohimbe's innate abilities with technology, it came as no surprise when they decided to go into business together in their surrogate homeland of Vinington. A gritty, working-class community teaming with a melting pot of hardworking people from West Africa's poorest nations, Tom felt drawn to Vinington's bustling — albeit disheveled — downtown. It was here that Tom and Yohimbe opened PLAY Technology, Inc., which Tom chose to memorialize after his parents and older brother (Paul, Larayna and Awayle), and Yohimbe simply name for himself.

"Just got a new load of credit card numbers, Tom!" Yohimbe's proclamation snapped his friend out of a coma-like gaze through the small space in the Plexiglas window that was enclosed in a metal grate. The storefront looked out onto Vinington's abandoned Main Street at midnight on a Wednesday. For reasons he couldn't fully explain, Tom found Yohimbe's cheerful disposition annoying. Perhaps it was how eager to please Yohimbe seemed, a trait that Tom could remember as far back as their childhood in Lagos, and which he regarded as a sign of weakness in his longtime friend. Tom was astonished at Yohimbe's willingness to open up their fictitious business and to prey upon the very people who could have been their opponents in football matches, — had civil unrest not come so suddenly to Nigeria. Tom considered himself the senior partner in the business, a fact that he repeated with it regularity to Yohimbe (who rarely complained) but was also careful not to put in writing in their incorporation documents.

"Great," Tom replied dryly, but with just enough inflection to ensure Yohimbe would consider this to be high praise. "Sweepstakes site?" Tom continued.

"No," Yohimbe chirped happily, "they're from the Amazon.com mirror site one of our associates created last night."

Community-Based Fraudsters

The brainchild of owners Tom Nakafe and Yohimbe Aglean, PLAY Technology, Inc., appeared to represent the perfect combination of leading-edge entrepreneurship and service to the community. Comparable to the myriad of bodegas that were a common sight in northern New Jersey, the bustling business offered the amenities of a first-class *groceria*, ranging from infant formula and diapers to a wide variety of *sofritos*, beans and rice. Lottery tickets, beer, wine and cigarettes were also available in abundance. Tom realized early on that if he could attract customers seeking their daily provisions, he might also be able to entice them into purchasing items normally beyond their financial reach, such as plasma televisions, digital cameras and computers. He did this by offering "easy credit" installment plans. In exchange for immediately receiving their new electronic items, customers would turn over their entire weekly paychecks to him, and he would provide them with in-store credit, which they could use to purchase groceries and other incidentals. Adding to PLAY Technology's substantial profit margin was its markup on "gray-market" products (i.e., electronics purchased outside of the United States devoid of warranties) and the 10-percent service fee collected for converting customers' paychecks into in-store credit.

Yohimbe was the more extroverted, albeit overly blunt, of the two partners. It was he who convinced the Vinington Business Owners Association that it would be in their best interest to allow PLAY Technology, Inc., to foray into other ventures, including providing low- or no-cost after-hours computer training to the seemingly eager residents of the community, offering income-tax preparation clinics and working with representatives of the U.S. Department of Housing and Urban Development. He also encouraged them to support his interests in the New Jersey Higher Education Authority, by providing seminars on housing assistance and student loans. Yohimbe's efforts at community outreach had proven so successful that he and Tom had been twice recognized in formal resolutions by the City Council as the model for corporate-civic partnerships. Indeed, the partners of PLAY Technology, Inc., had started planning a second store in nearby Jersey City. Kanja Wohmana — who was born and raised in Jersey City and served as the current manager of the Vinington store — would run the new location, along with periodic assistance from fellow employees Hank Kristmis and Robert deFatha.

Kanja, Hank and Robert had reason to celebrate the prospect of their business franchise opportunity with Tom and Yohimbe. The original PLAY Technology location in Vinington was a true success story, at least in terms of an illegal enterprise masquerading as a legitimate business and community-support organization. Over the course of the two-and-a-half years since Tom and Yohimbe established the company, PLAY Technology had generated more than 37 fabricated Section 8 housing claims, 18 fraudulent student loan applications and 11 false federal and state income tax refund filings, resulting in government payments of more than $811,000 to fictitious parties. About two dozen *sales associates* — the term Yohimbe preferred used to describe the community members who had essentially indentured themselves to the store by amassing significant debts and who received in-store credit for engaging in online credit card, bank and other identity phishing schemes for PLAY Technology — had netted nearly $322,000 for the company. When this hefty sum was added to the $76,000 and $22,000 in advance-fee fraud scams that PLAY Technology had successfully perpetrated on a prominent Essex County judge and a respected superintendent of schools, respectively, Tom and Yohimbe could boast profits of more than $1.2 million — a success story that would make even Horatio Alger blush.

High-Profile Victims

Entering its third year of operation, as PLAY Technology continued to grow in community prestige and profitability, its illicit activities also increased substantially. Many of the company's customers had purchased expensive electronic items that they simply could not afford — especially with the large service fees imposed on them for converting their paychecks into in-store credits. Few of them were therefore in no position to argue when Tom and Yohimbe began offering additional merchandise credits or preferred-customer discounts for attending their after-hours information sessions in computer training, public housing assistance and student loan applications. In reality, these courses were little more than data-entry production mills; participants would complete and submit online Section 8 lower-income applications and Free Application for Student Aid forms using the names and personal information of friends, coworkers and even data from patrons at the various retail establishments and hotels where a number of them worked. Many of these late-night training sessions would last in excess of five to six hours without breaks.

Yohimbe, the more technologically savvy of the two partners, occasionally identified a training participant who possessed an unusual aptitude for computers. These special customers would be retained by PLAY Technology as new associates and taught the art and science of Web site design and desktop publishing; after which they would put their newfound proficiency to use producing false identification documents (e.g., birth certificates, utility bills, etc.), generating fictitious bank checks and developing "mirror-image" Web sites of legitimate businesses that could be used to phish for credit card numbers and other personal information. Kanja Wohmana, Hank Kristmis, and Robert deFatha had each been initially discovered by Yohimbe for possessing such talents. They would still periodically pitch in and produce advance-fee (i.e., Nigerian 419 scams) e-mail distribution lists on the increasingly rare occasions when business was slow.

Unfortunately for the owners and associates of PLAY Technology, as the frequency of their scams increased, the number of consumer complaints of fraudulent charges for electronics on their credit card statements and new of lines of credit that they had not applied for rose, and the number of major banks receiving forged or counterfeit checks also grew. Targeted fraud analysis reports from the major credit card companies began showing a spike in disputed transactions emanating from the Vinington area. But these indications and warnings might not have resulted in law enforcement action were it not for the incident involving the Honorable Frank T. Highbottom, a well-respected Essex County judge.

According to Judge Highbottom, the matter began innocently enough. He had received an e-mail from an elderly widow in Lagos, Nigeria, whose late husband had been a Deputy Finance Minister for nearly six years. Upon her husband's sudden and mysterious death (purportedly payback for his public stand against corruption in Nigeria's banking industry), his widow had managed to conceal $7 million from the local authorities. In exchange for Judge Highbottom's assistance in relocating these funds from Nigeria to the United States (which involved a complex process of bribes to public officials and wire transfers abroad), she would provide him with 10 percent of the sum for his personal use. Although an embarrassed Judge Highbottom maintained that his motives were simply to assist a widow whose husband had "stood up for what is right," when his local bank threatened to foreclose on his lavish home and notify the media of his outstanding debts of more than $76,000, he grudgingly reported the matter to his long-time acquaintance, my boss, Randolph Morrisey, who was serving as the Special Agent in Charge (SAIC) of the Newark Field Office of the U.S. Secret Service. Among SAIC Morrisey's many responsibilities was managing the Interagency Nigerian Organized Crime Task Force (INOCTF).

Charged with investigating a wide range of criminal offenses emanating from West Africa or involving Nigerian nationals in the United States, the primary mission of INOCTF includes thwarting the financial crimes (e.g., fraud, forgery, phishing, counterfeiting and advance-fee scams) that had grown exponentially since the Nigerian military coup. To provide adequate investigative resources to address the complexity of Nigerian organized crime, a variety of federal, state and local law enforcement agencies — each of which brought its own individual resources and legal authority to the group — were assigned to the task force. As the lead for the INOCTF, SAIC Morrisey assigned me as the full-time intelligence analyst on the case. He chose me to lead the day-to-day case operations of the INOCTF for several reasons. First, while local police departments might assign detectives to run task forces, most federal-state-local combined working groups do not because analysts are the glue that holds the case together; whereas agents or investigators travel often or frequently rotate through different squads or other projects during the course of a lengthy investigation. Second, I already possessed more than 10 years of experience as both a military and civilian analyst specializing in drug trafficking, money laundering and financial crimes; many of these facets are common to INOCTF cases. Lastly, my doctorate in social science research methods ensured my comfort employing both qualitative and quantitative methods, including inductive data visualization. This analytic approach stresses reliance on an ever-expanding base of data that unites multiple databases to link what might otherwise appear to be unconnected information (e.g., financial transaction records, telephone call logs, business and personal e-mails, Section 8 applications, income tax filings and student loan applications).

The Secret Service agents and I worked closely with members of the Immigration and Customs Enforcement, U.S. Postal Inspection Service, Department of State's Bureau of Diplomatic Security, the Federal Bureau of Investigation, U.S. Housing and Urban Development's Office of the Inspector General, the Internal Revenue Service, Essex and Hudson County Prosecutor's Offices, the New Jersey State Police and the Vinington Police Department. The task force not only included special agents and police officers, but also intelligence analysts, linguists fluent in Hausa and Igbo and representatives of the banking industry and major credit card companies. The political star power of Judge Highbottom was enough to launch INOCTF into high gear. Its momentum was further accelerated when Dr. Frances Meyerson, the much-loved, long-serving superintendent of schools in West Orange, New Jersey, also sheepishly acknowledged she had been conned out of about $22,000. This was money that she believed she was giving to the family of a deceased teacher who had been killed in a pro-Democracy rally, in hopes of helping them escape Nigeria with their "modest" inheritance of $2.8 million, which they had managed to conceal from government officials. The e-mails she received — first from the murdered teacher's family and later from a "prestigious" law firm in London — certainly appeared legitimate, not unlike the electronic correspondence Judge Highbottom had received from the First National Bank of Lagos verifying the substantial assets of the grieving Deputy Finance Minister's widow.

Not reported by the media was the fact that in neither the Highbottom nor Meyerson cases were their actions wholly altruistic. Indeed, both had been assured by their contacts that they would be properly compensated by the aggrieved with sums in excess of $1 million. Of course, our task force knew this, as well as the fact that there was no Deputy Finance Minister's widow, no murdered teacher's family and certainly no millions of dollars in assets to be smuggled out of Nigeria. Regardless, this was the lucrative hook that kept advance-fee fraud patsies engaged until master perpetrators such as Tom and Yohimbe financially bled them dry.

Getting Our Hands Dirty

Task force work is not easy, and in the nearly 11-month investigation that ensued, the long hours of surveillance, seemingly endless dumpster dives (court-approved, warranted searches of trash receptacles to collect incriminating documents) and interviews with erstwhile associates-turned-informants for whom English was neither their first nor second language proved challenging. For example, collecting hours of surreptitious video often meant that we had to forego our children's sporting events, postpone wedding anniversaries and reschedule birthdays. Efforts to glean from dumpsters fictitious tax returns, W-2s and Section 8 applications seemed to take place in the worst weather imaginable and when the dumpsters were nearly overflowing with week-old sweet-and-sour chicken and rancid spaghetti (at least we hoped the long worm-like things we were sifting through were spaghetti noodles). The task force was fortunate to include two members of Immigrations and Customs Enforcement who spoke fluent Hausa and Igbo. They were contemporaneously tasked with communicating with the nearly two dozen confidential informants involved in the case and translating hours of audio and video conversations among Tom, Yohimbe and their associates picked up on the federally approved wiretaps in the store and on their telephones. Eleven months is a long time to devote to a case, which meant we had frequent turnover in agents and officers due to competing priorities within their respective agencies.

Fortunately, as an intelligence analyst, I was not subjected to this same frenetic travel rotation, and could ensure a continual investigative thread and maintain momentum on the case. Given the ability to focus specifically on this case, and by applying data visualization software to this large criminal enterprise, I was able to graphically depict relationships between quantitative and qualitative datasets — something that could not have been accomplished using traditional analytic techniques. In short, I was able to both account for and visually display the details of the case by linking more than $1.2 million in fraud losses and victims with PLAY Technologies, Tom Nakafe and Yohimbe Aglean. My analyses also linked Kanja Wohmana, Hank Kristmis and Robert deFatha to the scheme, along with 22 lesser associates. This graphic representation proved critical in enticing the majority of defendants to plead guilty or accept plea agreements (including Tom Nakafe), and to convict Yohimbe Aglean at trial.

Equally important, I provided this chart and associated findings to other law enforcement entities in the United States and abroad, including

INTERPOL. Such information-sharing efforts are critical in combating organized crime, because they allow intelligence professionals to inductively connect seemingly disparate pieces of information about criminal groups. In the case of PLAY Technology, providing this data to INOCTF offices in other states and countries led investigators to uncover a robust public housing fraud network linking Nakafe and Aglean to similar perpetrators in Cleveland, Ohio, and Saint Louis and Branson, Missouri, and an extensive advance-fee ring based in Lagos, Nigeria, with tentacles stretching to London, Toronto and Newark.

The Ultimate Betrayal

After nearly a year of dumpster diving, surveillance operations, financial link analysis, confidential informant monitoring and victim queries, the Newark-based INOCTF received approval from the Office of the U.S. Attorney for the District of New Jersey to execute search, seizure and arrest warrants for Tom Nakafe, Yohimbe Aglean, 18 of their associates and the "alleged criminal enterprise doing business as PLAY Technology." Immediately after the arrests, U.S. Attorney Rick Thatcher read a statement to the press, touting the "intense cooperative investigative effort between a wide range of law enforcement agencies and public and private partners, which has successfully disrupted a long-standing and complex fraud ring with connections to several other states and countries. As a result of the efforts of these fine men and women," he continued, "identity theft will be markedly reduced in the greater Vinington area, and the integrity of public housing and education programs will be restored."

Trials for Nakafe and Aglean were handled separately in the District Court of New Jersey. In a plea agreement, Tom Nakafe pleaded guilty to seven counts of a 17-count indictment. He pleaded guilty to conspiracy (18 U.S.C. 371), possession of five or more fraudulent identification documents (18 U.S.C. 1028), Internet (wire) fraud in connection with federally subsidized housing (18 U.S.C. 1343), Internet (wire) fraud in connection with FHA mortgage fraud application, making false statements and entries on federal student loan documents (18 U.S.C. 1001), money laundering via federal income tax evasion (18 U.S.C. 1956) and access device fraud (18 U.S.C. 1029). Nakafe was able to leverage the fact that he had put very little in writing to prove that he was not the senior partner in PLAY Technology. Indeed, much of his attorney's argument focused on his client's assertion that he was "simply a pawn" of the technologically savvy Yohimbe Aglean, who he claimed had masterminded the entire scheme. Ultimately, Nakafe was sentenced to 37 months in federal prison and ordered to pay approximately $412,000 in restitution.

Dumbfounded by his longtime friend's deception, Yohimbe Aglean chose not to accept a plea agreement and went to trial. After nearly four weeks, he was found guilty of conspiracy to commit Internet (wire) fraud in connection with federally subsidized housing (18 U.S.C. 371), Internet (wire) fraud in connection with federally subsidized Section 8 housing (18 U.S.C. 1343), access device fraud (18 U.S.C. 1029) and use of computers to engage in identity theft (18 U.S.C. 1030 and 18 U.S.C. 1028). He was sentenced to 37 months in federal prison, three years of probation following his release, and was ordered to pay more than $600,000 in restitution.

Aglean subsequently appealed his case on the grounds that some of the evidence introduced in court should have been suppressed. His counsel argued that one of the vehicles searched belonged to Aglean's cousin, who was not involved in any illicit activity, and that the evidence obtained therein should not have been considered by the jury. The appellate court affirmed the defendant's conviction, but vacated his sentence and remanded him for resentencing.

Defendant Kanja Wohmana pleaded guilty to theft of government funds (18 U.S.C. 666) involving the Section 8 assistance program. He was sentenced to two years of probation and ordered to pay restitution in the amount of $14,000. Hank Kristmis and Robert deFatha were each sentenced to six months of home detention and ordered to make restitution to the U.S. Department of Housing and Urban Development in the amount of $48,000. Each pleaded guilty to one count of theft of U.S. government funds (18 U.S.C. 666).

Twenty-two other suspects were deemed "unindicted co-conspirators." Many of them were the sales associates — the women and men who amassed large debts at PLAY Technology and were paying off their debts by engaging in the extensive after-hours fraud scams directed by Nakafe and Aglean. In exchange for their cooperation as confidential informants and for providing testimony against Nakafe and Aglean they were not charged. They also agreed to neither apply for, nor obtain, federally subsidized housing or educational assistance for at least three years.

Lessons Learned

While internal and external auditors appropriately focus much of their attention on identifying theft within an organization perpetrated by an individual employee or a few "bad apples," we must not discount the fact that — as former chief of the fraud section of the U.S. Department of Justice Herbert Edlehertz asserted more than 40 years ago — some businesses do exist purely for the purpose of engaging in fraud and other white-collar crimes. Based on

(continued)

(*continued*)

the PLAY Technology case and the myriad of other Nigerian fraud cases investigated each year, the imagination of those who would perpetrate such schemes cannot be underestimated.

Moreover, given the complexity of such enterprises, law enforcement officials would benefit from employing a variety of inductive analytic techniques including data visualization, link association charts and the continuum of money management to successfully identify schemes and bring the guilty parties to justice. We should remain cognizant that Nigerian organized crime is a growing octopus, with the body firmly embedded in the art of advance-fee fraud. However, its tentacles — some of which stretch to the United Kingdom, the United States, Canada and beyond — are often inextricably linked to other illicit offenses, including identity theft, access device fraud, bank fraud, heroin trafficking and money laundering. Accordingly, information sharing across federal, state and international borders is essential.

Recommendations to Prevent Future Occurrences

Small businesses are a stalwart facet of America's economic sustainability. However, if left unmonitored, such entities may prey upon members of their own communities. Accordingly, public officials should attempt to enhance opportunities for positive interactions between law enforcement and citizens through community policing and participation in civic organizations. Formal and informal training and awareness seminars — presented in a variety of languages representative of the community being served — may reduce opportunities for those who would prey upon their neighbors. Only through thoughtful research, serious investigative efforts and a steadfast commitment to educate all Americans, especially our most recent arrivals who are often the most vulnerable, can we reduce the impact of Nigerian organized crime and other types of Internet fraud for future generations.

About the Author

Hank J. Brightman is an Associate Research Professor of War Gaming at the U.S. Naval War College. He previously served as an Associate Professor and Chair of the Criminal Justice Department at Saint Peter's College from 2000 to 2008. Hank has more than 16 years of varied experience in law enforcement, investigations and intelligence analysis with the U.S. Department of the Interior, U.S. Secret Service and the U.S. Navy. The views and opinions expressed in this case study are the authors', and do not necessarily represent those of the Naval War College, Department of the Navy, or the U.S. Government.

Hack, Pump and Dump

NADIA BRANNON

Anatoliy Serov was intensely staring at his computer monitor. "Yes, there it is; place a sell order now. Sell order complete!" Anatoliy was jubilant, and he immediately called his girlfriend, "Lenchik, be ready by six — we are going to Onegin to celebrate." Onegin was a fashionable, high-end restaurant in St. Petersburg, Russia, and Anatoliy's girlfriend was understandably confused.

"Celebrate what? Tolik, are you crazy? Do you know how expensive Onegin is?" she asked.

"Yes, baby, I know. We are finally rich! I made 30,000 bucks today on the financial market, and this is just the beginning."

Anatoliy could have been mistaken for a successful investor, financial broker or lucky day trader, but in fact he was none of the above. He was a talented computer programmer working for a small development firm in St. Petersburg. And Anatoliy (along with a few of his work colleagues) had just successfully executed a pump and dump scheme with a new, high-tech twist. The Securities and Exchange Commission (SEC) defined these schemes as follows:

> "Pump and dump" schemes, also known as "hype and dump manipulation," involve the touting of a company's stock (typically microcap companies) through false and misleading statements to the marketplace. After pumping the stock, fraudsters make huge profits by selling their cheap stock into the market. Pump and dump schemes often occur on the Internet where it is common to see messages posted that urge readers to buy a stock quickly or to sell before the price goes down.

The SEC did not mention a more recent improvement on the scheme by my creative and computer-savvy compatriots, Anatoliy and his friends, which added the term *hack* to pump and dump.

The Perfect Storm

With unemployment rates reaching 40 percent in certain regions, former Soviet states were replete with characters like Anatoliy who had a good technical education, were extremely hungry to make it big in the new capitalist society but were unemployed or severely underemployed. It was the perfect storm for the development of some of the best hackers the Internet has seen. When a fraudster's command of English was limited to a profound knowledge of Perl, Java and C++ syntax and a familiarity with computer-geek speak, it was a bit of a challenge to create a persuasive media campaign to convince investors to buy penny stocks — a necessary step in a traditional pump and dump campaign. Anatoliy found himself in that position and decided, why not just hack into investors' accounts and make the trades on their behalf?

China Gold

Jeffrey Scott was strongly attached to his Saturday morning routine: coffee, newspaper and then the deeply despised yet necessary process of going through the pile of weekly mail. "Ah, there it is; my monthly statement from my brokerage account. Straight to the filing cabinet for you."

Jeff did not closely follow the market — the morning Bloomberg broadcast did not go down well with his leisurely cup of coffee. He was a conservative investor who had learned early in business school that investors cannot beat the market. Therefore, he developed an investment strategy that was plainer than vanilla: buy and hold, at regular intervals.

With a well-practiced gesture, Jeff stripped the statement of its envelope and shoved it into the designated pile, but then something caught his eye. "CGDC — China Gold Corporation." Jeff thought, "Chinese gold, that's interesting. When did I buy that? It must be part of some international growth fund that I hold. Let's see how it is doing — must be fairing really well." He thought that because at the time China was the darling of the investment world. The Chinese economy was experiencing explosive growth and many were rushing to invest or outsource their operations to China. Jeff scanned the statement for a moment and then his face became virtually indistinguishable in color from the paper he was holding. "This has got to be a mistake. Is this even my statement? A balance of $1,932.54? That can't be. I should have at least $120,000 in there."

Empty Nest Egg

Jeff ran to his computer and logged into his Internet brokerage account hoping to see that indeed it was a big mistake and his $120,000 was safe and growing daily. But no, $1,932.54 was starkly staring at him from the screen. What happened? How could that be? Jeff feverishly dialed his broker.

The broker promptly transferred Jeff to the fraud prevention department, where a representative informed him that he was a victim of a hack, pump and dump scheme. His online brokerage account was compromised by hackers who held stocks of China Gold Corporation in their own accounts in Latvia and St. Petersburg, which at the time was trading at about $0.005 per share. Hackers broke into Jeff's account, sold his holdings (the retirement savings that he proudly and painstakingly built up over the years) and purchased China Gold on his behalf, thus elevating the share price to previously unseen high levels. Shortly after, they sold their holdings of the CGDC, reaping thousands of dollars in profit. The customer service representative told Jeff the crime was virtually untraceable.

A Fad or a Ring?

Jeff Scott was not the only victim of the China Gold hackers — far from it. Not only were the accounts of other customers at his brokerage firm well stocked with China Gold, but those of many other firms across the United States and Canada were also victims of the same scheme. When the first few incidents of the hack, pump and dump scheme were reported, the financial community believed they were separate, unrelated incidents not worth worrying about.

But when a flood of similar Internet transactions suddenly rushed through the regulators' gates, my firm was brought in to investigate. Were these unrelated, copycat events that had become a new fad for the online criminal community or were they representative of a centrally orchestrated campaign on a massive scale?

Timing Is Everything

I was working for the private firm that was hired to investigate this case, and I was assigned to the team. We had a lot of questions to answer: How did they do it? What means did they use to hack into the systems? What vulnerabilities, if any, were exploited? Who was behind the attacks? And the ultimate question: How could we stop them?

We began by examining the server logs associated with access to the compromised accounts, including the Internet protocol (IP) addresses and thousands of connections stemming from them. What we immediately noticed was that most of the logins were coming from many, but consistently repeating, IP addresses in the United States — not what we were expecting to see. If this was a crime ring operating from the former Soviet Union — which was our working theory — we expected to see logins from IP addresses registered in Russia, Ukraine, Latvia and perhaps several proxy servers. However, the IP addresses that were used to illegally access the on-line brokerage accounts were registered to large U.S. corporations, the U.S. government or U.S.-based Internet service providers (ISPs).

After looking into the suspect computers and IP addresses more closely, we discovered that the addresses used were part of various botnets. A *botnet* is a group of computers (*bots*) that are controlled by a different, usually re-mote, computer to perform specific coordinated tasks. The computer that controls the bots is known as the *herder*. In this case, groups of computers had been infected with the same spyware program and were used by a herder to perform a number of tasks: login to the Internet brokerage site, guess account numbers, crack passwords, confirm that accounts were active and transfer funds.

When we analyzed server logs over a longer period of time, we noticed a peculiar pattern: The suspicious activity started with multiple logins from IPs in the United States (often coming from the same network) and ended with a single login from somewhere in Russia, Estonia, Latvia or Ukraine that executed the illegal trades. Even more strange was that some of the initial attempts to access accounts occurred within regular time intervals — a clear signature of an automated process. Therefore, we concluded that botnets were being used to break into online accounts and, once they were compromised, the criminals themselves placed trading orders.

The Monster Strikes Back

One of the standard procedures that our investigative team performed was to remotely scan the suspicious computers. Following this protocol, the team selected a few IP addresses at random and started monitoring the ac-tivity coming from them. However, within a few hours of our scanning, the targets went silent. The bad guys turned out to be extremely smart; they realized they were being scanned. As a result, we did not collect much evi-dence by that method. Then the next day, the team chose another set of IP addresses to monitor in the hope of collecting more information but sud-denly the unexpected happened. Our computer lab was attacked by the hackers. It was their way of saying, "We know who you are. Do not mess with us." That made us realize the fraudsters were extremely sophisticated and well organized. It also confirmed our theory that most of the fraudu-lent activity was related and committed by an organized group.

A Multi-Headed Hydra

The onslaught of hack, pump and dump schemes not only reached major financial institutions in the United States but a number of brokerage firms in Canada were also targeted. In response to these incidents, every victim institution introduced its own security measures, among them:

- Blocking the known suspicious IP addresses
- Continuously updating the list of known suspicious IP addresses
- Locking the online accounts after a certain number (10 or fewer) of unsuccessful login attempts
- Notifying customers after numerous unsuccessful login attempts
- Blocking online trades in known penny stock targets
- Generating alerts when orders for certain thinly traded securities were placed
- Using multifactor authentication methods, such as SecureID token, smart cards, and other similar technologies (physical devices the individual customers install on their computers to provide security protection)
- Automatically referring accounts to customer service when suspicious activity was detected

A large number of financial institutions joined forces and created an industry group to coordinate anti-fraud activities in real time. The group notifies participants of the recent attacks and modes of operation used by the fraudsters, IP addresses involved, securities traded and other pertinent information. The FBI and other law enforcement agencies have begun to dedicate significant resources to the investigation of these types of Internet securities frauds. As a result of these measures, several of the perpetrators have been apprehended and prosecuted.

However, fraudsters have become more sophisticated in response to increased preventive measures; their techniques and methods have evolved. They stopped logging in to computers that could allow law enforcement agencies to detect their physical location and began using proxy servers, which masked their location. Their trading activity also changed. As many financial institutions began to monitor trading in penny stocks, fraudsters moved to other securities that do not exactly fit the definition of *penny stocks* but whose prices can still be easily manipulated. These modes of attack are much harder to proactively detect because they cause a significant — but not unusual — fluctuation in the price of the stock, and thus are unlikely to raise a red flag.

Where Is the Head?

Why is the fraudulent activity that started several years ago and caused the largest fraud-related monetary losses to the industry still occurring? Why aren't the criminals behind the bars? Though some small fry — like Alexei Kamardin, a 21-year-old Russian student living in Tampa, Florida — have been caught, the really big fish — the Anatoliy Serovs — are still at large. This is due to several factors:

- Fraudsters' use of technologically sophisticated methods that prevent detection and identification
- Difficulty linking illegal trading activity in compromised accounts to the financial gains reaped by account holders in other financial institutions absent direct computer forensic evidence
- The international nature of the fraud
- Lack of cooperation of the Russian government and other foreign law enforcement agencies
- Corruption in the former Soviet countries

Many believe that the Russian Business Network (RBN), a cybercrime organization that originated in St. Petersburg, was behind most of the hack, pump and dump activity, but there is not enough evidence to prove it. RBN first started as an ISP that provided hosting to many shady and illegal businesses that distributed child pornography, phishing, spam and malware. It developed partner and affiliate marketing programs in different countries to provide a method for organized crime to target victims internationally. It is also believed that in response to law enforcement actions, RBN moved much of its operation to China. It presumably operates several botnets and is also known for distribution of fake antispyware and antimalware applications for the purposes of PC hijacking and personal identity theft.

The hack, pump and dump fraudsters used any number of the available cyber means of collecting personal identity information — phishing, malware, spyware and password-cracking algorithms to name a few — to access the online brokerage accounts of unsuspecting victims like Jeff Scott.

Lessons Learned

What are the key lessons learned here?

- The Internet is making our world much more efficient and connected, but it also creates exposures of a global nature.
- Computer technologies allow criminals to commit fraud that is large in scale (target multiple institutions and accounts) and that crosses national borders.
- The Internet also creates opportunities for the formation and growth of online criminal rings and communities.
- Criminals are increasingly using technologies and fraud schemes that make detection and prosecution extremely difficult.

Recommendations to Prevent Future Occurrences

What can you do to avoid becoming another Jeff Scott? The following computer-safety practices can make you safer — but never completely safe — in cyberspace:

- Install a properly configured firewall on your personal computer.
- Install antivirus and antispyware software (and update it regularly to protect yourself from recently identified threats).
- Encrypt sensitive information stored on your computer.
- Do not keep personal information on public computers (at the office, library, etc.).
- Do not install applications that you are not absolutely sure are legitimate.
- Do not open suspicious e-mail attachments, especially executables (file names that end in ".exe").
- Do not respond to phishing e-mails or Web advertisements.

Additionally, to protect yourself from hack, pump and dump schemes, you should consider the following rules:

- Do not share your Internet brokerage account information with anybody.
- Do not access your online account from public computers (office, airport, Internet café, library, etc.).
- Avoid using mobile devices to access your online account (iPhone, BlackBerry, etc.). Many of the compromised accounts that we reviewed had a history of access through mobile devices.
- Review your brokerage statements regularly and call customer service if you do not understand certain transactions.
- Use passwords that are hard to crack (avoid common words, combinations of your name/date of birth/Social Security number, etc.).
- If your brokerage firm does not already offer it, request a SecureID token to provide an extra level of security to your online account.
- Avoid linking your brokerage account to your bank account. If one of your accounts is compromised, the other could be as well.
- If you have multiple accounts, have separate passwords for them.

By far the most important safety rule is if you have an Internet brokerage account, make sure it is with a large, reputable company. The leading financial institutions in the United States have customer-protection guarantee, that compensate customers for the losses if their online accounts are compromised. Their security personnel work with consultants and investigators like me to detect and prevent fraud early and protect their customers.

About the Author

Nadia Brannon is a Principal with LECG, a global expert services and consulting firm. Ms. Brannon is an expert in database forensics, complex data analytics and data mining. Her clients include Fortune Global 500 corporations and major law firms worldwide.

Dangerous Learning Curve

AHMED R. KUNNUMPURATH

Obe Kofe was a 25-year-old Nigerian national who received a bachelor's degree in computer science from American University in Nigeria. However, after graduating, he could not find a suitable job in his home country and was looking for overseas positions, preferably in Saudi Arabia, one of the richest countries in the Persian Gulf.

His friend and schoolmate, Martin Gil, worked for a travel agency in Nigeria and had connections with overseas recruitment agencies. When Obe told him about his dream of working abroad, Martin immediately asked, "What about a job in Saudi Arabia? I know an agent there who could help you get a work permit." That was just the opportunity Obe was looking for. He jumped at the chance and told Martin, "Why not? I would love to! Please pass my name and information to your friend and let me know what he says."

Two days later, Obe had a phone interview with the Saudi recruiter, and the following week his work permit was prepared. Obe took the first flight he could to Saudi Arabia.

Once in Riyadh, the capital of Saudi Arabia, Obe discovered that his work visa did not ensure him a lucrative job and — much to his surprise — he had only been granted a three-month visitor's visa. However, he befriended some Nigerian expatriates who let him stay with them while he looked for work. After a week of fruitless job hunting, one of his roommates, Ian Smith, promised to find him a permanent position in his friend's company, which was Nigerian based. Obe took a clerical job for the time being.

Introducing Internet Banking

Ahli Commerce Bank (ACB) was founded in Saudi Arabia and grew into one of the leading banks in the Persian Gulf. It had more than 2,000 employees, 90 local branches and 20 overseas locations in Egypt, the United Kingdom, France and Jordan.

Although it was an old, established bank, it was also the first in Saudi Arabia to have a fully computerized system and to offer Internet banking to its customers. ACB purchased its Internet-banking program from Arizona Internet Banking Software, a leading Asian vendor, and it was a very sophisticated system. However, as new technology usually comes with a learning curve for those who have to use it, ACB's customers were slow to warm up to Internet banking, and the software had a few critical issues. But the customer base grew and slowly accepted the new online service, and even customers with little computer knowledge learned to appreciate the service as an easy way to make transfers and request account services. ACB introduced user identifications (IDs) and passwords for its customers and allowed them to transfer funds among their accounts and to third parties.

The Internet Banking Unit (IBU) at ACB, headed by Danny Alto, was a well-organized department that handled problems with Internet banking, user IDs, passwords and the execution and monitoring of transactions. There were two or three employees working at any given time in IBU; shifts ran throughout the day and during weekends and holidays.

Customers who wanted to apply for Internet banking services had to fill out a standard application form and submit it to their branch. Once IBU received it, a staff member checked the information provided, verified the signature and had a supervisor approve the application. Then the software program generated a user ID and password. Customers were issued their user IDs and passwords in separate envelopes that required signed acknowledgments of receipt. After the acknowledgments were returned to IBU, the user IDs and passwords were activated. An IBU employee called customers to tell them they could start using the Internet-banking features.

IBU's procedures required a senior staff member to verify via telephone the user ID and other details provided in a customer's application when the department received online instructions to transfer funds from one account to another. Only after confirmation was received would IBU execute the transaction. If an employee could not speak to the customer, a message would be left on the customer's answering machine under the assumption that the customer would receive the message and confirm the transaction later. However, it could be difficult for staff members to reach customers, so sometimes transactions were executed without following this failsafe. But IBU had not received serious complaints, and everything seemed to be going smoothly.

Control Lapse

One Saturday afternoon, ACB's customer service center received a call from A. J. Simon, a Belgian national who held an account with the Riyadh branch. A. J. claimed that $40,000 had been transferred from his checking account without his authorization. He did not remember requesting any such transaction in the past two days. He was upset and desperately wanted to know the reason for the transfer.

The call center employee checked A. J.'s account and saw that an online transfer for $40,000 had indeed been executed that day through an Internet banking transaction, and he forwarded the matter to ACB's IBU. Unfortunately, because it was a weekend, there were no supervisors available. However, the message was logged by an IBU staff member and flagged.

The next morning, when a supervisor was in the office, a thorough investigation was launched. I was an internal auditor at ACB and took the case. The records indicated that the transfer from A. J.'s account was initiated by a request to send the money to a third-party bank account in Jeddah. By the time A. J. discovered it, the transaction had been completed, and close scrutiny revealed that A. J. had not been contacted to confirm the transfer request.

The head of IBU, Danny Alto, called the operations department to recall the funds but was told by Jamie Edwards, the operations supervisor, that the payment had already been processed in the name of Obc Kofc to an account at International Commercial Bank (ICB) in Jeddah. Jamie requested the beneficiary bank recall the funds, but ICB had already closed for the day and was, therefore, unable to honor the request.

The funds could not be frozen, but Jamie placed a block on A. J.'s account to prevent further fraudulent transfers. IBU was ordered to provide a report of the Internet transactions that occurred during the past two days.

While we were investigating the fraudulent transfer from A. J.'s account, three other customers called to complain that they received text messages on their mobile phones informing them of unauthorized debits from their accounts. IBU was able to act quickly enough to prevent those transfers from being processed and requested that the operations department block them. A. J. and the three other customers were outside the country when the transactions were requested and they were all directed to Obe Kofe's account at ICB. We passed our information to the Saudi police and continued with our internal investigation.

Follow the Money

We found that two employees were directly involved in the processing of the fraudulent Internet transactions and decided to start our investigation by interviewing them. The first IBU staff member we spoke with, Mary Suzan, had been with the bank for one year. She told me the transfer request came through late in the afternoon and, although she tried calling the customer several times, she could not reach him, so she left a message on his answering machine requesting approval of the transfer. Mary admitted that when she left for the day, she forgot to mention the outstanding approval to her replacement; the employee who took over for her did not suspect anything unusual and forwarded the transfer request for processing. Subsequently, the operations department executed the payment.

We made a follow-up request with ICB to refund the amount transferred from A. J.'s account to Obe Kofe's accounts, but ICB informed us that Obe had already withdrawn $30,000, so the funds could not be remitted. We requested ICB freeze the remaining $10,000 until we could get a court order for the money. In the meantime, Obe tried to withdraw the balance using a different bank's ATM, but he received a message saying the request could not be processed and he should contact his branch for information. The next morning ICB received an angry phone call from Obe; he shouted at the branch manager and wanted to know why his account had been frozen. The branch manager asked Obe to visit the branch the next morning to discuss the issue. Obe agreed to go to the bank the next day, but he did not show up. We think he became suspicious and decided not to risk a visit. The branch manager tried to call him several times, but his phone had been disconnected.

Our IT security officer traced the Internet protocol (IP) addresses from where the transfer messages originated and found that, except for one request that originated in the UK, the messages were sent from Nigeria. However, the IP address did not help much in identifying the original fraudsters because authorities in Nigeria and the UK did not pursue the culprits. Riyadh's police service requested the IP address details and began its own forensic investigation.

We tried to review recordings of the defrauded customers' phone calls to the service department, but found out that full records were not available and supervisors were not reviewing the calls on a regular basis as they should have been.

Our investigation proved almost certainly that customer accounts were accessed by an organized group of hackers working outside the country who gained access to customers' stolen user IDs and passwords. The account data could have been compromised in a few different ways:

- The customers responded to phishing e-mails claiming to have come from ACB and requesting confirmation of their IDs and passwords.
- The customers checked their bank accounts on public computers — for example, in an Internet café or library — that had key logging software installed on them. The software sent their online banking IDs and passwords to the culprits.

- The customers did not have up-to-date antivirus software on their home computers, allowing them to be infected with spyware.

Whatever the case, customer negligence was a factor in each instance; they were unknowingly exposing their user IDs and passwords to cyber criminals.

A Slap on the Wrist Gone Awry

Police traced the fraud to one suspect — Obe Kofe — who turned out to be a small fish in a big pond of cyber criminals. Police took him into custody for questioning, but he said he did not know the higher-ups on the chain of command and denied involvement in a fraudulent scheme. However, he could not explain how A. J.'s $40,000 made it into his account or why he decided to withdraw it. As the interview progressed, Obe agreed to partially repay the withdrawn amount; he said he could not repay the full amount because he was unemployed and he requested a grace period of three months to settle. Police discussed the matter with ACB's upper management and legal counsel, who agreed that Obe could remit only $20,000 of the illegally withdrawn $30,000. ACB refunded the remaining $10,000 to A. J.'s account.

Obe disclosed vital information about others involved in his scheme to Saudi Arabian intelligence officers as part of a plea bargain that included his release from jail and deportation to Nigeria. We later learned that the Nigerian government managed to identify the masterminds of the crime and arrested them. Despite the fact that Obe received a light sentence in Saudi Arabia, only days after his return to Nigeria, he was killed in a car collision. Local authorities in Nigeria suspected that members of the cyber-crime gang whom Obe exposed in Saudi Arabia were involved in his death, but the incident was not investigated.

Lessons Learned

This was my first investigation of an Internet fraud and I was eager to learn how these types of crimes are committed and how to investigate them. We used system experts to retrieve IP information used in the transactions and interviewed the staff members involved to identify weaknesses in our system. The control step of sending text messages to clients before Internet transfers were executed turned out to be the most effective part of the process. It empowered the victims to identify fraudulent transactions and alert the bank, usually in enough time for ACB to stop the transaction from being

(continued)

(*continued*)

processed. However, there was a catch — if a customer's Internet account could be hacked, the phone number on record could be changed by the hackers.

This case also taught me how to investigate Internet fraud by locating the IP address used by the criminals to access the system. The IP addresses in this case were from Nigeria and the United Kingdom. Unfortunately, the local police in those countries did not attempt to locate the individuals behind the IP addresses, so that information resulted in a dead end. With more responsive outside investigators, however, IP addresses could be used to track criminals and prevent further losses.

I also learned of an inherent weakness in ACB's Internet-banking process — staff had to call the customers and confirm each transaction before it was processed. This manual intervention led to human errors and negligence. Proper follow-up on the calls was not necessarily made and the telephone recordings were inadequately maintained. In A. J.'s case, the staff member said she called his cell phone but it was turned off, so she left him a voice mail requesting confirmation of the transfer. A lack of internal communication caused the transfer to be completed before A. J. heard the message.

We also learned that customers were not protecting their user IDs and passwords as well as they could have. Computers should have up-to-date antivirus software installed to stop Trojan horses, spyware and other dangerous viruses from invading the system and stealing confidential information. We learned the importance of educating customers to prevent them from conducting online bank transactions on public computers. One of the victims in this case admitted that he used public Internet cafés in the United Kingdom while there on a business trip. In response to this need for education, management began to publish leaflets and brochures that illustrated proper precautions for clients to take to protect their online account information. After this case, ACB stopped allowing bank-to-bank transfers through the Internet. Online transactions are now limited to ACB accounts because they are much less risky.

Recommendations to Prevent Future Occurrences

ACB decided to enhance the senior staff's supervision of day-to-day processes to ensure transfer requests received online were confirmed by the callback procedure until an alternate solution is created. We also began requiring staff members to attend training and fraud awareness programs.

(*continued*)

Management decided to shift the responsibility of monitoring customer calls from the IBU to the call center, which allows IBU staff members to concentrate on other aspects of their positions. The call center operates around the clock, so it is easier for them to respond promptly to customer requests and confirm instructions. A callback time limit of 30 minutes has been established for transactions requested through the Internet.

Customers are also advised to have antivirus software installed on their home and office computers if they are using Internet banking. We also warned them to avoid conducting online transactions with their accounts from Internet cafés and other public Internet facilities. We are now limiting the right to use Internet banking to customers who have undergone proper training and are aware of the necessary safety precautions. New applications for access to Internet banking are more rigorously reviewed than in the past. Last but not least, ACB's management purchased fraud-alert software to monitor frequent online transactions in customers' accounts and to flag unusual patterns.

About the Author

Ahmed R. Kunnumpurath, CFE, CIA, has a bachelor's of commerce degree. He is an experienced banker with more than 25 years of extensive experience in the fields of financial control, internal control, internal auditing, anti-money laundering and financial fraud investigations in both conventional banks and Islamic banks. He currently works as a senior fraud examiner in one of the leading banks in the Persian Gulf.

The Sherwood Boys

PAOLO BOURELLY

A small group of British fellows decided to apply their knowledge of information technology, the financial markets and their sales skills to establish a large and difficult-to-penetrate criminal organization dedicated to collecting money from victims and washing it through offshore banks. A stock exchange crisis years ago — and an understanding of investors' desire to make up their lost assets — was the catalyst that led these criminals to create such an organization. The founding members were British, but the group later expanded to include fraudsters from many different countries. They called themselves Sherwood Last, Ltd.

John Yeung was a young man from Singapore who ran the Asian arm of the organization. As general manager of Asian Health Global, Ltd., a ghost company of Sherwood Last based in Singapore and Hong Kong, he received funds from "investors" and moved them to bank accounts in other countries. Peter Wolf, a British man in his thirties, felt safe in Southeast Asia, where he was assumed to be living and from where he had been moving funds out of banks in Caribbean paradises to others in emerging Asian countries. Chris Green, a British IT consultant, was one of those criminals who liked to depict himself as a hard worker, good father and loving husbands. Chris told Peter Holm, one of his victims, "I live in Jakarta with my family. I am working very hard to sort out your account situation, and will do all I can to resolve this problem."

The perpetrators all had U.S., British or Canadian accents. They used pseudonyms that changed every time they spoke to someone new. At any given moment, two separate Chris Greens could have been talking to two different victims. For example, there was a slip-up by David Smith — he first introduced himself to victim Jane Idol as Marvin Boyd and later as David Smith. She eventually realized it was the same person and triggered an alarm. But what his real name? Boyd? Smith? Neither? No one seemed to know.

The leading men were accompanied by ladies acting as secretaries, wives and who knows what else. They were from Japan, Malaysia, Hong Kong, Indonesia, Taiwan and the Philippines. They were hard workers and would send e-mails, call clients using Sherwood's Voice over Internet Protocol (VoIP) phone system and take messages for their bosses.

An International Assembly

Sherwood Last culled its victims from around the world. Those whom I identified were from South Africa, India, the United Arab Emirates, Italy, Sweden, Denmark, Germany, Slovenia, Latvia, Norway, Austria and Poland. They were not the only victims of this fraud, but they were the ones I was able to uncover in my investigation.

The victims were diverse and most of them were left without any money. In some cases I could see their suffering. John, for example, a handicapped retiree in Poland who hoped to earn some extra money to improve his poor living conditions, was left without a cent. Then there was Nick. I was writing a case report in my office one day when the telephone rang. On the line a voice with a South African accent said, ''Can I speak to Paolo Bourelly, please?'' ''Yes, speaking,'' I said. ''Hi, Paolo; my name is Nick Grant. I am a victim of fraud by Sherwood Last, Ltd. I have been left with no money, no job and my bank has closed my account.'' Mary was a kind Slovenian woman who was trying to shield her boss from pushy cold callers but ended up a victim herself. She told me, ''Paolo, I did something I did not imagine I could do. I lied to my husband, I transferred our money to those criminals and I even took out a loan to send them more money. Suddenly, I understood something was wrong but it was too late. I need your help, please.''

Then there were the more fortunate, but they were victims nonetheless. Marc, an affable German guy, told me once, ''Paolo, this is just one of my hobbies!'' Lucky him, he was too rich to care. And Arthur from Denmark just wanted a new toy. He told me, ''I wanted to buy my own jet with the return on the investment. When I realized I was scammed, I first went to Sweden to buy the jet anyway and then called you.'' Despite his wealth, Arthur still wanted his money back.

The Tentacles Start to Spread

Four years ago, representatives of Sherwood Last, and of shell companies connected to Sherwood Last, began calling people in Europe, Asia and Africa to solicit investments in the shared capital of large corporations traded on the stock exchanges of New York and Singapore. Among the companies supposedly traded were Sony, Microsoft, Devon Energy Corporation, Rio Tinto and

PetroChina Co. None of this was true; the callers were just trolling for money with which they could abscond.

These perpetrators selected their prey through the Internet. They made cold calls to companies and asked to talk to the managing director. In some cases they asked for a specific person, whose name they might have already researched online. During the first call, they did not leave a contact number or send an e-mail with their pitch. They normally called landlines, although in some cases they called the victim directly on a cellular phone, probably because it was available on the Internet. It seemed that many victims were found on the Web site Alibaba.com, where they had placed their company's advertisement.

John Green was receiving many calls a day from different men who told him that a big boss was going to call him back. He thought it was strange that so many different people kept calling to tell him the same story. John was lucky. This uncoordinated behavior triggered his suspicions before he transferred any money to the organization.

Many people who were contacted had, at the time of their first call, received a large amount of money from the sale of a business or a home or had just inherited money after the death of a parent. In other cases, the victim's wealth was well known in his community or had been publicized in the media.

One victim, Karen, recounted her experience for me, and I later found out other investors had similar stories. Karen received a phone call from a British man named Peter who introduced himself as a member of Sherwood Last, with offices in Singapore and Hong Kong. Peter offered to open an investment account with Sherwood Last for Karen to buy and sell stock at a 1 percent commission rate on the purchase or sale price. When Karen decided to start an investment, she received a new account application she had to sign and return. Once the account was open, Peter e-mailed her and suggested certain stocks for her to purchase. She then received a document indicating the shares to be purchased and another piece of paper that provided the banking instruction for the transfer of funds through the Internet.

Once Sherwood Last got the money, a new account representative named John e-mailed Karen a confirmation that her funds had been received. After a few weeks, Peter called Karen again and suggested that she sell her shares at a profit to buy yet another stock. To complete the transaction, Karen had to send more money to cover the difference between the new stock's purchase price and what she made on the sold stock. Again, she received two documents from Sherwood Last: one showing the new situation of her account and the other providing new Internet-transfer instructions. Karen requested, and Peter agreed, to sell a few of her stocks and transfer the money to her bank account. However, shortly after her request, Peter called Karen and told her that her account had been flagged by the U.S. tax authorities and that she had to pay 30 percent in tax on the amount she invested. Karen agreed to let Peter take the taxes out of her account and then transfer her remaining profits, but when she checked her account online the next day, it showed that her entire balance had been used to pay taxes. She tried calling and e-mailing every contact she had at Sherwood Last, but she did not hear from the company again.

In a different situation, which I learned from a victim named James, the investor refused to let Sherwood Last take the taxes out of his account. James told me he was suspicious about the taxes and asked Peter to provide him with the IRS information. James wanted to arrange to pay the taxes himself because he did not trust Peter, since he sprang the taxes on James at the last minute. However, Peter's response shocked James. He received phone calls and e-mails berating him; Peter told him, "You will never see your money until you pay us the tax. Your account has been blocked until the payment is received!"

In other instances, when a victim asked to withdraw his investment, Sherwood Last representatives stopped communication — for a few months. The victim would then be contacted by another Sherwood Last advisor who would tell him the previous account representative had been dismissed for misconduct. "Your account has some problems, but I am here to help solve them." After a while, the new advisor called the victim and proposed a sale and purchase — "to get your account back on track" — which kept the game going. In fact, there were cases in which this pattern was repeated throughout many years. The net of the con game was that when a victim parted with money, it was not seen again. Instead, the scammers would use various ruses to get the victims to fork over even more funds for taxes or additional investments. It was all a lie.

On the Case

I first became involved with this case when Nick Grant called me and asked me to check the office of Sherwood Last, Ltd., in Hong Kong. I was working as a private investigator and I specialized in financial crimes. Nick told me he had found my Web site online. That was the beginning of an investigation that has taken me across the globe to talk to law enforcement agencies and prosecutors' offices in several countries.

I began my investigation with the information Nick could provide me. He sent me the e-mails, marketing pieces and newsletter he received from Sherwood Last, and I quickly realized the perpetrators possessed good knowledge of financial markets. They were able to analyze available financial information about different stocks and different countries' markets.

Based on their analysis, they prepared company newsletters and distributed them to the victims via e-mail. Their analyses and reports on the stock markets were also published on a Web site they created solely for this purpose. This Web site incorporated dynamic information collected from available Internet resources, such as www.marketwatch.com and www.bigcharts.com.

Shell Companies

I investigated Sherwood Last to uncover the organization's leadership, when it was formed, where it was incorporated and other pertinent details, and I discovered that Sherwood Last was not the only company involved. My research showed that the people behind this fraud had been using several shell companies that were incorporated in different countries. Four of these were incorporated in the British Virgin Islands:

- Sherwood Last, Ltd.
- Sunshine Group International, Ltd.
- Top International Group, Ltd.
- Top East Asia, Ltd.

I found other companies but could not identify where they were incorporated:

- Asian Health Global, Ltd.
- TYC International, LLC
- SHT Associates, Ltd.
- Last Tiger Asia, Ltd.
- World Securities International

When a company is incorporated in the British Virgin Islands, the name of the real beneficiary can be hidden. Only the agent who filed the paperwork would know his or her name. To get a court order to disclose the name is very complicated and only in a few occasions has it been done. However, one of the companies associated with Sherwood Last — Truelies International Corp. — was incorporated in Panama, which was a big mistake on the culprits' part. Records of companies incorporated in Panama must show the names of the president, secretary and treasurer. The president is responsible for the actions of anyone carrying a power of attorney, which is the instrument used to hide the name of the real beneficiary.

In communications with the victims, the crooks usually said they were located in Tokyo, so I asked my investigation team in Japan to survey the purported offices of Sherwood Last. Koyoda, my chief investigator in Japan, went to Chiyoda-ku, the area of Tokyo where the office was supposed to be, and reported that the address corresponded to an executive center where many companies were hosted. However, Sherwood Last was not one of them. The day after, I asked Nancy, my best investigator in Asia, to contact the reception desk of the executive center in Tokyo and gather more information. Nancy, with her genial way of dealing with people, was told that Sherwood Last had used the executive center in the past, but moved out a few years ago. I suspected Sherwood Last was not even operating in Japan, but was only using it as a fake address.

In a lucky break for my case, the lawyers of the Hong Kong bank where Asian Health Global and Top International Group — two of the ghost organizations associated with Sherwood Last — held accounts provided Hong Kong prosecutors with substantial information in response to a different ongoing investigation. From the court papers, I saw that Asian Health Global had an office in Hong Kong and Top International Group was located in Singapore. I decided not to interfere with the prosecutor's office, so I did not conduct any further investigation in Hong Kong.

High-Tech Organization

I looked into the many Web sites created by Sherwood Last and its affiliated shell companies. The perpetrators used a privacy-protecting service in the United States to register their sites, which meant the registrar would not disclose the owner of the Web site without a court order. The registrar offered to host clients' Web sites in another country, such as Malaysia or Singapore, and remove or mask the IP of outgoing e-mails. These factors combined to make it essentially impossible to trace e-mails. I was able to look up the Web sites' domain names on www.whois.com, and discovered the year in which one of Sherwood Last's sites was created; that at least gave me some idea of how long the organization had been in operation.

I was amazed at how this scheme was conducted almost entirely online. The Internet was used to create and incorporate their ''companies,'' open bank accounts in offshore countries, create and manage Web sites, find information about potential victims, communicate market knowledge and transfer money around the world. The Sherwood Last fraudsters even called their victims using VoIP telephony and cell phone subscriber identity module (SIM) cards from countries that sold the cards without verifying the buyer's personal information. This meant tracing the calls was next to impossible.

Sherwood Last advisors gave investors a phone number to the executive center in Tokyo where an accomplice would take a message and forward it to Peter or John. Someone from Sherwood Last would then return the call from a VoIP phone number. It was clear to me that none of the victims knew the real identities of the perpetrators. Therefore, I thought, the only way to perhaps catch them was to record their voices. This was quite an experience for most of the victims. The first hurdle was the technology. They asked many questions, such as, "Can I use my cell phone? How do these things work? Which one should I buy? Will they know I'm recording the conversation? What will happen to my money if they find out?"

I provided them with a list of cell phones that were equipped with recording devices and would be suitable for our purposes. There were several on the market, but the recording option was not documented in the user's manual, and the store attendants were often unaware of the feature. A Swedish make had the best recording functionality while a Finnish brand beeped when recording, so an astute person on the other end could tell what was happening. In fact, when victim Jane Idol was trying to record a phone call using the Finnish brand, the Sherwood Last representative abruptly hung up once she started recording. Listening to the conversations was interesting; some perpetrators were incredibly brutal and rude to their victims while telling them they were not going to get their money back.

During the years that the scam lasted, many different people from Sherwood Last called victims to solicit transfers of money, and the representatives seemed to have access to information the victims had shared with other reps in the past, such as e-mails, documents, bank transfers, information on stocks purchased and contracts. This made me suspect that Sherwood Last had client relationship management (CRM) software in place. They demonstrated a strong knowledge of financial markets and innate business savvy. I had spent many years working for large, multinational enterprises, and I could see that this one was run as a professional and well-organized company — albeit fraudulent.

Offshore Banking

The scammers behind Sherwood Last opened bank accounts in offshore countries in the names of their shell companies and instructed investors to transfer funds to those accounts electronically. They were usually cautious in choosing their offshore banking spots to protect their identities, but there was one exception — Panama. Truelies International Corp. had at least two bank accounts in Panama. With the help of the local authorities, I was able to get the names of the signatories of those bank accounts. My suspicions about the nationality of the perpetrators were confirmed — they were British, Canadian and American.

Overall, I identified more than 25 banks involved in this scheme. A few were used as the correspondent banks to transfer funds to banks in offshore countries. The beneficiary of each of the bank accounts was one of the companies mentioned above.

The combined sum of money transferred by the victims was more than $8 million. Money was transferred to the United Kingdom, Cyprus, Malaysia, China, the United States, Panama, Latvia and the Netherlands Antilles. I analyzed the pattern of the transfers made. First, only three of the shell companies had a bank account in more than one country. Second, through the years, the perpetrators changed their country of banking preference. Third, they did not target British, U.S. or Canadian citizens. Finally, they asked the victims to transfer money into bank accounts located outside their country of residence, which made it more difficult for the local police to investigate.

The Search Continues

At the time of writing, I know the identity of only a few perpetrators, either because they were arrested, tried and sentenced for money laundering, or as a result of my investigations. A case such as this one would benefit from the full support of INTERPOL; however, I was the one, working as a private investigator, trying to facilitate the exchange of information among the authorities.

John Yeung, the Singaporean man operating Sherwood Last's Hong Kong shell company, is the only culprit arrested to date. He was charged with money laundering, pleaded guilty and was sentenced to two years and eight months in prison. Unfortunately, he could not be interviewed or questioned during or after the trial by lawyers representing the victims. His victims from Slovenia who initiated the lawsuit did not receive restitution.

Law enforcement and prosecutors in Panama, Malaysia, the United Kingdom, Austria, Germany, Latvia, South Africa, Norway and the United States are investigating other suspects.

Lessons Learned

The strongest lesson I learned from this case is that humankind is greedy. We are not satisfied with what we have; we want more with no effort. However, these events and others like them have taught me that shortcuts rarely take us to the pot of gold at the end of the rainbow.

As one British law enforcement officer told me, it is easier to run an international criminal enterprise than to fight it. Coordinating the efforts of several local law enforcement authorities is a daunting task.

I also noticed that the fraudsters kept the total amount of money scammed from a single victim to a level that would not make a large manhunt worthwhile. They also made it too complicated for the local police to

(continued)

run an international investigation — the company was incorporated in the British Virgin Islands, it had a bank account in Malaysia and it claimed to be operating from Japan. A good approach to such cases is to collect as many victims as you can find, amass the largest amount of money scammed and make the case appealing for the prosecutors. However, their interest in a case cannot be taken for granted.

Recommendations to Prevent Future Occurrences

Potential financial investors should consider the following points before contributing money to an investment plan.

1. Know the identities of the people you are giving money to. Do sufficient due diligence.
2. Analyze the promises. Do you really believe you can get that return on the investment? How many financial investment firms can reach that performance?
3. Only hard work can build a fortune, unless you join the bad boys' club.
4. If you still want to invest, ask the Securities and Exchange Commission where the company is located and whether it is licensed. The company should have a license in the country in which it *operates*, not in the country in which it was *incorporated.*
5. Do not invest a large percentage of your overall assets. You should diversify your investments to create a balanced portfolio.
6. Search the Internet for client reviews of the investment firm. But beware; they themselves can use the Internet to post excellent, fabricated reviews.

About the Author

Paolo Bourelly, president of International Security Operations Group Inc. (www.isog.org), is a private investigator who specializes in fraud, money laundering and corporate and criminal investigations. He has worked for organizations including Ericsson; the U.S. Navy; and agencies of the United Nations, local governments, banks and corporations. He has taught financial accounting and conducted homicide investigations for the Italian TV show *Second Chance.*

The Broken Nest Egg

DAVID ALAN WHITE

T he anonymity of the Internet and the embarrassment of victims offer shelter to many modern fraudsters. In this case, the victim waited six months to report the crime to his local sheriff's office and was unable to provide accurate information to trace the identity of his offenders. To hide their identities and facilitate the crime, the perpetrators used the names of real and legitimate-sounding fake companies to gain the confidence of the victim, Edwin van Clarke.

The fraudsters initially made contact with van Clarke in November through an e-mail purportedly from Perez and Hamilton Consulting, Ltd., in London. According to the e-mail, the firm was attempting to locate the relatives of a Belgian man who had died a year earlier and had left behind a savings account at Buchwald Bank with $8.37 million in it. According to the e-mail, the deceased and the recipient shared the same surname — van Clarke. The e-mail asked Edwin van Clarke three questions:

1. Are you aware of any relative whose last contact address was in Brussels, Belgium?
2. Who shares a similar name?
3. Whose date of birth on file was July 27, 1932?

Although van Clarke did not respond to the initial e-mail because he was sure it was a case of mistaken identity, the perpetrators were undeterred. They contacted van Clarke nine days later, on December 3. The second e-mail was purportedly from William Smythe, Global Head of Offshore Banking at Buchwald Bank. Smythe identified himself as the bank officer assigned to the account of Moser van Clarke, the deceased. The message and Smythe's title seemed legitimate, so van Clarke conducted an Internet search for a "William Smythe, Global Head of Offshore Banking at Buchwald Bank." He was pleased to discover that there was in fact a person by this name at the Buchwald Bank. Reassured and enticed by the possibility of easy money, van Clarke responded to Smythe's e-mail. Contact between the two continued until December 8.

In his first e-mail — and in a subsequent correspondence — Smythe told van Clarke:

> I do not want you contacting me through my official phone lines nor do I want you contacting me through my official e-mail account as this transaction will not be done under the clock of my employer. Contact will be through my personal numbers and also through this e-mail address, same could apply to you if you wish. My official lines are not secure lines as they are periodically monitored to assess our level of customer care in line with our Total Quality Management Policy. . . . Please observe this instruction religiously. Please again, note that I am a family man, I have a wife and children. I send you this mail not without a measure of doubt as to what the consequences, but I know within me that nothing ventured is nothing gained and that success and riches never come easy or on a platter of gold. This is one truth I have learnt from my private banking clients. Do not betray my confidence.

International Cast of Characters

Van Clarke was uneasy about the prospect of conducting business without the consent or knowledge of the bank, but the amount of money left by Moser van Clarke proved too strong an incentive for him to give up the idea. He strongly suspected that what he and Smythe were doing was probably illegal in some way, but he preferred simply not to think about that. On December 12, Smythe passed off van Clarke to Patrick Rodriguez, who was supposedly from Royal Asset Management. Another Internet search by van Clarke revealed that there was a legitimate company with this name. Rodriguez and Royal Asset Management's role was to "authenticate" van Clarke's claim through documents (driver's license, copy of utility bill, last-known address, deceased's last–known address and the deceased's mother's maiden name) that van Clarke would provide to Rodriguez. Van Clarke sent copies of the required documents by return e-mail.

In addition to Smythe and Rodriguez and the aforementioned companies, the scammers used the fictitious names of four companies and associated bank accounts in Hong Kong; two fictitious companies in Taiwan; and one company in Curacao, Netherland Antilles, as covers for the scam. In addition to Smythe there were eight other individuals used to collect funds supposedly sent to the United Kingdom.

Escalating Transfers   199

A Victim's Shame

Edwin van Clarke was 62 years old at the time Smythe contacted him. He lived with his wife in a single-family home in Naples, Florida, and had two grown children. The van Clarkes also owned a rental property in Naples. Van Clarke was a field supervisor for North Cabinets and was planning to use his portion of the inheritance to supplement his retirement. He later told me that he wanted to surprise his wife with the unexpected income.

Instead of increasing his retirement nest egg, during the next six months van Clarke would lose hundreds of thousands of dollars — without the knowledge of his wife. To be able to send the "required fees" to process the funds, van Clarke took out home equity loans on both his residence and rental property.

I was unable to determine when van Clarke knew he had been scammed. The fraud itself began in November and the last contact van Clarke had with the perpetrators was the next May, six months later. However, van Clarke waited until November — six months after his last contact with the perpetrators — to report the crime to the local sheriff's office. Even then, it was only his wife's insistence that convinced van Clarke to file a report.

What we do know is that on May 26, van Clarke received an e-mail stating:

> Dear Sir,
>
> I have just received a call from my Lawyer in Zurich that William Smythe has been arrested for Money Laundering and the illegal movement of funds from Buchwald Bank.
>
> The picture is still sketchy but he will get back to me.
>
> I tried to reach you but got your voicemail.
>
> Peter Harris.

This was the last contact van Clarke had with any of those involved in the scheme. From beginning to end, it lasted six months and cost van Clarke more than $206,000.

Escalating Transfers

This crime fell into two broad categories. The first was a fraud within a fraud. It was obvious from the start that van Clarke was not related to the deceased in any way and was not entitled to any inheritance — if there was one to be collected. I was working as an investigator at the sheriff's office when van Clarke first reached out to us in November. He readily admitted to me that he believed he was originally involved in a scheme that would net him a 30 percent share of more than $8 million. It was not until later that he came to the conclusion that he was not a participant in the scheme, but was in fact the victim.

The second category that this crime fell into was an advance-fee scheme, but it was different from any I had investigated in the past. From the very beginning, van Clarke was required to wire large up-front or advance fees in order to collect his portion of the inheritance. The other advance-fee schemes I had investigated began with the perpetrators asking the victim to submit small fees, which gradually increased over time, as the victim became more and more entrenched in the scam. The "fraud within a fraud" is the hallmark of many advance-fee swindles. The con intimates (if not states outright) that the proposed arrangement is illegal and is counting on the fact that the victim is willing to break the law. This will decrease the chances that the victim will tell someone else, even a spouse.

Van Clarke e-mailed Rodriquez copies of his Florida driver's license, electricity bill and his mother's maiden name. Two days later, van Clarke received an e-mail stating "Transfer of Title Mandate: Process Conclusion." The alleged purpose of this e-mail was threefold. The first was to congratulate van Clarke for successfully completing the "evaluation and verification process." The second reason was to inform van Clarke that an account had been set up in the Cayman Islands to receive the $8.37 million. The third and actual reason for the e-mail was to request the first of many advance fees from van Clarke; in short, to set the hook.

The first payment that van Clarke made was $18,850 — certainly not a small sum. However, van Clarke was so convinced of Smythe's and Rodriquez's intentions and authenticity that he did not hesitate to wire the $18,850 to the account of Royal Asset Management's bank in Hong Kong on December 15. According to van Clarke, this money was to cover handling, filing and transfer charges.

Two weeks later, van Clarke made a second wire transfer of $20,544.50 from his bank to the account of One Sky International, Ltd., also in Hong Kong. According to van Clarke, this was to cover his 25 percent share of the inheritance tax. It was at this time that van Clarke said he first questioned whether he was involved in a fraud. However, he ignored his doubts and convinced himself that the relationship was legitimate and continued paying the requested fees.

In January, van Clarke wired money to Hong Kong two more times. The first transfer was on January 17 for $15,000 to Fund Mind Investment,

Ltd. The cover story for this fee was that $35,980 was required for an antiterrorist/antidrug-smuggling certificate. Part of this money was to be returned 60 days after the receipt of the inheritance. The remaining $20,980 was to be paid by William Smythe. The second transfer, on January 23 for $8,980, went to the account of Future Lending Contracting Co., Ltd. According to van Clarke, this payment was requested to cover a shortage in funds that William Smythe was supposed to pay for the aforementioned certificate.

It should be noted that these first four transfers were to Hong Kong — not Europe, where the inheritance, banks and attorneys were supposedly located. When I questioned van Clarke about this, his answer was simply "That is where they told me to send the money."

During the early part of February the scheme shifted back to Europe; more specifically, it moved to the United Kingdom. Between February 6 and February 17, van Clarke wired funds nine times to five different people. These were made via Western Union and ranged from $1,000 to $2,200. These smaller payments, according to van Clarke, were to pay for an attorney to prepare and present legal documents to the British High Court to facilitate the transfer of the inheritance.

Reinforced Partnership

At this point in the fraud, van Clarke was told that he would have to fly to Lambeth in the United Kingdom to collect his portion of the inheritance. Although van Clarke believed that he was involved in a scheme to illegally collect an inheritance, he was told — and believed — that there would be a "signing ceremony" when he collected his money.

Shortly before the so-called signing ceremony was to have taken place, van Clarke received an e-mail that the inheritance claim had been suspended. The e-mail was purportedly from a London law firm, the first time it had contacted van Clarke. According to the e-mail, the suspension was due to the fact that the "funds are deemed to be deficient of the mandatory Cost Conversion charge which invariably mandated the termination of the transfer from your account in the central data-base monitoring system in Europe by the European Monetary Institute (EMI)." The e-mail ended with the notice that van Clarke had five days to "resolve this impasse." Regrettably for him, van Clarke believed this gobbledygook.

Again van Clarke was asked to split the fees with William Smythe — Smythe would put up $30,000 and van Clarke would provide $40,000. Van Clarke said that he was convinced of Smythe's legitimacy because Smythe kept sharing the payment of the required fees with him. Of course, there was no Smythe and no sharing, but the victim would only learn of that after he'd been scammed. Van Clarke transferred his share of the funds in February — not to the London law firm demanding payment, but to an account in Hong Kong in the name of Fund Mind Investments, Ltd.

Mounting Fees

Once his $40,000 transfer was complete, van Clarke received an e-mail from someone named Peter Tanner at Royal Asset Management requesting an additional $35,330 to cover a shortage of funds that Smythe was supposed to have paid. Van Clarke became suspicious of the situation and sent an e-mail to William Smythe based on these suspicions:

> William, please forward me a picture of yourself and your driver's license. I have no firm information on anyone I've dealt with these past months and that makes me concerned. I have to date sent funds after funds to different companies and individuals. I am not sure who these players are and am nervous to send additional funds. This last request [$40,000] was to end all payments and now your part of the transaction [$30,000] has disappeared and I am asked to burden the entire payment. I do not do business through e-mail and phone systems alone. I am especially concerned, as I have mentioned before, to have never received any original paperwork or agendas from anyone by: yourself, RAM, Berkely and now Peter Tanner. What guarantee is there that the funds I sent will not get lost and then where am I to get not only the inheritance but legitimate documents? Please send me the license and your picture and I will try to raise the funds Tuesday or Wednesday.

In response to this e-mail, van Clarke received a copy of a passport that appeared to be issued by the United Kingdom in the name of William Smythe. If van Clarke had done an Internet search of the William Smythe at Buchwald Bank, he would have discovered the photograph attached to the passport was not that of the real William Smythe.

Satisfied with Smythe's passport, van Clarke wired an additional $35,300 to Taiwan as requested on March 7. Eight days later, van Clarke received an e-mail from Patrick Rodriguez at Royal Asset Management confirming the receipt of the latest money. In this e-mail Rodriguez informed van Clarke that because there had been a problem with the original transfer of the $35,300 (which should have come from Smythe), the transfer fees had expired and another $8,000 was required to cover the lapsed transfer fees. Two days later, van Clarke wired the $8,000 to a bank in Taiwan.

At the same time van Clarke received an e-mail from Tanner requiring funds be sent to two individuals in the United Kingdom by Western Union. This e-mail stated:

> I apologise for my delay in contacting you, it is due to issues I uncovered at the remittance department.
>
> The Funds are ready for transfer but there is a statutory Wire Fee which you had already paid, but is now due again because the one you paid earlier has a 28-day validity.
>
> I tried to agree with them that you had paid but no wire was effected, but they explained once the 28-day validity elapses the charge must be paid again.
>
> In line with this you are required to immediately effect **TWO WESTERN UNION TRANSFERS FROM TWO DIFFERENT WESTERN UNION AGENTS**. [emphasis in original]

Western Union refused to wire the funds without physical descriptions of the recipients and held the money at their security department. The Western Union representative told van Clarke that frauds were being perpetrated against U.S. citizens and the funds were being sent to the United Kingdom. Van Clarke canceled the Western Union wire transfers and sent an e-mail to Smythe explaining the situation with Western Union. Van Clarke closed his e-mail with "If this is a big hoax I will be a joke, and probably my wife will leave me. I have used the equity in each of my properties." At this point van Clarke had wired more than $168,000 to various individuals.

During the end of March and through April, pressure was applied to van Clarke to provide additional funds. On April 5, van Clarke wired $8,000 into a bank in Curacao. According to e-mails between Smythe and van Clarke, this $8,000 was a portion of a $50,000 kickback to Peter Tanner, who was supposedly working to secure a release of the inheritance. Smythe and van Clarke each agreed to put up $25,000 toward this kickback.

Van Clarke's last large wire transfer, of $17,000, took place on May 1 to cover the remainder of his portion of the kickback. This money, like the previous $8,000, was wired to a bank in Curacao.

On May 17 van Clarke received an e-mail from Rodriguez at Royal Asset Management that provided him with the account information (account number and PIN number) where van Clarke's 30 percent of the inheritance was to be deposited. Between May 18 and May 25, van Clarke sent an additional $7,000, via Western Union, to two individuals to "dispatch a lawyer to see the Swiss Monitoring Team, who have put an embargo on the transfer" (e-mail from Tanner to van Clarke).

The last van Clarke heard from anyone involved in the fraud was on May 26, a day after the last transfer of funds. In an e-mail to van Clarke from Tanner, Tanner stated:

> Dear Sir,
>
> I have just received a call from my Lawyer in Zurich that William Smythe has been arrested for Money Laundering for the illegal movement of funds from Buchwald Bank.
>
> The picture is still sketchy but he will get back to me.
>
> I tried to reach you but got your voicemail.
>
> Peter Tanner

With this e-mail, the fraud against van Clarke came to a close.

An Unsatisfactory End

The investigation into this fraud was initiated six months after van Clarke made his last payment to the perpetrators. This made tracing the wires virtually impossible, even with the assistance of a federal agency, to which my sheriff's office forwarded the report. As the lead investigator on the case, I had access to most of the e-mail communications van Clarke had with the various players in the scheme, but the accounts were dead ends. The funds had been withdrawn and the accounts were closed months ago. In an attempt to establish the perpetrators identities, I contacted their e-mail providers, but they either required no identifying information from their customers, or what they had on file for Smythe, Rodriguez and Tanner was fictitious. I was not able to identify the perpetrators of this crime, which meant I could not recover any of the money van Clarke had sent them. When I last spoke with van Clarke, he was paying more than $1,500 a month on the interest-only loans he took out on his properties to fund the wires he sent overseas.

Van Clarke also told me that his wife was devastated to learn of the inheritance scam and has since taken over control of the family's finances.

Lessons Learned

Individuals need to learn that they cannot blindly trust the messages they receive in their e-mail inboxes. Unfortunately, gullible people are victimized by frauds like this too often. As the quote attributed to P. T. Barnum goes, ``There's a sucker born every minute.''

(continued)

The bigger issue raised by this case is, why would a 62-year-old, responsible, intelligent man like van Clarke become involved in such a scheme in the first place? He was a hardworking man with a family, a home and investment property. The only plausible answer is that he became overcome with greed. During my interviews with him, van Clarke readily admitted that he had no relation to the deceased. It was apparent that he knew that by attempting to gain control of the $8 million, he was violating the law in some fashion.

Unfortunately, van Clarke was unwilling to provide us with a reason for his actions other than he wanted to surprise his wife. I attribute this unwillingness to divulge a more in-depth explanation to the embarrassment that he was experiencing by having to report the crime in the first place and by taking part in the interview. The initial report to law enforcement by van Clarke was done at the insistence of his wife and made six months after his communication with the perpetrators had ceased.

In retrospect, it appears that the major lesson to be learned from this case is that greed can overcome many otherwise honest people.

Recommendations to Prevent Future Occurrences

Unlike frauds that occur in the business environment, where controls and segregation of duties can be implemented, one-on-one Internet-based crimes do not have such protections. There are few and apparently ineffective controls of Internet solicitations to protect individuals like van Clarke. Public awareness is the key to preventing Internet-based frauds. When all is said, this was a classic advance-fee swindle — much the same as the infamous "Nigerian frauds." Indeed, these scammers may well have been Nigerian — we will never know. Law enforcement agencies, with the assistance of the media, should produce public-safety advisories to educate individuals and consumers about the dangers of Internet fraud.

Sadly, education will not stop greed from overcoming common sense. I have investigated cases in which the victim was aware that a particular type of crime was occurring and still fell for the fraud, believing that it could not happen to them. Ultimately, the responsibility lies with individuals to scrutinize investment opportunities before handing over their hard-earned money.

About the Author

David Alan White, PhD, CFE, has been a law enforcement officer for more than 23 years and presently supervises an Economic Crimes Unit for a sheriff's office in Florida. Dr. White holds a bachelor's degree from Western New England College, a master's degree from American International College, a master's degree from Florida Gulf Coast University and a PhD from Northcentral University.

One More Lap to Go

SPYRIDON REPOUSIS

As I looked out my office window one afternoon, I noticed a tall woman walking with self-confidence down the street. Her hair was dark and wavy, and her black eyes were her most distinct feature. She was wearing a white shirt with a blue skirt and blue leather shoes. When she came a little closer, I could see her sun-tanned skin. This was the first time I saw Jane Lamog.

Jane was the proud mother of a 19-year-old and a 16-year-old. Married for 21 years to a quiet and low-profile man, Jane was pleased when she was promoted to branch manager at Meneo Bank in Aloa, Greece, at the age of 40. Before her work at Meneo, Jane was a clerk in the deposits department of another financial institution.

Although Jane had not graduated from college, she was a smart, hard-working individual who had taken the time to learn Meneo's operations. She was an open-minded and well-loved member of upper management and possessed excellent communication skills. She was the heart and soul of staff meetings and was extremely sociable. However, although she was an attractive, persuasive woman, she looked like she was hiding something behind her dark and mysterious eyes.

Jane strived to increase profits for the bank and was accustomed to working until 10 or 11 at night; she had not taken a vacation during her five-year tenure. Obviously, working under such conditions was not healthy. She could become aggressive with clients who were late on loan payments, and she exercised a killer instinct when she saw profit opportunities. Jane instructed her personnel that loans, deposits and withdrawals should first be authorized by her, even though the loans department and deposits department each had a head officer responsible for their own approvals.

Jane promised her clients the best interest rate and profits, saying ''Your money is my money. I handle and invest it with as much care as my own to get the best return at the lowest risk. Plus, you can access your accounts anytime, from anywhere with Internet banking.'' When I heard her motto, I thought of the James Bond film *Casino Royale*, where electronic wireless access was used by perpetrators to launder revenues from criminal activity.

Jane's branch was consistently among Meneo's best performing, and people believed that she was working hard in the bank's interest. Every change she implemented or new product she sold resulted in high profits. Other employees were encouraged to emulate her and live up to the example she set.

Meneo Bank

Meneo Bank was a dynamic financial organization with branches in the Balkan countries and in South Africa. It was founded in 1910 in Greece as a state-owned and state-managed bank. After being privatized in the 1990s, it continuously grew in size, market share, branches, number of employees and services.

After privatization, the company's management developed a strategic plan with the goal of establishing a strong presence in domestic and foreign markets. Following this plan, Meneo Bank acquired a domestic financial institution, Tillicoutry Bank, and took over a controlling interest in Tullibody Bank and Alva Bank.

Meneo Bank's management's plans may have changed a great deal over the years but its basic position remained quite simple: Initiate money transfers from one person to another. One of Meneo's most closely held secrets was the process for electronic money transfers, and management's efforts to introduce electronic home banking — financial services electronically delivered to the home — repeatedly resulted in massive expenditures and market penetration. The company invested heavily in technology. Information and trading messages flew across financial wires and the Internet, and it was getting easier to involve more people in the varied e-trading possibilities. These services were offered through Meneo's network of branches and through electronic banking (Internet, mobile phone, call centers and ATMs).

When I met Jane, Meneo Bank engaged in financial and banking activities as an institution with international presence and had more than 6,000 employees with a network of more than 800 branches.

Billy Lo Needs a Loan?

I worked for Meneo Bank as a credit officer. One rainy May morning, as I was analyzing a credit proposal and the financial statements of a company, I received an e-mail about a loan application that had been submitted by Jane's branch. When I read the e-mail, I said to myself, "We all need money and loans, but even Billy Lo?" Billy Lo was a wealthy, well-known individual in Jane's town, Aloa, and was frequently featured in the local newspapers.

Two weeks before I received the e-mail, I was visiting Aloa for the weekend and I stopped by Jane's branch to withdraw funds from my account. As I was waiting in line, I easily recognized Billy Lo in line behind me because I had seen his photo in newspapers many times. I overheard him saying, "I invested $300,000 with Jane and, as she promised me, I got a 6 percent return in a month." But there I was, faced with an e-mail and loan application for $200,000 supposedly from Billy. I wondered why he needed a loan when he already had plenty of money and assets. What was happening?

While in Jane's branch I had noticed other suspicious activity. She was behaving very strangely and was on the phone the entire time I was there. At one point she was even speaking on three mobile phones simultaneously, which struck me as odd because branch managers are only supposed to have one business cell phone. Jane had four in total.

I decided to start reviewing the deposit and loan accounts Billy held at Jane's branch, which was easy to do because my office computer had access to that information. When I investigated the financial products in which Jane was investing Billy's money, I realized that about 60 percent of it was invested in government bonds and the rest in stocks.

Then I examined the accounts of three other clients who used Jane's wealth-management service and discovered that Jane was investing the majority of their money in short-term government bonds but promising them the higher rates they could get from long-term government bonds. This was the first red flag for me.

The second red flag came from risky securities and returns. Jane was investing about 40 percent of her clients' money in risky stocks, which usually have higher average returns than bonds. But Jane promised her clients, in written statements (I had seen such documents online), higher constant returns regardless of market changes. This was against any financial theory and was too good to be true. It indicated to me that something fraudulent could be taking place.

I also discovered that Jane was investing clients' money in zero-coupon bonds that paid interest to the clients' bank accounts online every six months. But zero-coupon bonds, which are sold at a deep discount and redeemed at face value, do not make coupon payments (meaning they pay no interest) until the bond matures. This was my third red flag.

Another important red flag for me was Jane's way of life. Her known income was not enough to justify her expensive clothes and the lavish gifts she gave to upper management. She took out the auditors in her branch to high-end restaurants for lunches and to nightclubs on the weekends. But the auditors always said that the branch was free of fraud and operated properly. I was also informed that Jane had an affair with a male manager who helped her further her career and had sway with the auditing department.

People in the bank raved about her achievements and high profits in comparison to other branches. But I believed that there was a dark side to Jane and decided to conduct an unannounced, one-week investigation into the branch's accounts.

The Investigation

I phoned James, an old and trustworthy friend from my university who had a company in Aloa. I asked him his opinion about Jane, and if he had heard any rumors about her. James told me, "Although many professionals believe in her because they earn money on their investments, I do not trust Jane. I heard from a friend in a bank that she has a company abroad and works only for her personal interests." I thanked him and continued my investigation.

Jane had gained her clients' confidence because she delivered on her promises, regardless of how unbelievable they were; her customers made money. So clients trusted her to move funds from their deposit accounts, and they changed their investment portfolios based on her advice. Clients signed all the appropriate documents for the investments, and sometimes even signed blank papers that Jane could later complete on her own. She was offering her clients an interest rate twice as high as that paid by Meneo Bank on both sight and time deposits, and she paid the rate to customers in person or even credited to bank accounts in advance! Meneo Bank offered no deposit product that paid interest in advance; such a practice was certainly unusual.

I also noticed that the number of clients who opened accounts at Jane's branch was twice the average for other locations; her interest rates were a sure-fire way to attract new business. After gathering evidence of her abnormal and potentially fraudulent activity, I decided that it was time to talk to Jane. When I asked her about the double interest some of her clients were receiving, she became upset. She said there must have been a mistake and that she would look into it and correct the problem. That same day I presented the red flags and my evidence to upper management, and by the end of the week they had taken decisive action. Their solution was to remove Jane's branch from my jurisdiction.

People believed that Jane was a good person, and she was loved by upper management because her branch was always among the best in sales, profits and bank products. They didn't think she would commit fraud.

Under New Management

Three years later, the possible fraud in Jane's branch was still being ignored. But then it started to reveal itself decisively after a decline in the stock market and an increase in rumors about usury and fraudulent activities between Jane and the mayor of the town.

My new manager said to me, "I know you found important information about Jane Lamog's activities years ago. It would be good if you could cooperate with auditors and have another look." I returned to Jane's branch, where she was very friendly with me and offered to take me to dinner, an invitation I declined.

During my investigation, I received calls from clients who wanted to check the balance of their online accounts and asked to withdraw their money, but there were no records of many of these customers in the bank's electronic system. I asked them to bring any documentation they had to the branch; all had documents written by Jane declaring the amount they had invested and promising a 6–7 percent return. These were not produced from the official operating system, but from Microsoft Word.

In the end, I realized that Jane was pocketing the money that clients deposited without recording it to the Internet banking system. With this money she paid double interest to other clients. She was keeping separate books in her office, which I found with the help of Vicky, an internal auditor working on the investigation with me. With money from everyday and new depositors, she paid old depositors, creating a classic Ponzi scheme. But Jane had run out of money to pay her clients.

When the new deposits were not enough to pay interest or fulfill the withdrawal needs of clients, she took advantage of the online banking system to take money from one account to pay another: a lapping scheme. I interviewed John Bosackle, who was responsible for the deposits department and had been hired by Jane. He said that Jane always tried to persuade clients not to withdraw their deposits, but instead to capitalize them to avoid payouts. She also began offering more than double returns to keep clients from withdrawing funds. Her customers remained happy until the collapse.

Some clients told me they entrusted their funds to Jane completely because she told them to. She told them they were valued and respected customers who did not need to wait in line at the bank. Clients appreciated that they avoided lines and had more time to do other business.

John Bosackle also told me that Jane instructed the tellers what to do and how much money to credit to accounts. Bosackle, a 28-year-old man with a low profile and no opinion on what occurred in branch, worked as a clerk and did not consider himself to be responsible for protecting the bank's interests. I told him he was wrong and would have problems as a result.

Phishing for PINs

As the scheme grew, it became more difficult to redirect money to cover returns and withdrawals. I understood the crux of the fraud when clients showed me e-mails they had received from the bank. Jane had gained unauthorized access to clients' online bank accounts through the electronic banking system. She had fraudulently discovered personal identification numbers (PINs) of some clients by sending them e-mails that appeared to come from Meneo but were in fact well-crafted phishing e-mails. They told customers there was an error in the online system, and the bank had assigned them temporary PINs. To reset their PINs, they had to respond to Jane's fake e-mail with a new PIN. When clients changed their PINs, they gave Jane access to their bank accounts. I also saw e-mails that clients had received, directing them to a fake Web site that looked exactly like Meneo Bank's Web site.

By acquiring passwords and unauthorized access to about 25 accounts, Jane transferred funds from clients' accounts to her offshore company. Half of the money was sent through SWIFT (an electronic-payment system) to the Isle of Man, where Jane's offshore company was located.

The other half of the money was used to cover withdrawals and usury. The investigation showed that Jane was crediting sight-deposit accounts by providing loans to six clients through the Internet banking function and charging a monthly interest rate of 13–14 percent, which constituted usury. Most deposit clients told me that Jane was offering a 6–7 percent annual interest rate on new deposits — double the market rate and that offered by other financial institutions. However, at the same time she was charging for loans on the black market.

Prepaid Cards, Politics and Arson

I also discovered fraud with prepaid cards. Following the money flows, I found that Jane was accessing clients' online accounts to transfer their funds to her prepaid cards. The cards are multifunction cards that many clients use to replace several separate credit cards, and are supposedly very secure. Jane credited prepaid cards that she had at Meneo Bank and at other banks with funds from her clients' accounts. She benefited from fast online transactions to transfer money abroad and purchase luxury goods online.

Even the mayor of the town was involved in the usury and unauthorized use of money from loans. We discovered borrowing issued to the town but we could not trace how the funds were used. And not coincidentally, the loans were given by Jane's branch. Separately, the mayor blackmailed businessmen for loans and also to sell their assets to the offshore company in the Isle of Man.

An audit committee scheduled an examination of the town's economic department, but three days before the audit, a man was arrested during the night for trying to set fire to the finance department. The would-be arsonist confessed to sending gasoline and explosives through a mail courier to the manager of the finance department. He even procured keys to the offices so he could sneak in at night, set fire to the delivered parcel and destroyed the evidence he knew the audit team was looking for. Luckily, this scheme was intercepted by the police.

The Outcome of the Investigation

The mayor resigned, was arrested for usury and was sent to prison with many other fraudsters, but due to political interventions on his behalf, he was released before his trial. The trial was later canceled. Other trials associated with the case are still ongoing. The person who tried to burn the town's finance department was sent to prison for five years.

Jane Lamog and John Bosackle were arrested for usury, money laundering, bribery, fraud, theft and blackmail. Bosackle's parents sold all their assets to pay restitution for the fraud and keep their son out of prison, but to no avail. Bosackle was sentenced to five years in prison. Jane is still free, thanks to political interventions, and is awaiting trial although it has been several years since her arrest. Jane's fraud lasted for five years, and the final loss was $60 million. In the end, the bank repaid most of the clients' losses.

After this occurrence, Meneo Bank began requiring all branch managers to sign a document every three months that certifies that all procedures are being followed and that no fraud is taking place. These certifications essentially require branch managers to take personal responsibility for the operations of their branches and prevent them from delegating this responsibility to their subordinates and then claiming ignorance when fraud is uncovered.

The bank also improved measures to protect PINs, reduced the amount of money that an individual may withdraw daily from ATMs and online and released a statement warning customers not to reply to e-mails they receive claiming to be sent by the bank.

Lessons Learned

I learned that unauthorized access to bank accounts is a more dangerous and prevalent threat to clients than I previously thought, and that it needs to be fixed. Unfortunately, the bank learned the hard way — a $60-million loss. I also learned that no single employee should be granted exclusive trust, regardless of the profits he or she produces. On the contrary, high abnormal profits, above and beyond the average, are a red flag that upper management should take into account. I now have a greater appreciation of how important it is to investigate and audit complicated Internet fraud and maintain the chain of custody for all evidence gathered.

Recommendations to Prevent Future Occurrences

Based on the lessons learned, I made the following recommendations to my company. Most of them were adopted.

ENCRYPTION AND EXTRA PINs

- Use encryption for all Internet transactions, both secret-key/symmetric encryption and public-key/asymmetric encryption.
- Require that digital signatures be submitted with public-key cryptography, such as an RSA algorithm (so named after its founders, Rivest, Shamir and Adleman) or a digital signature standard algorithm. This will ensure the integrity and authenticity of the signature.
- Decrease the daily withdrawal limit online and from ATMs.
- Send text messages or e-mails to clients when money is withdrawn from their accounts.
- Use second PINs with a duration life of five minutes when conducting online transactions worth more than $500.

EMPLOYEE AWARENESS

- Enact a whistleblower policy with an anonymous hotline.
- Encourage employees to trust their instincts and report suspicious behavior.
- Conduct an independent assessment of employees' duties. Those with significant responsibilities should be evaluated by someone other than their immediate supervisor.
- Conduct employee-awareness training. Banks can implement a number of prevention tools and programs to combat Internet fraud, but if employees are unaware of them or don't know how to use them, the desired outcome will not be achieved.
- Train employees to recognize investment swindles, especially Ponzi schemes.
- Require job rotation to avoid unusually close association with clients.
- Look for employees and managers living beyond their means.
- Enforce standard days off. All employees should have their normal vacations and be replaced by other employees during that time.
- Train management to recognize fraud schemes.
- Train employees to notice and understand unlawful behavior.

AUDITING AND MONITORING

- Segregate duties.
- Pay more attention to tips or complaints from any employee or client — they are the most common means of detection.
- Conduct surprise audits.

CLIENTS

- Never reveal passwords to others.
- Don't trust anyone to help with your PIN or with electronic access to bank accounts.

(continued)

FRAUD EXAMINERS AND COMPUTER FRAUD TEAMS

- A good way to prevent Internet fraud is to operate a separate, independent computer fraud team that can conduct checks for unusual and unauthorized computer access (abnormal time, date, many attempts to get access through e-banking and Internet, etc.). The team should work independently and submit reports only to the board of directors.

About the Author

Spyridon Repousis, CFE, has an MS in Banking and Finance and is a senior credit officer in a private bank. Mr. Repousis has written seven books about banking, credit policy and finance and has worked in the banking sector for 13 years. He is a PhD candidate and has taught for 10 years as a part-time lecturer at the Technological Educational Institute (a state-owned, higher-educational institute) in Greece.

CHAPTER

Death and Taxes

GAY STEBBINS

James Snyder grew up in Humboldt Park, a crime-infested area of Chicago. He dropped out of high school at age 15 and began a life of crime, alcoholism and penury. Snyder married his girlfriend, Ann, at an early age and they had four children. A few years later, James divorced Ann and went into treatment for alcoholism and drug addiction. While in rehab he met Shelia, and within a year the two married. It was James's second marriage and Shelia's first. Five years later, Snyder, Shelia and their two young children moved to North Carolina to begin a new life, and Snyder's contact with his first wife and their four children diminished. Snyder moved his family into a paltry home in northeast Charlotte, another neighborhood known for crime and poverty.

James found it difficult to land a job in Charlotte that paid well because he had no real skills. He had not had steady work before and had made money in Chicago doing odd jobs. In North Carolina, he applied for and received welfare payments, but they were not sufficient to cover his and his family's cost of living. Financial need led James to seek out other means of support. His lack of education and simplistic lifestyle would not have made him a suspect in an elaborate Internet fraud scheme.

The Tax Man Cometh

The Internal Revenue Service's Processing Center routinely searched filed tax returns for fraud using various detection methods. The IRS processors had seen countless variations of tax scams, but they knew that fraudsters constantly thought up new schemes to try to cheat Uncle Sam. It became apparent through daily scans conducted by the Electronic Fraud Detection System that in one particular case, a vast number of tax returns were linked together by similar names, addresses, wages, withholding, refund amounts, IP addresses and bank routing numbers. Through the initial investigative inquiries, the processors determined that most of the tax returns had the commonality of claiming only Schedule C income with no expenses, dead dependents and the Earned Income Tax Credit (EITC). Schedule Cs are filed by small-business owners or self-employed individuals. Some of the other reviewed tax returns were filed with false W-2s that reflected inflated wages and withholdings. Many of the filers in the scheme turned out to be deceased with similar last names to the dependents listed on the returns; however, the Social Security Administration showed that none of them were related by blood or marriage.

The Name Game

The case was forwarded to the IRS's Criminal Investigation Division, and I was assigned as the lead investigator. After putting together an investigation team, including a computer forensics specialist, I went to the immediate task of identifying the perpetrator. I followed the money trail to find the bank accounts where the tax refunds were directly deposited. There were hundreds of them at financial institutions across the United States and they were in the names of many different people. But one name seemed to come up more frequently than any other — James Snyder.

The most significant connections that my investigation team discovered were the IP addresses from which the majority of the falsified income tax returns were filed. A summons was issued to the Internet service providers (ISP) that maintained the IP addresses. We learned that many of the returns were filed at a computer lab at the Charlotte employment services agency. I called them for more information and was sent a copy of a sign-in sheet they kept for people using the computer lab. The log showed the date and time that each individual used the computer. James's name was on the list for the dates and times the questionable returns were electronically filed.

Code Violations

Under Internal Revenue Code Section 32(a), the Earned Income Tax Credit is determined as an amount equal to the credit percentage of the taxpayer's earned income for the taxable year. The code further defines *earned income* as wages, salaries, tips and other employee compensation, plus the taxpayer's net earnings from self-employment for the taxable year. Snyder used false W-2s when he first started the scheme, but stopped quickly because he realized they could be verified. Instead, Snyder began claiming self-employment income, which he figured could not be confirmed by the IRS. By reporting only self-employment income on a Schedule C form with no expenses, Snyder was able to raise his claimed income to the limit that allowed him the maximum Earned Income Tax Credit, approximately $4,500 per tax return. We had yet to determine how many returns he filed, so we didn't know how much he netted.

Before filing the returns, James needed to open bank accounts into which the money would be directly deposited. Oddly, though, we discovered many returns that were deposited to accounts in other people's names. My team filed a summons for bank records and, after further investigation, I determined that most of the account holders were his family members. Many of them were located in Chicago, where James grew up and where his children from his previous marriage still lived.

It became apparent that James was filing fraudulent returns even after we started the investigation, so I began conducting weekly "trash runs" to look for active evidence. Trash runs involved going to James's house and discreetly picking up the garbage left on the curb. I would then take it to a facility where I could carefully search it for evidence. After a few weeks, my dirty work paid off. I discovered lists of names, Social Security numbers and bank account numbers that he used on the tax returns. These lists, combined with the other evidence my team had already obtained, was enough probable cause to get a search warrant on James's house signed by a judge.

When we executed the search warrant at James Snyder's home, he voluntarily opened the door and invited us in when we arrived — search warrant in hand — at 7:00 in the morning. After I identified myself as a special agent with the IRS, his response was, "I was waiting for you to come."

What's in a Name?

While the other special agents did a thorough search of the residence, I interviewed James. I informed him of his right to remain silent and said that he could choose to not answer questions until he had consulted an attorney. But James insisted he was ready to talk and confessed to filing the falsified tax returns. He did not try to cover up or make excuses for his behavior. Instead, he said he knew he was playing a game with the IRS and it was just a matter of time until we caught him.

When I asked James why he filed the fraudulent tax returns, he said he did it because it was easy. He started the scam by filing false returns for himself and his children by using fake W-2s. He picked up blank W-2 forms at the employment agency he worked with and filled them in himself. He obtained valid Employer Identification Numbers (EINs) from the W-2s of friends and relatives who had legitimate employment.

James then learned that if he added dependents to his fake returns, he could qualify for a bigger refund with the EITC. He told me that after a few failed brainstorming attempts, he hit on a way to find dependent information — searching the Internet for Social Security numbers of deceased individuals. He would look for deceased people with his last name, for example Patty Snyder, in hopes that the IRS processor would not question the legitimacy of dependents if they shared his surname. He assumed the fact that they were dead would slip by unnoticed. Nonetheless, he told me he was pleasantly surprised when the first returns with dependents were processed without a hitch and he received the tax refunds. I could not believe how easy it was for James to find Social Security numbers online, but he showed me that the information was readily available on Web sites that helped people who were looking for their ancestors.

Because he had no trouble obtaining refunds using Social Security numbers of deceased "dependents," James started using their identities as the primary and secondary taxpayers on returns as well.

James only used names that were similar to his or his friends and relatives so he could set up bank accounts in their names. He used many relatives, including his own children, parents, mother-in-law, cousins and ex-wife. He would have his fraudulent refunds deposited into the accounts, and then he could withdraw the money at his leisure. For example, James had a cousin named Jean Dudley. He asked her if he could help her open a bank account, and in return she provided him with the account information. Then he went to www.roots.com or www.ancestry.com and found the Social Security number of a deceased woman by the name of Jeanetta Dudley. Snyder used this information to file a fraudulent W-2 and claimed two dependency exemptions using other deceased Dudleys he found online. It did not matter that none of these individuals were related or alive. The refund for Jeanetta Dudley was electronically deposited into the bank account of Jean Dudley, and because of the similarities between the names, the bank was not suspicious.

James explained to me that his scheme primarily involved the use of the Internet. Almost everything he needed to perform his crime was at his disposal while sitting in front of a computer. He prepared the false tax returns online and filed them electronically. His final step was to enter the bank account information at the bottom of the tax return, because James used the direct-deposit option on each of his false tax returns. The IRS only allowed five tax refunds into one bank account; that was why he set up multiple bank accounts using relatives and friends.

James stated in the interview that the relatives and friends who held the bank accounts had no knowledge of the Internet scheme, and he primarily used relatives under the age of 18. He told them that he wanted to help them build credit and would drive them to the bank and guide them through the process of setting up a checking account. Once he had the account information, he took over from there.

Family Bond

Snyder's relatives in Chicago were interviewed, including his children, who said they rarely saw their father but that he came to Chicago several times to help them set up bank accounts. We showed the children copies of tax returns filed in their names and they said they had no knowledge of them. This was in line with what James had told me in his interview. His only contact with his relatives was helping set up their bank accounts.

Once James had his family's bank account information, he was able to control the money flow. He used ATMs and debit cards to spend the money. It was not readily apparent how he squandered his ill-gotten gain, but through our search of his home and interviews of friends and family, we ascertained that James spent a considerable amount of time at local casinos.

James also set up accounts in his mother's name; numerous refunds were deposited into them. When I visited her house in Chicago to conduct an interview, she refused to answer my questions. We were not able to gather enough evidence to prove her culpability.

Another bank account holder was a mentally disabled woman who lived on the same street in Charlotte as Snyder. He set up several accounts in her name by driving her to various local banks and showing her how to fill out the necessary paperwork, which clearly demonstrated a lack of due diligence on the banks' part. We identified another account holder in Seattle, Washington, so I made the trip out to meet her; she readily gave me information in the interview. She had been his girlfriend years ago and told me James had asked her for her bank account information so he could deposit money into it. When I asked her why he wanted to give her money, she said she "met his needs." I asked if she knew the source of the funds James deposited into her bank account, and she said she did not, so I showed her copies of the tax returns. They had the names of deceased individuals, but the account number used for the direct deposit was hers. I also showed her corresponding bank statements that listed a number of tax refunds directly deposited into her account by the IRS. I asked her why she didn't notice that the deposits were from the IRS and not James. Her answer was that she stopped looking at her bank statements years ago. She also told me that she only received part of the money, because James had access to her account and took out some. She did not know what he did with his portion.

Have a Cookie

The more relevant evidence obtained with the search warrant included personal computers, to which James had saved the results of his searches for deceased individuals' names, Social Security numbers and dates of birth. Our computer forensic specialist searched the computers and gave us the cookie file list from each. The lists showed Snyder's visits to Web sites such as www.ancestralfindings.com, www.MyTrees.com, www.ancestry.com and www.RootsWeb.com. I conducted a few searches of my own on these Web sites and was astonished at how easy it was to uncover identifying information for real, deceased people.

The computer forensic specialist was also able to show James pulling facts from Web sites and entering the exact same information on fraudulent tax returns. Moreover, evidence was uncovered of bank accounts used in the filing of the false claims, including enrollment for online banking.

We seized various handwritten documents, the most compelling of which was a purple spiral notebook. In it we found lists of the identities used on fraudulent returns, their dependency exemptions, birth dates, routing transit number (RTN) and bank account number where the refund was to be deposited — written in James's handwriting. A handwriting exemplar showed the handwriting in the seized notebook had "excellent similarities" to the handwriting taken in a sample James provided.

A Rose by Any Other Name . . .

James filed the fraudulent tax returns electronically, and many were traced to the IP addresses of his two home computers. Most of the other fraudulent tax returns were linked to IP addresses owned by local public libraries. Evidence of Internet use sign-in sheets tied James to the libraries' computers at the time the false claims were electronically filed.

Because James had a fairly common name, it was not difficult to find matches of deceased individuals with his name. He filed many tax returns using the name of "James Snyder" or "Jim Snyder." He used the matching Social Security number and date of birth for the name, both of which he obtained on public Web sites. The returns quickly went through, and he was pleased to have found another easy way to get fast cash.

We could not determine the exact number of returns prepared by James because we estimated that the IRS only intercepted a small percentage of his false claims and we probably did not locate each bank account he used. However, we did discover hundreds of false returns totaling more than $500,000. James also filed fraudulent state tax returns.

Although most of the victims of his fraud were dead, his crimes did have an effect on living victims. I met one woman who went through emotional turmoil after receiving a letter from the IRS regarding the tax return her deceased husband supposedly filed. The letter requested that her husband submit an amended return because there was an error on his. The woman's husband had passed away years ago, and she was understandably disturbed by the letter. I reviewed the return and saw that James had used the woman's husband as the primary taxpayer on a falsified return. He also added other deceased identities as a secondary taxpayer and dependency exemptions.

During my investigation I also met Lana Smith, a taxpayer in Oregon who went into the local Taxpayer Service Help Desk to find out why her daughter — who had died five months earlier — was being claimed as a dependent on a stranger's return. Ms. Smith was entitled to claim her daughter as a dependent for the prior year, but the IRS denied it because another person had already claimed her. The return was referred to the IRS's Fraud Detection Center, where it was linked to the Internet refund scheme I had been investigating. We discovered it was filed using the same IP address as many of James's other filings.

Paying the Piper

Although Snyder was the only person prosecuted in this case, we presumed that many of the adult relatives and other individuals who held bank accounts were aware of the fraud, at least to some degree. In particular, we thought one of his daughters was involved because a large percentage of refunds were deposited into her bank accounts. She had four accounts set up in her name, and each one had multiple refunds electronically deposited into it. She withdrew and spent the money herself. When I interviewed her, she firmly denied knowledge of the false claims. When I asked where she thought the money came from, her response was "My father put the money there for me." Despite our strong suspicions about her, the evidence against James was more convincing and as part of his plea bargain his daughter was not charged.

James was charged with false claims and identity fraud under Title 18, U.S.C., Sections 287 and 1028, respectively. He entered a guilty plea to the charge of false claims and was sentenced to prison for three years. The Assistant U.S. Attorney (AUSA) prosecuting the case told me that he had not seen a more complicated case of tax fraud using the Internet. The AUSA thought someone else must have helped James devise his plan because it was so complex, but I disagreed. Although he lacked education and was a seemingly inexperienced man with few notable skills, I believed he acted on his own and was able to find the resources he needed through the Internet.

Lessons Learned

This case taught me that a person with no education and little technical skill can navigate his way through the Internet to obtain readily available information and commit what seems to be a complicated fraud. James was able to execute his scheme because it was so easy for him to commit identity fraud online.

I think Web sites that provide sensitive personal information, whether for living or deceased individuals, should implement stricter security controls. James proved that anyone can go online and easily pose as someone else.

I was surprised to learn that James Snyder was able to accompany minors and his mentally handicapped neighbor to banks and establish accounts in their names. Stronger due diligence measures on the part of financial institutions could have eliminated some of the conduits James used in this scheme.

Stronger checks into the identities of tax return filers could also have brought this case to light earlier and reduced the losses. A system of verification checks based on Social Security numbers may have been able to reveal that some of the claims submitted were filed in the names of those who had already died. Finally, if the IRS did not readily detect false claims from a fraudulent tax return filed under the Social Security number of a deceased individual, what other fraudulent uses of a deceased person's identifying information are there?

About the Author

Gay Stebbins, CFE, is a retired special agent of the Internal Revenue Service's Criminal Investigation Division.

CHAPTER

Keeping It All in the Family

DAVID PETTERSON

Michael Flanders was 26 years old when he started working as the chief financial officer (CFO) for Condor Construction. This was the first sole-charge position the young accountant had held in his fledgling career, but he felt he was ready for it.

No one could accuse Michael of a lack of confidence. His good looks, natural charm and charismatic appeal endeared him to all he met. Michael was the person his younger brother, Daniel, most respected and from whom Daniel fashioned his own academic and professional aspirations. Together the two brothers were viewed as markers of success for their hard-working parents, Cynthia and George Flanders. Their sons were destined to be successful family men, men they would always be proud of. Pride was a foundation of the Flanders household.

When Michael first interviewed for the CFO position with Condor Corporation, he made no secret of his wish to succeed in both his personal life and his career. His parents had a small hardware store that both he and Daniel had worked in during their school vacations. Michael, while respecting his father's achievement of owning his own business, saw the store as well below the level of achievement that he wanted for his own life.

The Rise of Condor

Indeed Michael told Alan Campbell, the president and founder of Condor, that "I plan to be a millionaire by the time I'm 35 and, while that means I will have to work even harder than my father did, I know I can do it and I know I can succeed." Campbell was impressed by the young man. Himself a self-made millionaire, Campbell took pride in identifying "self-starters; people who can get up and go; people I can rely on, trust and work with. My sort of people."

The only nervousness that Campbell had about the young man was that although he was enthusiastic, he was relatively inexperienced. He did not want Condor to be the training ground for someone to "just get up to speed and then move on, leaving me with a critical gap in my management team just when we get to our business peak." However, when Michael announced that he was recently engaged to his childhood sweetheart and was looking for a long-term position upon which he could build a future and provide for a family, Campbell's concerns melted away.

Michael Flanders joined the management team of Condor Construction as its new CFO 10 days later. He inherited a mess. A certified public accountant (CPA) had been assisting the company on a part-time basis since the previous CFO resigned almost three months earlier. That position started out as a caretaker role "just for a couple of weeks while we find a new person" but continued on an ad-hoc basis for three months as the business juggernaut that was Condor went about its ever-expanding enterprise — and expanding it was.

Campbell had been approached by an English property finance company eager to capitalize on Condor's U.S. success. With the promise of "all the funding you need" Campbell paid scant attention to the finance function as he went about securing the funding deal of a lifetime. In the five years since starting business in the United States, Condor had grown from a team of four people to ten specialists, including Flanders. Sales of finished condominiums had just topped $120 million. Campbell saw the opportunity to do twice, maybe three times, the amount of business he was doing at present. The money would really flow!

Two weeks after he started, Michael was working late when Campbell came over and sat down at his desk. Over a couple of glasses of Jack Daniels, Campbell told the young man of his plans for the company and how, if he carried on the way he had started, that there was "a piece of this in it for you. What I will need," said Campbell, "is a fairly creative tax structure to deal with the profits that we will be making. I want to plan for that now so we are ready to go when the money rolls in. There will be a significant bonus in this for you if things go well." "You can rely on me," replied Michael, "I will treat your money as if it were my own." And, true to his word, he did.

Double Trouble

From the time that Michael Flanders commenced employment with Condor Construction, organized chaos — as Alan Campbell once described it — had degenerated to out-and-out bedlam. In addition to trying to come to grips with the business of the company and trying to catch up with the work that was left incomplete by the external CPA, the number of new projects the company was undertaking as active developments had doubled. Michael felt himself being dragged down by the ever-increasing workload. Fourteen-hour days and late nights had become the norm. The fun of the job had developed into the daily grind. To make matters worse, two further development sites had been purchased because "they were such a good buy," according to Campbell. There were no firm plans in place yet to develop these two properties.

The young CFO needed help and he knew it. However, he did not want the CPA back. That would have been a significant blow to both his ego and his pride. He just wanted someone who could work with him — *for* him really — a person he could trust to not question his judgment and decisions; someone like his brother Daniel.

Daniel Flanders was even less experienced than his older brother and he did not have Michael's creative flair. However, what he lacked in style he more than made up for in organizational skills. Determined, methodical and pedantically meticulous, he was everything that Michael was not and none of what Michael was. In short, the two brothers complemented each other perfectly.

When Michael first floated the idea of hiring his brother, it was met with firm rejection by Condor's CEO. Nathan Collingwood wanted an independent, externally recruited person and did not like the idea of siblings working together in any part of the company, and especially not in the finance department. However, even after Collingwood expressed his concerns to Alan Campbell about Michael's proposition, Campbell agreed to the hire; albeit on a short-term basis, "until the current mess gets sorted," said the boss.

"Michael went and talked to Alan privately about the hire one afternoon, and the next day Alan told me we would be taking Daniel on for six months or so," Collingwood said. "I don't know what they talked about, but nothing I said to Alan about it seemed to make any difference. Condor was his company; in the end the decision was his. So, 14 months after Michael joined Condor, we had the two Flanders brothers working for us."

Skirting Controls

With all of the development work underway, not to mention the two "stock" properties, it seemed to Campbell that every week Michael was coming to him looking for more money for one thing or another. In addition, the construction company that Campbell had contracted to build three of the four current developments was running into delays and their quality of work was dropping. If it continued, Campbell would not meet the standards required to achieve the market premiums that he thought the projects were capable of. Campbell realized that "more human resources are needed to get things back on track and we need it now." To address the needs, Campbell brought in contractors who had worked for his old UK firm. This required the establishment of offshore payments and wire transfer arrangements with Condor's bank, Belford First National.

Belford already had very firm instructions from Campbell regarding drawing on the group checking accounts. There were only four approved signatories and any two of these were required on all checks that were cut. For reasons of internal control the CFO was not one of the signatories. When it came to wire transfers, a tighter regime was put in place. Campbell insisted that he personally sign all wire authorizations and that the bank had to orally confirm the instruction with him before any wire transfers were actioned. With these controls in place, Campbell felt assured that no money would leave the group accounts without his knowledge or the agreement of approved persons.

The problem with Campbell's check controls came from the increased workload — often all four signatories would be out of the office at project sites when payments needed to be made. Within two weeks of his commencement as CFO, Michael was harassing the signatories to come back to the office to sign checks to meet various project and office expenses. Eventually, it became the practice to have three or four checks signed in blank and held in Michael's office safe, to cover "emergency payments."

A Discrete Tip

Alan Campbell was in England completing a week of meetings with his British joint venture partners when Condor's CEO, Collingwood, telephoned to say that he had received a disturbing call from Jeff Segar, the Security and Systems Compliance Manager at Sinclair Savings and Loan. Segar had told him that several large deposits had been made through the Internet banking function to one of Sinclair's customer's accounts. Segar told Collingwood the deposits had originated from accounts linked to the Condor Group at Belford First National.

Sinclair's anti-money-laundering software had flagged the transactions as suspicious because the sums transferred were then withdrawn by check from the Sinclair account the following day. Pressed on the matter, Segar told Collingwood that it was prudent for Collingwood to review the group's bank accounts for electronic withdrawals and to verify that each of these was made with proper authority. "I can't tell you whose account it's going into but I will tell you that we cannot see a reason why sums like this would be coming out of your accounts and going to this person's account."

Knowing that Campbell would ask, Collingwood pressed on with his questions of Segar and suggested the names of a couple of Condor's staff. "Like I said," said Segar, "I can't tell you whose account it is as that would breach privacy, but you might not want to talk to the people you just mentioned until you have made other discrete inquiries." The people Collingwood had suggested were Michael Flanders and Robert Petrino, the contracts and construction manager.

The Call for Help

It was 2:00 PM in San Francisco when Nathan Collingwood hung up with Alan Campbell. Collingwood was furious. Once before a contracts manager had "looked after himself" at the expense of the company and history, it seemed, was about to repeat itself. There was little that could be done in the way of making inquiries, subtly at least, until the staff went home for the day. Even then he had no idea where to start. Leaving the office, he walked down the quiet service alley that ran to the adjacent parking lot. Upon reaching his car — hot and stuffy after being closed up all day in the hot sun — he pulled out his cell phone and called Julia Meyers at Stern, Katz, Meyers LLP.

Meyers agreed to see Collingwood immediately once she became aware of the nature of the advice he was seeking. A junior partner in the profitable law firm (the Meyers in the firm's name came from her near-retirement uncle), Julia had earlier in her career worked in the District Attorney's (DA) office and had prosecuted her share of corporate fraudsters. In the 40 minutes it took Collingwood to drive to the Beachwood Boulevard office, Meyers had put together a must-do priority list and sketched out an action plan for Collingwood to follow. She had also alerted a private investigator that a client may need some urgent assistance and had contacted me, a Certified Fraud Examiner(CFE), to let me know she might need my services on the case. By the time Collingwood arrived at the law firm, the wheels had begun to turn in what would be a testing and consuming investigation.

Bottled water in hand, Meyers took Collingwood through her suggested approach. She reminded him that at present there was only a suspicion that funds may have been embezzled and until there was something more concrete than an unconfirmed telephone conversation with a "name no one" bank officer, that Collingwood should keep the information he had received to himself. Her composure reassured Collingwood as she mapped out the strategy.

Collingwood returned to Condor's office just before the end of the day. Robert Petrino had left for the day and would not be in until mid-morning tomorrow. As was his practice, Petrino called into jobsites at the start and the end of each day, which left him time to complete the paperwork side of his job during the middle of the day. As luck would have it, both Michael and Daniel Flanders had joined a new gym earlier in the week and that night was their second training session. By 5:20 PM the office was silent and, apart from Collingwood, empty.

Snooping Around

The first part of the plan was to look at the bank statements for the dates indicated by Jeff Segar from Sinclair Savings and Loan. It took Nathan almost an hour to find the bank statements because they were out of order in the files and not where he had expected them to be. Frustrated, he pulled together all the statements he could find, regardless of their corresponding accounts, and headed into the boardroom, one of only two private meeting rooms on the floor leased by the company. He was still missing some pages as he organized them into account order on the boardroom table. Small bundles of paid checks were attached to some of the statements, but some statements had none at all.

With all of the statements that he could find set out before him, he flicked through the piles of paper until he came to the most recent. "I saw them immediately. On the first account there were four transactions, all electronic debits. They totaled over $78,000. Two transactions, each for $25,000 were in the week preceding the call from Segar. As I scanned other group accounts for the same month I saw lots of transfers between the various bank accounts; movements in and out. So much activity was going through the bank accounts when I would have expected very little; something was wrong."

Collingwood worked through the bank statements and scheduled out just over $250,000 of transfers to Sinclair Savings and Loan. There were more pages missing than he had first realized. It was nearly midnight when he decided to call it quits for the night. He was tired, loaded up with coffee and had decided that he was getting nowhere. As he tidied up the last of the piles of bank statements before he left the room, he saw it: a canceled check. It was signed by himself and Robert Petrino. It was made out for the sum of $20,000 to Daniel Flanders. With a rush of adrenaline, fueled by caffeine, Collingwood examined the check over and over. He looked at the date; almost six months ago. He did not remember any payments being authorized for Daniel Flanders for $20,000. Daniel had barely started then. No, this was wrong. Locking the office, and despite the hour, he called Julia Meyers on her cell phone.

To his surprise Julia answered almost immediately. She had been waiting for some report on his snooping around, and while it was later than she expected, she was eager to hear what had been discovered. After listening without interruption to Collingwood's report, Julia suggested they move to the next step in the plan; to confront the suspected offenders and seek an explanation. Collingwood expressed his opinion that he considered Robert Petrino was in the clear, but Michael and Daniel Flanders had some explaining to do. They agreed that Julia would visit the Condor offices first thing in the morning and the two accountants would be interviewed. Julia would also alert the private investigator and me, in the capacity of a CFE, about the case's developments.

When Michael and Daniel Flanders arrived at work at their customary 7:50 AM, they were mildly surprised to see that Collingwood was already in. The two accountants, whose work area was directly across the office from the boardroom, were rather amused. Collingwood, in contrast to them, rarely arrived in the office before 9:00 AM. It was a point of some discontent, more with Michael than Daniel, that Collingwood was paid so much but seemed to do so little. They had often discussed that between Robert Petrino and Nathan Collingwood it was a toss-up as to who did the least amount of work.

Julia Meyers entered the reception-less offices of Condor Construction just after 9:00 AM and went straight to the boardroom. Reluctant to confirm Collingwood's view that Daniel Flanders was embezzling from the company, she agreed to a range of questions that would be put to the Flanders brothers. It took another two and a half hours before Julia was satisfied that the drafted questions sufficiently covered the concerns raised by the suspicious transactions. They agreed that the interviews would commence at 2:00 PM, when the accountants returned from their lunch break.

The Confrontation

It was not unusual for Michael Flanders to be called into boardroom meetings. Since starting at Condor he was often involved — too late in his opinion — in discussing new projects, capital-raising issues and tax implications of various proposals. The invitation to join Julia Meyers and Nathan Collingwood at 2:15 PM was clearly another such meeting. He picked up his leather-bound writing compendium, pen and the ever-present calculator and headed into the meeting, closing the door as he entered the room.

When he emerged 45 minutes later he was ashen and very quiet. Gone was the cheeky smile that endeared him to so many, replaced with a drained look that one might expect to see on the face of a mourner at the funeral of a close friend. As he left the boardroom he was closely followed by Nathan Collingwood, who walked over to the accountants' desks. "Daniel, do you have a minute? There is something I need your help with," Collingwood asked the younger Flanders brother.

The boardroom table was covered in bank statements and canceled checks. The air in the room was hot and stale. Daniel's throat was dry and he began sweating profusely. He took a gulp of freshly poured, chilled water from a glass Collingwood obligingly handed to him.

Julia began the interview. Skillfully, but not in an accusatory manner, she outlined the concerns "that Condor now finds itself faced with." Beginning with generalities and moving to specifics Meyers put the transactions in question to a clearly unsettled Daniel Flanders, pausing often to allow the young accountant time to offer an explanation. Meyers was met with a continual and assertive denial of any knowledge of the transactions in question. Aside from admitting that he was the person responsible for posting the ledgers and doing the bank reconciliations, Daniel Flanders offered no explanation as to what might have occurred.

His response was in stark contrast to that of his older brother. Michael Flanders had been dismissive of the questions put to him and offered a number of explanations for the missing money. He repeatedly told Meyers and Collingwood that "you do not understand the accounting process" and that "the transactions were part of the intercompany account-ledger balancing process affecting the tax position of the group — something that I am not at liberty to go into detail with you."

Both Meyers and Collingwood made notes of the questions and answers put to both of the accountants. When everything but the check for $20,000 had been discussed, Collingwood put forward a series of suggestions to Daniel Flanders regarding the purpose of the transactions. Daniel was emphatic. "If that is what you think has happened here then you do not understand the accounting process properly," he said. However, Collingwood had simply put forward the explanations offered by Michael not more than 40 minutes earlier. Finally Julia Meyers put the $20,000 check on the table. The color drained from Daniel's face. "It's not mine; I haven't seen it before," he said turning it over. But there, endorsed on the back, was an account in his name at Sinclair Savings and Loan.

Collingwood stood up and called Michael back into the boardroom. One last time he asked both men if they had anything more to say. Both said nothing. Moments afterward, they were suspended on full pay and they made their way out of the offices of Condor Construction for the last time. Five days later, Michael and Daniel Flanders submitted their resignations by e-mail to Nathan Collingwood.

Enter the CFEs

Now it became the job of the CFEs to try to ascertain what had happened, how it had happened and the amount missing. Julia Meyers had called me immediately after her first conversation with Nathan Collingwood to say that she might need my help on the case. I was the head of a forensic accounting firm and had experience in other embezzlement cases. That same day, I gathered a team of forensic examiners and we headed over to Condor's offices.

My team reconstructed, both in tables and diagrams, the electronic transactions conducted in each of Condor's fourteen bank accounts during the 18 months that Michael Flanders had been employed. We analyzed the computer system's audit logs and confirmed that a number of the electronic transactions were set up via the Internet during the work day using Michael Flanders's login name and password. Other transfers were originated off-site between the hours of 1:00 AM and 4:00 AM when there was no one at the Condor office. Regardless of the number of transfers that took place each week, an accumulation of funds ultimately ended up in an account at Sinclair Savings and Loan.

We also examined canceled checks and identified the ledger entries used to mask the embezzlement. Our complete forensic investigation lasted six months as information was sought, enquiries followed up and missing documents located.

Like Mother, Like Son

People wanted to know how the embezzlement occurred. Given the tight controls in place and Alan Campbell's strict instructions to Belford First National, how did these funds get transferred out? The answer, as is often the case, proved to be very simple. Soon after Michael Flanders started working at Condor, he needed to upgrade the firm's accounting software. The package upgrade, approved by Nathan Collingwood, was undertaken online and required a credit card payment. Michael used his own credit card and paid just under $900. Collingwood intended to cut a reimbursement check to repay Michael, but it was overlooked by the company until Michael's credit card statement arrived.

With a credit card account balance already running in arrears and no presigned checks on hand, Michael set up a direct debit from Condor Construction's main checking account at Belford to his own checking account at Westside Community Bank using the Internet banking system. That night the $900 direct debit went through and the money transferred to his checking account. It would be six months before he started drawing significant sums from Condor's accounts this way — a week after his brother Daniel began working in the accounting department.

The investigation also revealed that in the first six months of his employment, Michael Flanders had regularly cut presigned checks and deposited them into various bank accounts, including one in Daniel's name at Sinclair Savings and Loan, his own account at Westside Community Bank and an account at the Shelton Community Credit Union in the name of his fiancée. We discovered that Michael opened the Sinclair account in Daniel's name by posing as Daniel and using his brother's Social Security number as proof of identification.

The first fraudulent check occurred three weeks after Michael began at Condor. It was for $4,500, but as he became more comfortable with stealing, the amounts grew. On average, the fraudulent checks were for amounts around $10,000. By comparison, the electronic transfers were rarely below $10,000 and often exceeded $15,000. Also the check embezzlements happened less frequently (usually once a month) than the Internet transactions (one or two a week). During the month before Michael Flanders's employment was suspended, the amount embezzled online exceeded $78,000.

In all, some $1.6 million disappeared through the accounting alchemy of Michael Flanders. To hide his online embezzlement in the company ledgers, before the employment of his brother, Michael had created a number of fictitious intercompany accounts, loans and suspense accounts. In addition to coding entries to these, all of which were dutifully posted by his brother once he came onboard, entries were logged against unreconciled wages and salary accounts, equity accounts, fictitious construction costs, IRS tax provision accounts, personal drawings and the equity contributions of Alan Campbell. With complete control of the accounting and general ledger system and with no regular oversight, Michael was free to create as many fictitious accounts as necessary to cover his actions.

However, the biggest surprise to all of us came from the civil proceedings against Michael Flanders, when it was revealed that most of the funds he embezzled from Condor at First Belford went into an account at Sinclair Savings and Loan in the name of Cynthia Flanders, his mother. It was Cynthia who cut the checks on Sinclair Savings and Loan and deposited them into Michael's account at Westside Community Bank. Cynthia's account had been flagged as suspicious by the Sinclair anti-money-laundering software.

While law enforcement was notified at the outset of the investigation, it was not until our final report was submitted that the matter was taken up as an active file. State and federal agencies are considering filing criminal charges of embezzlement and money laundering against Michael and a criminal charge of money laundering against his mother. Civil proceedings were recently abandoned because the cost of litigation was beyond Campbell's and Condor's means.

Lessons Learned

It is of fundamental importance that responsibilities be defined and monitored within an organization, regardless of size. While trust is an important factor in ensuring a committed and cohesive management team, that is a far cry from blind faith.

Alan Campbell summed the situation up in a review meeting when he said, ``Responsibility for this rests with me. I sacrificed good governance and thereby good management practices for what I misguidedly took for autonomy and efficiency. In fact, not implementing the basic management steps of oversight and review has cost me and the company hundreds of thousands of dollars in legal and investigative costs, in addition to the embezzlement itself. Changes to a couple of management policies — practices that arose out of laziness masked as expediency — combined with a fundamental review of my monthly cash position may have prevented this fraud. If not, it certainly would have limited the damage.''

Clearly, red flags in the internal controls process were ignored. The protocols that surrounded the handling of payments by check became impractical due to the unavailability of authorized signatories when they were needed. The substitute process adopted was a quick-fix compromise rather than a business solution. It then became the standard practice, resulting in a permanent degradation in internal control. In addition, there was no follow-up or review of the presigned checks by the signatories to see what they were used for. This told the CFO that no one was going to look at the bank accounts. He was able to undertake the subsequent electronic fraud with confidence.

While Belford would reverse any direct debit within three working days if the customer requested it, the only person reviewing bank statements was the perpetrator. Even a casual or irregular review by the CEO would have raised flags about the number of electronic transactions. This action may not have prevented the fraud but may have limited the losses.

Recommendations to Prevent Future Occurrences

A review of the bank statements and the general ledger accounts each month would have identified the excessive movements among the various bank accounts, each of which should have been authorized by someone other than the CFO. All balance sheet accounts must be regularly reconciled and intercompany accounts balanced among each company. Suspense accounts should be cleared and a working paper prepared to support the entries.

(*continued*)

(*continued*)

Direct debit transactions must be treated as checks drawn on the bank account and processed in the same way: fully supported by properly authorized documentation. Employment policies must recognize the need for pre-employment checks, and hiring family members within the same area of company operations should be discouraged. The age and (in)experience of key staff should also be factored into the wider management function, ensuring that mentoring — if not audit oversight of their performance — takes place. Finally, and most critically in this case, no one other than the CFO understood how the Internet banking system worked. There was no communication with the bank about online debits and no company policy that limited the authority of the CFO to initiate transfers among accounts.

The losses that arise from embezzlement often go beyond the loss of the funds themselves. Racked with debt, fifteen months after Michael's fraud was discovered, Condor Construction filed for Chapter 11 bankruptcy protection.

About the Author

David Petterson, CFE, is a Regent Emeritus of the ACFE. Although based in New Zealand, Mr. Petterson works across the South Pacific, holds a bachelor's degree in business studies, and is professionally qualified as an accountant. He is the Principal and Managing Director of Forensic Accounting Services Ltd.

CHAPTER 26

No Security in Online Advance Fees

DR. IVO GEORGE CAYTAS

Hannes Wogner was a businessman and property owner in Germany who provided local representation and other corporate services for foreign companies. Among his most valuable contacts was Hassan Roban, a nightclub owner, architect and financial broker in Istanbul who had a lucrative sideline operation in loan sharking. Roban also controlled a network of financially insubstantial but loyal Turkish expatriates in Germany and elsewhere, and a few unlicensed brokers in London and New York. Wogner preferred to work through layers of straw men that usually involved Hernando Paria and his Belizean offshore company, China-Spanish Holdings Ltd. Wogner's contacts also included Londoner Marvin Gibbons, a father of six children who had successfully escaped prosecution by the Serious Fraud Office of England. Their mutual friend was Philipp Pepperman, an almost-retired attorney in a New York suburb with more than 50 years of experience who, for the last decade, had confined his law practice to serving as an escrow agent for investments that were structured, marketed and supposedly operated by members of this informal network based outside the United States. Their deals involved seven-figure start-up fees that, as the brokers claimed, were required by the banks issuing and trading the securities, and by other banks that provided capital for investors who did not have it available themselves. Pepperman's much younger wife was also an attorney at his firm but — other than one secretary — they did not have a discernible law practice, or any measurable business, aside from these highly lucrative escrows that conveniently carried neither risk nor liability for them. In the investors' agreements, risks other than gross negligence and criminal intent were to be assumed by the investors in exchange for expectations of phenomenal, "risk-free" returns that supposedly were well in excess of 100 percent annually.

This association of investment "experts" primarily found their victims through the Internet. They created impressive Web sites for their affiliate brokers and targeted investors with well-crafted online marketing. E-mail chains among various contacts led to introductions between potential investors. This sense of community and trust among participants was essential to the success of the scheme, but it was completely fabricated by the culprits.

Through their U.S. and Caribbean contacts — and an expansive group of straw men, nominee directors and other agents — Wogner and his brokers created a mushroom structure of offshore companies in the Caribbean, Ireland, and certain British Isles. Some of these companies sported elaborate Web sites to tout the highly lucrative investment schemes, yet they claimed not to do business with or offer investments to the public. This shifted the risk to their investors. Plus, the wording of investment agreements gave the brokers a wide buffer of legal protection that investors needed to wade through — and hurdles posed by offshore corporations whose veils needed to be pierced — before developing a picture of the organization and how it worked. The group was essentially a changing set of intermediaries with a fixed core of masterminds.

Formal Introductions

Johann Haumgartner Ltd. was a state-licensed Austrian investment advisory firm run by its founder of the same name. It also invested for its own account. Through a convoluted chain of Internet business brokers, Haumgartner was introduced via the Internet to a trader firm run by a man named Peter Schritt in Germany who claimed to act as a feeder for a federally licensed trader. However, Schritt said the trader's identity was confidential because of his extraordinary spectrum of access and abilities. Schritt had an open investment opportunity because one of his Internet investors — a German accountant named Kurt Weiler — was about to invest $1.2 million in Schritt's new program; Weiler needed other investors to contribute $3.6 million to collectively acquire a "lot" with Schritt's wondertrader. Schritt put Haumgartner and Weiler in contact initially through e-mail, Web-conferencing and other Internet-based communications, and eventually used Weiler to bait Haumgartner into investing. Weiler was a live investor to whom Haumgartner had the opportunity to speak and who would invest before him, which set Haumgartner's mind at ease. Schritt then held a Web-conference with Haumgartner, Weiler, China-Spanish Holdings Ltd. and Pepperman. The team was assembled.

In the middle of March, Weiler and Haumgartner entered into elaborate escrow and investment agreements involving a myriad of companies that had one thing in common: Their names suggested an affiliation of major banks, asset managers or sovereign wealth funds.

According to the plan, Weiler and Haumgartner were being given the opportunity to invest in a high-yield program that required a minimum of $100 million. These funds would not be encumbered; they would serve as collateral to underwrite bank-issued securities offered at a substantial discount. Those would be released into the secondary market at ordinary and prevailing terms and conditions. Because the securities were to be issued at such a substantial discount to Weiler and Haumgartner, the trade in the secondary market would yield sufficient proceeds to cover market fluctuations that threatened a loss.

If the investors did not have sufficient funds to participate, they could borrow the money from third parties for a monthly fee of 3 percent. To release the funds, an advance-fee equivalent to the first month's fee needed to be deposited in an escrow account of a law firm. Pepperman's law firm was nominated as the escrow agent.

Two weeks after they had transferred their advance fees to Pepperman via the Internet, Weiler and Haumgartner were e-mailed bank documentation (for which they had paid $4.8 million) and almost right away recognized it as fraudulent — the paperwork was dated two years ago. The next day the victims retained my firm's services to demand repayment of their advance fees or, failing that, to take legal action. Pepperman claimed to have already disposed of the escrow deposits to members of the group. However, as subsequent investigation showed, he used most of the money for himself.

Wide Reach

We found that Pepperman, Paria and China-Spanish Holdings Ltd. had been sued at least four times in the last three years in four jurisdictions under very similar allegations. Unfortunately, the incidents had not been reduced to judgment or even a disciplinary sanction. Coincidence connected one of our clients to Roban, who loquaciously provided information that led directly to Gibbons and Wogner. Discovery produced a map of documentary evidence exposing a far-flung fraud network with tentacles in Europe, Asia and North America.

Philipp Pepperman was a soft-spoken, avuncular, grandfatherly type who claimed naïveté when we spoke; he said his actions were those of an arm's-length escrow agent who had not provided legal advice or drafted the agreements. He had merely taken instructions in accordance with the escrow. At least that was his story, and he was sticking to it.

Hassan Roban was a man of many talents that apparently included running an extensive network of forgers, Turkish expatriates and people with access to the offices and letterheads of banks. Hannes Wogner was owner of substantial real estate in southern Germany and a number of corporate vehicles. These two were perhaps the best at maintaining appearances because as far as the investors' paperwork was concerned, they did not exist.

Discovery produced detailed information about the distribution of the funds placed in escrow by Weiler and Haumgartner. A day or two after Pepperman received the investment, he wired it to a dozen unlicensed entities, none of which provided any service whatsoever. Moreover, China-Spanish Holdings Ltd., the investors' counterparty to the escrow, had delegated its authority to Marvin Gibbons in London. In turn, Gibbons issued wiring instructions to Pepperman for more than $3 million of the escrowed money. Pepperman claimed to have verified the recipients of the transfers, but he did not request bank-to-bank confirmation.

As Weiler and Haumgartner suspected when they received their investment documents, the bank asserted that they were forgeries. Pepperman proved (and the bank admitted upon review of its e-mail records) that the bank received his transmission requesting verification. However, the bank claimed to have no record of the contents of the transmission or the outgoing e-mail produced by Pepperman that showed a statement confirming his inquiry.

Weiler and Haumgartner contacted Pepperman one day after they received their paperwork to notify him of their suspicions of fraud and requested that he return their undisbursed funds. However, he continued to disburse millions of dollars after they contacted him; it was clear that he acted in collusion with the recipients of the escrow disbursements. We conducted research at the county clerk's office of Pepperman's hometown and learned that he had transferred his property to his wife on the same day I issued my complaint against him, so we added Mrs. Pepperman as a co-conspirator and accessory after the fact.

After Haumgartner's and Weiler's Austrian and Turkish counsel conferred with Turkish and German prosecutors, Roban and two of his pawns (who had received $1.6 million of Pepperman's escrow disbursements) were taken into custody in Turkey and interrogated. Their bank accounts were inspected within three days. However, because Roban had connections in the local Turkish prosecutor's office, we had to bring in the Turkish national government from Ankara.

Shortly thereafter, German police raided the homes and offices of several transfer recipients in Germany, authorized surveillance of their electronic communications and confiscated evidence. Together with the records that Pepperman provided during discovery, Wogner then became a suspect.

The investigation was long, tedious and detail-oriented — along the lines of classical forensic accounting work — yet it proved relatively simple.

It was also costly, weighing in at about one-third of the amount of damages. A basic comparison of time lines showed that Pepperman, Gibbons, Roban and others could not possibly have acted in good faith because Haumgartner had notified them of his suspicions well before the last — and quite substantial — disbursement of his escrowed funds was made. Offshore corporations controlled by Wogner routed money through Pepperman's accounts without a discernible commercial reason. However, in so doing, the defendants violated the cardinal rule that successful frauds must follow: Preserve the appearance of integrity and credible deniability.

The Art of Delaying

Drawn-out settlement negotiations with Gibbons, Roban and Wogner proved useless. Almost four months after I received the initial complaint, we brought action in federal court for racketeering, fraud, breach of contract and various other torts. We notified authorities in Austria, Germany, Turkey, England and the United States and initiated disciplinary proceedings against Pepperman. Several criminal investigations are still pending. Pepperman's professional liability insurance, though unlikely to indemnify his victims, is paying for his legal defense. Until his $ 1 million coverage is exhausted by legal fees, he will doubtlessly drag out civil litigation. The cases will remain pending unless or until a settlement is reached by the financially solvent parties — Wogner, Roban and some European banks.

Marvin Gibbons agreed to settlement negotiations but failed to produce the funds when they were due; he requested more than six months of extensions to deliver, but he hasn't to date. A few weeks later, Pepperman and his wife requested settlement negotiations but they offered the barest minimum — with other people's money. Pepperman offered a $200,000 contribution from his liability insurer, and his wife offered to sell her property and provide a small portion of the proceeds. Both argued that they needed to retain assets to pay for criminal investigations and to secure their retirement. Despite my assurances that, to avoid criminal charges, they only needed to turn over evidence against the bigger players in the scam, Pepperman insisted that he had no incriminating evidence and had already given me the relevant information he knew.

After months of back and forth, Mrs. Pepperman agreed to settle for a small fraction of the claim, payable upon sale of her property over the next year. Settlement negotiations with her husband are ongoing but an agreement has been reached in principle. Pepperman's professional liability insurer will agree to pay 50 percent of the overall amount Pepperman and his wife owed in restitution, and Pepperman will have to liquidate his retirement assets to pay the other 50 percent.

This case could have set the standard for stalling and delays. However, the forthcoming settlement agreement with Pepperman will likely force other defendants to settle within 24 months or face criminal consequences. We sued and obtained default judgments against an array of intermediaries and business brokers to force them to cooperate with our proceedings against the wealthier — but far less cooperative — defendants.

Lessons Learned

Reliance on written representations of attorneys and other licensed professionals — but especially of unlicensed parties — is wholly insufficient for investors. It is equally dangerous to trust online investors whom you have not met in person. Bank employees and other individuals who appear to hold positions of public trust are not above collusion with criminals. The critical traits I observed in organized criminal fraud perpetrated through an international, Internet-based network include:

1. Perpetrators manage the risk.
2. Lawyers create significant buffers and delays.
3. Settlements seldom occur before the start of a criminal investigation.
4. Costs of criminal defenses often compete with funds available for settlement.
5. Settlement rarely achieves full restitution.

Recommendations to Prevent Future Occurrences

Innovative financial and business models are a cornerstone of investment returns that exceed market rates (at least until copycats catch up), but they are also a hotbed for fraud based on investor greed, manipulation and unverifiable key assumptions. Following are recommendations to avoid entanglement in such schemes.

VERIFY ASSUMPTIONS, TESTIMONIALS AND REPRESENTATIONS

An astounding number of frauds succeed on the weight of unquestioned and unverified assumptions. These work along the lines of "he has to know that he will go to prison if this is not true" or "this whole thing would not make sense if x, y or z were not participating, too." However, such fundamental assumptions can be dead wrong. The fact that someone would potentially face grievous consequences if he lies seldom stops someone from knowingly and willfully misrepresenting material facts. One

(continued)

explanation for this is found in the popular saying, "Possession is nine-tenths of the law." Once an investor has parted with money, recovering it can be nearly impossible; even partial restitution can take years and involve substantial legal fees.

Much of the same is true of testimonials. Con men understand the art of *distributed responsibility* — the more individuals involved in a scheme, the better. Each player can claim to have been one insignificant piece of the greater assemblage, and the mastermind can say he could not possibly have made so many individuals do his bidding. There are also ways for a fraudster to create this impression with only a few other participants if he has one key ally: a greedy investor who wants to believe. Once the culprit has made inroads with a potential victim, that person will accept the scammer's assertions at face value because they support the investor's desired outcome.

AVOID UNUSUAL OR COMPLEX STRUCTURES

A fraudulent investment scheme typically has an unusual, "tailor-made" structure because it defies comparison and makes it difficult to rely on precedent. This also substantially reduces the fraudster's risk in litigation because judges and juries have a tendency to find contributory negligence on the victims' part when they invest money in an uncommon and untested plan. The reasoning is that if a strategy were as good as it promised to be, the major market players would have seized it long ago. And that is usually true.

Complexity is important in many investment and securities frauds. The more specialized expertise that is required to comprehend the structure, the more difficult it is to detect flaws and risks. And that means more opportunity for the criminals to limit their personal liability.

AVOID CONCLUSIONS AND INFERENCES ABOUT RISK

One of the arguments most often offered by unlicensed financial intermediaries is based on risk. The argument compares events that seem remote and qualifies them as a *systemic risk*, such as the possibility that an asset will find no buyers on a given day in a public market. Such events — although they seem unlikely to the layperson — actually do occur. Statements about risk are typically made orally — not in writing — and are difficult to prove. However, they influence the victim's readiness to accept informal information as fact, although it was not put in writing.

STRICTLY AVOID WORKING WITH PEOPLE WITHOUT SUBSTANTIAL VERIFIABLE WEALTH

Proponents of investments that promise to yield returns significantly or consistently above market average should be verifiably wealthy — unless they admit to doing for the first time what they propose to do. Beware of penniless brokers advising millionaires on how to become billionaires — and in 180 days.

(continued)

(continued)

INVESTIGATE MISSION-CRITICAL PLAYERS

Investors victimized by Internet securities or investment frauds often did not conduct adequate background checks. And for understandable reasons — fraudulent investment schemes are frequently peddled through impressive-looking Web sites by unlicensed brokers who limit access to the "real players" behind them. The brokers claim to be protecting the people in the upper echelon who actually pull the strings and receive the lion's share of the proceeds. Investors will often have limited information on the brokers as well, because they have not met in person and trust the information found on the investment Web page. While there is ample legal basis to sue and prosecute unlicensed brokers under the U.S. securities laws, it is an expensive proposition unless a significant recovery is likely. Brokers are not promising targets of civil proceedings either, except for the evidence they might provide against their principals.

AVOID PROPOSALS IN AREAS WHERE YOU LACK EXPERTISE OR IN-HOUSE EXPERTS

Institutional investors do not keep subject matter experts on staff because they simply love to pay them. The risk of falling prey to a fictitious scheme in areas where one does not have expertise is great. This is one reason why otherwise successful, self-made professionals — such as doctors, dentists and entertainers — fail to recognize scams: their achievement in other areas creates a sense of embarrassment about their investment ignorance. Fraudsters often drown their victims in facts and figures to confuse them. Document overload also gives the investor the sense that the answers "must be in there somewhere," but too often they are not.

DO NOT DELAY CIVIL AND CRIMINAL ACTION; SPEED IS OF THE ESSENCE

The less time that passes between discovery and legal action, the better the outcome will be. Over time evidence will deteriorate, witness recollections will suffer or may be tampered with, material witnesses may move or pass away, documentary evidence may be destroyed intentionally or accidentally and money and other assets may be laundered or simply spent by the perpetrators.

About the Author

Dr. Ivo George Caytas holds two PhDs and has been a practicing attorney for 18 years in three jurisdictions. He is the founder of Caytas and Associates, a financial services law firm that serves domestic and international clients.

The G.I. Hacker

BRUCE L. OWDLEY

James Wilson was a proud military soldier who had been married for just under a year to his sweetheart, Linda. They had plans of expanding their family, but for the time being were happy with their short-hair terrier, Scrappy. James was pleased with his military career; he learned electronics and communications in the Army and enjoyed his assignment as a signal-corps technician. After his active-duty assignment ended, he continued his career in the Army Reserves and used his G.I. Bill to obtain several computer certifications. James was a fit, active young man who still donned his military-style haircut. He wanted to make sure his wife received every enjoyment and luxury life could offer, and promised Linda's father that he would strive to provide her with the finer things in life.

Linda was the daughter of a plastic surgeon and grew up in an upper-class, conservative, suburban neighborhood. Her parents did not allow her to wander very far from home or partake of any questionable or risky activities. She went to the best schools and had been brought up to be a refined member of upper-class society. Linda's father, Richard, did not think anyone was good enough for his sweet Lin, who he believed was destined to become a world-class surgeon. She graduated magna cum laude in premed from Stanford University and was accepted to Johns Hopkins University's prestigious medical school. But her future took a dramatic turn when she was introduced to James through a mutual friend. When they met, Linda was immediately drawn to his bad-boy persona, which her parents raised her to avoid. James had an arrogance that appealed to Linda, and she looked at him as both a challenge and a charity project. James told her of his future plans and insisted that he only needed the right opportunity and support to succeed. What began as an innocent flirtation turned into dating, and eventually James invited her to visit him at his Army base. While there, Linda had three of the most memorable weeks of fun and excitement that she had experienced in her sheltered life.

James came from a blue-collar family. His father was a veteran of the Vietnam War and worked in a manufacturing plant 12 hours a day; his mother did not finish high school after giving birth to his oldest sister; she was a career housewife. James grew up motivated to succeed by reflecting back on the hard times that he and his family went through, and made a promise to his mother that one day he would buy her a house with a back-yard. When he graduated from high school, he wanted to leave his home-town and expand his horizons, and he saw the Army as the answer. It would give him the opportunity to travel the world, be trained in a new career and receive money to go to college. And to top things off, he could follow in his father's footsteps and serve his country. James's family was very proud of him. Nevertheless, his accomplishments did not meet the standards of Linda's father — Richard expected his daughter to marry a doctor or lawyer and enjoy the same financial comfort in which he raised her. When Richard found out about Linda's relationship with James, he became angry and expressed his disdain of their relationship to both of them. The doctor was concerned that Linda would not finish college, which would ruin her career prospects. James, attempting to understand Richard's concerns, promised him that he would do everything in his power to make sure that Linda fin-ished medical school and lived the life that Richard envisioned for her. Her father just replied, "Sure. We'll see, son."

A New Beginning

Despite Richard's objections, Linda's mother was able to convince him to attend the wedding and give away his daughter. Shortly after they were mar-ried, James decided to leave the Army and pursue a career in the computer industry. Linda enrolled in medical school. When James spoke of his wife and their future, he passionately expressed that nothing in the world would prevent him from providing her and their future children with whatever they desired. James used his Army benefits to purchase a new home in the suburbs, which he referred to as their "temporary" home. It was a modestly built single-story home with approximately 2,800 square feet. Linda's father considered it meager, but it was James and Linda's starting point. James set up his own computer lab at home, where he conducted research into the industry and new trends on the Internet. He was most proud of the home–wide computer network he constructed. He had a cable line installed in his office to support a self-contained server that he used to host his Web site. He connected the desktop and laptop computers in the house to a single system, which he could monitor remotely. He constantly devised hypotheti-cal network problems and came up with different solutions to sharpen his problem-solving skills. One of his favorite pastimes was hacking into his own network from different Internet connections — friends, family members, even the local library — and then devising stronger protections against such hacks. After working various odd jobs with temporary agencies, James found an opening for the position of his dreams at a mom-and-pop network-servicing company that was undergoing growth and had the potential for future advancement.

James believed that his education and training made him one of the top candidates for the company's newest network engineer position. James knew the interview was going well when Eric Mathis, who co-owned the company with his wife, reviewed James's résumé, and then brought his wife, Rita, into the interview with them. James's practical experience in the military, along with his industry certifications, proved to be influential in his hiring. Eric and Rita were especially impressed when James explained how he installed his own server network and practiced with the various scenarios he created. He seemed to have a unique grasp of Internet-based threats to network security, which the Mathises considered a valuable asset to the company. The couple was excited about bringing James on board; they thought they had found the right person with the ideal desire and dedication. A week later, James was hired and began his new career. He told Linda, "Baby, our worries are over. You just focus on finishing school; I have found the golden egg."

During his first week at work, James was given an organizational chart of the company's administration. There were already potential management slots being created due to the enormous growth of the company. James's ambitions began to soar and he set his sights on upward progression — more responsibility and more money. He was strongly motivated to help his mother buy that house he promised her and to prove to Linda's father that he was worthy of her. James worked overtime on a regular basis, not only to keep up with his workload, but to get a better understanding of how the company functioned. He had his eyes on the prize and he wanted his bosses to know that he was a dedicated employee.

The Mathises

Mathis Network Technologies was founded to manage and maintain network servers for small- to medium-size companies that did not have internal IT departments. Mathis Network gave their clients a reliable backup system in case of a disaster and was more cost effective for their customer base than it would be to purchase expensive equipment and hire on-staff personnel. The company began as a daydream Eric had while working as a technician at a computer-manufacturing company. He learned electronics on the job from a technician who took him in as an apprentice. Since that experience, Eric also tried to help young people who were hard working and wanted to make something out of their lives. Eric enrolled in business courses and undertook entrepreneur training provided by a community program.

After developing a sound business plan and obtaining a commercial loan, Eric and Rita started Mathis Network Technologies in a small office in a strip mall. Eric would drive out to businesses in his little Chevy S-10 pickup truck and work on their computers and network problems while Rita managed the office. As the company grew and attracted more clients, they moved into their own 8,600-square-foot building with four floors. They eventually employed more than 500 people, working in shifts around the clock. Eric and Rita were considering taking the company public, so they asked James to help redesign the Web site to increase visibility and expand market share, a step recommended by their bank. The bank also suggested that they hire more management with advanced education.

The Mathises had a big decision to make — to get the loan to expand the corporation, they needed to hire a few MBA-type managers. But they already had dedicated network engineers with a zeal for the business who anticipated moving up. Despite their loyalty to the current staff, Eric and Rita knew what they had to do for the company to move forward. Eric interviewed several highly qualified managers with MBAs but he was having trouble finding someone who also had a knack for the industry; those who did, frankly, wanted more money than Eric was willing to pay. Finally, a candidate with a bachelor's degree in computer science and an MBA applied for the position — Eric and Rita hired her almost on the spot. A few weeks later Eric took Marcy around the office and introduced her to the staff as the new operations manager.

Sabotage

I was going through my morning rituals — coffee, e-mail, voice mail — when the lieutenant brought me a new case file and said, "I believe you're going to like this one." As a police investigator I usually received relatively standard — cookie-cutter, even — fraud cases, but on the humid spring day when I read the report filed by Eric Mathis, I was forced to switch up my routine and take heed of the peculiar circumstances. I reviewed the initial report. This was an opportunity to wear my Dr. Holmes hat and get into some real investigative work, especially for an Internet fraud; these crimes were still relatively new at the time and I looked forward to expanding my skills. Eric Mathis stated in his report, "A former employee is trying to put me out of business. He has sabotaged my company's network and shut down my operations, which affects several of my clients.''

Following the IP Trail

I drove over to the Mathis Network Technologies' office and met with Eric and Rita Mathis to get a more detailed overview of the incident. Eric began by describing James as a brilliant employee, but said he also suspected James had serious personal issues. As I gathered more details, Rita suggested that pressure from his wife may have been a problem for James. She said that Linda didn't work and was used to having the finer things in life. And from water-cooler talk around the office, Rita had surmised that James needed a promotion not only to build a bigger house for Linda, but also to show his father-in-law that he could be a good provider. Eric then mentioned James's upbringing and said that James had to work hard for everything in his life. Eric said that was one of the reasons he hired James — his determination — was exactly what Mathis Network Technologies needed. Eric told me that he knew James was disappointed to be passed over for the operations manager position, but Eric "explained to him that it was a business decision. I told James he could go back to school and then I would be glad to bring him up. But I believe he wanted instant gratification. Four to six years of college was not in his plans.''

A year after they hired Marcy as operations manager, James's focus and priorities seemed to change. He showed up late to work, left early, called in sick on a regular basis and became outright disrespectful to his superiors. The final straw came when a customer complained about James to Eric, stating that records had been altered without his authorization and that James was his account representative. When Eric questioned James about the incident, James became irate and combative. Eric said he had no choice but to call the police to escort him from the premises: That was the end of James's tenure with Mathis Network Technologies. The day after James was fired, Eric and Rita began to get calls from clients complaining that their networks had been terminated and that they were losing money by the minute.

The Mathises looked into the compromised accounts and discovered that someone had used the Internet to hack into Mathis Network Technologies' system and then shut down their customers' networks. I learned that an outside Internet protocol (IP) address had been used to access the Mathis server on the night James was fired. I contacted the domain name service (DNS) that Mathis Network Technologies used and obtained the IP address that was used to access the company's server; it was serviced by One-Stop Cable Company. My next step was to request grand jury subpoenas to obtain the physical address where the IP address originated. After the subpoenas were granted, One-Stop turned over its records. It was no surprise that the IP address came from James Wilson's home in the northwest suburbs of town.

Surveillance and Searches

I decided to drive by the Wilson residence to ascertain the activity and routines of Linda and James. Then I was able to obtain a search warrant for the premises from the district judge, and I was trying to get the lay of the land before executing it. Based on significant amounts of circumstantial evidence, I chose a foggy summer morning to execute the search warrant.

With the assistance of several other officers, I entered the Wilson residence with the search warrant to find James and Linda inside. It appeared that James was preparing to leave for the weekend for Army Reserve duty. We gathered digital evidence including CDs, DVDs, thumb drives, cameras, cell phones, laptops, and desktop and server computers. Our forensic experts packed it all and took it to our computer forensics lab for examination.

Angry Intent

Later I called James into my office to give him an opportunity to give his perspective of the events. I read him his Miranda rights and proceeded with the interview. James began to rant about Eric and said he did not receive the respect he deserved at work. "I should have been promoted to a supervisory position long ago, but I was overlooked for someone who had less experience but who had graduated from a well-known school with a master's degree. I was the only employee who worked overtime when Eric needed me to; everyone else always made up excuses."

I asked James how he felt when Marcy was hired and he practically screamed, "I felt betrayed! I needed that raise; that job was mine! Eric knew that I needed more money to buy a new house. But the final straw came when I told Eric and Rita I couldn't work one weekend that they scheduled me because I had Army Reserve duty. They called the commander of my reserve unit and asked him if I really had a drill that weekend. Then they started telling him my personal business and work habits."

I asked James how he knew what the Mathises told his commander, and he admitted to fixing the network to notify him whenever Eric or Rita called the base. He said once he received a notification, he tapped into the phone line and listened to their conversation. I was stunned by this admission and asked him, "You mean that you hacked into a government network and listened to other people's conversations? Does your commander know you did this?" And suddenly James wasn't so forthcoming. He said he didn't want to talk about it anymore and wanted to consult with a lawyer.

I pieced together my digital and Internet evidence and the facts I gathered from my various interviews, and determined that James became disgruntled when Marcy was hired and decided to take revenge on the Mathises. He started by tapping their phones and listening in on private conversations, but he took it to a new level after he was fired. He returned home, box of desk miscellany in hand, and used the Internet to remotely launch an attack on his previous employer's network. Once he gained access to Mathis Network Technologies' systems, he began shutting down Mathis's largest clients, one at a time. James knew which clients to target first, and he knew exactly how to compromise the networks. After all, he helped set them up. I compiled a report of my findings and presented it to the district attorney. After reviewing my evidence he was pleased to have such a well-packaged case. "Looks like you did your homework, Bruce. This guy is going to take a long ride."

A warrant was issued, and James was arrested at home early one morning. He was tried in court for breach of computer security, a second-degree felony. During the trial, evidence showed that James's actions caused a monetary loss of more than $100,000 for Mathis Network Technologies. The district attorney also proved that James's actions were intentional and malicious. James was sentenced to 10 years in prison and received a $10,000 fine. The district attorney also forwarded a copy of my report and a transcript of my interview with James to the department of defense for investigation because he tapped into phone calls made by military personnel. He faces possible additional federal charges of unlawful access to stored communications. In the meantime, he has been dishonorably discharged from the Army Reserves.

Lessons Learned

I learned a great deal about investigating complicated breaches of computer security and Internet hacking. I now realize the importance of obtaining digital evidence as soon as possible, due to the potential loss of information. I also learned how important it is to document every step of the investigation and not leave out any details. And to obtain a search warrant, it pays to know how to properly video, photograph and document physical evidence. It is important to attempt to learn the behavior patterns of the perpetrator to establish his motives and his potential for doing other harm.

Recommendations to Prevent Future Occurrences

I made the following recommendations to Mathis Network Technologies, which might also be helpful for other companies that are vulnerable to Internet hackers.

1. Create a more secure system of network passwords.
2. Limit employee access to client account information.
3. Use a computer certificate program to only allow access to the network from designated machines.
4. Implement a computer network compliance policy.
5. Devise a plan to protect network security from outside Internet hackers.
6. Hire an ethical hacker to test the system on a regular basis and determine any weaknesses.
7. Consider having potential employees who would work in certain positions undergo a psychological evaluation prior to hiring them.

About the Author

Bruce L. Owdley, CFE, is a police investigator for the Houston Police Department's Financial Crimes Unit. He enjoys working on computer crimes and has become the de facto computer-crimes investigator in his unit. Bruce has a bachelor's degree in computer science, with a minor in business, and is currently pursuing a master's degree in strategic leadership. Bruce is a Certified Fraud Examiner and a Certified Fraud Specialist.

CHAPTER

28

The Wrong Suspect

JYOTI KHETARPAL

The culprits in this case had different motivations, methods and expectations but they shared one trait — they were united by their decision to commit fraud. Some were disgruntled employees at recruiting companies hoping to branch out and open their own businesses. Others were stressed-out recruiters who had unrealistic budgets and time constraints placed upon them. And still others were simply unscrupulous business owners trying to save a buck. The one thing they had in common was that they targeted the same victim.

Serve.com was founded by Linden McNally to provide online recruitment and related professional services to corporations. Serve established and maintained a network of 60 offices nationwide and employed 2,500 people; it was considered the nation's leading job portal. The client list included employers, screening companies, consultants and job seekers, and it was strictly an Internet business. It had a Web site on which corporate clients could place recruitment classifieds and it offered online tools for conducting searches in résumé databases and applicant screening programs. These services required Serve's customers to be able to download large amounts of data from the Web site.

Serve also provided lists of consultants, including their addresses, the top 100 companies in the country, the industry leaders and so forth; these services were mainly used by individuals. Individuals made online payments and either downloaded the compilation or requested it in printed form.

Serve began outsourcing the processing of online payments to its bank, and suddenly discovered problems with fraudulent transactions, which were costing Serve not only financially but in damage to its reputation as well. Media reports began claiming that Serve's employees may have been involved in the fraudulent transactions.

A Call from an Old Friend

I was enjoying a lazy Sunday afternoon in the peak of the winter season when I received a phone call from my old friend Linden asking if I could help out with a problem his company was facing. He said that since he contracted Serve's online bill-pay services to an outside bank, the payment rejection rate increased from 2 to 16 percent. Linden was worried that existing clients might be downloading subscribed data from Serve's Web site but then disputing the payments.

Linden stated that reputable corporate clients were availing themselves of Serve's downloadable products but, at the time of payment, they disputed the transactions. He suspected somebody in the organization was involved in fraud, but said that he could not discuss much over the phone. I tried to calm Linden down and we arranged a meeting at his office for the following day.

The Big Picture

A little basic research on the Internet gave me fair idea of the products and services offered by Serve, the nature of the company's online transactions and the clientele. Although I was told that the problem was with rejections of online purchases, the details were unclear to me.

I met with Linden in his office the next day. He told me that long-term customers had recently begun rejecting payments because they claimed the transactions were unknown to them. The rejection rate had surged almost 700 percent from the acceptable threshold levels of the previous few months. He also said that upper management at Serve suspected Michael, who was a member of the IT team, was somehow involved. Michael was in charge of account maintenance and management was considering firing him, depending on the outcome of a parallel investigation that was being conducted on Michael by an independent agency. They were trying to determine whether there were discrepancies in his lifestyle and income.

Linden said that Michael was a hardworking employee who got along well with other staff members. Linden did not personally suspect that Michael was involved in the increased payment disputes, but so far the evidence pointed to him. To begin my investigation, Linden gave me Michael's personnel file. He had been with the company for nine years, was promoted gradually and was even awarded "employee of the month" recently. I told Linden that we needed to conduct a thorough investigation before blaming anyone, which meant I was going to study Serve's entire payment process to find loopholes that could indicate the possible malfeasant involvement of employees. Linden walked me through Serve's operational procedures, starting with the creation of a new account through the client's online payment for services or products. The process outwardly seemed standard and was monitored with proper checkpoints.

I asked Linden if his organization had prepared comparative analyses or a matrix to pinpoint the problem area, but he said no. Linden was able to give me the data on past and current rejections during our meeting and promised to send other information by the end of the week. We arranged a follow-up meeting in another two weeks.

I found the problem intriguing. Serve was a well-established company. Its processes seemed to include proper control checks and segregation of duties, the staff members appeared to be of high integrity and the clients were respected employers and recruitment consultants. I had seen nothing yet to raise suspicions toward anyone in the chain of operations, including Michael.

Focusing on the Details

To begin my investigation, I reviewed the current rejection files Linden gave me. I asked my team to analyze the rejections in terms of rate, type and amount to prepare a matrix. Three days later, the results were in and we were surprised by what we saw. The facts were pointing to the element of the chain that we least suspected — Serve's corporate customers. I did not reveal the results to Linden immediately but asked him to send the other data as soon as possible.

After I received the records for the past year, my team compiled a matrix of the rejections; the results did not change. We noticed a trend in the rejection rates. At the beginning of the year, the problem was individual account holders downloading résumés or other basic information about job seekers from Serve's Web site but then denying the transactions and refusing to pay. Gradually the problem shifted from individual accounts to small-time consultants and eventually we saw the large corporate customers denying payments. The trend was shocking because we thought the corporate customers would probably be more organized and trustworthy.

Our initial analysis and discussions indicated that the culprits were mostly employees of Serve's corporate customers. They had acquired their employers' login details and were able to misuse them because authorization was not required to purchase products online. These employees were divided into two categories: those who used the main identification (main ID) and those who created sub-identifications (sub-IDs), whether through their personal or work e-mail accounts.

I discussed my team's findings with Linden during our next meeting and he was thrilled that we had identified the root of the issue. He had a razor-sharp mind and knew the company inside and out; he had a fair understanding of what I was trying to establish. Our initial discovery ruled

out Michael as a suspect in the fraud. He was an IT employee who had no
contact with clients. Linden was happy to clear the name of an honest
employee whose integrity had been challenged due to process faults. Linden ordered the independent investigator to discontinue the investigation
into Michael.

Collaborative Investigation

I requested that Linden allow two of my team members to work with his IT
department and Michael. Linden readily agreed. I sent Alex and Christine
to Linden's office to have a structured walk-through to understand the technical processes related to creating corporate account IDs, confirming
service requests, downloading data after online payments and tracing the
necessary audit trails. The report created by Alex and Christine clearly
depicted the following problem areas:

- Limited information was requested from clients at the time the pri-
  mary accounts were created.
- Once they had an ID for a primary account, customers could create
  unlimited sub-IDs with limited connections to the primary account.
- Clients did not have to provide authorization at the time they pur-
  chased products or services from Serve's Web site.
- There was a significant lack of controls in the ordering process.
- Serve did not maintain a database of disputed payments.

Our analysis of the rejections indicated that established accounts were
being used by dishonest employees of good clients to make unauthorized
purchases. Part of the problem was that Serve's upper management insisted
new customers be granted nearly instantaneous access to the company's
Web site and downloadable products, which meant that Serve's employees
did not have time to conduct thorough checks of new clients when the
accounts were opened. Also, because it was easy to crcatc sub-IDs that were
piggybacked to one main corporate account, a scam artist only needed to
uncover the main account ID, and could then create an endless supply of
sub-IDs with which to make purchases in the client's name. Our investigation revealed that 94 percent of the rejections were due to unknown transactions. The question turned to how to curb it, considering the large
number of users. Linden and I had various discussions and came to the
conclusion that half of the problem could be resolved by correcting the
account-creation process. To fix the other half, we asked the IT department
to write new algorithms that would send an e-mail to the main-ID holder of
an account when a sub-ID attempted to download data from Serve.com.

Once we had identified the culprits and knew that the problem was most severe with the corporate customers, Serve's management chose to send an official notice to its large clients explaining the problem. The notice stated that Serve was working to improve its enrollment process and would soon be asking the clients to protect their accounts by following a few additional but necessary steps.

Lessons Learned

Linden and I learned a lot about investigating Internet-based frauds from this case, including the importance of screening for fraudulent intentions in the initial stages of account creation. We noticed that many small recruitment clients created their accounts with the intention of defrauding Serve. They created a main account with multiple sub-IDs and used those to download résumés. When they received the bill for the downloaded information, the clients disputed the transactions because they came from sub-IDs. The burden of proof was on Serve to establish the legitimacy of the purchases, so the clients were easily getting out of payment obligations. These deceptive clients falsely claimed that their account information was leaked by Serve's employees or that its Web site was hacked.

Serve's upper management wanted new clients to have access to the Web site in a matter of minutes, which compromised the integrity of the approval process. We learned that there were critical control steps left uncompleted, which unscrupulous customers took advantage of, costing Serve both in profits and reputation. Providing world-class service is important, but it should not come at the expense of control procedures. Clients should not have been given opportunities to indulge their fraudulent intentions.

We discovered that employees at some of Serve's corporate clients were given strict targets and tight budgets on their recruitment assignments. The employees, struggling with management's restrictions, were fraudulently creating sub-IDs to download data from Serve, only to have the company dispute the charges. Employees were creating these sub-IDs using dummy personal e-mail accounts, but because they were attached to their employers' main IDs, the payment was billed to corporate clients associated with the main IDs.

On the Internet, too, the customer is always right. The moment a client refuses to recognize a transaction, it is the merchant's responsibility to prove it. Linden decided that, going forward, when Serve received a disputed payment, management would review the process for operational deficiencies rather than treating it like an isolated case.

Last but not least, do not accuse a loyal employee of improper actions until the investigation is complete and he or she is found culpable.

Recommendations to Prevent Future Occurrences

Fraud can be managed with a combination of prevention tools and techniques. The following recommendations were implemented at Serve after my investigation to keep frauds to a minimum.

KNOW YOUR CUSTOMER

To establish long-term clients at Serve, we created a three-step account-creation process to replace the old one-step process and function as the Know Your Customer (KYC) check:

- Account creation
- Confirmation
- Authorization and access

Linden and I wrote a checklist for creating accounts and compared it with the existing list. We saw that the existing list had significant deficiencies:

- A business e-mail address was the only identifier requested from new clients.
- Confirmation and authorization were only sent to the provided business e-mail.
- The unique account personal identification number (PIN) was communicated to the client through the same business e-mail.
- The type of data the client intended to download was not categorized.
- The range of associated sub-IDs was not defined.

SAFETY STEP

We introduced a safety step at the time of account creation with three options. Most of the corporate accounts were billed to a corporate credit card, and the card number was stored at the time the account was created. A person with access to an account ID or sub-ID could download information from Serve.com and the corporate card would be billed. The new safety step allowed clients to log-in and browse for information only with the ID, but:

- Clients needed to enter a credit card number each time they downloaded data.
- A computer system generated the PINs for account holders and those were then communicated to the corporate client over the telephone after the account was established. These PINs needed to be entered to download data.

We knew clients would be hesitant to spend extra time for safety steps, so we added a disclaimer that if they did not set up their accounts using this optional procedure, purchase disputes would not be entertained by Serve. Therefore the burden of any fraudulent downloads would be on the clients who did not opt for the safety step when they created their accounts.

(continued)

ALGORITHMS

We made flow charts showing missing checks and asked Serve's IT department to create algorithms to address the problems. We identified the following issues:

- *Unlimited sub-IDs were linked to a primary ID.* Customers established as many sub-IDs as they wanted. We changed the process to require customers to define the number of sub-IDs they allowed when the account was created. If sub-ID creation exceeded the limit, a notification was automatically sent to the main account holder. The following steps were also introduced to control sub-IDs:
  - Sub-IDs shared the name of the main ID. Hence if a main ID was adrian@job search.com, a sub-ID could be adrian-naomi@jobsearch.com. The name on the sub-ID had to follow the name on the parent account.
  - Requests for sub-IDs from personal e-mail addresses were prohibited. The system used to allow sub-IDs to be created from Gmail or Hotmail, but new restrictions limited creation to business e-mail addresses.
- *There was a lack of controls in the ordering process.* A detailed analysis of disputed payments showed that the data was not the type normally downloaded by the client or it was done with fraudulent IDs. The IT team added the following confirmation steps to the ordering process:
  - If the order was from an individual account not associated with a corporate client, an e-mail was sent to the account holder to confirm the order. Once the order was confirmed, the client had to enter the account's PIN, which was generated in the safety step.
  - When a request came from a sub-ID for the first time, an e-mail was sent to the main ID to authorize it.
  - When accounts were opened, clients were asked to supply the range of services and type of information they anticipated downloading. When a client requested a new product or service, an e-mail was sent for confirmation.
  - Only users with existing IDs could download products.

NEGATIVE DATABASE

A database of disputed payments was created in response to this case, and it included the account ID, individual user's name, credit card number, reference data and any other relevant information from the transaction. If a future dispute matches an entry in the database, the dispute will be rejected.

WEB SITE CONTROLS

Linden introduced additional controls over Serve's Web site. He minimized the number of people involved in maintaining the site and added more firewalls. He also adjusted the PIN-generating feature online to make if fully automatic and restrict employee access.

(*continued*)

(*continued*)

RANDOM TESTING

Our first random test was of the online system used to create IDs. We tried creating fraudulent accounts to find loopholes in process. When we discovered problems, we sent them to the IT department and they came up with solutions. We then randomly tested the authenticity of purchases made by customers. This step was implemented as a recurring test and was done with different client categories and for different types of services.

FRAUD HOTLINE

Many of Serve's clients reported that they wanted to provide the company with a list of ex-employees who they suspected may have been using a sub-IDs, but they did not have a way to get in touch with Serve. Linden established a hotline to fill this need.

TRAINING

Trainers are now sent to corporate clients' offices to show them how to use Serve's products and Web site effectively. The trainers make the clients aware of the importance of protecting their IDs, inform them of the safety step that Serve recently implemented and provide them with ways to contact the company later if they want to report suspicious behavior.

CONCLUSION

This case made it clear to me that threats from Internet fraudsters are continuously evolving to form new fraud avenues. To keep fraud and its perpetrators at bay, it is important to roll out new technologies, identify appropriate regulations and educate consumers of the dangers they face.

About the Author

Jyoti Khetarpal is a qualified chartered accountant in India with more than 12 years of corporate experience with organizations including Dun & Bradstreet and American Express. She has been instrumental in outlining risk management methodology, analytics and assessment. Jyoti is currently working with Alea Consulting to provide reputational due diligence, corporate (fraud) investigations, intellectual property protection, KYC and other related services.

Dribbling on the Internet

TIMOTHY D. MARTIN

Practice had gone an hour longer than usual and Jeff was getting nervous. The Littleton High School Cougars had done well this season and were headed to the state basketball championships. Seventeen-year-old Jeff Wilson was a tall, good-looking kid and the star of the basketball team. He was outgoing and well liked by his classmates and teachers alike.

Coach Mather called his name again and Jeff snapped out of his thoughts. The coach was saying something about the players not letting up at this point in the season. Jeff didn't understand why the coach was pushing so hard when the players had done so well this year. Finally the whistle was blown and the players headed for the showers, but Jeff went straight out the door to his motorcycle. His parents would be home soon and he had work to do.

When Jeff arrived after basketball practice, he was relieved to find that his parents were not there yet. He rushed into the house and dropped his gym bag and schoolbooks on the floor. He needed to check his e-mail before his parents came home. The computer was in his parents' bedroom. When he entered their bedroom he saw his younger brother sitting at the computer chatting with his online friends. His annoyance was apparent when he told his brother to get off the computer, as he was in a hurry to use it. He locked the door as the younger boy left the room.

Logging into his Web site, he was nearly petrified when he saw the number of new e-mails he had received, each asking the same thing — "Where is my money?"

Jeff checked his E-Gold account to see how much was left in it. At the moment there wasn't nearly enough to cover the requested refunds and profit payments, so he checked his DMS account to see if prices had improved since the previous Friday — things looked worse. Prices were continuing to decline and his account had lost another 15 percent. He had less than what he had started with. Jeff's original plan had been to invest the entirety of the UWI money he had received but, after the significant gains DMS had reported last year, he thought he could invest just half of it and still show his investors acceptable returns. They certainly wouldn't be able to tell that he had spent the rest on himself.

This year was different. The markets had fallen and the options he purchased were losing money. He was down to a quarter of what he had invested and prices were still falling. Things just weren't happening like he had expected. If only he hadn't wanted that motorcycle so much.

Jeff was nervous. The sweat was running down his neck and forehead. The state championships were in three weeks, the whole school was counting on him and he didn't need this kind of stress. How was he going to come up with the money to pay these people back? What would happen if they found out who he was? What would happen if they found out he had spent their money on a new motorcycle? What could he do? He heard the garage door open — Mom and Dad were home. He quickly signed off the Web site and shut down the computer. The investors would not be getting a response that night.

The Disgruntled Investor

I was at my desk in the Idaho Department of Finance one morning when I received a call. The man on the other end of the line identified himself as Rob Miles from Denton, Florida, and said he wanted to get some information on Universal Wealth, Inc. (UWI). He said that he and his wife had made a sizeable investment with the investment firm and he was concerned because he hadn't heard from them since he transferred his money. Miles had sent e-mails to them but had received no response.

I asked him how he became acquainted with the company. Miles said he was looking for an investment that would give him a better return than he was getting at his bank. A friend referred him to the Web site of the Internet-based investment company UWI, which promised returns of 20–50 percent on a low-risk investment. Miles gave me the company's URL and told me that his research indicated the Web site was operating out of Australia.

I reviewed UWI's Web site briefly while Miles and I were on the phone. It showed that the firm had offices along the East Coast of the United States and in the United Kingdom but did not disclose the specific locations due to "security issues." I asked him what made him decide the firm had ties to Idaho. He stated that the Web site gave the names of a number of options-trading firms as advisors, one of which was DMS Options Trading (DMS).

Miles contacted them for information on UWI, and the representative he spoke with said that DMS did not have an account by that name but the company had received a number of calls about the firm and they were looking into it. A DMS employee called Miles back a few days later and told him the UWI Web site was operating out of Idaho and suggested he call the Idaho Department of Finance. So Miles called me. I told Miles that our records had no registration or licensing information on UWI but that I would do some investigating to see what I could find.

Suspicious Web Site

After reviewing the UWI Web site, I could tell it was put together quite well but the text was poorly written. I couldn't determine if the information had been written by someone outside the country who wasn't fluent in English or if the author simply wasn't trained in professional writing. I had seen hundreds of Nigerian advance-fee scams with their poorly written letters and e-mails, and at least this wasn't that bad.

The Web site claimed that UWI was an international investment program "open only to qualified, accepted, private UWI members." It said that the program was exempt from U.S. and British securities laws and that the company's traders "invest and trade in stock options based off of trading signals received by professional licensed advisories."

The UWI Web site made several claims about the company, its investment process and the returns that the investors could expect. I found the following representations.

- UWI has been in business for seven years and has more than 500 members.
- UWI offers one basic program that has a fluctuating return based on the performance of the funds traded.
- By joining UWI, you will be entered into a pool of investors just like you.
- The funds will be invested into stock options. These trades will be made based off intra-day signals received by three different professional option advisors.
- These investments would normally require large sums of money to operate; however, as a group our money can be pooled together and we can participate in trades that are typically only available to the wealthiest investors.
- The returns average a rate of 20–50 percent per month. That means you could earn 100 percent of your money back in two months.

Investors were required to make Internet transfers to UWI using E-Gold deposits. As the Web site explained, E-Gold was an alternative digital currency with a low transfer cost and real-time clearances that provided privacy and legal benefits. UWI also claimed the deposits were backed by "100-percent real gold." E-Gold acted as a third-party escrow system where investors deposited funds and used E-Gold digital currency to make purchases on the Internet. Other restrictions were that UWI accepted only investments of $1,000 or more, and withdrawals were limited to one per month. The Web site provided a table representing the organization's performance for the previous seven years.

Year One — 263% returns

Year Two — 198% returns

Year Three — 502% returns

Year Four — 318% returns

Year Five — 312% returns

Year Six — 427% returns

Year Seven — 387% returns

An Australian Diversion

My next step was to determine who owned the Web site. My Whois search indicated a private owner with an Australian domain registrar, so I tried to find the owner on an Australian Whois Web site. That did the trick. UWI was registered to Jeffrey Wilson in Littleton, Idaho. His name and address were listed along with the date the Web site was set up.

The next day I received a call from Dan Marcella of DMS Options Trading in Boca Raton, Florida. He informed me that DMS was receiving a large number of inquiries from investors who had put money into a company called UWI. They were telling him that they believed DMS was somehow connected to UWI. He said he had conducted an internal investigation and had no evidence of a connection to UWI. He then reviewed investor accounts that may have had trades similar to those mentioned by the complainants, and the only match he found was Jeffrey Wilson in Littleton, Idaho. Dan told me he gave that information to several of the investors and suggested that they call the securities regulator in Idaho, and he was calling now to follow up.

Marcella provided me with the information he had on the investors who had called him and gave me information on Wilson's account. He said that he would send me the account documents and e-mail correspondence.

After I looked at it, this information appeared to confirm Wilson's involvement with UWI.

When I hung up with Marcella, I searched the Internet; the National White Collar Crime Center's database; and state, national and foreign securities databases, but none of them contained information UWI. I checked the CLEAR AutoTrax database and other public databases, but again found nothing.

Mounting Pressure

The following day I received two more calls from UWI investors. Their stories were the same — referrals to UWI, Internet investments made with E-Gold and then no further contact from anyone with the firm. I searched the Internet for Jeffrey Wilson, but the only information I could find was on a high-school basketball player in Littleton, Idaho, a star athlete who was leading his team to the state championships.

A check of the Idaho driver's license database verified that his address matched the one on the UWI domain registration, but I thought that couldn't be right — his driver's license showed that he was only 17 years old. He was a teenager; he couldn't possibly have the knowledge and skills needed to run an international options-trading firm. Perhaps his father or some other relative had the same name. I found a driver's license for David Wilson, age 46, and Margaret Wilson, age 42, at that address.

Perhaps it was time to bring Jeff Wilson in.

Home Visit

The next few days were difficult for Jeff. He was withdrawn and preoccupied and had been avoiding the computer. He didn't know how to respond to the growing number of unhappy e-mails he was receiving. Coach Mather was pushing him harder and harder. Jeff couldn't concentrate in class and he was behind on his homework. His dad was on him for forgetting to shovel the snow from the driveway and his mom was worried because he was not hungry. Then it happened — a sheriff's deputy was at the door asking to see Jeffrey Wilson. Mr. Wilson called Jeff to come down and explain what was going on, and the deputy handed Jeff a subpoena from the Idaho Department of Finance requesting that he appear in Boise in 10 days. His face was white and his throat was dry. Jeff's father shut the door and seemed confused and angry. He demanded to know what was going on. Jeff led him into the master bedroom and logged into his Web site.

A few days after Jeff was served his subpoena, I received a call from Harold Madison, an attorney in Portland, Oregon. He said that he was an

attorney and a relative of Jeffrey's and he wanted to know why Jeff was being subpoenaed. I asked if he was representing Jeffrey and Madison said
for the time being he was. I told him we had reason to believe that Jeff was
involved in violations of the Idaho Securities Act, stemming from his operation of a Web site through which he solicited and sold unregistered securities to investors throughout the United States. Madison said that he
believed Jeff had only been involved for a few months but he didn't know
how much money was brought in. He asked if he could attend the investigative testimony by telephone, but I told him both Jeff and his attorney
needed to appear in person. He said he would advise Jeffrey on how to
respond but he would probably be turning the case over to a local attorney
in Boise.

Man-to-Man Chat

On the day Jeff Wilson was expected to give a sworn statement, he appeared
at our offices with his father and John Rivera, a Boise attorney. John asked
if he could sit in on the meeting, and I consented. The court reporter swore
in Jeff and I informed him of his constitutional rights before questioning
him about his involvement in UWI.

I asked Jeff if he had an educational or occupational history in investments and he replied that he did not. I asked him if he was the one who
created UWI and its Web site. He said that he was. I asked him if anyone
else was involved with him in this business, and he said no but he had a
cousin who knew about it. His cousin was about the same age as Jeff.

When I asked Jeff how he came up with the idea for UWI, he explained
that he had seen similar Web sites on the Internet and was interested in
what they did. He even made a small investment in one to see what happened. I asked him if he made a return on his investment, but he had not.
Jeff then began looking into similar Internet securities and investment services and realized that many of them offered very high returns with low
risk and paid a monthly return. They didn't look too complicated and Jeff
decided that he could set up something similar.

UWI's investors would deposit money into his E-Gold account and he
would withdraw the money and deposit half of the funds into a UWI bank
account and the other half into his personal account. He then opened an
account at DMS in his name and deposited the investors' money in DMS's
high-yield program. I asked him why he put half of the money in his own
account and he said he wanted to have money in reserve to pay the investors' monthly return if he needed to. To relax Jeff a little during the interview, I switched topics and asked him about school, his friends and his

basketball team. I have found that for some people this method works better than continuing to increase their stress level.

We then turned to the Web site he created. He had made several representations on the Web site that were highly suspect. On the home page, Jeff wrote that the program was only offered to a select group of investors. When I asked why he claimed the firm was located in the Northeastern United States with offices throughout the world, he said he thought it sounded more prestigious. I questioned him about the monthly returns of 20–50 percent he quoted to the investors — he just made up the numbers. As for claiming UWI was a low-risk investment, he said he thought it would bring in more investors.

To conclude our interview, I asked if he felt what he did was wrong. Jeff said he realized it was but at the time he didn't think about it. He also said he thought returning the investors' money would be the right thing to do, but he didn't know where he was going to get the cash.

After the interview was over, Jeff's father asked what we intended to do with his son. I told him I couldn't say but that we would review the facts and notify them of our decision. Mr. Wilson looked at Jeff and said he would certainly be working to pay back the investors. He would also be reconsidering Jeff's computer use, his ownership of a motorcycle and his involvement in basketball.

When he returned home, Jeff's life changed. He got a part-time job and went to work after school. He had to miss the basketball championship and sold the motorcycle.

Cease and Desist

After reviewing my evidence in the case, I started writing the report using a standard format that included the subject's name, the entities involved and a description of the events. I specified the laws, statutes and violations and listed the possible counts that could be filed with the court. I submitted my final report to my supervisor for review and we concluded — based on Jeffrey's age and the amount of money he scammed from investors — that we would not send it on to the attorney general for civil or criminal prosecution. Our securities statute allows the Director of the Idaho Department of Finance to issue administrative orders, so we decided to issue a Consent Order to Cease and Desist, which outlined the facts of the case, stated our findings of violations and provided for the admission of the violations. The order required restitution to investors and the payment of a fine in the amount of $2,000. Jeff signed the order and agreed to its findings and terms.

Lessons Learned

It is evident from this case that there is no age requirement to commit fraud. I have investigated cases in which the perpetrators were in their seventies or eighties, but I was surprised to see someone this young. As technology has developed and become more accessible, the younger generation has embraced it and has access to more technology than anyone before them. Given these factors, we may expect to see more and more young people involved in Internet fraud.

Parents need to be aware of what their children are doing online and monitor their Internet use. With advanced technology comes a responsibility to guard against its misuse. In the same vein, it remains the responsibility of investors to do their due diligence before parting with their money.

Recommendations to Prevent Future Occurrences

The Idaho Department of Finance has teamed with other agencies and organizations — such as the Investor Protection Trust and the Financial Literacy Coalition — to provide savings and investment education to high-school students throughout the state. These programs provide training to teachers, students and parents in recognizing, preventing and avoiding financial fraud. Students are taught the importance of protecting themselves from fraud and about the penalties that may befall them if they become involved in perpetrating a scheme. We have received great responses from these programs and we believe our efforts have been successful.

About the Author

Timothy D. Martin, CFE, is a securities investigator with the Idaho Department of Finance. He has more than 20 years of investigative experience with the state of Idaho specializing in investment fraud. He has extensive experience in undercover investigation and asset identification and recovery. Mr. Martin is an expert witness and has provided testimony in numerous court cases in the areas of securities and commodities fraud. Mr. Martin is the state agency representative to the National White Collar Crime Center (NW3C) and serves on the state of Idaho's advisory committee for homeland security.

Behind the Mask

CHRISTIAN ANDRÉ CHMIEL

Czeslaw Ovseenko was a very elusive man. Both Internet research and official inquiries sent to authorities failed to uncover much information about him. In fact, he was barely more than a phantom. There was nothing distinguishing about him, and he kept himself hidden in the background. The photograph in his passport — the only known picture of him — showed a 33-year-old Ukrainian citizen with a face like a child's. But whether the photo really depicted Czeslaw Ovseenko or an imposter, no one knows. Even his residence at the time of this case was uncertain. It was assumed that he was either in Malta, Ukraine or Russia.

But one thing was certain — Ovseenko had to be a technically skilled programmer who was familiar with the production of highly sensitive and complicated software. Even if people did not know his name, the name of his software program was well-known to millions of Internet users. It was so famous that one of the leading software manufacturers offered a bounty of $250,000 for him. Why? Ovseenko not only had broad knowledge in the field of software programming, but he also had a high degree of criminal energy.

Online Sys-Tec Limited, based in Malta, was a software company that specialized in the development, programming and sale of antivirus software. It was founded by a group of software developers and programmers who previously worked together on a large technology project. The majority shareholder in Online Sys-Tec was a woman named Helena Sarantakos. Interestingly, she was not only the owner of the company but also the managing director and held the position of a secretary.

Helena's company offered software products to individuals and businesses to analyze the content of a Windows-operated PC in order to detect and remove malicious programs and files that had surreptitiously been installed on the computer. It was supposed to keep the PC clean and protect it from being infected by such malicious programs again. It purported to scan a computer, identify the invading programs and remove them.

The company offered its products only online. Its Web site featured the current software program and its capability, and customers were able to buy it directly online using their credit cards. The product did not need to be shipped because it was downloaded directly from the Web site. What was sold was aimed mainly at Internet users who had little or no experience in the fight against computer viruses and Trojan horses. Scare tactics were the primary marketing ploy on the Web site.

Picture-Perfect Compliance

I was working as a compliance manager for an international bank that provided credit cards and other financial services to businesses. At the end of November, I received a letter from the United States with a credit card application for a new Internet-based merchant — Online Sys-Tec Limited. The fact that it was sent from the United States but based in Malta did not seem strange to me because several merchants have their headquarters outside Europe. At the time, I did not know that this would be the first unusual event in a series.

Enclosed with the application was a detailed business plan that said:

> Online Sys-Tec Ltd. is currently offering an anti-virus product that can be purchased online from the product Web site quickly and easily. The product is a removal utility that will help fight all kinds of spyware, adware, browser hijackers and dialers that are some of the most annoying and pervasive threats in the Internet today. By simply browsing a Web page, you could find your computer infected with one of the above-mentioned malicious programs. The most important step you can take is to secure your system, ideally before something happens. "Virus-Smash" is the most powerful protection program available.

After reading that the software "is the most powerful protection program available," I thought it must be well known but I wondered why I had not heard about it. I decided to conduct a Google search for the product to see what I was missing out on, as opposed to starting the official compliance examination I run on new merchant applications. The results of my online search surprised me. Only 21 results were found on the term *Virus-Smash*. I began to suspect that the software might not be "the most powerful protection program available." I had a hunch that something might be wrong.

According to my employer's usual compliance procedure, I first ran a background check on Online Sys-Tec. I investigated Dun & Bradstreet's database and had a closer look at the company documents. I was interested in the fact that Helena Sarantakos was not only the managing director of Online Sys-Tec, but was also the managing director of 70 other limited companies registered in Malta. The company documents included a power of attorney signed the same day that the company was registered. With this document, Czeslaw Ovseenko was empowered to act in any capacity for Online Sys-Tec Limited. This power of attorney made me think that Helena Sarantakos was just a stooge and Czeslaw Ovseenko was the true owner.

Next I ran a check in the databases of two major credit card companies. First I searched for the company's name and the managing director but there were no matches for either. After that I searched for a match of the company's address, and more than 100 different results were displayed. This led me to the realization that the Online Sys-Tec was probably a shell company. My last step was to run a search for Czeslaw Ovseenko's name, and I actually got a result, which surprised me. Previously, Czeslaw Ovseenko was the managing director of a company named Zarbol Limited, which was located at the same address as Online Sys-Tec. Because of excessive charge-back problems and suspected credit card fraud on the part of Zarbol, the merchant had been terminated. This was the point when I began to deepen the investigation.

Occupational Curiosity

As a compliance manager, I am expected to be skeptical about many things. Because some inconsistencies had already appeared in my first analysis, my natural curiosity was aroused and I launched even more checks. First I wanted an overview of the products that Online Sys-Tec offered. I took a closer look at the company's Web site, which, in the end, would have been connected to our payment system. The Web site looked very professional. Routinely, I checked the product descriptions, the checkout process, the privacy statement, the imprint and the terms and conditions. I was amazed. The Web site was completely compliant in each aspect and requirement of credit card organizations. This was more than unusual. Normally new merchants need to make many changes before we consider them to be in complete compliance with the requirements of credit card organizations. Someone appeared to have done his homework in order to avoid any possible suspicion in case of a review.

However, I did discover a problem with the Virus-Smash software. To have a comprehensive picture of the company, I naturally wanted to test the software program's functionality. After I downloaded the 52-megabyte free version of the software, I was not able to run it. Each time I started the installation process I received an error warning and then the installation would be terminated. I tried to install the software on different computers but each time I had the same result.

Next, I expanded my search on Zarbol Limited in Dun & Bradstreet's database. Unfortunately, the credit rating information for the company was just as meaningless as the information I had found for Online Sys-Tec. Zarbol had been founded and liquidated eight months later. The company's official purpose was the trade of electronic goods. Both the business purpose and the length of time it was in operation indicated that Zarbol Limited might be the predecessor of Online Sys-Tec Limited.

I thought that Zarbol was my key to more information, so I ran a Google search on the name. Unfortunately, only a few general results came up, such as the Web site the company had used when it was in operation. Zarbol also appeared in a report titled "The Secrets of Cybercrime" (http://hostexploit.com) which described in detail the actions of a fake antivirus software program, along with screenshots. The report further said:

> The fake anti-virus campaigns work on two levels. The first is installing malware that downloads up to 30 other independent Trojans and key loggers. The second level is the direct billing. Here the victims are misled or forced to buy the dangerous product with their credit card.

The report also provided the number of visitors to Zarbol's Web site each day; there was an average of 40,000 from the United States alone. If Online Sys-Tec Limited was actually the successor of Zarbol Limited, two things were clear. It could be a dangerous product that was used under certain circumstances to collect credit card information. In addition, the software was in a position to generate surprisingly high traffic and to spread extremely fast. I needed to find proof for the connection of these two companies.

Passing of the Torch

After I was unable to run the software program provided by Online Sys-Tec and verify its function, I knew I needed other proof of the connection between these two companies and their apparently fraudulent intentions. My first approach was to compare the Web sites of Zarbol Limited and Online Sys-Tec Limited, based on the URL I already found in my Google search for Zarbol. Unfortunately, the Zarbol Web site had been shut down when the company closed and was unavailable. That left me with two other options to compare the Web sites: the Google cache and the Internet archive (www .archive.org).

The search engine Google stores a copy of every Web site it searches when creating a search index, the so-called Google cache. It can be viewed by individual users and is especially helpful when a Web site has been deleted by the operator. The problem is that the cache will be overwritten when the page is searched again, and the user will only see the latest state of the Web site prior to its closure. This fact was probably known by the employees of Zarbol Limited; when I tried looking in the cache I only received the message "It works!"

I had better luck with the Internet archive (also known as the "Wayback Machine"). In contrast to Google's cache, the archive not only stores the most recent copy, but also keeps records of the previous versions of the Web site. These records allowed me to compare Zarbol's and Online Sys-Tec's Web sites. Visually, there were obvious differences but, interestingly, the menu structure and the content were identical.

This confirmed my suspicion that Online Sys-Tec was the successor of Zarbol, so I instituted further inquiries to gather more evidence. I examined the Internet protocol (IP) address of Online Sys-Tec's domain more closely. For this I used a handy Web site known as the Robtex Swiss Army Knife, which allows users to search multiple features of any Web site. The first request I made was to determine the owners of the domain. The Whois search I conducted through Robtex indicated that the domain name was registered to a so-called privacy service. They are typically used to conceal a domain's true owner and are often used by shell companies. Privacy services are also used by "high-risk" ventures, such as adult entertainment or gambling, not by pure e-commerce businesses.

This raised the question of why a dealer who was selling antivirus software would conceal his identity. To get more information about the domain holder, I contacted the privacy service by e-mail. Unfortunately I was told that the information I was seeking would be provided only to investigative governmental authorities. This direction of my search hit a dead end.

Next, I decided to look into the IP address. To do this, I first had to identify to which domain it was registered. Again, Robtex was able to provide this information. I then conducted a reverse IP search, which would display any other domains that were registered on that the same IP address; unfortunately, this yielded no results. Undaunted, I tried to cross-check the e-mail server that both Web sites used and found out that Online Sys-Tec's Web site used the same e-mail server as the former Web site of Zarbol.

As the final step, I conducted a test purchase of Online Sys-Tec's software. After I completed the ordering process on the Web site and paid for the software with an immediate bank transfer, I promptly received a confirmation e-mail. There was nothing remarkable about it, except for one small thing: The signature of the automatically generated confirmation e-mail said "Zarbol Limited."

Details Emerge

I presented my evidence to my supervisor for review before handing it over to the control department. According to my research, this was not a minor offense; it seemed that thousands of Internet users had already fallen victim to Online Sys-Tec's scam. Because of this, I suggested that we submit the case to the federal authorities. However, if we were going to hand over the case for possible prosecution, I wanted to ensure that I had not misinterpreted the results of my audit.

My boss and I reviewed the documents that Online Sys-Tec Limited had submitted with the application for a credit card. A closer look at the business plan showed that it had been written very generally, so we conducted a plagiarism test to determine if the text had been copied from a publicly available source, such as another company's Web site. We used an Internet tool called Copyscape to conduct our search. The Web site uses various search engines to look for matches of the provided text on other Web sites.

From this search, we identified four more companies, which were purportedly involved in the sale of antivirus software products. They were based in either Malta or Cyprus, sometimes even at the same address as Online Sys-Tec Limited. Our suspicion hardened that we were dealing with a much larger fraud case than we originally thought.

Since we had four more names, we performed a fresh Internet search on each one. We discovered thousands of complaints from duped Internet users who purchased the antivirus program. A query to credit card organizations identified one bank that had already been affected by this scam — it had lost tens of millions of dollars.

We also uncovered information explaining how this scam works. The Internet user was offered a free virus scan and only had to install it. After downloading and installing the program from the Web page, the software told the user that his computer was not infected by a virus. Depending on the particular site, the program would sometimes tell the user that he did in fact have a virus, but that the software had removed it. Thus the customer thought the process was finished.

However, after about three to seven days, the software reported that the computer had become infected by a virus or a Trojan horse but this was just a ploy for the user to enter his credit card data, allegedly because only the purchased version of the software could remove the virus. If the user ignored this warning, the same message would appear two days later. Over time, the period between the warnings drastically reduced, until the individual could no longer use his computer because the message was popping up every two seconds. Eventually the frustrated user invariably purchased the software just to be able to stop the pop-up warnings and use his computer again.

Alternatively, the user could call a toll-free number to report problems. When presented with complaints of the pop-up warnings, customer service representatives consistently offered the same solution: For a small service charge of $21.99, the software would be disabled and the pop-ups would stop. This was presented to the individual as a preferred alternative to buying the software at full price. Not surprisingly, the user only had to furnish his credit card information over the phone.

The strength of our combined evidence convinced my supervisor to hand over the investigation to the federal authorities. As of this writing, a warrant has been issued for the arrest of Czeslaw Ovseenko, but he has proven difficult to locate. As unfortunately happens in too many Internet fraud cases, the perpetrator's anonymity allows him to slip away.

Lessons Learned

Through this case I was able to gain new and valuable experience in the field of online investigation. Particularly interesting to me was the precision and care required when auditing the sale of digital goods. During the audit I discovered a report titled "The Secrets of Cybercrime," which showed me how quick and easy it was to conduct millions of dollars in fraudulent sales with a worthless software program. I was surprised at how small the percentage of purchasers who reported the fraud was — less than 10 percent.

With the constantly changing Internet technology and the possibilities of anonymity, it is not difficult to become victimized by Internet fraud. Whether the victim will become aware of the fraud remains a question. Also, online marketing can reach hundreds of thousands — if not millions — of people at once, meaning frauds for very small dollar amounts become profitable when committed against a large population.

I also discovered the importance of not informing our potential customers, in this case Online Sys-Tec Limited, about our research results before they were complete. To do so could have prompted Ovseenko to obliterate the traces of his fraud, an easy task to complete on the Internet.

Recommendations to Prevent Future Occurrences

After investigating this case, my company implemented a few more standard checks to the application process for new e-commerce merchants. These steps could serve other financial institutions well.

COMPLETE COMPLIANCE

Even if a Web site looks exceptionally professional, it should not be above suspicion. If the Web site is 100 percent compliant to the requirements of the credit card organization, it should be considered very unusual and a red flag. If something looks too good to be true, it usually is.

TEST PURCHASES

Perform test purchases of new e-commerce merchants and their products to determine whether the dealer can actually deliver, whether the products correspond to their descriptions, how long it takes for the customer to receive the product and how the merchant responds to complaints or returns. Digital goods should be tested extensively by the IT department, particularly when only one product is sold on a Web site.

PLAGIARISM TESTS

To determine whether the merchant has already sold a similar product on different Web sites and to identify those other sites, conduct an online plagiarism test using specific product descriptions, frequently asked questions and terms and conditions. Previous patterns of behavior can be uncovered, which may indicate how the merchant will behave in the future.

WHOIS LOOKUP

Review the Whois database for information about the beneficial owner of a Web site. Especially in the field of e-commerce, the owner's name should match the merchant information provided in the contract agreement. If another person, firm or privacy service is registered, it should be regarded as suspect and looked at more closely.

REVERSE IP AND SEARCH ENGINE CHECKS

Web sites of new online merchants can be subject to reverse IP and search engine checks. These searches could reveal whether other URLs are operated by the merchant, and the URLs that deliver e-mail to the Web site's mail server can be analyzed. A search engine may uncover negative reports or messages about the merchant or its other Web sites.

The best recommendation for compliance and risk managers to prevent fraud is to stay up to date with new research methods and opportunities, to be suspicious when it seems necessary and to perhaps be even more suspicious when it does not seem necessary. Who knows? Someone could be lurking behind the mask.

About the Author

Christian André Chmiel studied at the Euro-FH in Hamburg, Germany, and at the University of Lincoln, Great Britain. He works as a compliance manager at Wirecard Bank AG in Germany and specializes in online investigations for fraud prevention in the acquiring business. His e-mail address is c.chmiel@gmx.de.

CHAPTER

Online Pharmacy

JON COHEN

J effrey Stevens knew in an instant that he had died and gone to heaven. How else could he explain his good fortune? After struggling for years to earn an income that could feed his seemingly insatiable appetite for the finer things in life, Stevens had just stumbled upon what he could describe only as a goldmine of financial opportunity. The native Canadian had recently immigrated to the United States, but not to just anywhere. He moved to the land of a narcissist's dreams — Southern California — the home of the eternally optimistic, the place that invented sculptured bodies, where nearly everyone was on a perpetual diet. Where better to fulfill his fantasy of striking it rich in the world of weight-loss clinics and body-care elixirs?

Stevens was the oldest child in a home of four boys and three girls, just another mouth to feed for his middle-class parents. His father eked out a meager income selling linen supplies to hotels and restaurants, often stretching his workday into nights and weekends. His mother was left to raise the seven children as best as she knew how, constantly wondering where the next dollar was coming from. Jeff decided at an early age that he wanted a way out and scrounged around for opportunities to build a get-away nest egg. Although he struggled to graduate from high school, Jeff was blessed with a wealth of common sense, street smarts and a golden tongue. He used these attributes, along with his muscular physique, to convince people to buy what he happened to be selling at the time and gradually amassed a tidy sum. One day he felt confident enough to take his earnings and embark on a new venture, one that he believed was destined to bring him untold wealth. After months of developing and refining it, he eventually hatched a business plan, resulting in an enterprise that grossed more than $51 million in 18 months.

In a small town more than 300 miles from Stevens's native Montreal suburb, a tall, gawky man with jet-black spiked hair shared a similar dream.

David Crane, the son of a domineering father and an introverted mother, had been a recluse throughout his time at Peterson Senior High School. While lacking the social graces to compete with the "popular" kids in his class, Crane was a bright student whose talent for preparing undiscovered cheat sheets brought him considerable acclaim. Crane excelled in math and computer science classes, and was rewarded with a full scholarship to McGoughan University, in the heart of Toronto. He soon warmed to the academic and social environment of the large campus and transformed his appearance, trading heavy black-framed eyeglasses for contact lenses and committing to a daily regimen of weight training. As he grew physically and intellectually, a sense of inner confidence took hold and his demeanor underwent a dramatic change.

Following graduation, Crane began the first of a series of jobs in the information technology (IT) field and over time built an impressive résumé with successful performances at several IT startup firms. Restless for greater challenges and a higher standard of living, David put out feelers to acquaintances in California's Silicon Valley. He soon found work in the exciting and competitive e-commerce field, creating software templates for a variety of businesses. With a new girlfriend and a rosy employment outlook, Crane was at a happy place in life. Only a few years later would he look back on this time from his prison cell and wonder how it had fallen apart.

Standing before the Stanford Medical Society's elite membership at their annual symposium, Samuel Melendez was thrilled to be presenting yet another announcement of a research breakthrough in the treatment of obesity. As an alumnus of a prestigious university, he felt honored to grace their presence and deliver a speech he was certain would be well received. Melendez lived to hear the heartfelt congratulations of his colleagues for his achievements and basked in their compliments. He was a shy man who desperately needed the praise they so readily bestowed upon him. It was a different environment from the one he was accustomed to as a child growing up in a Mexican town near the border of Texas. His father was an illiterate man who toiled in the migrant farms of South Texas, picking fruit and vegetables for meager pay. His mother worked part-time as a neighborhood seamstress and devoted equal energy to raising their three children.

Samuel was the middle son of three mischievous boys; he managed to distinguish and separate himself from his two brothers and school friends in elementary school. His mother often remarked that Samuel was a special gift from above because he was bright, handsome and possessed a resolute quality — none of which were in abundance in the Melendez family. As Samuel developed a sharp intellect, his parents convinced Hector and Maria Arguelo to take him into their home and raise him as a son. The

Arguelos were distant relatives who worked in the lush orchards of Orange County, California, and lived in a rented three-bedroom apartment. The purpose of Samuel's move was twofold. First, it enabled him to attend the highly regarded Orange County school system, which placed him on track for greater academic success than he could achieve in Mexico; and second, it gave the Arguelo family — desperate for money to feed their growing family of twelve children — a steady stream of undeclared income from Samuel's parents.

In due course, Samuel proved himself to be the boy his family expected. He garnered one award after another for his high marks in school and excelled in nearly every course he took. Taking a special interest in the natural sciences, particularly chemistry, Samuel became a model student. Upon graduation from high school, he was offered a full scholarship to Vilpaso University. Racing through his college coursework, Melendez graduated summa cum laude in three years and enrolled in the university's highly ranked medical school. After graduation, he embarked on a career path that was filled with increasingly frequent accomplishments, awards and financial wealth far beyond his childhood dreams. By the time he met Jeff Stevens, Melendez had done much more than he ever imagined but still felt somehow professionally unfulfilled. But he recently suffered from a series of poor financial investments, and a sense of panic had begun to set in, combined with a deteriorating lack of self-confidence.

Two more players would join this band of unlikely accomplices that would later be charged with committing a massive Internet prescription drug fraud. Mansour Jibril, a rather naïve yet brilliant physician who traveled to the United States from his native India; and Stefan Gorbonich, a shrewd businessman cloaked in the white coat of a respectable neighborhood pharmacist, rounded out the group.

Supply and Demand

Located in Southern California, The Physician Group (TPG) was founded in 2001 by Jeffrey Stevens, although Samuel Melendez was also listed in corporate documents as a cofounder and the chief medical officer. Stevens envisioned TPG as a multilayered business venture that marketed a diverse product line capable of yielding huge profits — all through e-commerce. Beginning with printer inkjet cartridges, contact lenses and diabetic testing kits, the firm broadened its offerings to include so-called lifestyle products, such as pills developed for the treatment of male erectile dysfunction and weight loss. Although prescriptions were technically required for some of TPG's products, Stevens counted on his long-term relationship with Dr. Samuel Melendez to overcome this hurdle.

Melendez and Stevens met each other in the early 1990s when diet clinics were springing up almost daily throughout Los Angeles, and a miracle weight-loss product called Fen-Phen was all the rage. This trend shaped their business idea, and the two men established a one-stop diet shop. With Stevens assuming the role of chief administrator, Melendez served as medical director and the outward face of their first clinic on Sunset Boulevard near Hollywood Beach. Until the bubble burst and Fen-Phen became discredited as a dangerous drug, their little enterprise had grown to six outpatient clinics and achieved considerable financial success and public acclaim.

The TPG business model was designed to deliver a variety of products directly to the consumer, bypassing more expensive distribution networks and parasitic middlemen. Through direct shipping, storage and handling costs were significantly reduced and the term *speedy delivery* became both the goal and mantra of the company.

Customers were willing to pay for this convenience with price markups usually exceeding five times what they would pay for a prescription at the corner brick-and-mortar pharmacy. The hitch with the latter was the need for a valid written prescription from a licensed physician, which usually meant a trip to a doctor's office and frequently a physical examination. For the typical street junkie, that was neither financially feasible nor desirable. Often lacking health insurance and unable to convince physicians to prescribe whatever drugs they wanted, many drug abusers opted for the Internet choice. Even if it meant scrounging around for the extra money, the ability to order exactly what they asked for was highly preferable to playing by the rules.

TPG's Clientele

Molly Williams was a 27-year-old high school dropout who spent time on the cruel urban streets. Molly learned at an early age to fend for herself; she fell into a pattern of skipping school to hang out with a rough crowd and quickly slid into a life dominated by drugs. To her friends, Molly seemed to be in a race to sample as many different street drugs as possible. She rotated through various stages of criminal behavior, incarceration and/or drug rehabilitation, and then she went back on the streets to begin another cycle.

During one of her many stints in rehab, a friend told Williams about procuring drugs online. Williams learned how to log into an available computer (for free at the local library) and order whatever prescription drug she wanted. Initially, Molly used stolen credit cards and arranged to meet the delivery service in front of abandoned houses in her neighborhood, but she soon graduated to paying cash-on-delivery (COD) at the shippers' local outlet. No one checked Molly's identification, but just in case, she carried a driver's license belonging to her friend Janine, whom she closely resembled.

After more than 14 months of this practice, Molly was arrested for passing a forged check at the local mall. As a repeat offender, she was incarcerated and agreed to cooperate with the local police — which meant being admitted to yet another drug rehabilitation program. However, in her fuzzy-minded state, Williams forgot that she had a wealth of illicit loot in her apartment. She was stunned to later learn that police, upon executing a search warrant, had discovered a variety of documents and physical evidence indicating a conspiracy to defraud area pharmacies and to facilitate drug trafficking. From these meager beginnings, a complex international investigation was eventually launched by the Drug Enforcement Administration, the Internal Revenue Service and the U.S. Postal Inspection Service that culminated in the dismantling of the largest Internet-based prescription drug fraud in U.S. history at the time.

Online Marketplace

Stevens had been searching for a new way to exploit the rising e-commerce marketplace after his stores collapsed because of the Fen-Phen scandal. He finally stumbled onto the Internet prescription drug trade and was impressed with the unusually high profit potential. After meeting with some industry insiders, Stevens developed a business model that he confidently predicted would provide an unending revenue stream. Recalling his street-hustler days, the Internet venture seemed like an easy plan to put in action. He enlisted a group of Internet-based "affiliates" — a loose network of people who would do most of his grunt work. Stevens and David Crane then furnished them with product templates and insisted they link only to the TPG Web site. The templates listed TPG's product menu, which was made up of controlled drugs like diet pills and loosely regulated, noncontrolled substances. The menu also included a line of unregulated merchandise, such as diabetic testing kits and contact lenses.

Stevens quickly recognized that the highest profits were made on controlled substances, like weight-loss drugs and mood adjusters (depressants, stimulants or pain relievers). For example, one pill of Phentermine could be sold online for as much as five to six times its unit cost. Patients were willing to pay the premium to avoid visiting the doctor, where a suspicious prescription request might be rejected. And Stevens, ever the savvy marketer, allowed his affiliates to adjust the retail price of each item to stimulate demand.

Because the affiliates' Web sites were linked to the TPG Web site, they actually did little work. The entire backroom process — taking customer orders and payments, routing orders to physicians and pharmacies and ensuring prompt processing and shipping — were handled through the TPG server. Like most well-oiled machines, the business depended on a lubrication substance; for TPG, it was either credit card numbers or cash, processed upfront or via COD transactions with commercial shipping vendors. Once the money began rolling in, TPG electronically transferred payments to the affiliates, physicians and pharmacies in a seamless, fluid operation.

Deflecting Blame

For the perpetrators, the scheme placed the risk squarely on the independent contractors. As the first link in the chain, the affiliates tempted potential customers with imaginative Web sites, competitive prices and attractive specials. They became the online public face of the business. The next link in the chain, physicians, operated without any patient interaction — a highly desirable post for a busy practitioner — thus the competition for slots was initially fierce. Only when they were fully involved and had become dependent on the income stream did both the physicians and pharmacists recognize the legal jeopardy in which they had placed themselves. Participating in an Internet prescription fraud scheme exposed them to significant risk, not the least of which was the loss of their hard-earned professional licenses. Any finding of criminal misconduct or professional negligence could subject them to a variety of sanctions, including an end to their careers, public ridicule and scorn.

However, doctors are just as susceptible to greed as the rest of us, and Stevens had no trouble finding professionals to join his enterprise. Plus, the doctors were assured payment for their services because the patients could not complete the medical questionnaire until their credit card information had been verified or a COD order was processed. Only later — when stories leaked out about doctors under investigation for fraud, malpractice and financial irregularities — did the pool of applicants dry up. However, once on board, the desire to make a lot of money overcame many physicians. In fact, Dr. Mansour Jibril later told my partner and me that he had become obsessed with increasing his earnings. On one occasion he actually suffered a seizure while sitting in front of his computer. The good doctor surmised that he had been reviewing questionnaires online for 20 consecutive hours and his brain temporarily short-circuited. When he awoke, Jibril took a full day to recover, but he was more concerned about lost income than potential damage to his health.

The pharmacists assumed the upfront expenses for inventory, order processing and shipping. By contrast, TPG had little overhead, few staff members and a small physical footprint. Its main function was to ensure a smooth transition among the affiliates, doctors, pharmacists and their customers. This was where David Crane and his IT staff of two came into play.

The only potential legal hazard foreseen by Stevens, Crane and Melendez was with the medical questionnaire. Stevens convinced Melendez to list as few questions as possible on the form and place only two items in the software templates that could trigger a red flag. These items were the patient's age and body-mass index (BMI). Without conducting a physical exam or a face-to-face consultation, the physician would approve the prescription order online if no red flags were triggered. If a patient didn't appreciate the deliberate ordering flaw and entered a lower age or higher BMI than the program allowed, a pop-up window would prompt the patient to change the numbers to conform to the program limits. And with the affiliates, physicians and pharmacists focused on making a profit, their moral and legal concerns were quickly cast aside. We calculated that on the day Dr. Jibril suffered his seizure, he had reviewed as many as 2,200 applications for prescriptions. Jibril earned more than $15,000 that day alone.

The Tip of the Iceberg

During the execution of their search warrant at Molly Williams's apartment, Winterboro police officers found prescription receipts that had been filled at various local pharmacies, blank prescription pads from two local physicians and more than a dozen empty prescription bottles from local and out-of-state pharmacies. Officers and federal investigators didn't realize at the time that the empty pill bottles would be the most crucial items they uncovered. Finally, several fraudulent identification cards were found, including Pennsylvania driver's licenses, commercial check cashing cards and county library cards.

Within weeks of the search at Molly's apartment, federal agencies around the country began receiving reports of drug overdoses by individuals who bought prescription drugs online. But it took the death of 14-year-old Joshua Tendler for the media to take notice. Network news reports soon relayed the details of Tendler's death to a nation awash in prescription drugs. The further reporters dug, the more troubling circumstances they uncovered. Hundreds of tales describing similar incidents began to emerge as a pill-obsessed populace grappled with the magnitude of the problem and attempted to gauge its effect. Industry experts were contacted to provide additional insight into the scope of prescription-drug abuse within the population; however, one voice remained silent. The law enforcement community, as was its custom, refrained from public comment while agents waded through volumes of evidence. We were able to link similar transactions to various Web sites that used the same payment processing center as Tendler, which was based in Canada. Further inquiries yielded hits on the most frequently accessed Web site for ordering prescription drugs at the time, one that was tied to more than 6,000 affiliate partners. That Web site was owned and operated by TPG.

Defining the Crime

I was detailed to the Drug Enforcement Administration (DEA) and from the beginning my partner and I suspected a much greater scheme was at play than the simple identity theft and prescription drug fraud indicated by the evidence in Molly Williams's apartment. I contacted Assistant U.S. Attorney (AUSA) William Grimley, an experienced cybercrimes prosecutor, and asked for his assistance with the investigation. Initially, Grimley expressed reluctance to prosecute the case because no obvious specific federal statute existed to outlaw the sale of prescription drugs over the Internet. And although we could cite several drug distribution laws that we believed were applicable, Grimley and many of his colleagues in the Justice Department were hesitant to proceed without a uniquely crafted regulation to address the offense. However, my partner and I, along with many other investigators around the country, persisted until this — and several similar investigations — were green-lighted for aggressive prosecution. The prime arguments we used to convince federal prosecutors were the existence of similar laws on the books in several states, and an enlightened view of existing federal drug statutes pertaining to street drug dealers and international drug-trafficking organizations.

We began our inquiry with a thorough review of the Molly Williams case file. Looking for potential leads and evidence, we quickly decided to focus on two issues: the empty prescription bottle labels, and the money trail emanating from the in-state and Internet purchases evidenced by some of the prescription bottles. What followed was a whirlwind of activity, including the issuance of dozens of subpoenas and search warrants. This was accompanied by information uncovered during interviews of more than 85 employees and other witnesses and reviews of tens of thousands of e-mail transcripts.

The most valuable information came from TPG employees. During these interviews, we learned the identities of numerous contractor employees, including 9 pharmacists and 14 physicians. Because of their fear of incarceration should they be found criminally culpable, a number of employees eagerly furnished us with valuable information. For example, IT administrators at TPG used backdoor passwords to alter system software and hide or change various data. They purchased a standard software program but then tweaked the package to fit their specific needs and resold the modified version to other start-up Internet marketers without revealing the backdoor-access capabilities that had been added. This enabled TPG to monitor its competitors' transactions and alter its product pricing to gain a competitive advantage.

Following the coordinated execution of 14 search warrants in eight states on a sunny spring day, the U.S. Attorney's Office in the Eastern District of Pennsylvania issued letters to a number of TPG principals and critical staff members advising that they were targets of the investigation. In short order, several high-level employees agreed to cooperate with us and we were able to corroborate various aspects of the case. We amassed documents, e-mail transcripts and assorted evidentiary items that illuminated TPG's organizational structure and business model. We lawfully accessed customer records at financial institutions and investment firms. We married financial leads obtained from e-mails with credit card records and other transactions to assess the extent of TPG's revenues. At the end of the process, we estimated that TPG received more than $51 million in gross revenue.

This was not a typical fraud scheme. Although a number of institutions and firms had been defrauded (for example, credit card processors and bank-issued credit card entities), others benefitted financially from the run-up in manufacturing, distribution and financial activity generated by TPG's scheme. Drug manufacturers and wholesalers in particular realized double-digit sales growth on an annual basis in certain product lines. Failing to question customer activity, disregarding warning signs of unusually rapid growth in product ordering and abandoning due diligence policies enabled firms to boost their own bottom lines and revenue projections.

Sentencing

At the final phase of the investigation we seized more than $7.2 million in currency, real estate and other assets from TPG executives, physicians and pharmacies. This resulted from a comprehensive analysis of the records at more than 40 U.S. financial institutions and investment houses. At any given time, tens of millions of dollars flowed among the conspirators, and it was only through good fortune and timing that we were able to seize the funds we did. We also froze and recovered almost $9 million in accounts held by the culprits in Canada, Europe and several Caribbean countries.

The further we delved into the activities of TPG, the more it became apparent there were two categories of victims/offenders. The first group included victims in the classic sense — adults and juveniles who obtained controlled substances without following the usual lawful path to obtaining a prescription drug. After interviewing a number of patients, family members and health care professionals, we compiled a list of subjects who had already received prescription drugs lawfully while under the care of a physician but had also made Internet purchases. The second group consisted of subjects who fit the pattern of drug abusers but had found an alternative source online. Members of both groups had experienced drug overdoses from the products they purchased from TPG. Clearly, these were cases where the costs incurred were incalculable.

More than two years after our investigation began, a federal grand jury issued an 82-count indictment charging Jeffrey Stevens, David Crane, Samuel Melendez, Mansour Jibril, Stefan Gorbonich and five other co-defendants with violations of federal drug and money laundering statutes. Jeffrey Stevens rejected a plea deal and opted for a trial. David Crane, however, pleaded guilty and provided significant testimony at Stevens's trial. In return for helping the government, Crane was sentenced to 18 months in jail, less time served — far below the 10-year sentence he had been facing. Crane also agreed to pay a fine and forfeit the remaining proceeds from his illegal activity.

Mansour Jibril suffered considerable anguish following his indictment and was hospitalized on several occasions for stress and depression-related symptoms. Although financially strapped, Jibril had the wherewithal to hire two former federal prosecutors to negotiate a plea arrangement. At sentencing, Jibril expressed deep and apparently sincere regret for his conduct, which moved the court to hand down a sentence of 37 months of incarceration along with the forfeiture of nearly $1.2 million to the government. The judge commented that Jibril originally faced a 10-year term, but the overwhelming correspondence received by the court attesting to Jibril's otherwise fine character, along with the defendant's extensive cooperation with the investigation, warranted a sentence reduction. This mountain of community support, however, did not sway the state medical board — it rescinded Jibril's license to practice medicine, effectively ending his medical career.

Samuel Melendez was a broken man. His family members turned their backs on him, a once-promising medical career was over, and he was left impoverished. None of these facts gave the court any pause. The judge invoked the full measure of the law and sentenced Melendez to 10 years in prison and the forfeiture of any remaining assets.

Stefan Gorbonich, relying upon the advice of his attorney, delayed his hearing until the other defendants had been adjudicated. Thinking he could diminish his role in the eyes of the court, Gorbonich enlisted a vast network of supporters to provide glowing character testimonials. The judge was unmoved by this contrived strategy and sentenced Gorbonich to 45 months of incarceration and the forfeiture of more than $620,000.

Of the remaining defendants, the judge reserved the harshest penalty for the most egregious party, Jeffrey Stevens. He was found guilty of drug trafficking and money laundering; at sentencing he offered little in the way of remorse or explanation for his conduct. In fact, he was openly disdainful of the government's efforts to portray him in a negative light. The judge sentenced Stevens to 12 years' of incarceration and the forfeiture of $3.1 million in assets, including his newly built Southern California home.

Lessons Learned

Our persistence spurred the reluctant prosecutors to pursue a judicial solution in this case. We used existing federal laws and legal concepts in new ways to achieve prosecution. No single law packed a comprehensive deterrent effect to warn both the public and potential offenders about the serious nature of the Internet sale of prescription drugs. The prosecutors said that the legislative process failed to keep pace with legal concerns brought on by new technology like e-commerce. However, we were able to find courageous prosecutors willing to roll the dice and rely on their experience and confidence to pursue the criminal cases. In numerous jurisdictions, investigators had to educate and cajole reluctant and inexperienced prosecutors to recognize the magnitude of the problem.

As technology gains a greater foothold in our society, law enforcement will have to adapt to combat these new schemes, educating both a skeptical public and professional community, and prepare for increasing threats to health. Relying solely on traditional investigative techniques will be an inadequate response to the future perils we face.

Recommendations to Prevent Future Occurrences

Parents are the first line of defense to ensure their children's safe use of the Internet; minors can and have bought illegal prescriptions. Constant monitoring of online behavior and usage is the most appropriate means to prevent predators from creeping into the lives of juveniles. The best method of detection is maintaining an open dialog with your children. Alert them to potential dangers and teach them proper Internet usage.

(*continued*)

(continued)

Legislation in both local and federal jurisdictions needs to keep pace with and anticipate future advances in technology. It is extremely difficult for investigators and prosecutors to address life-threatening issues with laws that were written decades earlier.

As a result of this and similar investigations, the U.S. Congress passed the Ryan Haight Online Pharmacy Consumer Protection Act of 2007. The law was subsequently signed into effect by the president in October 2008. It was enacted to address the problems of online prescription drug trafficking, abuse and availability. According to Administrator Michele M. Leonhart of the DEA, "This landmark piece of legislation will bring rogue pharmacy operators out of the shadows by establishing a clear standard for legitimate online pharmaceutical sales. The legislation will allow customers to know they are doing business with a trusted, legitimate pharmacy, and give law enforcement the tools we need to identify illegitimate online pharmacies."

About the Author

Jon Cohen, CFE, retired in 2007 following a 27-year career in law enforcement, with assignments at several federal, state and local agencies. He is a graduate of Temple University and earned a master's degree from Fairleigh Dickinson University. Mr. Cohen earned his CFE in 2008 and is an active member of the Philadelphia Area Chapter of the ACFE, serving on its Board of Directors and as Chapter Secretary.

The Porn Procurement Process

LT COL ROBERT J. BLAIR

*A*merica Happy Company probably sounds odd to anyone who has not been to the Middle East. If you've never had the opportunity to stand in swirling sand as fine as powdered sugar and watch plumes of gas burn at heights of 100 feet all around you, then the awkward, broken English used in the region probably clangs jarringly as it hits your ears. But luckily for Middle Eastern business owners and contractors, when Americans are fighting a war and looking for a company to supply fresh produce and ''American-style'' ketchup in the middle of a 135-degree endless beach, we don't grade on grammar or syntax.

As the Air Force officer in charge of procuring basic provisions for troops — such as food, beverages and toiletries — I was more concerned with the quality of a company's products and services than its name. America Happy Company was one of many vendors operating out of the region that bid on my contract, and it was able to supply our essentials for less money than the closest competitor. So I awarded the contract to it, regardless of its inelegant name.

The Air Force Procurement Process

U.S. Central Command Air Force (CENTAF) is responsible for U.S. Air Force troops in the Middle East. After the September 11th attack in New York City and the Pentagon, our CENTAF budget skyrocketed from $230 million per year to more than $2 billion annually. We were investing in an ever-expanding infrastructure in the giant sandbox, and we were responsible for establishing necessary Air Force bases and adequately equipping them.

It is said that the Army builds portable, inexpensive camps because it is a mobile beast, consisting of a tent city with a strong perimeter and a few outhouses surrounded by barbed wire. Then, a few days or weeks later, all of that is pulled up and moved to a new location as the Army takes over more and more land in a mission to overtake the enemy.

The Air Force philosophy and mission are completely different than the other branches of service. We build more permanent bases with runways and even — dare I say it — indoor plumbing. We stay on those bases long term and launch our airplanes to do battle, only for them to return later for maintenance and refueling. Our camps come with a 1,000-foot runway capable of withstanding hundreds of hard landings daily. Because of that permanence, it costs more to build an Air Force base than an Army post. Thanks to our more traditional amenities, Air Force bases often play host to Army troops taking their rest and relaxation. In the end, because the Air Force spends more money establishing on-site facilities, we are a bigger target, not for just the enemy, but for unscrupulous contractors and vendors.

The process of choosing suppliers is one of attrition. The military makes potential vendors complete stacks of forms and conducts background checks to ensure we do not buy barbed wire from Iran or bread from terrorists. Then the companies submit bids for contracts, and many factors weigh into who is selected to provide particular services or goods. The Air Force also has a board that meets with contracting personnel, comptroller representatives and operations staff. The operations guys are there to ensure the soldiers' needs are met. The contracting and comptroller personnel are there to discuss past work the vendors have provided and weigh the bids based on cost, experience and quality provided. Often, the same big companies get many of our contracts because they understand our process, have good performance histories and can deliver on their promises. When we ask a company to provide electricity and water in the desert — 100 miles from the nearest living thing — we can't just hope it will deliver; we like to see a proven track record. If the vendor fails to deliver, it means fines for the company but, more important, it means U.S. troops are stuck in the middle of the desert without water or electricity — it means people can die. That is why acquisition officers and comptroller personnel in the military take their jobs very seriously. We are not working toward a profit, but to keep our people alive while ensuring victory for our commanders and our country.

As the Financial Comptroller for CENTAF, I had an immediate staff of 15 financial managers at Shaw Air Force Base, and another 85 or so spread throughout the sandbox from Qatar to Kuwait to Iraq. My staff and I oversaw about 50 bases through a network of local and international contracts. The Air Force uses a system of contracting that includes separation of the duties. Acquiring local contracts for goods and services that support the base, picking up and paying for those supplies and reconciling the accounting books are all separate functions performed by different employees. It's similar to the system that a bank or retail store in Smalltown, USA, would use to separate the responsibilities of daily operations. In addition to this division of tasks, the Air Force financial managers conduct audits and hold random checks of invoices and accounts to ensure that everything is copasetic. Sometimes those checks smoke out parasites trying to take advantage of good ol' Uncle Sam. It was my job to stomp on those nasty little bugs.

Small Transactions Pack a Big Punch

It was a normal day in the Air Force; I started at 0530 with a run and was in the office by 0700. My team and I held a video teleconference (VTC) with Air Combat Command (ACC) in Langley, Virginia, that morning. ACC is CENTAF's big boss and controls our flow of money from the Pentagon. We discussed our upcoming operations and how we planned to tackle the myriad funding obstacles of the day. Overall, it was a constructive teleconference, and we all left it feeling ready to attack what the day had waiting for us. After the VTC, I circled the troops and we divided the day's workload based on everyone's respective talents.

I was preparing a briefing on funding issues in Kuwait for our commander, General Buzz Moseley (a legend in the Air Force). My deputy was preparing to receive 50 finance troops who were coming to town later that month. We had to train them to take over for 50 tired troops who were packing their bags and chomping at the bit to go home. The rest of my office was moving money where it needed to be and reviewing the activities of our agents to make sure they were keeping all their projects on track. I had my noncommissioned officer (NCO), Master Sergeant Mike Linville, doing a review of invoices from a vendor with which we had been having problems. The vendor was making too many food deliveries to the dining hall and we were having to pay rent on a dozen freezer trucks that were sitting outside in the heat, running all day and night to keep meat from spoiling. Mike was trying to figure out why the vendor kept bringing more and more meat, and how to make it stop. During one of his random checks, a few small amounts stood out on the spreadsheet of multi-thousand-dollar purchases of food and supplies. Mike came to me scratching his head and we took a look together. I used our internal accounting systems to dig deeper into the transactions and found the source of several of the small expenses: Barnyard Honeys and Barely Legal Teens. My years of experience and the knowledge I gleaned from dozens of CFE training sessions slapped me in the back of the head and told me something was wrong. After ''$200,000 for barbed wire, $320,000 for concrete, and $400,000 for tents,'' the entry of ''$400 for Big College Boobies'' just didn't compute.

Refund Request

My first concern was to recover the money. I did some quick research on the Internet using the credit card details and found contact information for the electronic publishing company that maintained these Web sites. Next, I went down the hall and met with one of our CENTAF lawyers to discuss the legal implications of using a government credit card to buy pornography. We looked into the rights of the card holder (the U.S. government) and the rights of the Internet publisher. The lawyer and I discussed the theft of the card and the consequences faced by the thief. He provided me with legal references to use when talking to the company about refunding our money. Then he advised me that neither the FBI nor the courts would prosecute a case (even a slam dunk) over a $2,000 theft like the one we had discovered. The best we could hope for would be to identify the culprit, let him know that we had found him and discipline him.

The credit card used in the illicit purchases was assigned to an NCO who had returned home a few months ago. MSgt Linville called the NCO's senior enlisted advisor (or *shirt*, as we say in the Air Force) and discussed the situation. A shirt is usually a high-ranking enlisted officer assigned to a unit to act as a big brother to the young enlisted troops. He supports the troops, offers advice if they are having personal issues, helps the commander relate to his subordinates and generally has his thumb on the pulse of the unit. When we contacted the NCO's shirt, he said he knew his troops well and that the NCO who was assigned the credit card was a stand-up guy with a family and no history of problems. He didn't have DUIs or other criminal charges; he didn't have any money issues and had never been in trouble before. In fact, he and his wife had just had a baby, and he was busy passing out cigars and being a goofy new father. After clearing the NCO of suspicion, we turned our attention to our vendors. We decided that if the perpetrator wasn't a troop, the next likely suspect was an employee at one of our contractors. Who had access to the card number?

The illicit literature was purchased from a company called Porn-4-You. I contacted the provider to explain the theft and decided to go into the conversation politely, but with an air of authority. I found out that more than 1,000 new pornographic Web sites appeared on the Internet everyday and suspected that this one didn't want a Department of Defense (DoD) investigation into its screening process for customer credit cards or an Internal Revenue Service audit of their books. When I mentioned that I was a DoD agent and Certified Fraud Examiner (CFE) calling from a government line, the tech was quick to put me through to a supervisor with some clout. He was very cooperative and provided me with the e-mail address and system password used to make the transactions on the NCO's credit card.

He also disclosed the customer's expense history, and he authorized a refund to the government credit card for all charges. He even offered me a free trial account with Barnyard Honeys (which I politely declined).

Establishing Contact

My next step was to contact the perpetrator, we'll call him Harry, using the information the Internet publisher gave me. I set up a dummy e-mail account in the name PORN4YOU@hotmail.com, intentionally mimicking the Web site from which Harry purchased his smut, Porn-4-You. I sent Harry an e-mail informing him that he was our lucky winner of a year of free literature. I included his Porn-4-You password and went over some of his past usage so he would think I was legitimate. I kept the e-mail short and happy and made sure he understood that I didn't need a credit card to offer him a free year of material. I gave him a choice of Biker Babes, Barnyard Honeys or College Co-Eds and told him he had 30 days to respond before I moved on to the next name on my list. I got an e-mail the next day saying he was very excited about his prize and would love to access Biker Babes for a year. I waited a few days (because I'm a busy smut peddler) and e-mailed him back that, because we did not require a credit card, we had to certify that he was over 18 years old. I asked Harry for his name and a physical address to which we could send his prize certificate and a card for him to certify his age.

I waited a week with no reply from Harry, and then resent the e-mail. Harry replied that he didn't have a permanent address for me (that would have been too easy) but would still like the prize. He offered another credit card. I told him that I'd talk to my supervisor about a waiver of the age certification since he had a history with our company. However, by that point I already had what I needed — his computer location. I pulled the Internet protocol (IP) address from the e-mails he sent to me and ran it through the IP lookup service at www.whatismyip.com. I discovered that Harry was in Saudi Arabia, at his *work* computer.

Just Deserts — and Ketchup

The computer Harry used to access and purchase pornographic material with a U.S. credit card belonged to America Happy Company in Saudi Arabia, one of our regular vendors. I had contact information for the sales department, which I used to reach the loss prevention department and notify it of the theft. I informed the company's management that subsequent problems would result in its removal from the federal trade list of companies cleared to conduct business with the U.S. government. They weren't too happy to learn that. This would mean certain death for their enterprise

and inspired them to track down their "inside man" to prevent future occurrences. I gave them Harry's IP address and his contact information that I
received from the Porn-4-You manager. It took less than a day for them to
call me back and tell me they had fired Harry and had a letter of apology to
the U.S. Air Force in the mail. They even offered me free ketchup!

Although I could not bring charges against Harry, because the amount
of the fraud was not large enough to interest prosecutors, I was satisfied
with the outcome of the case. America Happy Company had been a trusted
contractor with a proven track record, and it was to everyone's benefit to
retain our professional relationship. Management took the proper steps
to remove Harry from the company and implemented control procedures
to prevent future occurrences.

Lessons Learned

I briefed my staff about the case and told them it was a solid validation that
our accounting checks were working properly and that due diligence was an
essential duty of all personnel. I gave MSgt Linville a day off to reward him for
noticing the discrepancy and bringing it to my attention. Not only was this a
bonus for his perseverance, but it was also an incentive for my other staff
members to follow his lead.

America trusts us to protect the freedoms of our great country, and that
trust brings with it the responsibility to meticulously oversee the personnel, contractors and resources that the job demands. I pay taxes too, and I certainly
don't want my tax money used to purchase Barnyard Honeys for some creep
perusing pornographic Web sites at work — regardless of the amount of
money involved.

Recommendations to Prevent Future Occurrences

The Air Force is set up like a business. We have audits and stakeholders (the American people). We have safeguards in our acquisition process just like those in place at
large retailers or Las Vegas casinos. And just like every business, we are susceptible to
fraudsters who search for weaknesses in our systems to can gain an unfair advantage;
wiggle out a few bucks that they didn't earn; take liberties that they shouldn't; and, in
this case, look up Lady Liberty's skirt. And also like any business, we need to have
prevention and detection controls in place to disclose such behavior as soon as it is
attempted.

(continued)

A CENTAF airman was simply doing a routine, weekly review of the books when he discovered Harry and his porn habit. Good accountants everywhere conduct similar reviews of their spreadsheets to see if anything looks wrong. It's a skill that is fostered and grows with experience and time. In the case of Harry, we caught the problem early. Given more time and success, his abuse would have spread to more risky and expensive endeavors. One thing I've learned from experience is that a successful thief can change his methods to steal more. Undeterred, like a cancer, his efforts will spread and grow until they consume the host body. That's where the fraud examiner comes in to play. Due diligence is the key. A proper set of checks and balances, scheduled reviews and audits keeps everyone honest and can even unearth a Dirty Harry in the desert.

About the Author

Lt Col Robert J. Blair, CFE, CGFM, is the branch chief for financial plans and policy under General David Petraeus at U.S. Central Command. He is the senior Air Force representative for funding support of $30 billion for U.S. and coalition efforts in Iraq, Afghanistan and Pakistan.

CHAPTER

33

Gambling on a Profit

ANTONIO IVAN S. AGUIRRE

Frank Schultz was a fresh recruit and a rising star in the accounting department of Nasdall Bank's West End branch. He had become accustomed to the star treatment even before he began working at Nasdall; Frank took pride in his multiple most valued player (MVP) awards in the intercollegiate basketball tournaments he played in, representing State College. He loved flaunting an image of being linked with pretty girls, fabulous cars and extravagant nightlife. However, when Frank was recruited straight from graduation as an assistant accountant for Nasdall Bank, he was not ready to let go of the illusions of his good times in college. For him, life should not be a bore, even in the financial world. "Let's create excitement," he told himself.

During his university days, Frank masterminded a gambling game that he introduced to his school buddies. The players bet online, using an Internet hosting facility, for the last winning digit of the scores of their favorite National Basketball Association (NBA) team, and whoever hit the correct score would get the pot money. The winner would receive his take through an online credit to his bank account. The losers had to pay their share through an interbranch deposit to the dealer's account. The dealer, Frank, enjoyed a 10 percent commission and deposited the remaining 90 percent to the winning bettor's account.

At first, it was just a game for fun. Almost every participant would regularly bet $5 per share of a winner's block; not enough to really hurt one's pocket. But it later became a lucrative business for Frank. He received his 10 percent commission weekly, which helped him create his high-flying lifestyle. Starting with a handful of about 20 bettors, the game quickly turned into a campus craze and captured a market of 70 participants, then 200 and eventually 300. Nobody knew exactly whom they were betting against. In reality, the players were dealing with an out-of-school punk, Curtis Harris, who acted as Frank's middleman. Frank was very clever about covering his tracks by avoiding direct contact with his "clients." The online betting game masterminded by Frank became so popular in the underground world that it branched out to several other schools in the region. Most bettors were college students who were also basketball fanatics. One good thing about such a client base — everyone was mum about the betting because they did not know with whom they were dealing. They would simply receive their winning shares or pay their shares when they lost. For them, it was more fun than off-track betting on horse racing because the basketball game provided a high chance of winning combined with certain excitement and challenge. And the score was fair and square — each player could watch the results live on TV or through the Internet.

After college, Frank Schultz went on to earn a name for himself in the banking world, starting out as an assistant accountant at Nasdall . He satisfactorily passed the six-month probationary period and earned the trust and confidence of his colleagues. He spent a great deal of time learning the ropes of his new career in the accounting department. He easily learned and became acquainted with the software packages used in his department. Schultz familiarized himself with the accounting processes of his branch and the head office and he absorbed the intricacies of the job. He envisioned himself working as a top-notch executive in the bank within the next five years.

However, the lure of the easy money he made during his college days did not leave his mind. Frank was still itching with the way he pulled away substantial sums of money through his online gambling without being detected. As a result, he decided to continue after graduation and while working with Nasdall. He soon became obsessed with the thought of bringing his online gambling scheme into the banking world. He started to build a network of friends in the bank, including Henry Flanagan, a bookkeeper at his branch. Henry, who was an avid basketball fan, became a frequent drinking buddy of Frank's.

The Wrong Bet

One evening when the two were out to happy hour together, Frank took the opportunity to propose his Internet gambling scheme to Henry. At first, Henry was hesitant about the idea but later became convinced that the plan was "flawless." Soon after, Henry became Frank's middleman for the Nasdall Bank bettors and was able to capture a sizeable market; he recruited almost 100 banking personnel in 19 branches in the area and later expanded to almost 500 bettors from 60 branches. It wasn't clear that this online betting game using Nasdall's Internet banking procedures violated the rules of employee conduct. The employees who were patronizing the game looked at it as a fun game and a stress reliever. However, Frank had decided to set the minimum bet higher than his college levels — after all, he was dealing with working professionals now. He upped the entry bet to $40 per share and the pot sometimes reached $20,000 per week. Furthermore, the "fun game" got out of line when Frank — not content with his 10 percent commission — and Henry bet huge sums of money and incurred a heavy loss of around $20,000 in one week. Frank's losses reached $100,000 in that particular month, which forced him to get creative about ways to pay them off. His flawless modus operandi had quickly turned into an abyss of gambling debts for both Frank and Henry.

Aware of their predicament, they devised a plan to siphon out funds from bank deposits to cover their debts. Frank spotted a weakness in the recording of accounting adjustments against deposit accounts. They posted fictitious entries using a "correction advice" against several deposit accounts and credited through the Internet banking facility the proceeds to a fictitious conduit account. Exploiting this weakness, Frank and Henry were able to amass an aggregate of $1.2 million in a period of three months.

Nasdall Bank had been engaged in commercial banking for more than 50 years and gained an excellent reputation for its efficient service and trustworthy employees in the Midwest. The company implemented a hands-on management style and invested sizeable sums of money into technological development. It had 900 branches and employed 12,000 employees nationwide. Never in their wildest dreams did Nasdall's management and executives expect that one of their well-screened employees would become a bad egg.

Frank Schultz came up with a clean record during the reference check by the personnel department at the time he was hired. His scholastic record showed decent grades and his popularity as a collegiate basketball star did not pass unnoticed by the hiring staff.

The Tip-Off

As the head of the special audit group at Nasdall Bank, I conducted regular investigations into the bank's fraud cases and red-flag issues. In my more-than-a-decade tenure with Nasdall, most of the cases involved petty and white-collar crimes with fairly small losses. However, the amount eventually uncovered in this case looked serious enough to call for a top-down reorganization in the West End branch.

This situation was brought to my attention during a visit I made to the branches in the West End area, including the one where Frank was employed. I was speaking to staff members about the reporting duties of the control and marketing officers, which apparently prompted an employee to confide in me. After the meeting, he approached me to say that he sensed something wrong in the recording of Internet-related transactions at his branch. He suspected some people in accounting were engaged in unsound financial practices.

When I returned to my office I mentioned the tip to my special audit staff. After a thorough trend analysis of the balance sheets of the branches in the area, my team uncovered many long-outstanding, unreconciled entries in the West End branch. There were entries from suspense accounts without corresponding transactions. Based on these suspicious patterns, I decided to send an investigation team to the branch to do a little more digging.

Unchecked Manipulation

Frank Schultz turned out to be a quick study in the Internet and intranet facilities of his branch. He became skilled in Internet usage while in college and was able to spot the loopholes of his branch's system and software package. These loopholes allowed him to siphon funds without being detected . . . initially.

My investigation team conducted a discreet review of the statement of conditions (SOCs) of five branches in the West End area. We noticed an unusual increase in the amount and volume of interbranch credit adjustments conducted through Internet-banking controls in the past three months. This was unusual because the bank used interbranch credit adjustments to post entries during offline mode. For example, credit adjustments would be made for interbranch cash deposits that were not posted, interest expenses and service charges, and this accepted practice did not cause substantial accumulation. Such postings could only be done with the correction advice (CA) of the bookkeeper and had to be approved by a designated branch accountant, which required an override password. After passing these controls, the batch amount would be posted by the bookkeeper using the Internet process for interbranch transactions.

The team tried to verify the supporting details of the SOCs and uncovered various fictitious CAs issued for interbranch credit adjustments. The recipient branch used the CA as the basis for a memo authorizing credits to a bank employee's account and to another bank client. It turned out that these recipient accounts were winners and losers of Frank's online gambling game and the settlement was made through a fictitious deposit account.

Frank and Henry (both acting as bookkeepers) dispatched by fax several fictitious CAs to branches within the West End and advised the bookkeepers at each branch to post the corrections. The bookkeepers un-wittingly complied without knowing that Frank had forged the signature of the accountant on the correction advice. He immediately perforated the original copy of the correction advice to reduce the audit trail. The submit-ting branch's audit team recovered only faxed copies of the CAs Frank sent and was unable to vouch for their authenticity. The accounting department of Nasdall had not maintained a logbook of correction advices and failed to assign particular sets of CA forms to individual branches for accountability. My team further discovered that there were no cash deposit slips to support the CAs marked as "unposted cash deposits."

To make the scheme work, the branch's bookkeeper (Frank or Henry) posted the fictitious adjustment by crediting a savings account using various transaction codes that were standard at Nasdall, such as "credit memo — others (CMOT)" instead of "cash — savings account" to avoid using a self-responding ticket (SRT). If they did use an SRT, they would need proof of cash and it would be reflected in the book balance of branches and estab-lish an audit trail. The use of the CMOT transaction code did not require interbranch accountability. Under this operating practice, the bank's com-puter system automatically generated an accounting entry for transactions still in process against savings accounts. To conceal their transactions, Frank and Henry manually reversed the fictitious entries in the branch's general ledger by debiting the amounts as service charges or interest expenses on deposits. This step would credit (reverse) the in-process ac-count. To avoid detection, either Frank or Henry forced the balances re-flected in the reconciliation statement of the deposit accounts so they would match the books.

Bouncing the Accounting Ball

The following two cases illustrate their methods for posting accounting entries. In the first case, they forced a fraudulent credit to the gambling conduit account and covered it up as an interest charge. In the second case, they charged a returned-check fee on a fraudulent check transaction:

Case 1: Internet entry using CMOT code to post a credit adjustment

- Debit: In process — transaction systems (IP-TS) $ 9,750
- Credit: Savings account $ 9,750
- Manual reversed entry (posted by Frank or Henry) by
  charging fictitious interest
    - Debit: Interest expense — demand deposit $12,187.50
    - Credit: In process — transaction systems (IP-TS) $ 9,750.00
    - Withholding tax payable $ 2,437.50

Case 2: Excess amount posted as a reversal of income intended for other branches on outward return checks (system entry using the Internet banking code for Cash — Service Charges (CASV) used to post a $500 credit adjustment)

- No system entry made
- System entry on fictitious charges on return check and services charges
  - Debit: Due from clearing outward $5,000
  - Credit: Demand deposit $5,000
  - Debit: Demand deposit $1,100
  - Credit: Service charge fees — others $1,100
- Reversal of income using manual entry (by bookkeepers)
  - Debit: Due from head office (for one returned check) $4,500
  - Debit: Service charge — others $1,000
  - Credit: Due from clearing outward $5,000
  - Credit: Savings account $ 500
- Should be:
  - Debit: Due from head office $4,500
  - Debit: Service charge — others $ 500
  - Credit: Due from clearing outward $5,000

The fraud perpetrated by Frank and Henry indicated weaknesses in Nasdall's internal controls of the interbranch transaction process, which was compounded by the negligence of the branch officers. My audit team discovered that the branch accountant approved correction advices without verifying the nature of the transaction and did not require supporting documents. Also, the branch head approved correction advices with credit memos — without verifying the memos.

Furthermore, the team learned that Frank connived with Alexander Horn, the information technology engineer at the West End branch, to acquire unlimited access to the bank's Internet-transaction processes. Alexander, who was actively engaged in Frank's online gambling scheme, provided the password and the conduit account for the gambling settlements. He was a necessary player in the successful execution of the fraud.

Frank and his associates were able to post fictitious credit adjustments using the Internet banking procedures of three branches of Nasdall in the area for their personal gain. They accumulated $1.2 million through 165 transactions in amounts ranging from $500 to $10,000. Their scam lasted three months. Our audit team analyzed the movement of cash deposits and withdrawals in the conduit account that Alexander established, and our report showed various Internet-banking fund transfers among employees of

Nasdall Bank and the bank's customers. We traced numerous inter-branch fund transfers involving 35 deposit accounts under the names of Nasdall employees, including tellers, loans clerk, IT personnel, branch cashiers and accountants in 47 branches. It showed how rampant Frank's online gambling was among Nasdall's staff.

In summary, Frank and his cohorts siphoned money from the bank using accounting-initiated unposted entries and manipulating the income and expense accounts through Internet banking. They exploited the company's lax controls on Internet transactions to perpetrate a fraud that remained undetected for a considerable period of time. The bank was able to recover its loss of $1.2 million only after litigation.

Calling the Bluff

My team was able to trace and document Frank's fraud, committed in cahoots with other employees of the bank. The team used the following audit procedures to detect fraudulent interbank and interbranch credits. To follow the audit trail, we checked and verified:

- Unposted items made with correction advices, especially for inter-branch and on-branch credit adjustments
- Source documents (e.g., deposit slips and credit memos) to support unposted credit transactions using correction advices
- Manually posted entries and reversals of entries made by the bookkeeper in the transaction journal for unposted transactions
- Credit memo adjustments made by the counterparty branches to support entries made by bookkeepers
- Original and duplicate copies of correction advices to detect tampering
- Overridden entries made by the bookkeepers for any unposted transactions
- Deposit accounts of the recipients of illegally acquired funds to identify the individuals involved in the fraud

We interviewed Frank Schultz, Henry Flanagan, Alexander Horn and other employees involved in the online gambling scheme. Frank admitted that he masterminded the online gambling as a fun game but that it turned out to be addicting and got out of control.

Alexander Horn confessed that he provided the supervisor override codes for posting online entries and created fictitious accounts as a conduits for gambling, specifically betting on winners of basketball games. He further admitted that his account was used to receive bets (deposits) from various Nasdall employees and to make payments to winners (withdrawals). He revealed that he used his account as a conduit for the fraudulent activity of Frank and Henry by depositing part of the fictitious credits made by them to winning bettors and then transferring a portion to the account Frank maintained at a Nasdall branch outside the West End area. Alexander was also involved in recruiting several IT personnel from other Nasdall branches to help facilitate gambling settlements online.

This was further collaborated by bookkeeper Henry's admission that he worked with Frank and Alexander to forge documents, create fictitious unposted entries and infiltrate the bank's Internet processes using override codes. Henry also admitted their illegal gambling activities using Alexander's account to temporarily park settlements.

The fraudsters also revealed the involvement of Curtis Harris — a personal friend of Frank's and former partner in his college gambling organization — in brokering the gambling bets of bank employees and some clients.

Several Nasdall employees admitted that they placed bets for the online game but denied they knew about the fraudulent activities of Frank, Henry and Alexander. They expressed regret at having been involved with this activity, which we pointed out was in violation of Nasdall's employee code of conduct.

Chasing the Crooks

My team submitted a painstakingly prepared audit report to the chief legal counsel at Nasdall and circumspectly coordinated with the police and legal authorities. The following individuals were identified as the perpetrators:

- Frank Schultz, Assistant Accountant — committed forgery, misrepresentation and falsification of commercial documents using the Internet and e-commerce.
- Alexander Horn, IT Engineer — created a fictitious deposit account to serve as the conduit for illegally acquired funds and used this account for the settlement of gambling receivables and payables.
- Henry Flanagan, Bookkeeper — committed forgery and falsification of commercial documents using the Internet and e-commerce.
- Curtis Harris, third party and close associate of Frank Schultz — served as middleman for the gambling operations that included the use of illegally acquired money from Nasdall Bank.

The bank terminated Frank Schultz, Henry Flanagan and Alexander Horn for cause.

By the time formal criminal charges were filed against them, the foursome had disappeared. As a result, warrants for the arrests of Frank Schultz, Alexander Horn, Henry Flanagan and Curtis Harris were issued. Only Frank was arrested immediately; he was ultimately sentenced to 10 years of incarceration. The others went into hiding. After almost a year-long manhunt, Henry, Alexander and Curtis surrendered and were each sentenced to five years in jail. The Nasdall Bank employees involved in the online gambling activities were sanctioned by Nasdall as provided for in the employee code of conduct.

Lessons Learned

As difficult as Internet-banking fraud cases are to prove (due to the complexity of implementing the e-commerce laws), my audit team generated a case report using the audit trail of Nasdall's Internet and intranet transactions that was ultimately used as evidence in the four prosecutions. The judicial system appeared lacking when it came to imposing severe sanctions on white-collar criminals, such as Internet fraudsters, as compared to palpable straightforward cases such as bank robbery.

From the perspective of the banking system, we recommended that call-back or review procedures be performed by officers on credit transactions before they are posted to the system. This will ensure that Internet or electronic banking transactions are verified and validated by appropriate authorities.

Recommendations to Prevent Future Occurrences

To strengthen internal controls over Internet transactions, I recommend the following:

- Unposted credit adjustments based on Internet transactions should be duly validated, verified and approved.
- Credit adjustments should be supported by original documents and posting media.
- Additional security functions should be implemented on Internet and intranet access (including control of password) by bank employees.
- Review offline and unposted transactions through call-back procedures.
- Strictly enforce the employee code of conduct.
- Regularly rotate jobs in critical accounting and bookkeeping functions.
- Review policies and procedures of online banking transactions, including the establishment of audit trails on "paperless" transactions.

About the Author

Antonio Ivan S. Aguirre, MBA, CFE, CPA, CSI, is a chief resident auditor under the Office of Internal Oversight Services (OIOS), United Nations. He previously worked with the largest bank in the Philippines as the head of special audit and acted on several occasions as an expert witness against numerous white-collar and organized crimes.

The Solitaire Trader

SHABDA PRAKASH

Samuel Ghosh grew up in a small village outside Kolkata, the old industrial capital of India in West Bengal, on the banks of the Ganges. Ghosh prided himself on being a family man and a hard worker; after completing an MBA, Samuel was hired at Solitaire Bank and moved up the ranks to become an assistant branch manager. Sam married Geeta, a human resources consultant he met while in college, and became the proud father of a sweet baby girl. Samuel was very religious and regularly attended church. His professional aspiration was to establish his own brokerage firm. A workaholic, Sam engaged himself part-time at a small brokerage firm in the evenings after he finished his working day at Solitaire. He wanted to learn the tricks of the brokerage trade and build up the start-up capital for his dream business.

Solitaire Bank was incorporated in Mumbai, the financial capital of India, to provide premier banking services. Within five years, the bank grew from 10 branches and one regional office to 890 branches across the country with four regional centers.

Unauthorized Transfer

I was one of three internal auditors working at Solitaire Bank's Kolkata regional office. Our team was responsible for the audit and compliance functions of 234 retail branches. My fellow auditor, Rakesh, and I used to travel from one branch to another to perform auditing work. One day we were on a train to a visit a branch in Patna when — the moment the train started moving — the regional audit manager called my cell phone and said that our branch in Bihta received a complaint from a high-net-worth customer that an unauthorized debit of $200,000 was transferred from his account through the Internet-banking system. He wanted me to go to the Bihta branch and do a quick review of the case. I left Rakesh in charge of the Patna audit and took the first train to Bihta.

When I arrived at the Bihta branch, the first thing I noticed was the size. There were only 10 employees, but it was a very profitable branch because there was a rich local cashew market in the area. I met with the branch manager, Gopal, over coffee and learned that the customer who lodged the complaint did not know why $200,000 was debited from his account. The complaint was sent via e-mail and had come only to the branch manager. The customer's complaint said:

> I have been dealing with your bank for the last three years. Your Relationship Manager (RM), who is also your Assistant Branch Manager, is very helpful and has always given me personalized service. However, I have been asking about a debit of $200,000 into my account last month and have not gotten any reply. Earlier as well, at least four or five instances have happened wherein the bank posted erroneous debits, but your RM has always taken care of it and I was given back credits and interest, too. This time it's taking long and your RM is not responding. If you could look into it please and resolve it at the earliest.

We had provisions at Solitaire that if a customer was erroneously debited, he was given the interest he would have earned and an acknowledgment of the mistake. It was sent with a letter of apology from the branch, which was also required to post an error-rectification entry to the customer's account when these actions were taken. I generated a report of the error-rectification entries posted by the Bihta branch in the last year and was surprised that there were only four entries and none pertained to the account in question. I asked for copies of the apologies sent to the customers and, adding to my confusion, I was told that there were none on file for the year. Something was fishy.

Not for the First Time

I started looking into the statements for the customer and discovered that two or three times a month Internet-banking transactions were originated from his account to the Bangalore branch and then reversed before the end of the day — without an explanation.

After scrutinizing the Bangalore account that was receiving the transfers I could not believe the entries. Each day there were Internet transfers into the account totaling no less than $1 million. They were from several Solitaire accounts, and were reversed before the end of the day without documentation. In addition to the deposits, there was one debit transferred out of the Bangalore-based account every day and credited to an Internet-trading account. The value of the debit equaled the total amount of credits made from various Solitaire customers' accounts. As Solitaire's corporate auditor, I had access to the reports and account statements from the bank. I generated a printout of the Internet-trading account in Bangalore, which showed that the account had income of $750,000 in last six months.

I looked up the personal details on the trading account and called the contact number on file; the phone was answered by a kind-sounding woman. When I said that I was calling from Solitaire Bank, she asked me to get in touch with her husband, Samuel Ghosh, who was the assistant manager at the Bihta branch. She told me that he had opened the trading account to buy mutual funds for tax benefits and that Samuel handled the transactions.

The Enemy Within

Shocked that the assistant branch manager was apparently behind the offense, I scheduled an interview with Samuel Ghosh. He was a successful assistant manager and enjoyed good relationships with each department of the bank. His superiors were happy with his work and he was respected by his subordinates. I, too, had shared their feelings about him — we had gone on business lunches together several times. Sam had a keen understanding of Solitaire's controls and was even considered for an internal audit position at one time.

As an assistant branch manager, Samuel had access to customer information and he knew that the default usernames for Internet banking accounts were the customers' identifications. If customers forget their passwords, they could create new ones online. While changing their passwords, the customers were given a verification call on the phone number listed in the bank's records. This number could be changed online by an employee to ensure the bank had the most up-to-date information. As the result of a systemic limitation, there was no audit trail of such changes made by employees. Samuel knew that if he changed a customer's contact number to his personal cell phone, a Solitaire employee would call him to confirm changes made to the Internet-banking password associated with that account. This allowed him to change customers' passwords, confirm the changes through his cell phone and then access online accounts using passwords of his choice.

After transferring funds from customers' online accounts to his trading account, he would attempt to log into the victims' accounts incorrectly three times to exploit another feature of the Solitaire system — three incorrect login attempts disabled the password. Therefore, the next time a victim customer tried to access his account online, he would be prompted to create a new password. Samuel also replaced the original contact number in the online records after transferring the funds, so the customer received the second confirmation call from the bank. Samuel usually posted transactions under $50,000 because he knew there was no oversight process for Internet transfers below that threshold.

Samuel chose high-net-worth customers who held large balances. When the customers complained of erroneous debits, he reversed the transaction and credited the amount back to the account before the end of the day because those were not checked and there was no tool to generate a report. Samuel knew the control limitations and exploited them to his advantage. However, he was caught when the market collapsed — he lost too much money in his trading account in one day and could not afford to transfer the funds back to the customer's online account. After trying to reach Samuel multiple times with no response, the customer contacted the branch manager to complain.

Tea for Two

After understanding the process behind the scam, I asked Samuel if he would meet with me for a discussion over tea. When I brought up the transfers to his personal account, he initially claimed that he and his friends had a profit-sharing agreement for the proceeds of the trading activity. When I smiled and said I was going to have to call his friends to confirm his statement, he broke down and confessed. It was one of the easiest confessions in my career. I asked him, "Sam, you were such an excellent banker. Why did you do it?"

He looked at me and put his cup on the table. He was silent for a minute and then mumbled, "Money has such a crazy nature; it started with my part-time brokerage firm assignment. While working there, I realized my clients made huge sums of money based on my recommendations. Why couldn't I do the same? I started doing day-trading with my small savings but quickly realized that to make the big money I needed to start my own company; I needed significant funds to do serious trading. I started *smurfing* by taking small amounts of money from a lot of different accounts to amass a large sum. I became greedy and thought it was easy to make money that way. I felt justified because I was a critical member of the management team and was not being fairly compensated. I also figured that I was not harming the bank or any clients. I was just borrowing the funds for six or seven hours a day; I always gave the money back at the end of the day."

I could see the regret on Samuel's face. I asked, "Did you only do it to earn money to start your own business? Did you have other reasons?" He looked at me and tears welled up in his eyes. "Are you okay?" I asked, pushing a glass of water toward him. He gulped half of the glass and looked into my eyes, but didn't say anything more. I told him that I would have to refer the matter, along with my detailed report, to the legal department. He uttered in a choked voice, "I understand; I have even sent a few cases of fraud to the legal department myself. Nothing can be done; I do not expect anything now."

There was a silence for while. He started to speak again, "My wife had no faith in my dreams, and she used to ask why I wanted a brokerage firm. She would say, 'Can't you be satiated in life? We both have good jobs with handsome salaries. We have a beautiful house; what else you want?' I was so lonely and frustrated that I lost my ability to differentiate between right and wrong. The only thing on my mind was to get enough money together to start my firm and show everyone who did not believe in me that I could do it."

I asked him why he didn't mention his goal to a senior bank official. I suggested that he might have been able to get a loan from Solitaire to start the business, but he responded, "Who has time to hear about my project? This organization is driven by deposit targets. We have to work 24/7 to meet them, and people here are only concerned with performance, which is judged by strict parameters."

His comment gave me insight into Solitaire's corporate culture. We were so engrossed in our work routines and tough competition that we forgot that our performance was driven by people. I realized that the psychological satisfaction of our employees was essential element in preventing internal frauds.

A New Direction

After gathering the documentation and Samuel's written confession, I turned over the evidence to Solitaire's legal department. After reviewing the report and evidence, management and our lawyers terminated Samuel and passed the case to law enforcement. Samuel was eventually sentenced to two years in prison. The last I heard of him, he had been released and moved in with parents in his childhood village to learn farming.

Lessons Learned

My supervisor and I learned a lot about investigating a complicated Internet fraud case. For one, we learned how important it is to maintain the chain of custody over crucial evidence. Our in-house counsel was a great help in that regard. We also learned that there were critical internal control deficiencies in Solitaire's Internet-banking processes.

Fraud can occur only when there is an opportunity. It is the result of poor internal controls and the fraudster abandoning his values to pursue his desires. Culprits often overcome feelings of guilt by rationalizing their actions. Most of us consider ourselves to be good people, even if we occasionally do something wrong. To convince ourselves, we rationalize or deny our small ignoble acts. This process can aggregate over a period of time and allow us to justify actions that are harmful to ourselves, our employers and society.

Recommendations to Prevent Future Occurrences

I made the following recommendations to management at Solitaire as a result of this case.

1. Install a central customer complaint department and a tool that allows customers to submit complaints themselves.
2. Remove the ability of branches to change customers' information on a real-time basis. Now these must be requested by branch employees and will be processed within 24 hours by a central team.
3. Branches should verify reversals to identify unauthorized transactions.
4. Emphasize ethical behavior through training. Formulate and mandate strict adherence to a code of conduct by employees.
5. Ask employees about their goals or objectives in life and offer institutional mentoring.

About the Author

Shabda Prakash is a risk manager at a financial institution. He has experience in retail banking, wholesale banking, corporate banking, financial operations, retirement planning services operations and investment banking.

The Big Brother He Never Had

CHRIS A MCCULLOCH

Dmitri Ivanov lived in a dark, cold, windowless basement room in Russia with several family members. Dmitri was only 21 years old, dark haired, with a thin small frame and stood about 5'9". He was not someone people noticed. Nothing made him physically stand out among other young Russian men. But what he had planned and plotted so meticulously for months would make him known on the other side of the globe in a matter of days. While his family was extremely poor and he came from humble beginnings, Dmitri was smart, very smart — especially when it came to computers. And he had big dreams. So, from his cold, dreary room in Russia, he plotted and schemed, knowing he would need hundreds of people from around the world to help him.

Dmitri did not finish high school, and nothing held his attention for long until he started learning about computers. Libraries in Russia gave the local school children access to computers. Dmitri went to a public school as a boy but did not excel. He frankly thought it was a waste of time and did not see a future in an education. He saw people struggle daily around him despite their education, so he did not focus on schooling. However, as a young teen, he quickly caught on to technology. He was curious about how things worked behind the scenes and he tackled the hardware aspect of computers first. He learned to physically piece them together from bits of other computers. He would find old, worn, discarded computers and use parts from them to build new ones. Then he started learning software programs and taught himself how applications worked. He quickly learned the codes used in programming.

The Internet brought a new world to the Russian's fingertips that otherwise would have been out of his reach. Dmitri started making connections with people in many different countries. He first began by socializing and reaching out to strangers to talk about movies, music, daily life and world events. However, Dmitri quickly became bored with these chat rooms. He discovered a secret cyber-underground of Web sites that only trusted members could access. People were granted access only after being verified several times by a referral. Dmitri felt proud that he had received access to these chat rooms. It made him feel like he was not just a poor, small-town Russian boy with no future. He saw an opportunity and he was going to take it.

The cyber-underground is often used for criminal activity. In this arena, people can talk openly about how to commit crimes, how to avoid getting caught and what to do if that happens. Dmitri had developed into a big player and he began recruiting trusted people in various countries around the world, spanning Russia to Canada to Peru to the United States.

Oleg Alekseev lived in Coral Gables, Florida, with his mother, Judith. Oleg was a college student studying for a business degree. By most standards, he appeared to be an average, run-of-the-mill student. Judith had emigrated from Russia several years ago with Oleg. He spoke with a heavy Russian accent, which separated him from other American boys. As he grew up, Oleg isolated himself because he did not feel included in activities with other teenagers. He started spending time on Web sites that connected him to his heritage; he felt more accepted by other Russians. Soon he started visiting chat rooms and was introduced to Dmitri Ivanov. Through many months of conversations on every imaginable topic, Dmitri and Oleg became very trusting of each other. In fact, Oleg considered Dmitri to be the big brother he never had. While Oleg was trying to become Americanized, Dmitri was trying to get him to hold onto his Russian roots. But unbeknownst to Oleg, Dmitri had other plans for him, too.

The American Dream

Glenn Copeland was a New York go-getter. He was not the kind to let the world pass him by. Glenn did not like to wait for things to happen — he made his own opportunities. While he had a normal childhood by typical standards and was a graduate at an average East Coast college, Copeland did not want the predictable future of going to work for corporate America; that environment moved too slowly for him. He was full of forward-thinking ideas and did not want to work for someone else. But, like others before Glenn, he entered the corporate world anyway. And true to his nature, he was a misfit. There was too much red tape, too many meetings to think about ideas, and this slowed down accomplishing them. He climbed the corporate ladder but still felt that he wasn't following his calling in life. So when he was 35 years old he went out on a limb with a partner and they started their own company. It was a provider of simple and inexpensive ways for businesses to pay their employees via direct deposit instead of with a check. However, the service quickly became outdated, so when Glenn was 40 he started his own company called eTransfer.

Glenn realized that companies had employees who did not have bank accounts or could not cash a paycheck without exorbitant fees, so his new venture began providing prepaid debit cards as an alternative to checks and direct deposit. Besides payroll cards, eTransfer provided the opportunity for employers to give bonuses or other compensation through cards instead of checks. Glenn believed it provided a safer method than checks because check fraud was so prevalent.

eTransfer was based in New York City but had a technology office in Miami. Glenn held several bank accounts in the company's name in multiple states, but used Arch Bank for its processing for the last four years.

A Window of Opportunity

On October 2, a normal Tuesday morning, the manager of the electronic banking department at Arch Bank, Nathan Wertz, was notified of an unusually large overdraft in the checking account of eTransfer. The account was overdrawn by $5.2 million from transactions that were processed over the weekend. Considering that the most eTransfer ever processed nightly was around $20,000, Nathan knew something was wrong and began looking into the situation.

At the time I was working as an investigator at Arch Bank. I was in my office when my boss came over to say that something was brewing in electronic banking and there was an overdraft of more than $5 million. Normally, I did not handle electronic banking investigations or overdrawn accounts, but the amount certainly was an attention-getter. For a bank of our size, it was an astronomical amount. I was told that I needed to attend a meeting being held soon in a nearby boardroom. After learning the basics of what had occurred from Nathan, I contacted my colleague at the Secret Service, Special Agent Dave Barker. I gave him the information I had at the time, and he told me to update him when I had more to report.

An unusually large number of people attended the initial meeting. In addition to Nathan, his manager (an executive of the bank), our corporate lawyer, the head of the technology department and several of his staff members, the manager of compliance and the manager of the risk department attended. On the phone were two anti-fraud specialists from MasterCard International, our processor.

Nathan began the meeting with the initial information he had uncovered. He had an internal report showing that four prepaid debit card numbers issued by eTransfer had been used repeatedly during the last couple of days. The statistics seemed too unbelievable to be real. Due to the size of the loss, everyone assumed there was a weird computer glitch. The report showed that the four card numbers were duplicated and disbursed to a network of perpetrators who initiated approximately 9,500 transactions in 8 to 10 hours late Saturday evening through Sunday morning.

Cash withdrawals had been made at multiple ATMs around the world. There was an average of 1,800 transactions to each of the four accounts ranging from $200 to $2,400. Most of the transactions were processed internationally; approximately 30 percent occurred in the United States.

The Perfect Storm

We began a complete forensic investigation into Arch Bank's and eTransfer's systems, and MasterCard. Separate teams of IT experts reviewed them to find a point of compromise and to pinpoint the date the attack started. Glenn Copeland agreed to fully cooperate with our IT specialists to isolate the security breach.

Hours turned into days for everyone involved. We ultimately determined that the only compromise had occurred on eTransfer's end. Arch Bank and MasterCard were completely untouched. We also figured out that eTransfer's system was invaded a few days before the withdrawals began, using malware. Keylogging software was then installed a couple days later to capture the credentials of the system administrator. When transactions were sent to eTransfer for approval, the malware instructed the security system to ignore the account balance fields and the PIN fields; therefore, transactions were being improperly authorized.

We later learned that the crooks had been lurking in the eTransfer system since June, apparently waiting for the perfect time to strike. If Glenn had run a program to sweep his system for malware, the hackers would have been discovered in time to prevent the fraud. In the beginning, they were able to capture the administrator login and password, learning from monitoring his activity that he worked every day. Then they were able to penetrate his corporate e-mail activity. From that information, they discovered he was going on vacation starting October 1. They saw their window and went to work getting past the encrypted data, printing cards and formulating a plan of attack. They had the perfect storm of opportunity that they had been waiting for.

A Picture Is Worth a Thousand Words

We pulled the usage reports and tried many ways to analyze the data to find the common denominator. We finally settled on lumping the cities together and sorting by ATM location. From there we tried to map the distance and travel time between them. At that point, we sorted by bank, so that we could contact it with one request for multiple transactions. For example, we pulled each Bank of America item on Long Island, New York, and then requested pictures and video surveillance from those transactions. We continued this by state, by bank and by city. The Secret Service helped tremendously in this endeavor and most banks responded to our request fairly promptly. As we started receiving pictures, we spotted the same individuals at different machines. In some photos, we saw the suspects with buckets of money, passing them off to other people outside the camera's range. Realizing we had too many transactions at too many ATMs across the country, we decided to focus on heavy concentrations of cash withdrawals and on locations where we had clear images of the suspects. The Secret Service then ran the pictures through their databases, sent them to other law enforcement agencies and circulated them among agents to see if anyone was identified.

After reviewing pictures of the suspects making ATM withdrawals near Tallahassee, Florida, the Secret Service noticed one young male who looked like he was college age. The withdrawals were made at an ATM on a college campus. The Secret Service took copies of his pictures to the local banks, including one on-campus branch for students. One of the tellers said, ''I know him. He's a student and comes in here often.'' She could not remember his name, so the agents asked her to call them if he came in again. The very next day, the suspect in the picture went into the bank. Not only did the teller instantly recognize him from the picture, but he was wearing the exact same clothing as he was in the picture. What were the odds?

The teller called the Secret Service agents as soon as the young man entered the bank, and the agents promptly responded. At the bank, they reviewed video surveillance of the suspect and confirmed that it was the same person in their pictures. After obtaining his identifying information, they went to the college campus administration office to confirm that he was a student. The college administrator gave the agents his home address, which was where they found him doing homework — just like any normal college kid. They asked if they could talk with him about something that occurred at the college. Within two weeks he was the first suspect arrested. Who was it? Oleg Alekseev. A search of his home found $57,627 in cash, which was seized by the Secret Service. We still do not know exactly how much he withdrew, because Oleg himself did not know the total.

The Secret Service said Oleg was cooperative, but not immediately. Once Oleg realized there was no doubt that he was on the video, he became more compliant. He explained that he had become friends with someone from Russia named Dmitri Ivanov over the Internet and that the scheme was Dmitri's idea. He told them about months and months of e-mail conversations with Dmitri spent gaining each other's trust and bonding about their Russian roots and desire to get ahead in life. Dmitri had shared his love of computers with Oleg, and described the conditions of his life in Russia, among other things. Oleg told the agents that he still communicated with Dmitri but had not met him. The Secret Service agents asked him if he had saved any of the e-mails so they could look at them, and he said yes but that they were in Russian. The agents called back to headquarters to say they needed forensic specialists to retrieve the computer; they knew not to take it anywhere or even unplug it before it was properly preserved for evidence.

When the Secret Service IT personnel dug around in his computer, they obtained hundreds of e-mails, including deleted ones, that showed the communications between Oleg and Dmitri. Dmitri was very careful to not give out identifying information, so we did not have a reliable way to track him. We knew from the conversations with Oleg that the suspects at ATMs were only mules; they were not the masterminds. Oleg was convinced that because he and Dmitri had become so close and because he looked to Dmitri as a brother, that once the agents contacted Dmitri, he would help Oleg out of trouble. But as it would turn out later, Dmitri was just fine leaving Oleg and the others to take the fall.

Oleg told the agents that he kept half of the withdrawals and sent the other half to Dmitri in Russia. Through Oleg, we learned that the counterfeit cardstock used in the debit cards was created by an external source that Dmitri found online. While a legitimate prepaid debit card would have colorful corporate logos, 16-digit account numbers and so forth, the counterfeits were plain white cards that lacked insignias. We learned that they were ordered by the thousands very cheaply and shipped globally. Distribution centers waited for directions regarding what to encode and then shipped the cards to a contact that had multiple addresses. This person then distributed the cards to the mules to begin withdrawing funds.

Remittances to the Motherland

The scheme to get the money back to Russia was interesting but not overly complex. After withdrawing the cash, the mules went to any Bank of America branch and deposited the cash into a previously designated business account. As far as Oleg knew, everyone had been given the same account number. Whatever amount of cash they deposited had to end in 30 cents. For example, if Oleg had withdrawn $20,000 using his fraudulent eTransfer debit card, he would keep half and deposit $10,000.30 into the Bank of America account. The 30-cent deposit indicated to the business account holder that he was to wire the funds to Russia. The business owner was also Russian and had become friends with Dmitri online. The owner had an import/export business, so it was the perfect cover for funds being deposited across the country, as well as for large amounts of money being wired out of the country. The business owner had not met Dmitri nor asked him a lot of questions. He also kept a portion of the funds before wiring them to Russia.

The Secret Service did not have enough evidence to track down Dmitri, so they asked Oleg to continue communicating with him to gather more information. Oleg agreed to cooperate in exchange for possible leniency in his own criminal case.

The Secret Service installed a myriad of tracking software on Oleg's computer, but wanted it to look like Oleg was still just chatting with Dmitri. They had to make conversations appear normal while trying to push a little harder for identifying information. They also had to ensure that Oleg did not tip off Dmitri about the surveillance because they were communicating in Russian. However, by this time Oleg had become very cooperative and wanted to reduce his trouble. He finally realized that Dmitri was not coming to his rescue.

Mixed Results

The agents we were working with suggested topics of conversation for Oleg to engage Dmitri in, and they had him ask about other schemes in which Dmitri may have been involved. They tried to collect enough details about his life to find him, prosecute him for this case and prevent him from committing similar ones in the future. Oleg and Dmitri stayed in contact for months. At one point, agents had narrowed down Dmitri's location to one area in Russia and were working with the Russian equivalent of the Secret Service — the Federal Security Service of the Russian Federation — to gather more evidence.

I had to e-mail the Russian agent numerous times to explain the case, details and loss. Honestly, I had not heard of the Russian agency before, so I looked it up online to see if it was legitimate. The Secret Service agent I was collaborating with assured me that they were the good guys. The Secret Service also met with them in Russia to try to bring about the prosecution of Dmitri. The Russian Federation requested formal written letters from Arch Bank to explain the cause, the loss and why they should get involved. Ultimately, they said that although they wanted to prosecute Dmitri, he had a connection to the government, and they could not proceed. They did not explain the situation to us, and it seemed like something out of an old movie. We had hit a wall.

In August, only 10 months after the crime began, Oleg pleaded guilty to fraudulent use of an access device. He was sentenced to 12 months of incarceration, five years of probation and to pay restitution of $20,000. To date, he has paid about $13,000.

In the 12-month investigation of this crime, it was impossible to track how much time bank personnel, law enforcement, vendors and lawyers across the country and around the world put into the case. The civil side alone cost several hundred thousand dollars in forensics and attorney fees. There were civil and criminal suits. Glenn Copeland was forced to file for bankruptcy to shield himself and his company from further financial costs. He had to lay off several of his employees due to his financial loss, and eTransfer suffered reputational damage in the industry. Arch Bank filed suit against him and eTransfer. It is still too early to determine any outcome in civil court. There was no criminal wrongdoing on the part of Glenn or anyone at eTransfer. They were also seen by the law as victims.

Several hundred people perpetrated this fraud, and we were unable to catch most of them. However, the Secret Service had their first arrest within two weeks, which was amazingly quick work. I cannot say enough positive things about the professionalism and responsiveness of the Secret Service in this situation. The agents obtained pictures of suspects from various banks in the United States and Canada and sent them to various law enforcement agencies to identify other culprits. From the pictures they were able to identify and arrest 12 additional suspects, who either pleaded guilty or were found guilty at trial. But the alleged ring leader, Dmitri Ivanov, is still free. We certainly made our best case to the Federal Security Service of the Russian Federation, but as of this writing, Dmitri is still being protected. Of our initial loss of $5.2 million (not including the additional fees) we have recovered only about $300,000. We do not expect much more restitution than we have already received. Regrettably, in all too many situations like this one, crime pays.

Lessons Learned

I learned that when it comes to technology, nothing is safe. I also learned that through the products and services banks offer, the financial institution can become the victim along with the customer. Although our bank systems were not hacked or even compromised, because our customer was, it placed the burden on us as the processor. We also learned the value of having multiple layers of experts review not only new contracts with customers, vendors and other processors but also review renewed contracts for loopholes. And I was reminded again of the value of networking and knowing the right connections with law enforcement to get a case moving quickly. We also learned the very hard lesson that justice in the United States is not always the same as justice around the world.

Recommendations to Prevent Future Occurrences

If any financial institution is dependent on its customer's technology, management should not only have their own technology experts conduct a field investigation, but also hire an outside company to perform due diligence. They need to prepare for the what-if scenarios, because hackers are searching for that one small window of opportunity. Subject-matter experts should review technology-related products and services. Having only lawyers and contract experts review them is insufficient. Rely on the experts to point out the weaknesses, and weigh those risks with serious thought, so that your company can learn from our mistakes.

About the Author

Chris A. McCulloch, CFE, is a corporate security manager for a midwest bank and has been in fraud investigations since 1997. She is an expert in internal and external fraud prevention and investigations. She has worked in the banking industry since 1986 and has been a board member of the Midwest Financial Fraud Investigators for ten years. Chris has been interviewed as an expert for various media, including TV, newspapers and the *Code Red!* radio show. She received an FBI commendation in June 2009.

CHAPTER

Wanted: Your Money

JONATHAN WASHER

At first he seemed like a friendly businessman looking to fulfill customers' wants and needs through the various services and products he offered on different Web sites. But Blake Styles of Cape Coral, Florida, was quite the clever con artist. He seemed to have just what you needed (or could get what you wanted) for a reasonable price. He sold guns, scopes, binoculars and camera equipment online, and later branched out to offer professional services to CEOs and CFOs looking for employment and to corporations searching for executives — for a nominal fee. He found the employment services side of business picked up significantly when the economy took a turn for the worse. Blake used several different Web sites to entice his victims. He would keep one active until the complaints from swindled customers rolled in and the Internet hosting company banned him. When this happened, he simply moved on to a new hosting Web site and targeted new victims. His modus operandi did not change, only the names of his victims.

Blake advertised his items for sale on several Web sites as an individual. But he also used his company name to offer employment services to CEOs, CFOs and other executives. Blake's communication with each customer and subsequent victim was steady and seemingly professional. His method of correspondence was typically e-mail through free services, such as Yahoo! or Gmail, which required no verification of the user's identity.

Blake Styles ran Theodore and Styles, Inc., based in North Fort Myers, Florida, just outside Cape Coral. The business address was a nice piece of property, conveniently located in a busy strip mall on a main road past the Cape Coral city limits. The company's mailing address was assigned a suite number that turned out to be a mailbox rental service offering PO boxes and other shipping and receiving services to individuals. Theodore and Styles seemed to be doing quite well. Mail delivery was steady from people across the country. Blake also used other rental boxes to keep mail related to his Internet dealings away from his personal residence. Theodore and Styles even had a nice Web site that explained its services for executive searches and included a photo of the owner, Blake Styles, on the home page. The Web site also showed logos or seals of international companies — some Fortune 500 corporations — that were reportedly previous clients of Theodore and Styles. The Web site claimed to have helped the companies locate their CFOs and CEOs. There were no reliable letters of recommendation from these companies, only graphics on the site with statements from Blake Styles claiming they were previous clients.

Blake was clever in advertising his services on the Web site. He attempted to cater to larger corporations in search of VPs of finance, CFOs, CEOs and treasurers. To do this, he quoted current laws, such as the Sarbanes-Oxley Act, to stress the importance of using his executive search service to find qualified professionals. The victims had no idea that his representations weren't true. And sadly, if any of the victims had done the most basic research into Blake Styles or Theodore and Styles, they would have clearly seen him for the fraud he was.

United Online

Blake Styles was not selective when choosing the victims for his various scams; they ranged from retirees to skilled tradesman to professional executives. Blake orchestrated his scheme via the Internet, so he mostly dealt with victims outside Cape Coral and Lee County, Florida; they were spread across the United States and came from Wisconsin, Massachusetts, Connecticut, Iowa, Texas, New York, Colorado, Indiana, Ohio, Georgia, Kentucky, Oregon, Montana, Florida and Wyoming. In many of these states, there were several victims who were scammed with multiple Web sites run by Blake that offered items for sale or auction, such as firearms, scopes, binoculars and camera equipment.

The least amount a victim lost to Blake was $275; the most was $4,500. Each was required to pay him for the merchandise or service with a money order, cashier's check, or personal check. Once Blake received the payment, each victim reported that communication from him began to trail off. The victims became incessantly persistent; they called and e-mailed him day and night to ask when they would receive their items or their money back. After many excuses from Blake, he stopped contacting the victims completely. He changed his telephone numbers and ignored the e-mails or changed his e-mail address. As anyone would expect, the victims became angry. And angry Internet customers tend to express their feelings online. They began to blog on various Web sites that they were victimized by Blake, and fortunately for them, they had a lot in common, because many of them bought the exact same item. At this point, I had already received one report about Theodore and Styles, undertaken a little investigative groundwork and communicated with two victims. This was enough for them to get my name out in the blogosphere as a point of contact for other victims. Within days, I received dozens of calls wanting to file complaints against Blake Styles for an Internet-based fraud.

The Reports Were Piling Up

It was another warm, moderately humid morning for the end of October, one day before Halloween in Fort Myers, Florida. I arrived at the office at 7:45 and got settled in my cubicle at the economic crimes unit (ECU) of the Lee County Sheriff's Office, turned on my computer, checked my e-mail and noticed another wave of new cases in my bin, assigned that morning by my lieutenant. At the time, there were only four full-time detectives and we were carrying more than 100 cases each, with no sign of it slowing down. My lieutenant tried to assign cases to each detective based on our investigative strengths. I was quite knowledgeable in most fields of fraud investigation and was studying to attain my Certified Fraud Examiner's (CFE) credential, so I was assigned a lot of the high-profile cases, as well as long-term investigations.

I began to go through my new assignments, and right away one grabbed my interest. It was an Internet case where the suspect, Blake Styles, had reportedly defrauded several victims who tried to purchase different firearms and scopes through a Web site. Each of the five victims had several things in common: They bought an item from Blake Styles, they sent him money in the form of a check or money order and they did not receive their merchandise. The victims became known to each other by filing complaints through the Web site's blog. The combined cash loss was in excess of $6,500. I made contact with each victim and requested they forward their correspondence with Blake Styles to my e-mail address. When I began to read them, I noticed a pattern. He acknowledged receiving the victim's funds, but had an excuse or reason beyond his control for not shipping the merchandise. Due to the fact that the sale and shipping of firearms required a federal firearms license (FFL), Blake would attempt to pass blame for the shipping delay to the FFL holder — usually a local pawnshop. Since I had five victims from one Web site, was it possible a crime didn't occur? Could there have been a simple problem with the shipping of the merchandise? Or was this the beginning of a larger scam with more victims yet to come forward?

A Long-Term Plan

The preliminary investigation progressed slowly. I was dealing with multiple victims from different parts of the country and it was difficult to get their documentation in a timely manner. I needed the victims to forward a sworn statement, copies of payments made to Blake and/or his company and any correspondence they shared with Blake and each other when blogging about their thefts. It took nearly a month to receive the proper documents. I began to send out subpoenas for e-mail accounts, bank account information and other relevant records. A few months later, not to my surprise, I received yet another complaint against Blake Styles. This time he was using a different Web site to sell a high-priced camera lens. The victim sent Blake the funds via a post office box, but the customer did not receive the item. I made contact with the victim and requested his documentation to add to my case file. Now, with six victims and one suspect, was it possibly a coincidence? I didn't think so.

Throughout the next year and a half, I received numerous reports of theft by Blake Styles and his Internet companies. In total, I received 17 reports and had 21 victims on record, with an estimated financial loss of more than $25,000. It seemed obvious that Blake Styles was engaged in an organized Internet scam to defraud people of their money.

A review of the bank records showed that the checks the victims sent Blake were deposited into an account at a bank where I had a good contact. He was an ex-law enforcement officer who was now the fraud investigator at the suspect's bank. To speed up the case and see if a subpoena for surveillance photos of any transactions was necessary, I sent my contact copies of the deposits made by Blake. He said the bank might have a video of the transaction. I immediately requested that the state attorney's office issue a subpoena for the bank records of Blake's account and the surveillance video. After a review, it was clear I was looking at the culprit's bank records. I viewed the surveillance photos of a man making a deposit at a drive-up window and compared it to Blake's driver's license photo — it was a match.

It was also helpful that the suspect put his picture on his own Web site for us. The photograph he had displayed on his professional services Web site also matched the license and surveillance photo. This was key evidence for me in the case. One of the most difficult tasks in solving an Internet fraud is identifying the suspect because there is almost never a witness to the crime. Further review of the bank records confirmed Blake was the sole account holder and signer on each account he had with the bank.

I met with the clerk of the pawnshop that Blake mentioned in communications with customers — the one he claimed could not ship their firearms because there was a problem with the pawnshop's FFL. The clerk said Blake was a frequent customer and had purchased and sold items back to the shop dozens of times in the past several months. However, Blake had not made any arrangements with the shop to receive or ship firearms. The clerk provided a printout of the shop's transactions with Blake. There were a lot of firearms on the list, the same ones he was advertising for sale on several of his Web sites.

After obtaining a subpoena for Blake's mail, I met with a manager at the location where Blake received mail and checks from the victims. He immediately recognized Blake's name and confirmed he was a frequent customer and the sole recipient on the mailbox account. Blake provided his driver's license to open the account.

Additional records were subpoenaed from the Web sites he used to sell his products. Each site provided records with an Internet protocol (IP) address and history I was able to trace back to Blake. He was smart, up to a point. When I looked into the phone numbers he gave his victims, the telephone companies could only provide me with limited information. Blake had purchased throw-away trac-fones that did not have to be registered to an individual user. Because these phones and many other wireless companies offer prepaid services, it is often difficult for an investigator to identify the owner of a phone number. I made several attempts to contact Blake Styles, but he would not speak with me. He refused to answer the phone or return my calls, and his answering message usually said he was "traveling out of state."

Time Is Running Out

Fraud investigations take a lot of time. They also require patience and understanding from the victims regarding the amount of time needed to properly investigate them and bring them to a successful conclusion. As I type this, the Lee County Sheriff's Office ECU received yet another report against Blake from a victim in another state. He seems to use these schemes to make his living and, based on the information and facts obtained, he was positively identified as the individual who bilked more than a dozen individuals in excess of $25,000. Blake has been successful in eluding arrest by law enforcement thus far. Since he has been known to come back to Lee County periodically, he should worry every time he does and ask himself, "Is today the day I am going to jail?" The clock is ticking, and he is running out of time. With the dedication that we exert to identify, combat and prevent fraud, con artists and fraudsters cannot be elusive forever. Blake Styles will be arrested for his crimes; it's just a matter of time.

Lessons Learned

There are many lessons to be learned from this case, both for investigators and victims. For investigators, the main lesson is to request additional assistance early in cases that require serious financial analysis. Due to my unit's

(continued)

(*continued*)

heavy caseload, Blake's case was forced to sit dormant for more than a month because we lacked the analytical support. Today, we have more analysts in our unit than before and are attempting to hire more. This lesson was learned and corrected.

For the victims, this case points out many protective measures to be taken before purchasing products over the Internet. Customers should ask the following questions about a business or individual seller before buying anything online:

- What is the physical location of the person/business?
- How many people are employed?
- Can I send payment via a secure Web site, like PayPal or VeriSign, or directly to the bank instead of by check, money order or wire?
- Is the company registered with the Better Business Bureau?
- Are there records on file with the secretary of state or county clerk?

One of the biggest downfalls victims tend to have when making a purchase on the Internet is to forget the saying, ''If it sounds too good to be true, it usually is.'' When victims find something they have wanted for quite awhile, they let their guard down and violate common, good-sense business practices. Most fraudsters have been doing this for a while and know how to exploit people. The victims in this case didn't notice red flags before the transactions; it was only after they sent the money that they began having doubts. By that time, this suspect had already moved to a new target. The victims did not ask background questions, request references or ask for verification from the seller. Consumers who purchase products or services on the Internet should learn from these mistakes.

Recommendations to Prevent Future Occurrences

When we are online, we can hide behind a computer monitor and do whatever we like. And in some respects, that makes the Internet a useful tool. It is an information highway for a reason. We can find our favorite recipes, locate lost classmates, post photos of a fun event on a personal Web page, purchase a coveted item or apply for a job. Blake Styles knew this, as many other fraudsters do.

Individuals need to be wary when using the Internet. They need to take the extra time to verify who they are dealing with. *Do not* rush into buying anything. If someone is using a high-pressure sales tactic, you probably don't want that item. There is a reason why a person or business is trying to offload something as quickly as possible.

(*continued*)

Think — that is the strongest piece of advice I can offer to anyone wanting to use the Internet. Think before you post something; a future employer or colleague just may see it and not like what they see. Before you buy a product online, think: Do I need this item? Where is the seller located? Is this a legitimate, properly registered business? Why is this person so insistent on a check and will not take a payment from a secure and insured Web site like PayPal? Public records can tell consumers a lot — if they take the time to look.

Have the person you are dealing with verify his or her identity by sending a copy of a state-issued driver's license or ID card. Check online to see exactly where the business is located. By doing this, many potential victims have realized the company was operating out of a retail mailbox store, which should raise suspicions. The suite number Styles used was actually a PO box number.

Hardships in the economy and technological advances are accompanied by new breeds of criminals ready to exploit the situation and make a buck. This is what we have to watch out for as consumers and proactively deter and detect as anti-fraud professionals.

About the Author

Jonathan Washer, CFE, is a sergeant and supervisor of the Lee County Sheriff's Office, Economic Crimes Unit (ECU), in Fort Myers, Florida. He has been with the sheriff's office for nearly 15 years and was one of the founding members of the ECU. Despite being the supervisor, Sergeant Washer takes an active role in investigating cases of fraud and educating others on the prevention of fraud.

37

The Business of Making Money

BILL MALONEY

Jerry Taylor lived a charmed life. He grew up in an upper-middle-class neighborhood. He was a standout in high-school lacrosse, went to a good college and was making a good living as a stockbroker. In his mid-twenties he settled down and married a local girl and they had two kids — a boy and a girl. They lived in a nice house, in a nice neighborhood, in a nice North-east community. Life was good. That was until the National Association of Securities Dealers (NASD) took away his license for cheating and then not paying his fine.

What's a man to do when life kicks him like that? Jerry knew exactly what to do — keep on cheating. The whole NASD thing was just a big misunderstanding and if they weren't going to see it that way, he'd have to go on his own. First things first, move out West where no one knew him. He knew that with his experience in the financial arena, it would be no problem to buy a house out West, refinance it, inflate the price a few times and then move on and walk away from the loan. Jerry also knew he needed some operating capital, and forming fake companies would pay for the leases on the brand-new cars he and his wife drove. After all, a man needs to get around. He also figured that fake companies would be the perfect capital-generating projects. He could lease office equipment and apply for business loans to misappropriate for his personal use. Even better than creating fake companies was impersonating Fortune 500 companies. As long as the financial institutions did not conduct proper background checks, he would be approved for large lines of credit based on the companies' reputations.

However, Jerry knew that when his fake companies started failing and he started defaulting on loans, the creditors would come after the leased vehicles and office equipment. Unfortunately for the creditors, the assets weren't located where Jerry said they were on his loan applications, so it would take a while for the repossession teams to find them. Jerry was clearly a man who got around; one of his vehicles was recovered in Las Vegas. When an arrest warrant was issued for him in California, Jerry knew what to do — move to Florida.

With a wife and two young children, Jerry wanted a little stability but considered doing business on his own, with his own money, to be a little too risky. So Jerry decided to go back to his roots — using other people's money to fund his endeavors. Convincing other people to invest their money and take the financial risk for him was a start, but Jerry thought it would be even better to take people's money without them knowing. That way, they wouldn't say no. So Jerry simply went online and applied for a loan through Money Online Finance Company to pay for his new office and business supplies — the full $ 10,000's worth.

Jerry was familiar with the Internet and knew that a large, international company like Money Online wasn't going to check too hard to see if he had the proper paperwork and a creditable cosigner with attachable assets. The Internet offered a certain anonymity that Jerry relished. The application process was quick and easy, and if the Money Online employee on the receiving end was lax in conducting due diligence, Jerry would have a much better chance of being approved than if he applied for a loan in person.

Jerry chose Betty Sue to be the Vice President of his new company and cosigner on the loan. He found her online and was able to unearth enough of her private identifying information to add her to his loan application. Of course, it would have been nice for Betty Sue if she knew about Jerry, his business or the loan, but Jerry figured that with her in the hospital with a chronic illness, what she didn't know wouldn't hurt her (more). That is, until she recovered and was released from the hospital, Jerry defaulted on the loan and Money Online came looking for her. When Betty Sue was first contacted by Money Online, Jerry had already moved again, from Florida back to the Northeast. He decided to take the Internet identity-theft skills he practiced on Betty Sue and apply them to bigger fish. He had set his profession sites on a new target — corporate identity theft.

Online Money from Money Online

Money Online Finance Company was a bank holding company. For more than 100 years, Money Online provided lending, advisory and leasing services to small- and middle-market businesses. It was headquartered in New York City and was a Fortune 500 company. Money Online was a full-service, regulated state bank. It had relationships with top players in industries such as technology, office products, health care, printing and other diversified industries.

Money Online was a leading provider of vendor financing solutions to companies around the world. Its main services included designing, implementing and managing customized financing solutions to help with the sale of products for manufacturers and distributors. The company provided lease financing directly to end-user customers. Money Online was able to develop and execute structured financing relationships with industry-leading manufacturers, distributors, software vendors and service providers worldwide.

Money Online loan processors saw multiple applications each day, and because most applicants submitted the forms and documentation online, the processors were detached from the applicants. Unless employees made a conscious effort to perform due diligence on every application, it was easy for falsified information to slip past them.

Not-So-Excellent Technology

Excellent Computer Technology, Inc., was started in the early 1980s. The company provided information technology solutions and a full range of computer services to companies of all sizes, including network design and installation, centralized management and remote-access solutions. It also provided small businesses services ranging from the strategy and assessment planning to design, development and implementation of computer systems and ongoing operations and support. They offered Internet services such as e-mail access, Web design, Web site hosting, firewall security and e-commerce solutions. The only thing Excellent Computer Technology, Inc., did *not* do was sell computers.

One day Jason Mitchell, a customer service representative, approached Valerie Rosales, Excellent Computer's general manager, with a problem: A Money Online loan processor called to speak with the sales manager to confirm the final details of a contract for the sale of computers — a contract that Excellent Computer Technology knew nothing about. Jason and Valerie discussed the supposed contract, the details of the deal and the involved parties. When all the notes were compared, a fraud in progress emerged. Valerie contacted the detective division of the police department and requested assistance.

The Master Impersonator

I was working as a police detective when Valerie called to report the suspicious contract at Excellent Computer Technology. After interviewing Valerie and reviewing the paperwork and e-mails she had related to the contract, I determined that someone had found the name of Excellent Computer Technology's sales manager and assumed his identity for the purpose of arranging contract financing between Excellent Computer Technology and the perpetrator's company. A little research into the documents showed that the offender not only assumed the identity of Excellent

Computer's sales manager; he also fraudulently posed as a Fortune 500 company. I contacted the company listed on the contract as the purchaser of the computers, but no one there had heard of the transaction. As my investigation proceeded, I discovered that numerous other finance companies were also approached to provide this third-party financing.

Acting as the sales manager for Excellent Computer Technology and the president or purchasing director of the Fortune 500 company that was supposedly requesting the equipment and the loan, Jerry convinced the financing company's processor that he or she had a viable business deal and the processor would send a check to Excellent Computer Technology. The check, however, would be intercepted and neither business would be the wiser — until the loan went into default months later.

My team and I started the investigation by obtaining a list of the parties and companies involved and reviewing their e-mail and paperwork. We ran them through data analysis software to develop backgrounds and patterns of information. When the supporting documents supplied with loan applications didn't pan out, we were able to identify suspects. While running our analyses, other information about individuals and companies was developed. This led us to the name of our prime suspect — Jerry Taylor — a man who kept appearing in our reports. We hit the jackpot one day when we discovered his real driver's license on a loan application; he must have gotten lazy that day. We also learned that he had active arrest warrants issued for him. As we developed more information about Jerry and cross-checked it against information already obtained, we conducted more computer analyses.

We gave Money Online some of the identifying data (name, address, driver's license number and so on) we had uncovered and asked the management team to analyze their records for other contracts with the same information. They found other contracts that had already gone into default and were in the process of being sent to civil collection. There were also several contracts in various stages of approval.

When we heard of this, we devised a sting operation using one of them as the bait. The financing request was for $150,000 for computers and peripherals, supposedly to be purchased from Excellent Computer Technology. Money Online issued a check to Excellent Computer Technology for more than $150,000 to the address Jerry provided and we tracked it. When he picked up the check at the post office, he found a few police detectives waiting to introduce themselves. We positively identified the suspect as Jerry Taylor, arrested him and went to his "office," where we found the brand-new luxury convertible he was driving. This led to search and seizure warrants for Jerry's banking records.

Jerry's crime was uncovered because a finance company representative needed to confirm the final details of the contract before sending the check but he couldn't find the phone number on the paperwork Jerry provided. Rather than look for it, the representative called information and got the direct — and correct — number.

Missing Checks and Double-Checks

That simple act of independently looking up the company's phone number foiled Jerry's crime. Other finance companies that had been approached but not swindled conducted these types of independent checks as part of their normal screening process. When the public records differed from the information provided by an applicant, the company refused the financing application. If the representative had relied on the contact information provided in the application, the phone would have been answered by Jerry and the check would have gone out in the mail. In fact, it would have been the third check Money Online sent Jerry that month! The other two checks he had already received were for $50,000 and $30,000. Obviously, Jerry was feeding his family well.

Admittedly, Jerry did have to expend a bit of effort for his money. With his background in business, he knew to do his homework. He formed a shell company that appeared — on paper at least — to be legitimate. He opened a Dun & Bradstreet account to search for ideal companies to pretend to be and to obtain the necessary information to accurately portray them.

He even leased office space, equipment and vehicles in the shell company's name. Of course, the leases were in default after only one month, but Jerry knew it would take the finance companies another couple months to determine the defaults were the result of deliberate nonpayment. So he moved the leased equipment and office furniture into storage and sold it privately. When the lessor's personnel went to repossess the property, they found an empty office and a bitter landlord. It was about six months before the car company went after the leased vehicle — five months too late. By then Jerry had moved his family to another state and the car company was left with the useless and inaccurate identifying information provided on Jerry's lease.

Unfortunately, Jerry still obtains vehicles for himself and his wife this way. The leasing companies don't usually prosecute for auto theft on company-leased cars. When Jerry was caught, his BMW convertible hadn't gone to collection yet; it was only behind in payment. Despite being advised of Jerry's history and the fact that all the lease paperwork was invalid, the leasing company did not want to prosecute him for the fraud. Neither did the insurance company that Jerry had the vehicles insured under (and had the bill sent to a third corporation). They just canceled the policy and said that because he didn't have an accident claim during the insured time frame, they didn't want to get involved. Even when his many loans, leases and rentals went south, the victim companies did not process the defaults as civil collections until months after Jerry had disappeared.

Boring, Boring, Boring

After reviewing the paperwork and e-mails and interviewing the loan manager at Money Online, I learned that they had six different contracts with Jerry (all for different fake companies) in various stages of the loan lifecycle. It was one of them that started the investigation. The contract was to be the third check issued by Money Online and was for $150,000.

Unrelated to our investigation, Jerry had written several bad checks at a grocery store and had warrants out for him. When we arrested him at the post office, we first mentioned his outstanding warrants. He was more than willing to discuss the "misunderstanding" of the bad checks. After all, he pointed out, a man has to eat. However, as soon as we brought up the larceny involving Excellent Computer Technology, Jerry smiled and said, "I'd like to speak with my attorney before going any farther."

Jerry was charged with larceny in the first degree and writing fraudulent checks. He was held on a $150,000 bond, but his wife posted it as soon as he was arraigned; he spent a day and a half in jail. The prosecutor allowed a plea bargain when Jerry pleaded guilty to fourth-degree larceny. When I asked the prosecutor why he settled for such a low plea, he told me, "Fraud cases are inherently boring to prosecute and present to a jury." Even though there were two other charges of first-degree larceny against Jerry for the two checks he had already received from Money Online, the prosecutor said that the deal had been made and he wasn't going to go to trial for a fraud. He said that he would tell the defendant to make restitution for the other two checks but, to date, no money has been repaid.

We found evidence in Jerry's vehicle of his plans to impersonate various Fortune 500 companies. In total, he attempted to defraud investors and businesses of more than $600,000. I contacted the FBI and turned over my evidence because they were conducting a separate investigation into Jerry's actions. The agent I spoke with said that if restitution for the other two checks hadn't been made at the conclusion of their investigation, they would incorporate it into their charges.

Lessons Learned

The first and most important lesson learned in this investigation is for financial institution employees to "do it yourself." Conduct due diligence and verify the information a potential customer provides. The Money Online representative who

(continued)

independently looked up the phone number for Excellent Technology exposed Jerry's fraud. Other finance companies I interviewed did not give Jerry loans because they had done the same.

This case also demonstrated the importance of taking the time to coordinate with the necessary agencies, companies and departments to investigate a suspected identity thief. A large amount of the fraud losses we uncovered were treated as civil — not criminal — matters. Many of the managers I spoke with at various defrauded financial institutions were surprised that I — a police detective — was proactively investigating Jerry and admitted they probably wouldn't have thought to involve the police if I hadn't contacted them. Although almost all of Jerry's actions had elements of a tort (which is the basis for a civil lawsuit), there was a clear pattern of deception that also made them a crime. By explaining this to managers and pointing out that a criminal conviction would help their civil cases, I was able to change the view of management at several companies. (Since civil and criminal actions are separate, both can be pursued independent of each other.)

At the same time, I learned that not everyone is going to be as enthusiastic about investigating and prosecuting identity theft as I was. Some companies did not want to be involved in a criminal investigation and preferred only to pursue a civil claim and ''turn it over to collection.'' I was also introduced to the sad truth that many district attorneys view fraud as ''boring'' and don't want to deal with it. Some prosecutors just want a conviction — any conviction — regardless of the cost or the negation of justice. If a defense attorney knows this about the prosecutor, he or she can simply threaten to have the defendant go to court so the prosecutor will agree to a lesser charge. However, to be fair, in my career I have seen a few prosecutors realize the necessity of prosecuting fraud.

Constant interaction, communication and monitoring are required from the victims, companies, investigative agencies and prosecutors to bring about a satisfactory resolution in an identity theft case. Lack of coordination or information-sharing and a reliance on the other guy to conduct your due diligence help the identity thief get away with his crime.

Recommendations to Prevent Future Occurrences

Be persistent! Following the paper trail can be tedious. The path is bureaucratic and time consuming, and the results are often not what you wanted. But if you keep at it, your efforts and actions can sometimes bring about a positive change that makes it harder for the next thief to do it again.

Coordinate the investigation and work as a cohesive team. Plan the investigation to determine who will do what and the charges to be brought. Develop solid evidence

(*continued*)

(*continued*)

so that the charges stick and the suspect is in a more difficult position to negotiate a plea.

Build a case based on state jurisdiction before considering a federal level. Develop strong local charges and coordinate them to be prosecuted together. (Local cases can often be prosecuted federally *or* — but not *and* — vice-versa.) If the violation is big enough, the feds may be interested in assuming the investigation. This case was initially turned down by the feds because the dollar amount was too low, even though it was occurring over the Internet and through interstate mail but they became interested after we discovered other Fortune 500 companies involved that raised the losses. Federal prosecutors have stringent guidelines but if local cases are strong, the feds might be able to help. However, if they assume the investigation, it becomes harder for local jurisdictions to incorporate and add their cases.

Lastly, monitor the prosecution and the plea deals being made. The prosecutors' attitude toward fraud is important — they may not always have your best interests in mind. In this situation, the plea deal had been completed without any input from the police or the victim or an attempt to gather more facts about the case. Had that been done, the end result might easily have been different.

About the Author

Bill Maloney, CFE, has been a police detective for the past 21 years of a 29-year-long career with the police in a Northeast city of about 100,000 people. He has been married to his wife, Vicki, for the past 27 years and is the father of three fantastic children, Michael, Meghan and Kelly.

CHAPTER 38

Failure to Deliver

TODD J. DAVIS

Norfolk Keen decided to turn his life around by starting his own business. Keen was a single man in his early thirties with short, cropped hair and was a little overweight. He had the appearance of having lived a hard life; he had a few scars on his face and looked at least 10 years older than he really was. When Keen decided to start fresh, the Internet was booming and he had heard stories about other people who made a fortune on the Web. He decided the best option for starting his own business was to open an online retail store; he wouldn't have to maintain normal retail hours and he would be his own boss. Keen lived in an area known for electronics and he envisioned himself employing his extensive knowledge in this field to develop a commercial enterprise. Keen had a high-school GED and grew up working in electronics retail stores and manufacturing plants, but he did not keep jobs for very long. He also tinkered with electronics throughout his life and saw the potential for his new endeavor to grow with his knowledge and passion.

Keen had a difficult past and was in and out of the criminal justice system for various drug-related charges and other offenses. He thought his new business would provide him the stability and focus to beat his addictions and to bring in a steady income. He planned on dedicating the time he used to occupy with drugs to making his new business successful. He bought a computer, rented a small storage room in the busy downtown business district and contacted local distributors to offer their products for sale online.

Norfolk Keen created his Web site, www.IntricateElectronics.com, and began listing items for sale. He specialized in small replacement parts that were inexpensive, hard to find and used in many different large electronic devices. He charged a high markup on the products because he knew customers would have a hard time finding them anywhere else. His Web site looked professional and he had divided the products into categories like mechanical, parts, tools and others. His intentions were genuine and he saw the business venture as a way to give back to his community and make a comfortable living. Many of his products were made in and around the city by companies he knew from growing up and working in the area. He took on the business himself with little help from others—except the occasional assistance provided by his new girlfriend—and excitedly shipped his first orders and contacted his customers if there would be a delay for any reason. However, Keen did not know the laws and regulations he needed to follow to start a business and did not incorporate with the secretary of state.

After his Web site had been up and running for a few months, Keen began having personal problems. He returned to his old drug habits and used the money he earned from Intricate Electronics to pay for his addictions. He stopped shipping products after collecting payment for them; eventually the number of unshipped orders outgrew completed orders. He began lying to buyers who contacted him and tried to stall them as long as possible. Keen had customers who were trying to repair family heirlooms with parts sold on his Web site and they were not interested in a refund. To them, the rare parts were more important than the money.

Sentimental Value

Allison Reynolds was an elderly woman who had limited experience buying online. She logged in to Keen's Web site to look for a replacement part for her family's antique Wurlitzer jukebox. She found exactly what she was looking for—a power cord—and placed the order. The Web site indicated the credit card system was not working and that she would have to send a check for $42.09, which she promptly did. The check cleared one week later and she eagerly anticipated her order. The jukebox had been nonoperational for years and, with a large family reunion coming up, she hoped to have it working for everyone to enjoy. A month passed but the power cord had not arrived, so Allison sent an e-mail to Keen asking for the status of her order. She did not receive a reply and sent two more e-mails, which also went unanswered. She then sent a certified letter to Keen outlining her experience and asking for a refund or shipment. Two weeks went by but she did not hear from Keen or receive her power cord. Allison and Keen lived on opposite sides of the state, and she did not have a driver's license, the only reason—as she later told me—that she did not drive to Keen's office to pick up her order in person. Allison finally filed a complaint against the seller with her local Better Business Bureau.

Connor Jenkins was an avid guitar player and proud of his extensive guitar collection. He was looking for new knobs to add to his Gibson Les Paul guitar. He found the exact ones he was looking for on Intricate Electronics. And although the price was higher than he hoped, he was willing to pay more because he had been unable to find those exact knobs on any other Web sites during his six-month search. Connor paid $36.78 through his PayPal account and awaited their arrival. After a few weeks Jenkins started to wonder why he had not received the order. He called Keen, who claimed to have just returned from a vacation to find his business in shambles; Keen assured Connor Jenkins that he would locate the order and fulfill it as soon as possible. Jenkins normally gave people the benefit of the doubt and had no reason to suspect Keen, but after three more weeks passed and he had not received the knobs, he became suspicious. He called Keen again, who said his computer system had crashed and asked Jenkins to e-mail the order confirmation so Keen could ship the parts. In his e-mail, Jenkins wrote that Keen had two weeks to deliver the guitar knobs or he would be contacting local law enforcement. Two weeks went by, but Jenkins still did not receive the order. Because he lived halfway across the country from Keen, Jenkins contacted Keen's local police department and filed a complaint.

Collecting Complaints

I was a consumer fraud investigator with the Attorney General's Office and was often contacted by police departments to investigate cases involving Internet retailers. After consumers began filing complaints against Intricate Electronics, I was initially provided with 30 to 40 of them and I quickly discerned a pattern: consumers ordered products on his Web site, paid online using credit cards or PayPal or mailed personal checks or money orders, but they did not receive their merchandise. When the customers contacted Keen, he promised to send their purchases promptly, but failed to honor that promise. On other occasions he told customers that he had been out of the country and returned to find his business in a state of chaos. He assured the purchasers that they were in good hands and offered to either provide a full refund or ship the merchandise right away. He also told many customers that his system had crashed and the orders had been lost.

Several of the orders were for low-cost items, so to develop a stronger case I expanded my search for complaints beyond those provided to me. I believed there were many more victims who had not come forward to the police and may have reported complaints to other agencies. Here is a list of complaints I discovered:

Attorney General's Office	39
Better Business Bureau	89
Federal Trade Commission	20

Internet Crime Complaint Center   9

Local Police Departments   13

Total complaints filed   170

After looking into the 170 complaints against Intricate Electronics and eliminating the duplicates filed with more than one agency, I was left with 126 separate frauds from 40 states with losses ranging from $9 to $849. I contacted a random 38 consumers to determine the current status of their complaints and to understand what deceptive business practices may have been committed by Keen.

I then held a meeting with Assistant Attorney General Christian Jackson to discuss how to proceed. Our goal was to get Keen to promptly ship the products to his customers or have him issue them a full refund. We decided to keep the case in civil court.

Jackson sent Keen a certified letter outlining his offenses under state law, including failing to deliver purchased items to consumers, offering refunds to consumers and not honoring them, making false and/or misleading statements to buyers regarding the delivery of their merchandise and failing to respond to e-mails and telephone inquiries from customers.

The letter was to notify Keen of the intention to take legal action against him and to give him and his attorney the opportunity to meet prior to the start of litigation. It advised Keen that a settlement would have to include an appropriate judgment filed in court, would bar future unlawful conduct and would require the payment of restitution and penalties to injured parties. The letter served as a formal notice that if we were unable to resolve the matter to the consumers' and our satisfaction, a civil complaint would be filed against Keen.

Still No Response

I continued to update my case file and maintained an open line of communication with the agencies that originally sent me their complaints. As my investigation progressed I received 16 more complaints and added them to my file. My goal was to have the most comprehensive list of complaints possible. During my investigation I searched the Internet for key terms, phrases and Web sites similar to Keen's. In one of my searches, I came across a Web site that appeared to share the same layout and format as Intricate Electronics. I checked the registration of the site and found it was to Keen's home address but in the name of his girlfriend. I found three more complaints relating to the Web site under Keen's girlfriend's name that alleged the same pattern of behavior. I added these complaints to the database I was maintaining and had a total of 145 complaints.

Jackson did not hear from Keen regarding the certified letter he sent, so he filed a complaint and preliminary injunction in superior court. Keen did not hire an attorney and, in response to Jackson's filing, requested a "quick and easy resolution to the order." Jackson's civil action contained the facts of the investigation, injunctive relief sought, statement of facts for the case and arguments based on a statutory mandate to protect the public interest in trade and commerce. The preliminary injunction was sought to ensure that Keen could not continue to commit his fraud. We also created a press release to inform the public of Keen and to prevent more potential victims from falling prey to Intricate Electronics. We sought restitution for Keen's customers as well as civil penalties, costs and fees. The lawsuit further requested an injunction to prohibit Keen from transferring or dissipating assets that could be used to pay restitution. I wanted the court to hear customers' stories and was able to include several affidavits from consumers with the court filings.

Accepting Responsibility

Keen agreed with the preliminary injunction because he knew what he did was wrong and said he fully intended to ship his customers' orders or refund their money. He admitted that his system did not crash and he had an active database of orders that were pending shipment. Keen provided us with an accounting of outstanding orders, which far exceeded my database of complaints. Apparently many of Keen's victims did not file complaints; this is not uncommon. Keen's list added another 60 customers to my database, bringing the total to more than 200. We worked with Keen to create a schedule for him to ship the products.

Keen began shipping orders and providing refunds while we were still negotiating with him, but we continued to monitor his actions. We filed a final judgment by consent in court that both the court and Keen signed. The terms of the final judgment were as follows. Keen shall not:

- Fail to deliver any merchandise within four weeks if payment has been received, unless a later delivery date has been agreed to by the buyer.
- Accept orders for merchandise that is not in stock or is not readily available by a third-party supplier.
- Make false or misleading statements to consumers in connection with the offering for sale, sale or delivery of merchandise.
- Offer a refund of the purchase price of a product and then fail to provide that refund.

Further stipulations were made regarding what Norfolk Keen should do going forward and included:

- Post delivery and refund policies clearly and conspicuously on his Web sites.
- Maintain and monitor his e-mail address and telephone number for the purpose of responding to consumers' inquiries.
- Post his contact information on his Web sites.

Keen agreed to pay a civil penalty of $5,000 in two partial payments—one at the filing of the judgment and the other four months later. Keen also said he would make restitution to outstanding customers either in merchandise or refunds. If he received any additional complaints in the future, he would provide a full refund within 30 days of receipt of the written complaint.

The case received much press in the local newspapers and radio programs. The community felt as though Keen had wounded its local heritage but also felt vindicated that he entered into the agreement, made restitution to his consumers and paid a penalty. The case received national press due to the large number of people who were victims and because online retail sales were increasing at such a high rate. The media wanted to warn and educate others about the possibility of becoming a victim of online fraud.

Keen was allowed to continue operations of Intricate Electronics and since our settlement, only a few complaints have been filed against him and he has promptly rectified them. I have maintained contact with Keen's local police department and heard that he has not committed any unlawful acts since my investigation—he has been clean on his drug tests and his business is going well. He even recently opened a retail store in the downtown area of the city.

This investigation was my first large case involving Internet consumer fraud. Normally the cases I investigate have occurred in my region, where I have contacts in the police departments and other agencies. For this case I had to cast a larger net to find as many complaints filed against Keen and Intricate Electronics as possible.

Lessons Learned

Keen learned from this case that he must maintain accurate records of his transactions and reply in a timely manner to his customers. I suggest that Internet retailers follow the guidelines we set forth for Keen in our final agreement. They should maintain communication with consumers, be up-front and honest about the products they have in stock and clearly post on their Web sites a reasonable shipping time frame. If a customer orders an out-of-stock product, the retailer should notify the buyer and provide an estimated delivery date.

Recommendations to Prevent Future Occurrences

Consumers should maintain accurate records of their Internet purchases and monitor their accounts to know when online purchases are debited to their credit cards or processed through an Internet payment service. They should also verify the amount of the purchase. Customers should read the retailer's shipping policies, document the contact information and conduct an Internet search for complaints filed against the company. If there are complaints, customers should determine their nature, if responses were filed and if they have been resolved. Should they still have concerns about the company, they should contact their local Better Business Bureau, state consumer protection department, Federal Trade Commission, local police department or other agency that monitors consumer complaints against Internet purchases.

About the Author

Todd J. Davis has been a CFE since early 2009. His background includes eight years of campus policing including becoming a sergeant. He was an investigator with the Attorney General's Office for four years and has more than five years of experience conducting criminal fraud investigations. He holds many instructor certificates.

CHAPTER

39

Cyber Psycho

ERIC A. KREUTER

— In cyberspace, no one can hear you scream.

Connie Delvecchio was raised by her parents in a tiny Pennsylvania coal-belt town. She had a younger brother and shared a bedroom with her older sister. Connie was a sociable child with disturbing antisocial tendencies. Her family often treated her as if she were invisible, because, frankly, they saw her as a disruptive, creepy girl. When she was young, Connie frequently stole her sister's clothes and later stole money from relatives with unwavering denials. Since childhood she displayed an innate ability to lie unflinchingly and with age, her psychopathic behavior became more pronounced and intimidating. Connie didn't express guilt or remorse for the wicked things she did; indeed, she seemed to derive pleasure from her actions.

Before turning 16, Connie was sexually precocious. After playing in a high-school basketball game against state police, Connie snuck off with a married officer named Max, who was twice her age, and easily seduced him into having sex with her. This provided her with blackmail leverage over him, and their lives remained entangled for the next 25 years.

Connie was quick-minded and clever. She was seen as troubled and unsettling by most of the people in her life, but those who knew her best found her frightening and evil. She married soon after high school, had her first child (Clarissa) at age 20, and had her second child (Anne) at age 25. In her mid-thirties Connie became a licensed practical nurse. Two weeks into her first job at a regional hospital, she was arrested for stealing hundreds of syringes of Demerol. Her coworkers claimed that she also stole narcotics from patients. She was fired and her license was revoked.

Connie was a self-medicating drug addict. Throughout her life she attempted to mask her psychopathic behavior by alleging migraine pain. She used headaches to excuse her hysterical antics and to obtain both sympathy and Demerol. She used this pretense even though Demerol is rarely used for emergency treatment of migraines. Dozens of times, Connie coerced Clarissa, a minor without a driver's license, to drive her at odd hours to distant emergency rooms because all the nearby hospitals knew to watch out for her. Clarissa reported: "She had me driving because she was completely out of it." Using her medical knowledge and often-stolen identities, Connie convinced the doctors to inject her with high doses of Demerol. "She faked it really well," said Clarissa, who drove home as Connie passed out in the back seat in a narcotics-induced stupor.

One by one, her family members abandoned Connie. Her tumultuous marriage of 25 years finally ended, and her ex-husband moved across the country. Clarissa relocated and ostracized Connie; "My mother is dead to me," she declared. Anne remained under tight maternal control until Connie was sent to jail for violating her probation by committing one of many felonies. Anne went to live with her father and didn't see her mother again. Even Connie's siblings severed their relationships with her. Barbie, her sister, felt Connie was always an untrustworthy thief, dating back to her youth. Barbie recalled how, as their father was dying, "possessions from the home were disappearing as he was getting closer to death." There have even been allegations that Connie accelerated his death. Connie made statements that she "put him out of his misery."

Flying into Danger

Robert Friedman grew up with two brothers in a stable and loving home in New York, close to a major airport. Robert's mother was a well-educated teacher, and his father owned a small business. Robert was engrossed with children's television shows that depicted pilots rescuing people. He watched *Superman* and other shows about flying. He built small planes out of balsa wood and liked to watch soaring birds.

Staring out his bedroom window, Robert began to decipher the traffic patterns of approaching aircraft. He took a flight in a glider at age 14. After that, he was dedicated to becoming a pilot. By the time he was 16, Robert was flying solo and he obtained a private airplane pilot's license at age 17. He was flying small planes before most teenagers drove cars. Robert went on to earn a degree in aeronautics. His skills developed as he advanced from flying small aircraft to working as a flight engineer and a pilot on large commercial airplanes, such as the Boeing 727. He attained his ultimate career ambition when he was hired as a pilot by a major carrier at age 32.

Robert was trim, handsome, amiable and very helpful to those around him. As an eligible bachelor, he had a lot to offer. He trusted people and would put himself at risk, even to help strangers.

The challenging and rewarding life of an airline pilot, while exciting, involves the strain of living out of a suitcase and being away from home. Robert's career required total concentration and dedication, and his record was unblemished. He enjoyed life, had accumulated some investments and was optimistic about the future. Having relocated to Philadelphia at age 40, Robert wanted to settle down and meet new people. He purchased his first computer in 1995 when home Internet use was just becoming popular. Robert visited chat rooms in an attempt to connect with local Philadelphians, and used a screen name that combined his initials and the word *Philly*.

Robert did not know what instant messaging (IM) was until he received his first message from a woman using a provocative screen name, who later identified herself as Connie. She asked him about baseball, thinking Robert must be a Phillies fan due to his screen name. As she was a fan of the Atlanta Braves, Connie wrote, "My Braves are beating up on your Phillies." She also said she was a nurse from a small town in western Pennsylvania. After the exchange of many e-mail messages and IMs, Robert and Connie began speaking on the telephone. Connie portrayed herself as a simple, small town, wholesome girl with a dash of sexuality. She said she played on a woman's softball team, which Robert found appealing.

After discussing everyday topics for several weeks, Connie began to mention an increasingly complicated and dangerous situation in which she was involved. As her stories became more detailed, they also became more incredulous, but she told them in a believable manner. Though Robert's interest in Connie had waned, he had concerns for her well-being. Wanting to help, he listened to Connie's tales of her complicated life.

Intimidation and Bullying

Shortly after Connie opened up to him about her troubles, Robert began receiving e-mails from unfamiliar people. Some of them said they were members of law enforcement in Connie's hometown. Others were just regular people, and still others claimed to be celebrities. Over the course of many months, more individuals contacted Robert by e-mail and some claimed to be government agents. Connie said she was working with them, albeit reluctantly, in a criminal investigation.

The cyber identities revealed that they knew a lot about Robert, which unnerved him. Collectively, this widening network of connections said Connie was helping them take down a Philadelphia-based organized-crime ring run by mobster Joey Merlino. Connie intimated that she was coerced by Max, the police officer with whom she had an affair when she was a teenager, to help the investigation because of her stated friendship with Mark, a major league baseball pitcher. Merlino's crime syndicate was purportedly involved in gambling operations during professional baseball games in collaboration with certain players, who agreed to alter plays on Merlino's command. Mark was one of the players allegedly involved. Robert listened kindly but wondered what was real. When he asked questions, things just got worse.

Robert was puzzled at how so many unfamiliar people knew intimate details of his life, as if he was being secretly investigated, and that they were all connected to Connie. They pressured Robert to maintain contact with Connie and insisted it would help the investigation. Robert wanted out of the entire situation, but he wanted to help Connie — he saw her as a damsel in distress. And that was how she wanted him to see her.

Robert was intimidated and bullied by his online connections, and the messages they sent him rapidly became more intense. Connie started acting hysterically, which threw Robert off track. He was feeling increasingly trapped and completely unprepared to defend himself against a cyberspace attack.

Connie had created an elaborate network of fictional online characters, each with a distinct personality, who confirmed each other's stories. Robert responded to each identity without knowing that Connie was behind them all. The personal information the characters revealed to Robert about their lives increased the veracity of the scheme.

Robert was overwhelmed by the conflicts and drama of this new Internet world. He struggled to maintain a full flight schedule, and was often juggling his career with Connie's needs. He was losing sleep and was deeply troubled.

Home Invasion

Max began to pressure Robert to let Connie move into his apartment. Max said he wanted to create the illusion of a relationship between Robert and Connie, and that Connie was needed in Philadelphia to meet Mark and Merlino, the crime boss. Max presented this idea to Robert allegedly as part of his plan to bring down Merlino. He said that pretending Robert and Connie were in a relationship would serve the investigation and that if Robert cooperated, the situation would soon be over and he would have his peace and quiet back. Money was regularly taken out of Robert's personal bank accounts without his knowledge or consent. Because of this, the situation became much more real to him.

Robert was horrified by this request and flatly refused it. He told Max by e-mail that the game had gone on too long and that Max and his agency could "go to hell." He already lost a year of his life and he wanted out. Robert wanted no part of Max or the agency he supposedly worked for.

Max replied quickly. Robert was told in no uncertain terms that he must bring Connie to Philadelphia immediately. If he didn't, Max would never be out of Robert's life; he would slowly be destroyed, both financially and professionally. The extreme threats were very direct, and Robert took them seriously. He gave into Max and agreed to let Connie move into his apartment, but only for a week or two. Max assured him that was all that was needed, thanked Robert, and told he would not regret it.

In early June, Robert flew to Connie's town, rented a car and picked her up. They loaded up the car with her clothes and drove to Philadelphia. Robert was feeling hopeless but thought, "At least things can't get worse."

Despite assurances from a host of online identities that Connie would only be living with Robert for a few weeks, she stayed for more than a year. By then, most of Robert's savings had been depleted by various demands and extortions from the cyber identities. He also discovered that credit cards were opened in his name, most of which were maxed out, ruining his credit. He was desperately trying to sort through the confusing information presented by Connie to figure out the truth.

Connie came back to Robert's apartment one afternoon in what struck Robert as an authentic state of horror, and said that two members of Merlino's mob forced her into the back of a limousine and burned her inner thighs with a cigarette. She said they wanted her to stop cooperating with the FBI investigation. Hysterically, she told Robert, "They burned me about 10 or 15 times." Although her shock seemed genuine, Robert asked her to show him the burns, hoping to finally catch her in a lie. After acting wounded by his lack of trust, she showed him multiple fresh burn marks. In tears she added a threat for Robert, "If they would do this to me, what do you think they would do to you or your family? Or maybe your little nephew?" It was surreal for Robert. He did not know who to believe or where to turn for help.

Robert was slowly drawn deeper into a bizarre world of what appeared to be government investigations and organized crime. Robert experienced disbelief, thoughts that organized crime really was involved and suspicions that he was being targeted by a combination of hackers and stalkers. As if to confirm his worst fears, the local news was filled with stories of police corruption.

Who's Crazy Here?

Robert finally decided to report the events. He went to an FBI office with his father and filled out a complaint form; he was asked to present his identification, including his pilot's license. More than a year after Connie moved into his apartment, he finally sat down for an interview with two young agents.

Special Agents Johnson and Dexter listened to Robert's story and asked him to return the next day with whatever supporting documentation he had. He brought about 75 pages of threatening e-mail messages and relevant bank statements showing the fraudulent accounts. After reviewing the documents, the agents contacted Connie by telephone to corroborate Robert's complaint, but she told them, "Robert likes to make up stories. Nothing criminal is happening." She convinced the agents that she thought Robert was mentally troubled.

The agents did not run a criminal background check on Connie; instead they believed her and assumed Robert was making a false report. They contacted the FAA and recommended he undergo a psychological evaluation. The FAA suspended Robert's first-class medical certificate pending a psychological and psychiatric evaluation, which meant he could not fly for medical reasons.

Robert was devastated by the news. After he was evaluated by a forensic psychologist, Robert's parents and Connie were interviewed. Connie claimed that nothing Robert said was true and, despite Robert's parents corroborating all that their son said, the forensic psychologist determined that Robert was delusional and should not be allowed to resume flying, effectively terminating Robert's career. The forensic psychologist's report was submitted without the opportunity for Robert to review the contents or submit additional facts in support of his case.

Piecing It Together

Robert evaluated everything that happened since Connie first contacted him. His life was destroyed, yet he was determined to find out who was responsible and why he had been victimized. He left Connie in the apartment in Philadelphia and moved to Queens, New York, with her guarantee that she would move out shortly. Robert finally got her to leave by threatening to turn off the utilities. She left and Robert sold the apartment, and the e-mail from Connie and the Internet characters gradually stopped.

Robert devoted his time to analyzing the archived e-mail and printouts; luckily he had the foresight to preserve much of the information from the beginning. He noticed that a particular word was misspelled frequently in the same manner by Connie and the online individuals. That supported Robert's suspicion that Connie was the mastermind of a plot against him.

Robert hired a private detective, who found out Connie was living in a halfway house. In addition to conducting extensive interviews with Connie, the detective also served her with Robert's lawsuit for monetary damages. Connie revealed to the private detective during one of their interviews that she burned herself with a cigarette to make her story more credible and to "keep Robert under control and make him afraid." The private detective convinced Connie to write a confession and address it to the FBI. Robert submitted her letter along with other supporting evidence, including Connie's past criminal record, to the FBI with a request to correct his file and retract their urgent warning to the FAA, but for unexplained reasons, he was ignored.

After his psychological evaluation, Robert had been placed on mental disability by the airline. To receive benefits under the disability policy, Robert was required to undergo psychotherapy. Very quickly his new therapist ascertained that Robert was not suffering from delusions of any kind. He was, however, deemed to have posttraumatic stress disorder as a direct result of the actions of the FBI and the previous forensic psychologist. Unfortunately for Robert, his treating therapist committed malpractice and bilked his patients' Medicare accounts. This abuse and similar conduct with many other patients led to the treating psychologist being investigated for insurance fraud. He was imprisoned and lost his professional license.

Overdue Answers

A few years after these events, Robert contacted me for help with his tax return. At that time, I was a partner in an accounting firm. I met with Robert to discuss his taxes. He wanted to address the financial losses he suffered from Connie's online extortion, but he did not know if I could help. He explained everything that happened to him and told me his previous accountant simply ignored his theft losses when compiling his tax return. After he explained what had happened to him, I became interested in his story and wanted to use my forensic skills to help Robert. We developed a good rapport and a strong sense of mutual trust in my eventual role as forensic examiner.

Robert's world was turned upside down. He described the events with an impassioned plea for help. I was in the third year of my doctorate in clinical psychology and was interested in the details. Robert gave me substantial, organized information to review, and he seemed credible, but I thoroughly examined all his documentation before accepting his claims. I became convinced that Robert was the victim of an elaborate Internet extortion scheme, and was further harmed by a shallow FBI investigation and an incompetent forensic psychologist.

I embarked on a forensic mission to help Robert recover his money and to achieve vindication for him being wrongly suspended from his job. I conducted dozens of interviews of Robert, his family, witnesses, and prior and subsequent victims of Connie. The other victims' stories enriched my understanding of her as a psychopathic criminal. Each was harmed differently, but all were devastated.

Connie's daughter, Anne, even put me in direct contact with Connie. Anne explained to her mother that I was studying victimology and wanted to understand her better. My hope was to initiate dialogue with Connie and convince her to provide written statements that would clear Robert. Connie told Anne, "Have him e-mail me if he has the guts to do so." After my initial e-mail to Connie, asking for open dialogue, she replied, "Only via e-mail, since we are both so good at hiding behind a screen." We exchanged about 50 e-mail messages and IMs, in which she readily admitted what she did to Robert and others. She openly discussed her wrongdoing, "I have admitted I have hurt people terribly; I've made bad, bad decisions; I have screwed up my life in many ways, and made the same mistakes over and over." She said she was a troubled person, but also blamed her victims, trying to pawn off responsibility for her criminal behavior on drug addiction, but this was yet another veiled effort to hide her psychopathic personality.

My scores of interviews and Connie's direct stories of her childhood fit with her adult psychopathic criminal profile. As a child, she stole from her family. She said: "The first experience I ever remember was taking pennies for an ice cream sandwich from my mom's drawer. I stole stupid little things just to see if I could get away with it. It was the high of the act itself. I usually didn't need the object. My version of the truth is usually pretty distorted. I have always, since I was a child, had a problem deciphering between the truth and what I want to believe."

When she returned to the topic of Robert, she was brief: "Look, Robert is a victim of a credit card scam, that's all." She was completely unconcerned about ruining his career.

Connie's behavior toward me alternated between a soft, cooperative attitude and anger. Much of what she said distorted the known truth and was meant to throw me off track. When she was feeling agreeable, she admitted to the use of other online identities. "I became involved in Max's persona with the help of the real Max. I had no intention of doing this, but Max was coming over all the time and we ended up having a lot of fun online, never thinking anyone would get hurt. Then Robert happened along and Max didn't like him e-mailing me, so Max messed with him a lot, and I followed suit. Then I took on the persona of an old friend who lives in DC, and that's how it began. I never meant to hurt anyone, but I know it has." However, one could argue with her statement. A characteristic of a psychopath is the inability to have deep empathy for people.

Where's the Justice?

Robert's civil lawsuit against Connie was successful, resulting in a judgment ordering Connie to pay restitution for the $57,000 she stole from him.

Together with accumulated interest, the unpaid amount totaled more than $100,000. To date, Connie has made no effort to pay even a small portion. Robert has made several attempts to work through the legal system to discover sources of income earned by Connie or assets that she may have accumulated, but she continues to skate by without being held accountable for the theft.

My work with Robert led to a deeper understanding about how Connie orchestrated the Internet-based scheme. I attended Connie's hearing for yet another violation of probation. She was jailed for six months. The investigation of Connie's abuse of Robert led to the discovery of similar criminal acts she perpetrated against an elderly man. Today, Connie is living with still another elderly man who has life-threatening pulmonary disease. I contacted his relatives and explained Connie's background, but the man's family is disconnected, and they didn't seem overly concerned about his well-being.

Robert eventually unwound the complexity of the events that occurred in his life, but not in time to avoid being considered psychotic by the FBI. Having such a track record, even though it was later proven to be false, ruined his ability to report the crime through another agency. No one would accept his case because his credibility was so tarnished.

I calculated the financial loss sustained by Robert and prepared a casualty loss claim in connection with Robert's income tax return, but originally it was denied. I visited the Internal Revenue Service (IRS) and explained what had occurred. I convinced the IRS agent to allow the loss, and Robert received a large tax refund as a result.

In addition to filing a suit against Robert's treating psychologist, a few law firms evaluated the potential for filing suit against the forensic psychologist, but did not represent Robert in this matter due to the statute of limitations having run out. Thus, the forensic psychologist escaped accountability for his actions.

Lessons Learned

In the hands of a psychopathic criminal, the immense power of the Internet is extremely dangerous. The proliferation of Internet-based scams requires careful discernment of messages, advertisements and solicitations. If potential victims know about the various types of schemes that are perpetrated online, they will be less vulnerable to them. Today there are many warnings about the dangerous criminals who lurk in cyberspace, which could have spared Robert his ordeal had he read about them. Fortunately, law enforcement has become much more receptive to investigating Internet-based crime than it was when Robert reported his case.

(continued)

(*continued*)
    Developing a deeper understanding of your own vulnerabilities can lead to more robust defenses against attacks from deceptive and exploitive people, but strong analytical skills can also lead potential victims to overestimate their ability to spot potential scams. Such overconfidence can prove disastrous.
    Inaccurate forensic reports can be harmful. Forums for people who have been harmed by these quacks may help victims correct their records and enable them to move forward in their lives. For example, an appeal board in place to review Robert's forensic psychological report might have cleared his name.

Recommendations to Prevent Future Occurrences

Regard Internet messages from unknown sources with skepticism. If you do become drawn into suspicious online activity, maintain a backup file of all the messages you exchange because they may become evidence if a scam is uncovered later.

If a crime is detected, a thorough investigation should take place. The victim's report should be validated and all available documentation should be reviewed. If the initial investigation proves the credibility of a victim's report, the fraud examiner should try to help the victim recover stolen assets and achieve meaningful vindication.

When conducting an investigation of this type of fraud, it is important to interview as many witnesses as possible who can corroborate the information provided by the victim and provide insight into the perpetrator. Evidence of criminality can be evaluated by the police.

Obtain documentation from witnesses for purposes of authentication and to support files and documents. This also will lend credibility to the information contained in evidence.

Following tried-and-true procedures when conducting an investigation will give you the best chance of recovering damages but, unfortunately, there is no guarantee of success. In the case of Robert, he may have been redeemed on paper and by the court's decision, but his reputation, career and finances were irreparably damaged.

About the Author

Eric A. Kreuter, PhD, CFE, CPA, CMA, CFM, CFFA, SPHR, is a partner with BST Valuation & Litigation Advisors, LLC in New York City. He conducts forensic investigations and provides litigation support, including expert reports and testimony. He serves on several professional and nonprofit boards. Dr. Kreuter has authored several books, book chapters and numerous articles.

Drag Queens and Drugs

PETER J. DONNELLY

A few years ago I was a lead investigator on a widespread case of identity theft and related crimes in the Dallas/Fort Worth Metroplex. The case spanned several local jurisdictions and affected more than a hundred victims. It would eventually involve the combined resources of several federal agencies and local police departments, and would touch the lives of celebrities and everyday citizens. The investigation would wend its way through the streets of Dallas into the unusual world of transvestite beauty pageants. It would expose the persistent activities of the most desperate criminals and demonstrate that extensive fraud can occur in the streets just as easily as in corporate boardrooms. While the losses were not as staggering as those attributed to recent Ponzi schemes, they were nonetheless economically devastating to the victims involved.

High-School Reunion

Norman Vincent Hardeman, James Untermeyer and Teresa Newman were part of two loose-knit groups in the inner city of Dallas. All the members of the groups, with one exception, had attended Skyline High School in Dallas and had grown up with each other. Most, including Hardeman and Untermeyer, were convicted felons with criminal records that involved violence. Newman was one of the few otherwise innocent accomplices who were duped or forced into abetting a criminal scheme.

In addition to being a seasoned con, Hardeman was also a locally well-known transvestite who had made a name for himself on the Dallas drag-queen circuit. He was a convicted felon and a habitual offender with a drug problem. James Untermeyer was also a convicted felon, and he and Teresa Newman, his girlfriend, shared Hardeman's weakness for drugs such as heroin, crack cocaine, and methamphetamines. Hardeman and Untermeyer headed up separate identity theft rings, but they frequently employed the same individuals and undertook the same types of schemes. Most of the money they made went to support their extensive drug habits. They were relatively uneducated but wise in the way of the streets, with a native intelligence and drive that would have served them well in legitimate occupations.

Equal-Opportunity Fraud

Identity thieves do not discriminate when choosing their victims. As my investigation revealed, seemingly disparate individuals and organizations can become unknowing members of a fellowship created by unscrupulous criminals. National celebrities, airport car-rental companies, and banks found themselves among credit card issuers, online merchants and ordinary citizens who were victimized by this identity theft ring. Even police chiefs were not safe.

I was working as a postal inspector in the Dallas/Fort Worth area and was visiting the local police station one afternoon. We had just wrapped up a joint identity theft investigation and were rehashing the details when a police lieutenant walked in and complained to us that his chief's identity had been used to obtain several fraudulent credit cards. The chief didn't know who had gained access to his personal information or how; he had not experienced mail theft or other losses attributable to burglary or theft. But it was obvious to everyone in the room that the perpetrator had not chosen his victim wisely. The investigation was underway quickly, and we soon identified additional victims, including some celebrities.

The Investigation

The investigation was conducted by the Southwest Financial Crimes Task Force, led by Postal Inspector Keith Tyner and involved the U.S. Postal Inspection Service; the Secret Service; the FBI; the Federal Deposit Insurance Corporation's Office of Inspector General; and detectives from the Dallas, Fort Worth, Irving, and Plano, Texas, police departments.

Following the initial report from the police lieutenant, our first step in the investigation was to contact the issuing credit card companies, which included large, well-known department stores. We solicited information about any other, similar fraudulent applications the stores may have received, and discovered 23 new victims from this request alone. We began looking for common denominators linking the initial 24 victims. Though some had suffered car burglaries, home burglaries, mail theft and purse snatchings, the only apparent similar element we found was that the handwriting on most of their fraudulent applications bore striking similarities, indicating that the same writer had probably completed the suspect applications.

Another common denominator surfaced when we interviewed the victims. All had, at least once, made installment credit purchases directly or indirectly connected to a national finance company. When investigators receive such information about a financial institution, we aggressively pursue the possibility that a company employee leaked the identities of customers. We found that the finance company had suffered three burglaries at their Dallas offices. The burglaries were unusual in that the burglars did not take items of obvious cash value, such as easily fenced computers and other office equipment. Instead, the burglars took the "smart" inquiry terminals furnished by a major credit bureau. The credit bureau informed us that each terminal carried in its internal memory 300 individual credit records, including names, dates of birth, Social Security numbers, addresses and, sometimes, employment information.

The credit bureau's investigators assured us that such data was properly encrypted and required secure password access. Those investigators, however, had never dealt with former inmates of the Texas prison system, many of whom were given computer training as part of a rehabilitative effort. For example, at one point, Texas prison inmates were doing data entry on real estate property transfers under a private contract and had access to deed and property transfer files, including mortgage applications. When this program became public knowledge, it was promptly terminated.

Although we could never directly prove that our targets stole or accessed the smart credit bureau terminals, the data recovered from the fraudulent applications we were accumulating matched that in the terminals' memories. Previous investigations of similar schemes conducted in the Dallas area identified dishonest employees at car dealerships who were providing the same type of personal identifying and financial information to their cohorts. The crooked workers would assist in the preparation of the sales paperwork, including retrieval of credit reports. We believe the actors we eventually identified in our case were schooled in how to access credit information by the dishonest dealership employees, who, when caught, were dismissed or given minimal sentences if they were prosecuted.

We developed our suspects by reviewing automated credit card loss reports and comparing them with local police complaints on suspects who had committed credit card abuse or uttered counterfeit checks. This tedious but necessary step in the investigation was made easier by crime analysts from several of the Task Force agencies who prepared spreadsheets to illustrate the patterns for us. We compared the suspects' physical descriptions with bank and store surveillance videos, some of which were sharp and clear; others were almost useless. The problem was that we were dealing with a highly transient population of "tweakers" or drug abusers. It was not unusual for them to often change locations, with long-term motels being the most frequent residential choice. It was also not unusual for a drug abuser's appearance to change significantly over time.

The Low-Tech Side

We discovered a low-tech side of the crimes as well. Early in the scheme, the perpetrators accessed public records, including voter registrations. At the time, anyone could say they were representing a political group verifying voter lists and gain access to voter registration cards, which listed personal identifying information. We believe this was how our police chief's identity was stolen.

While more sophisticated perpetrators used fraudulent credit cards to get cash advances from automated teller machines (ATMs), our criminals weren't that savvy. What stood out in our spreadsheets was the use of the cards to order from online merchants expensive electronic goods, auto parts, cosmetics and clothing, all of which could be readily converted into cash for drugs. One major online computer dealer cooperated fully, supplying us with complete records from the initial order to the ultimate delivery of the equipment to the customer. Another online computer dealer, although it suffered significant losses from the fraudulent credit card orders, refused to cooperate without grand jury subpoenas — citing its status as a financial organization — even though the customers were fictitious and the company ultimately suffered the losses. Naturally, we concentrated our efforts on the more cooperative company. We had enough on our plate already.

Our spreadsheets revealed still another common denominator — one address on Waycrest Avenue in Dallas's Oak Cliff neighborhood was used for multiple deliveries of fraudulently ordered merchandise. We identified the resident as Teresa Newman. I prepared a test mailing containing a "preapproved" credit card application in the name of our police chief, with a return address of a Post Office box we controlled. The test letter was delivered to the Waycrest address and, in almost no time, the completed application was returned to our PO box. The application bore the same handwriting as the fraudulent applications we had previously discovered.

Closing in on the Suspects

Intercepting a shipment of a fraudulently ordered DVD player going to the Waycrest address, I assumed the role of a uniformed U.S. Postal Service letter carrier and signed out a truck from the nearest post office to attempt a controlled delivery. Hidden in the back of the truck were two Dallas police detectives, a Secret Service agent, and another postal inspector. The accommodations for my passengers in the cargo area were a bit snug, and I inadvertently gave them a jolt when I clipped an overhanging tree limb with the truck's tall roof. My riders actually thought we struck another vehicle and vowed never to ride with me again.

At the Waycrest address, I delivered the parcel to Teresa Newman. She signed as the wife of the police chief, using his name, finishing the signature with a distinctive flourish we had seen on the fraudulent applications. After she signed, I signaled my passengers, who confronted Teresa. When interviewed, she denied all knowledge of the scheme, even when presented with evidence of prior deliveries to the Waycrest address. A written, sworn, statement of her denial was taken by the Secret Service agent and the postal inspector. It was a win/win situation because, in the face of the other evidence, the denial was a reflection on her credibility and an indication of guilt; Newman could be charged with lying to federal agents under the False Statements section of the U.S. Code.

A photograph, fingerprints and handwriting samples were then taken from Newman. But she made no attempt to disguise her handwriting, finishing many of her words with that same distinctive flourish. Handwriting samples were taken in all the known victims' names. Newman stated that she was just receiving the packages for a friend in the neighborhood whom she knew only as James, and who lived around the corner from her on Arborcrest Avenue. Newman surrendered two other pieces of mail she had received in the police chief's name.

Our local and regional forensic labs could not handle my expedited request for handwriting examination, so I had to send the request to our national lab in Dulles, Virginia. They, too, were under a heavy caseload and farmed the request out to another regional lab. Although the known handwriting of Teresa Newman appeared to be a layover for much of the writing on the suspect applications, the documents examiner issued a somewhat disappointing qualified opinion, stating only that he believed Newman was the probable author of the suspect writing. Even though a probable opinion from a lab expert carries more weight than a lay opinion, the qualified opinion can be explained fully only by the examining expert on the witness stand. This restriction on the qualified opinion coupled with the fact we had not yet identified Newman's coconspirators made the Assistant U.S. Attorney we contacted uncomfortable charging Teresa Newman with conspiracy, mail fraud and credit card abuse. Instead, Newman was arrested by the Dallas police and charged with forgery and credit card abuse. As we expected — since Newman had no prior criminal record — she agreed to cooperate and provided the names and addresses of the people who had involved her in the scheme, including her boyfriend, James Untermeyer. The four people's names she provided, including Untermeyer, were all recently released convicted felons. None of the addresses she provided, however, checked out.

Searching for Clues

A Plano police detective on the task force queried the Texas State Pardon and Parole Board and found good addresses, which were one or two numbers different from the ones Newman provided. Untermeyer, who lived on Arborcrest, proved to be a key player in the ring. We obtained state arrest warrants and executed them over the next several weeks. In a consent search incidental to Untermeyer's arrest, an address book was found and photocopied, a standard practice in all such investigations. Two of the four suspects were females who had previously been arrested by Dallas Police for using fraudulent credit cards at the Dallas Galleria shopping center.

Thirteen credit cards illegally obtained online using stolen identities had been delivered to the Waycrest address. Seven cards had been mailed to the Arborcrest address, and one to Rupert Street in Dallas. Eleven cards were sent to an apartment building with common mailboxes on Highway 135 North in Kilgore, in east Texas. Three of the same victims' names appeared on the cards sent to the Waycrest and Kilgore addresses. The fraudulent credit cards were obtained online from major department stores, gas stations and banks.

We arrested the four individuals identified by Newman as having participated in the scheme. Two of the suspects denied any knowledge of the fraud; the third blamed Newman, but the fourth, James Untermeyer — seeking a deal — told us everything. Untermeyer went through his address book and identified Norman Vincent Hardeman on Twyman Avenue in Dallas as being involved in a similar scheme.

Address books were recovered from the other suspects and copied as well. They can lead to the identification of new suspects and further intelligence. It is also not unusual to find suspects in possession of notebooks and other records with victims' identifying information and credit account numbers and balances. This is done so that the bogus cards and accounts are not overused, exposing the crooks to greater danger of being caught. Often the information and account numbers are used as street currency to buy drugs.

The Task Force investigation was now starting to focus on Norman Vincent Hardeman; however, because we had no reported fraudulent credit card activity connected to his address — and because surveillance is labor intensive — the investigation fell into inactive status as other cases took priority. The intelligence on Hardeman, who had an extensive criminal record, was filed away for future reference. He was off the radar screen for now, but not forgotten.

The Junkyard Dogs

A few months later, the Junkyard Dogs, also known as the Dallas Police Auto Theft Unit, called me about an investigation they were conducting into the rental of luxury cars at DFW airport using fraudulent credit cards. One of the names used was a victim from the Waycrest Avenue scheme. Perpetrators were fraudulently renting luxury cars and selling them on the streets of Dallas for about $2,000 each — not a bad price for an almost-new Lincoln Town Car, which was the preferred make and model in the scheme. The Task Force was back in business.

Surveillance videos and still photos obtained from the rental car agencies revealed well-dressed female suspects renting the vehicles. When we interviewed one of the rental clerks, she described one of the suspects as the "ugliest woman I've ever seen," and mentioned the gaudy costume jewelry she was wearing. This presented problems: Female suspects are less likely to have felony records and can often alter their appearance (such as by wearing wigs) easier than males. Nevertheless, the still photos were circulated with local police departments and at interagency intelligence meetings.

A Dallas County deputy constable working hot checks saw one of the photos at a forgery investigators' meeting and identified the suspect as Norman Vincent Hardeman, a transvestite he had previously arrested for uttering forged and insufficient funds checks. Hardeman's address was verified through the Pardon and Parole Board as the same Twyman Street address we had on file. The Junkyard Dogs set up surveillance on Hardeman's house. Their persistence and patience paid off when they spotted two new Lincoln Town Cars at the location. The plates came up as recently stolen from a DFW Airport car-rental agency. The clerk who described the "ugly woman" handled one of the rentals. A Dallas detective put Hardeman's mug shot in a photo spread and he and a postal inspector showed it to the clerk. The clerk declared that the photo of Hardeman "had to be the ugly woman's twin brother, no doubt about it." Because the witness was so positive, and because Hardeman's only known relative was an older brother living in Galveston, Texas, the Junkyard Dogs got a search warrant for the Twyman Street address.

Early the next morning, assisted by the Dallas Police SWAT team, the Junkyard Dogs and I executed the search warrant on Hardeman's residence on Twyman Street, where he was living with two other men and a woman. Computer equipment and other evidence were seized, including printouts from an online public database that included the names, home addresses, drivers' license numbers, dates of birth and other personal information of 294 people. Among the victims were a national civil rights leader, a former astronaut, current NBA and WNBA basketball stars, a former major league baseball star and two rising female pop music stars. The discovery was shocking, but quick work by the Dallas Police and Secret Service revealed that none of the celebrities had suffered any financial loss due to the compromise of their personal information.

Lesser-known victims were not so lucky. Hardeman and his associates selected victims with affluent-appearing addresses in the Dallas and Houston areas, and credit cards, drivers' licenses and blank checks were found in those victims' names. We figured Hardeman and his associates researched the celebrities just to see if they could do it, and then wisely declined to use those names further due to the heat it would bring.

A Treasure Trove of Evidence

We also recovered more than 230 pages of Internet searches of public databases; nine computer criminal histories; and the names, inmate numbers and institutional addresses of inmates in the Texas prison system. Much of the information was contained on the hard drive of Hardeman's computer. Many of the searches were requested using the name Kasper, an alias we knew Hardeman used. The hard drive also contained images of stolen and altered drivers' licenses and we found a counterfeit credit card among Hardeman's possessions.

Norman and his roommates' closets were full of women's clothing, including evening gowns, feather boas and stiletto high heels. Norman and his friends had won beauty pageants for drag queens and had the trophies and photo albums to prove it. We even found the clothing used at the car rental agency. Hardeman and his roommates had dressed as women on their criminal forays to confuse eyewitnesses.

Under Hardeman's mattress I found an Intratec semiautomatic pistol with a magazine loaded with 9mm ammunition. We also found matchbooks and flyers from topless clubs in Dallas and Arlington — the same clubs that Untermeyer was known to frequent. We discovered that Hardeman owned a bar in Dallas, which was unusual for a convicted felon. We dutifully provided this information to the Texas Alcoholic Beverage Commission and also passed along the information about Hardeman's recovered gun to the Bureau of Alcohol, Tobacco, and Firearms. In addition to the loss of approximately $300,000 suffered by the car rental companies, we discovered that other stolen checks had been used, resulting in losses to those individual victims and their banks.

Prosecution

Untermeyer, Newman and their associates were charged with the state offenses of theft, credit card abuse, forgery and engaging in organized criminal activity, which is Texas's conspiracy statute. Because of Untermeyer's criminal record, which included violent crimes, he received considerable prison time — more than he would have gotten if prosecuted federally. His confederates received lesser prison sentences. Teresa Newman received 10 years' community probation as a first-time felony offender.

Hardeman and two of his associates faced similar state charges and received significant prison time. Because he had a prior record as a habitual offender, Hardeman received 99 years. The state sentences handed down were considerably longer than if the fraudsters had been prosecuted in federal court. I testified at a parole hearing for Hardeman several years later. He had been diagnosed with a terminal illness and had applied for parole so he could live with his brother in Galveston until his death. It was granted. A year later, curious as to whether Hardeman was still alive, I ran a criminal history on him and found he had been arrested on a local forgery charge and died in the county jail.

Restitution was ordered in all the cases; however, the ill-gotten gains of both rings were used to buy dope, and there was no property worth recovering.

Lessons Learned

This case taught me that, while not Wall Street wizards, street criminals can be persistent and ingenious. Street criminals who commit fraud and other paper crimes are often fueled by drug addiction and they use the proceeds to buy more illegal narcotics. As such they are desperate and should not be considered nonviolent. Many of the perpetrators in this case had convictions for violent crimes in their past. And one of the main players, Hardeman, had a loaded gun ready to go, should he have chosen to use it.

No online database can be considered 100 percent secure. Underestimating the common criminal and assuming that he or she does not have the intelligence and persistence to eventually defeat security measures is dangerous thinking. No system is impervious to attack by individuals who have nothing to invest but their time and desperation.

As identity theft has grown, I have learned that we all leave a tremendous amount of personal financial information in the public domain, just from our day-to-day business dealings, and there are plenty of criminals eager to seize this information for their own gain. Identity theft, credit card fraud and check fraud are easy crimes to commit and have a low risk of exposure for the perpetrators compared to robberies and burglaries.

This case exemplified the value of teamwork in law enforcement, especially between local and federal agencies; it has proven time and again to be effective in combating complex street crime. There were no turf battles or clashes of professional egos in this case.

I also learned that luck plays a significant role in criminal investigations. Although luck can never replace preparation and investigative skill, it is a welcome partner in any endeavor. Had it not been for an observant deputy constable and Dallas detectives willing to think outside the box, this case may

(continued)

(*continued*)

well have had a much different conclusion. Luck is an elusive factor and must always be exploited fully when encountered.

Investigators need to be flexible when encountering disappointments and setbacks; we must also have a Plan B. In this case, it was the ability to effectively pursue local criminal charges when federal charges could not be pursued.

Recommendations to Prevent Future Occurrences

Since this case was investigated, the Gramm-Leach-Bliley Act and the Driver's Data Protection Act have taken full effect, requiring greater protection of Social Security numbers and other identifying information. This has led, for example, to the redaction of Social Security numbers and drivers' license numbers from many records available to public and business communities.

Public Internet databases have been cleaning up their act, as well. Customers who seek comprehensive personal and financial information from such providers now undergo a vetting process. For example, one provider now requires extensive documentation of private investigation licenses and evidence of legitimate business activity before it provides information.

Our team also sent a recommendation, via a special report, to the Postal Inspection Service Headquarters. We suggested that credit bureaus and other companies that furnish smart terminals for business computers should incorporate software to wipe the machines' internal memories clean if they are disconnected from a power source for a specified period of time, such as 15 to 30 minutes.

The first line of defense against identity theft and fraud is still the individual consumer; we all need to maintain control of our personal information and monitor our financial accounts. In this regard, there is no such thing as too much public education.

About the Author

Peter J. Donnelly, CFE, of Keller, Texas, is a retired postal inspector with 38 years of law enforcement experience on the municipal, county and federal levels. Mr. Donnelly has a master's degree in public administration and is a Master Texas Peace Officer. For the last 10 years of his federal career, he worked almost exclusively on identity theft and related fraud cases. He is the author of "Identity Theft: Hunting Down and Nabbing the Thieves," which appeared in the July/August and September/October 2004 issues of *Fraud Magazine.* He has taught identity crimes classes for the Texas Commission on Law Enforcement Officer Standards and Education. He can be contacted at pjdonn48@msn.com.

CHAPTER
41

Wire Transfers from Nowhere

KENNETH C. CITARELLA
LAURA A. FORBES

The Internet is often used by people who want to connect with new acquaintances, new business partners and even new lovers. In the darker corners of the Internet, however, criminals engage in anonymous communications to peddle services and sell contraband. Among the unlawful commodities available online are stolen identities complete with valid credit card information. Identity thieves harvest this information through phishing and pharming scams, in which the thieves trick unwary consumers into revealing their personal information, and then sell data to others to misuse for their own fraudulent purposes. Completely separate groups, unknown to each other except by their Internet screen names, can team up in this fashion and cause considerable harm to honest citizens.

In this case, one gang operating largely in the Northeast United States bought stolen identities and credit card information from a group of professional identity thieves operating overseas. The U.S. gang consisted of 13 young men of college age, most of whom were high-school classmates in a small town not too far north of New York City. At the time, five of them resided in Ravenna, a small city in upstate New York, and eight lived downstate, in Hudson's Landing, a New York City suburb. They were ethnically and economically diverse, but shared an affinity for computers, the Internet — and fraud.

The upstate members were Brian Noonan, Bart Grayson, Chuck Colty, Karl Kollins and Marty Brim, all of whom were officially registered at a local college, but for whom attendance seemed to be a forgotten obligation. Internet fraud provided them with a lucrative diversion from earning an honest living. The downstate suburban group consisted of Mike Peters, Andy Hook, Art Eason, John Mullins, Al Higgins, Walt Guss, Chris Morton and Miguel Salsa.

Each member of the U.S. gang had a specific job function. Mike Peters was at the center of the conspiracy. He was the most experienced *carder* among them all; an expert at using stolen credit card and personal information to obtain wire transfers through Money Transfer Services, Inc. (MTS), an international financial services company. Hook, Eason, Mullins, Guss and Morton were runners whom Peters sent to various MTS offices to collect wired funds. Peters paid a runner $100 for a successful retrieval of this money, which ranged from $200 to $1,000 per transaction. Peters even had a friend, known only as "Greg," who operated as a runner in California. Hook and Eason also spent time with Peters driving through wealthy neighborhoods looking for cars from which they could steal electronic equipment. As will be described later, this proved to be their downfall.

Noonan, Grayson and Colty were all carders in their own right, like Peters. Using the same overseas sources as Peters, they purchased stolen personal and credit card information via the Internet and then charged cash advances against credit cards for wire transfers through MTS. They also all served as runners for each other.

Outside of their screen names and the Web sites they used at the time, nothing was known about the number of or identities of the overseas phishers.

The Mathematics of Profit

The individual consumers who were victimized in this scam were as diverse as America itself. They only had two characteristics in common: They owned a credit card and fell victim to a phishing ploy. They came from at least seven different states scattered between California and New York. The exact number of individuals involved will never be known, but their credit cards were collectively used for probably more than 30,000 attempted or successful fraudulent wire transfers.

Phishing is one of the most common Internet scams; you've probably gotten many of them yourself. Phishers send fraudulent e-mail that mimic actual communications from banks or other financial institutions to their credit card holders. Phishers painstakingly duplicate the logos, colors and layout of genuine e-mail messages sent by the issuing institution. Some individuals, lulled into a false sense of security by the genuine appearance of the phishing e-mail, believe it to be a legitimate communication. With their guard down, unsuspecting cardholders accept the e-mail at face value. They believe the false assertion that a suspicious attempted charge requires a "reverification" of their account data and use a link in the e-mail to go to a Web site to "reenter" their personal identifying information and credit card number. They completely overlook the fact that their bank already has all that data readily on hand. Once the consumer has entered his or her personal and credit card information, everything is in the hands of the phishers to do with as they will.

Phishers cast their hooks blindly to massive quantities of e-mail addresses that are easily obtained online. Once the fraudulent e-mail communication and the mailing list are prepared, the cost of distribution is negligible whether 100 copies are sent or 1 million. In the latter case, a positive response rate of only 0.1 percent would mean that 1,000 consumers gave away the key to their financial identities. These are the mathematics that create the profits associated with e-mail advertising of any nature. Neither the phishers nor the carders cared where the actual credit card owners lived. All they wanted was an American identity and a valid card number.

The New York–based gang of carders victimized MTS offices throughout the state, using as many stolen identities as they could secure from their anonymous overseas providers. Because of the presence of one runner in California, several MTS offices in that state were victimized as well.

A Pattern Emerges

Trying to pinpoint when a widely dispersed fraud scheme was first uncovered is like trying to determine precisely when water begins to boil. All of a sudden, things were happening everywhere — puzzled consumers began to wonder about charges for wire transfer fees and cash advances posted to their credit cards. They reacted the way we all would, by calling their credit card issuer and asking why the unauthorized charges appeared on their statements. Once consumers started to make those calls, it was only a matter of time before the boiling point was noticeably reached. The credit card issuers began to react once they realized the charges were not isolated events but a pattern. Their security and investigations departments, staffed by experienced fraud examiners who were assisted by pattern-detecting software, contacted their counterparts at other financial institutions and reached out to law enforcement.

MTS, of course, was also on task. As reports of disputed charges began to come in from various offices, data was gathered and analyzed. Security personnel distributed information throughout the corporation to alert branches to what certainly appeared to be a coordinated fraud. Patterns of names began to emerge from the early chaotic reports. When the fraudsters assumed false names to use in their dealings with intended victims, they often used names similar to their own or to those they used elsewhere. This made it easier for them to devise and remember new names. MTS branches had security cameras, but the runners often wore dark glasses or hoods to disguise their features. Nonetheless, some useful images were captured.

The various security departments cooperated and provided all of their information to the federal agency coordinating the investigation. Eventually, enough information was assembled to enable the investigators to understand exactly what happened, what some of the runners looked like and the pattern of their aliases. The investigation focused on the activities around Ravenna. The pattern of behavior indicated that the perpetrators were likely younger rather than older, were certainly quite computer savvy and knew the ways and means of Internet-based identity theft very well.

They were also very bold and not deterred by failed attempts. The growing body of data enabled MTS to deny many requested transfers. The gang attempted more than 30,000 fraudulent wire transfers, every one of which required a valid-appearing but stolen identity and credit card information. For each transaction MTS accepted, a runner with identification had to be dispatched and made to appear as if he were picking up money from the victim. In all they attempted to process $1.4 million in wire transfers, and succeeded in stealing more than $200,000. Fraud had become the full-time occupation of the upstate and downstate groups. No wonder they seldom got to class.

Their actual identities, however, continued to elude those on their trail and awaiting the kind of mistake that would provide a clue to who they were.

A Fortuitous Error

Mike Peters, Andy Hook, and Art Eason were busy one evening cruising wealthy neighborhoods in downstate New York, looking for easy marks. Their crime scenes of preference were vehicles parked near the street in the driveway of upscale houses. When they found one such location, they would pull over and leave one member behind the wheel while the others peered through the windows of the parked car for valuable electronics behind unlocked doors. In the course of a night, they often found several victims at diverse locations, not leaving clues behind for law enforcement to follow. Distraught victims only knew in the morning that their valuables were gone.

On this particular night, they found a laptop on the backseat of a car in the town of Mt. Benton, a short drive north of New York City. For Internet fraudsters, a stolen laptop can be a valuable commodity, and, of course, the price was right.

The next morning, Fred Hart walked out to his car and found the laptop issued to him by his corporate employer missing. Embarrassed for having left corporate property so foolishly exposed, he dutifully reported the loss to his employer and to the Mt. Benton Police Department. In truth, no one expected to ever hear about that laptop again. But, several months later, a gang member began to use it to access the Internet. There is often one such critical and fortuitous error that resolves sophisticated frauds.

Fred Hart's corporate employer had equipped each employee's laptop with theft-detection software from Laptop Protection, Inc. (LPI). When one of those laptops connected to the Internet, it automatically sent its unique identification number to LPI. After Hart reported the theft, the corporate IT department notified LPI and that laptop's identification number was added to LPI's list of stolen laptops. It was just a waiting game to see if the laptop was used.

It sat unused for several months until Peters sold it to Brian Noonan to use in their scheme. Noonan knew there was a risk of theft-detection software on the laptop and removed the original hard drive and installed a new one. Fortunately, the LPI software had been installed by the laptop's manufacturer into the computer's basic input/output system (BIOS) and not on its hard drive. It is often referred to as *firmware* — software permanently residing on memory and designed to be the first steps taken at boot up. The BIOS tells a computer how it is configured and how its various components should interact. Despite Noonan's clever attempt to avoid detection, he didn't have a chance.

Thus when Noonan used Hart's laptop, like a lost ET it called home and provided its identification number. More important, since it was now on the LPI list of stolen laptops, the computer automatically provided its Internet protocol (IP) address and uploaded selected contents of its hard drive that revealed how it was being used. LPI forwarded that information to Hart's employer and through them to the Mt. Benton police. Detective Alan Mitchell was assigned to the case. Knowing he needed assistance beyond the capabilities of his small department, Mitchell contacted the Westchester County District Attorney's Office High Technology Crime Bureau for assistance. From our perspective, this is where the case began.

Mitchell came to see me, Assistant District Attorney Laura Forbes, because of my experience in computer crime and identity theft. From that moment on, although they didn't know it, time was running out for the identity theft gang.

Among the files the laptop uploaded to LPI were temporary files that recorded the Internet communications among members of the U.S. gang, and their contacts with the overseas phishers. The entire identity theft plan and the larceny from MTS were laid out in jargon-laded chats that, once understood, provided a roadmap for their crimes. The laptop also contained a series of personal information profiles — called *fulls* — that gang members had legitimately purchased on the Internet. Every consumer discloses a considerable amount of personal information during the course of financial transactions. Marketing research companies collect as much of that information as they legally can and compile it into what can be a comprehensive report on any given individual. They in turn resell that information to the purchaser as a full. It may contain a consumer's name, date of birth, Social Security number and residential address. Equipped with this pedigree information, as well as the credit data compiled by phishing, the gang members would be able to assume another online identity and order money through MTS for in-person pickups.

We did not need to secure the permission of a court to acquire this invaluable evidence. Since the laptop was stolen, its unauthorized users had no privacy rights to the computer or its contents. As long as their Internet communications were not monitored in real time, neither federal nor state wiretapping laws were violated. A perfectly lawful report on an ongoing crime was being provided to law enforcement every time the laptop accessed the Internet. (The legality of the theft-detection software was not an issue at the time of this case but the law continues to develop, so this should be reviewed before such evidence is used in any new investigation.)

Armed with this information, we were able to identify the locations at which the laptop appeared to be used through the IP addresses. We then issued subpoenas to the Internet service providers (ISPs) for the name and street address information for every account that was using the laptop. The information we received indicated that the computer had been used all over the country in a matter of days. Clearly this did not seem accurate. Whoever was using the computer had managed to disguise his actual IP address. However, several weeks into the investigation, we figured out that the IP addresses used consistently came from three locations: the upstate apartment where Noonan lived with Grayson and Colty; the suburban apartment where Mike Peters lived with his parents; and Noonan's parents' apartment in Westchester. Noonan had gotten lazy and, because of that, he was now identified.

A background check of Noonan revealed a suspicious activity report generated by MTS when he was observed with Andy Hook making more pickups in one day than is usual for customers. The same background check also revealed that Noonan went to high school with Mike Peters, Andy Hook, Art Eason, John Mullins, Al Higgins, Walt Guss, Chris Morton and Miguel Salsa.

Combining Forces

When Detective Mitchell contacted the Ravenna Police Department in upstate New York, he was notified that there was already an ongoing investigation by the department and a federal agency into an identity theft and fraudulent wire transfer scam involving our targets. We quickly assembled a multiagency meeting to hammer out the protocols for proceeding with a joint investigation. We mutually agreed on each agency's role and on the criteria for determining which future defendants would be prosecuted federally versus locally. When the information — painstakingly compiled by the credit card issuers, MTS and the local and federal investigators — was combined with the uploaded files from the laptop, we were able to attach names to faces and the investigation took a giant leap forward.

The main two locations, the Ravenna apartment and the Peters's residence in Hudson's Landing, were placed under regular surveillance and its residents were identified. We reviewed the evidence we had and I began drafting a search warrant for the Ravenna apartment. Approximately five months after Hart's stolen laptop began to be used as part of the identity theft and wire transfer fraud scheme, law enforcement was prepared to strike.

Early Morning Surprises

In the predawn hours of an early winter day, investigators from the Ravenna Police Department, the Westchester County District Attorney's Office, the Mt. Benton Police Department and the federal agency burst into the Ravenna apartment, surprising its sleeping inhabitants — a state Supreme Court justice had authorized a no-knock search warrant. Because of the clearly demonstrated computer skills of the suspects and the ephemeral nature of digital evidence, we had strong arguments for requesting that the court permit the police to enter the apartment without having to knock on the door and identify themselves. If the suspects had programmed some destructive code into the laptop, then the seconds that would pass from the time the police knocked on the door until they had located and secured the laptop could have proved fatal to the evidence it contained. The court agreed.

Noonan, Grayson and Colty were all asleep in the apartment when the police entered. They were completely surprised. The law enforcement agents quickly secured the premises and located the laptop. Some high-quality electronics were also seized that might have been purchased with stolen money. All three gang members were interrogated and Noonan began to come clean. The investigators and I interviewed Noonan for hours that day. We never revealed the presence of the LPI software in the laptop's BIOS. Based on the extremely detailed information we had about the scheme, Noonan believed that the gang's communications had been wiretapped and concluded there was no reason for him to withhold any information. We did nothing to dissuade him from that faulty reasoning; indeed, we used it to our advantage. His attempt to avoid theft-detection software worked against him for a second time. Not only did he fail to remove it, but his misplaced confidence in that effort caused him to wrongly conclude that we had even more evidence than we really did. Because of his false conclusions, we were able to confirm our understanding of Noonan's activities, as well as get details on his coconspirators' conduct.

Noonan told us that Peters was the ringleader of the entire scheme, but he proudly hailed himself as the more skillful fraudster. He stated that Peters was the one who devised the scam but that he, Noonan, was the one who perfected it. He also stated that he was originally spoofing his IP address to make it appear that the computer was somewhere else, but he admitted that he later grew lazy and cocky and stopped hiding behind false IP addresses. Noonan also implicated every other member of the ring: Mike Peters, Andy Hook, Art Eason, John Mullins, Al Higgins, Walt Guss, Chris Morton, Miguel Salsa and his roommates. Noonan made sure that as he mentioned the names, he pointed out that none of them were as clever or computer savvy as he was.

We decided that Noonan's statements, when combined with the information previously assembled regarding Peters and the use of the laptop in the family residence, provided enough evidence for a search warrant for his coconspirator's residence. In a few days, the same agencies executed the warrant and found Mike Peters, a sister and his parents at home in the early morning. The parents were extremely defensive and denied their son had done anything wrong. Peters had nothing to say. But in the bottom of his bedroom closet, pushed deep into the toe of a sock, was approximately $40,000 and a counterfeit New York driver's license, which was shown to MTS employees when Peters picked up money using that false name. Mr. Peters claimed the money was his, resulting from a recently liquidated investment, but the police decided that a stray sock in a son's closet was an unusual place to store such proceeds. They took the sock and the money and Mr. Peters didn't come up with proof of his alleged investment.

The Outcome

In all, six members of the gang were prosecuted at the state or federal level. As commonly happens in cases like this, there was less evidence against the more peripheral players and many of them escaped prosecution. Mike Peters pleaded guilty to state larceny and identity theft charges, forfeited the $40,000 found in his sock, and was sentenced to up to four years in state prison and to pay an additional $33,000 in restitution. Brian Noonan pleaded guilty to state identity theft charges and to federal wire fraud charges for which he was sentenced to four and a half years in federal prison. Walt Guss pleaded guilty to a state identity theft charge, paid $6,000 in restitution, and was sentenced to 5 years of probation. Three other members pleaded to lesser charges.

To date, no charges have been brought against the overseas phishers.

Lessons Learned

We can only speculate how long this fraud could have continued had Noonan not started to use the laptop Peters stole. Investigators can't deny the significance of mistakes made by their targets. But from this case history, several other important lessons are obvious.

Foremost among them is that the entire crime was completely preventable. If consumers had not fallen victim to phishing, their identities would not have been stolen and thus available for sale online to the Peters/Noonan gang. Considering the costs incurred by the various credit card issuers to investigate this matter and cooperate with law enforcement, it seems likely that increasing their efforts at identity theft protection would be money well spent. Every consumer who is educated about the various Internet identity theft scams and avoids being deceived reduces fraud loss to the financial institution and investigation expenses. Increasing consumer education by mail inserts or e-mail notices is step number one.

Second, this case benefited from the remarkable cooperation of several law enforcement agencies and corporate security departments. Such a lesson cannot be emphasized too often. Law enforcement agencies easily fall prey to turf wars. Corporations sometimes withhold information that they deem too embarrassing or sensitive. Such conduct decreases the likelihood of a successful investigation.

Last, the presence of BIOS-installed theft-prevention software was critical to the case. Businesses that issue laptops to their employees should install some kind of theft-prevention software. Although most laptop thieves lack the technical awareness to suspect the presence of theft-prevention software, it certainly makes sense to have that software in the BIOS rather than on the hard drive.

Recommendations to Prevent Future Occurrences

The core lessons to be learned from this case are obvious. First, credit card issuers must increase their consumer education efforts. The costs of e-mail alerts, security reminders included within monthly statements and similar notification procedures are trivial compared to the cost of investigating and absorbing fraud losses. Phishing scams and other identity theft techniques are well known to security departments. Efforts must be made to prevent identity theft before it occurs. Making consumers more aware of how they might be deceived is the cornerstone to that objective.

Second, financial institutions should have cutting-edge fraud detection systems. Patterns of activity within an account and across accounts that are uncharacteristic of established consumer behavior must be monitored and analyzed. The more quickly a credit card issuer can detect fraud, the more quickly it can be cut off and reported to law enforcement for investigation.

Third, information should be cooperatively shared among financial institutions and law enforcement agencies and the entities involved in the case must keep their attention focused on the objective of stopping fraud and convicting the fraudster. When information is withheld by a corporate victim or law enforcement agencies do not cooperate well, the criminals win.

About the Authors

Kenneth C. Citarella, Esq., MBA, CFE, CCS, had a distinguished 28-year career as a white-collar and computer crime prosecutor in the Westchester County (NY) District Attorney's Office, which he concluded as Deputy Chief of the Investigations Division. Ken prosecuted investment frauds, larcenies, embezzlements, anti-trust violations, public corruption, forgeries and many other economic crimes. Also a pioneer in computer crime prosecution, Ken obtained convictions for computer intrusions, malicious software attacks, a software time bomb, spamming, digital child pornography and the use of the Internet for child exploitation, among other cases. Now with the Corporate Investigations Division of Prudential Financial Services and an Adjunct Professor of Law at New York Law School, Ken has lectured widely before professional, legal, academic, corporate and community groups on computer crime and fraud-related issues.

Laura A. Forbes, Esq., is a Senior Assistant District Attorney with the Office of the Westchester County District Attorney. She is currently assigned to the High Technology Crimes Bureau of the Investigations Division, in which she investigates and prosecutes Internet and identity theft-related crimes. She was previously assigned to the Economic Crimes Bureau. Laura received a JD from Pace University School of Law and a BS in Business Management from Marymount College.

Glossary

advance-fee fraud: a type of confidence fraud in which a victim is persuaded to provide a fraudster with money in advance of earning more significant funds. Common advance-fee frauds include Nigerian 419, black-money and inheritance scams.

auction Web site: a business model in which potential buyers bid on items for sale online

back door: a program that creates an opening on a computer to remotely access files without the owner's knowledge

BIOS (basic input/output system): software that permanently resides on a computer's memory and is designed to be among the first steps taken when a computer boots up. It tells a computer how it is configured and how its various components should interact. Such software is often referred to as *firmware*.

blog: a Web site, usually maintained by an individual, that is updated regularly with commentary, personal information, video or photos. Also known as a *weblog*.

bot: a single computer that has been infected with malware and forms one part of a network known as a *botnet*

botnet: a group of bots that are infected with malware and controlled by a different and often remote computer, known as a *herder*, to perform specific coordinated tasks

broadband telephony: see **VoIP**

carder: an individual who is an expert at using stolen credit card and other personal information to obtain fraudulent wire transfers

confidence and consumer fraud: an online fraud in which the perpetrator breaches the victim's trust to cause a financial loss. Common confidence and consumer scams include advance-fee schemes, online auction fraud and solicitations for charitable contributions.

cyberterrorism and sabotage: the deliberate disruption of computer networks through the Internet with the intention of causing harm

e-commerce: commerce that is conducted via the Internet

e-mail: electronic mail sent via the Internet

executable (file): a file that causes a computer to perform specific tasks as opposed to a file that contains data. Fraudsters often attach executable files containing malware to e-mails sent to their victims. Such files usually end in the extension ".exe."

firmware: computer programs that reside permanently in a hardware device

full: a collection of personal information that can be legitimately purchased on the Internet and used to steal an identity

hacking: illegally gaining access to a computer by reprogramming or reconfiguring it or by cracking a password

herder: a computer that remotely controls bots in a botnet

HTML (hypertext markup language): a programming language used to create documents on the Internet

identity theft: a type of fraud in which someone obtains another person's identifying information, such as a credit card number or Social Security number, and uses it for personal financial gain

instant messaging (IM): a form of real-time communication using a shared network, most commonly the Internet. IM is also used by hackers to send viruses.

Internet protocol (IP) address: a series of four three-digit numbers separated by periods (such as 190.023.067.235), which identifies the Internet service provider and account identification for every computer connected to the Internet

Internet service provider (ISP): an organization that provides Internet access and related services

Internet telephony: see **VoIP**

investment and securities fraud: a type of fraud designed to entice victims to purchase nonexistent, misrepresented or manipulated investments or securities online

malware: malicious software that can infect computers and cause damage and steal information, such as spyware, worms, viruses and Trojan horses

metadata: data that provides information about data. Metadata is used to describe the properties of information, such as file name, size and date of creation.

meta tag: a coded element on a Web site that describes the content of the page. Meta tags are most commonly recognized as hidden HTML tags that describe attributes of a page's content. Such attributes include keywords and descriptions. A search engine may refer to a Web page's meta tags when indexing.

online auction fraud: the use of an online auction Web site for a fraudulent purpose. Common auction frauds include non-delivery of goods, selling stolen or illegal products, product misrepresentation and price manipulation.

online payment fraud: a type of Internet fraud in which the online purchaser pays for products with a fraudulent check, an invalid credit card number or a fraudulent escrow account, resulting in a financial loss to the seller

password sniffing: searching network information and messages for passwords

pharming: a series of actions that redirects victims to a fraudulent Web site designed to look like a legitimate organization's site for the purpose of collecting private data

phishing: a fraudulent attempt to acquire private information from an individual via SMS text messages, e-mail or instant messages from a sender purporting to be a trustworthy authority

SIM (subscriber identity module) card: a removable device in a cell phone that stores the user's identifying information

smishing: a form of phishing conducted through cell phones via SMS text messages

SMS (short message service): communication tool that allows users to send and receive text messages, usually via cell phones

smurfing: misappropriating many small sums of money to create one large sum

spyware: a form of malware that collects information about computer users and their actions without their knowledge

Trojan horse: a form of malware that is designed to appear harmless to victims and gives hackers access to their computers

virus: a form of malware capable of copying itself and attaching to other programs

vishing: a form of phishing conducted via VoIP communications

VoIP (Voice over Internet Protocol): technology that enables voice communications over the Internet. Also known as *Internet telephony* or *broadband telephony*.

war driving: the practice of seeking out unsecured wireless networks for anonymous Internet access to commit crimes

Web application: a software application that is accessed by a Web browser over the Internet rather than being installed on a computer

weblog: see **blog**

Whois search: an investigation tool used to uncover the registrant of a domain name or an owner of an IP address

worm: similar to a virus, a worm is a form of malware that can copy itself without needing a host program

Index

Italic page numbers indicate a definition